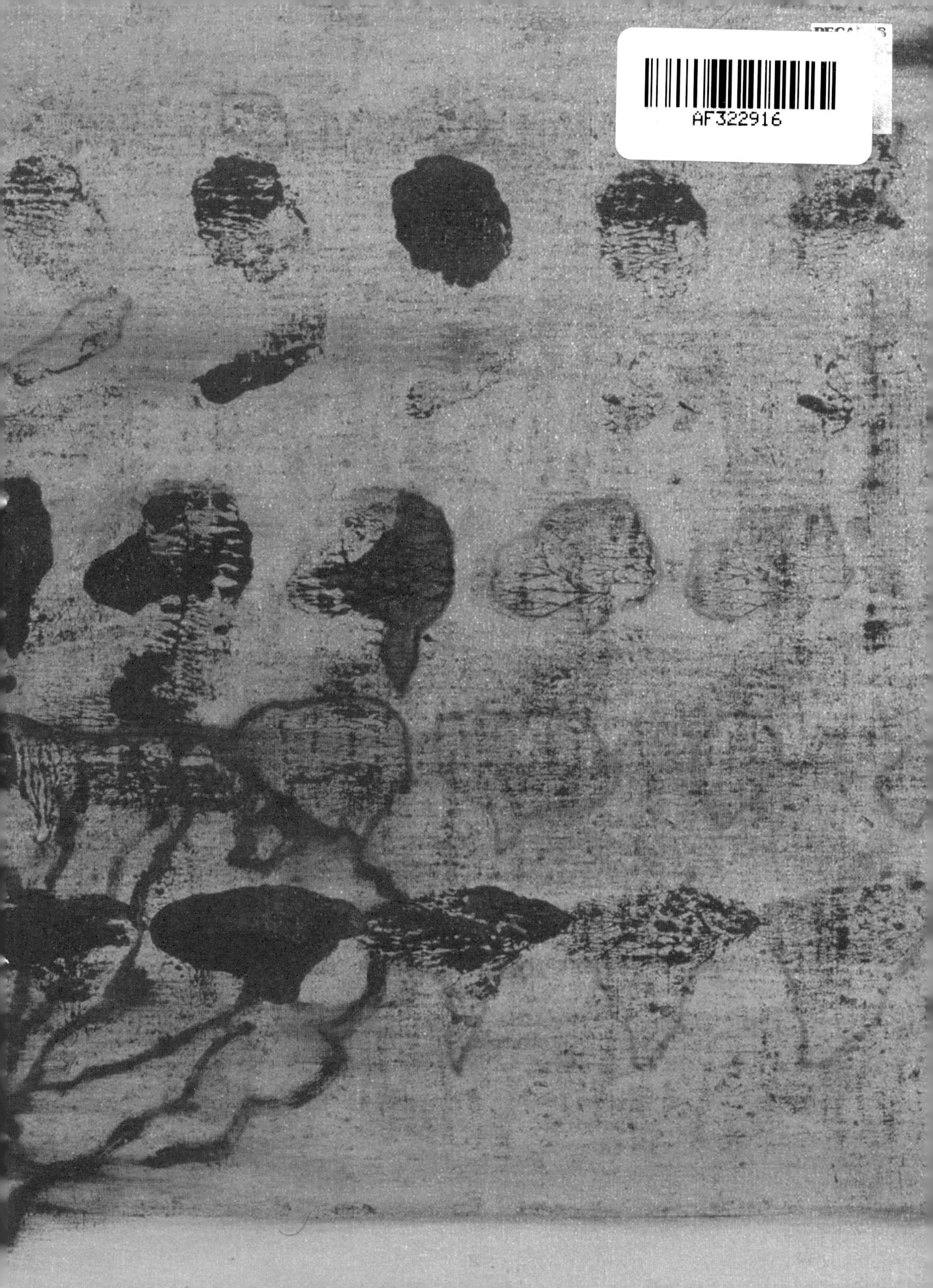

Sue Hubbard is a freelance art critic, award-
winning poet and writer. Her art-writing
career has spanned more than 20 years. For
ten of them she wrote regularly for 'Time Out',
moving on to 'The Independent on Sunday',
'The Independent' and the 'New Statesman'.
She has written numerous artists' catalogues
and contributed to a wide range of art magazines.
She has taught and lectured in various art schools,
and in 2000 curated the successful Arts Council
touring exhibition, 'Chora', with the artist and
writer Simon Morley.

An award-winning poet, Sue Hubbard has
twice won the London Writers' Competition,
as well as third prizes in the National and the
TLS poetry competitions. She has published two
collections of poetry, 'Everything Begins with the
Skin' (Enitharmon Press) and 'Ghost Station'
(Salt). The Poetry Society's first Public Art Poet,
she was responsible for London's largest public-
art poem at Waterloo Station. Her first novel,
'Depth of Field', is published by Dewi Lewis, and
her short-story collection, 'Rothko's Red', by Salt,

Sue Hubbard

Adventures in Art

Selected Writings
1990–2010

"We cannot believe in art if we do not
believe in some kind of unchanging
attitude toward, or timeless standards
of, what is beautiful, what is important
and what is essential to life." **Sol LeWitt**

Other Criteria

So what, in a contemporary western society, is art for? And why have I, as a poet, spent 20 years writing about it? From Charles Baudelaire to Frank O'Hara, poets have written on the subject. John Ashbery credited journalism with altering his writing methods, and many of my own poems are based on paintings. The process of looking involved in writing a poem, the long maturation, the editing, the elimination and constant reappraisal, is not so different from the techniques employed in making art. Ashbery did not write as an expert or an art historian but, like any

good journalist, as an informed observer, and for a general audience. This allowed for a certain freedom and freshness of vision. The pieces he wrote were not always chosen, but rather responses to what he was asked to write about. The same has been true for me. All the pieces that appear in this book were commissioned (which is why some major names are missing), and in the process of their writing I have discovered what I think. My aim has been to help readers find what is worth looking at and why, and to provide them with a few hooks and crampons to allow them the means to make their own way across the slippery and often treacherous slopes of modern and contemporary art. Exploring relationships between visual and verbal meaning, and the gaps between word and image, have been abiding preoccupations. I have been less interested in esoteric quarrels over theory, practice and methodology than in trying to discover what Susan Sontag has called "new modes of sensibility". My own art-writing career during the last 20 years has coincided with one of the most explosive periods of British art.

Art was born of a need to create magical-religious symbols and signs that allowed sense to be made of a threatening, fearsome world. In the west, it evolved into a way of telling stories about the systems put in place to control and comfort those without the means of understanding and questioning those systems. For moderns, mindful of God's slow death, the point and purpose of art switched from glorification and didacticism to doubt and self-questioning, from technique and skill into the realm of dreams and self-expression. God was no longer in his heaven and all was, after two world wars, obviously not right with the world. As a result, the point and purpose of art became more pluralistic and complex. Where once, great religious paintings had been used as the focus of prayer or examples of splendour and wealth, art began to respond, at the beginning of the 20th century, to those things that characterised modern society – industrialisation and technological change. With the proliferation of huge impersonal cities, the individual felt lost and alienated. Speed, scientific innovation and doubt filled the now God-shaped void. By the middle of the last century, art had turned inward. Uncomfortable with claiming any moral high ground in an increasingly uncertain and unstable world, it became emptied of ideology and talked largely of itself. As Susan Sontag wrote in 1965: "The most interesting and creative art of our time is not open to the generally educated; it demands special effort, it speaks a specialised language... The most interesting works of contemporary art are full of references to the history of the medium; so far as they comment on past art, they demand a knowledge of at least the recent past". As Harold Rosenberg pointed out, contemporary paintings are as much acts of criticism as they are acts of creation. Art gurus such as Clement Greenberg demanded that art be stripped of any narrative potential, of any language or reference that strayed outside the boundaries of art. As there was no longer any consensus as to which story should be told, the only safe ground was that of formalism. With the final collapse of that last great utopian enterprise, Marxism, along with the failed protests of the French students in May 1968 and the ensuing death throes of socialism overseen by Thatcher, Reagan and Blair, what was there left to believe in?

The poet Ezra Pound's credo to "make it new" had been the battle cry of Modernism. Newness was also to become the mantra of its younger sibling Postmodernism. Notions of what could constitute art were drawn as much from popular culture and mass production as from "high" art. Yet with this apparent process of democratisation, where old hierarchies were broken down, the culture of capitalism began to reduce art, suggests John Berger, "to market commodities and to an advertisement for other commodities". No other artist exemplified this shift better than Andy Warhol, with his appreciation of the

market and the effects of cursory and, at times, transient fame. Art began to leave the confines of the museum and the gallery and take to the streets in the form of performance and happenings. Ever since the display of Marcel Duchamp's infamous urinal in 1917, the boundaries of art have been stretched to include anything an artist chooses to call art. While Duchamp's daring led to a vital re-evaluation, ultimately we have arrived at a position whereby if art can be anything and everything, does it any longer amount to more than a hill of beans? In his lecture 'On the Nature of Abstraction' given at the Rice University in Texas in 2000, Robert Irwin suggested that "art" "has come to mean so many things that it doesn't mean anything anymore". In the 1980s, the French philosopher Jean Baudrillard wrote: "Behind the whole convulsive movement of modern art lies a kind of inertia, something that can no longer transcend itself, and has therefore turned in upon itself, merely repeating itself at a faster and faster rate".

The populist question "… but is it art?" proffered by many when confronted with what Harold Rosenberg termed an "anxious object" (such as Tracy Emin's 'My Bed' or the Cuban artist Felix Gonzales-Torres installation at the Serpentine in 2000, where visitors were encouraged to help themselves to toffees strewn across the gallery floor) gets us nowhere. The only worthwhile question is whether a work is challenging, whether it reveals something that has not previously been understood, and whether it extends perceptual, sensual, intellectual and emotional understanding of what it means to be human. Judgements about contemporary art are never fixed, but evolving and fluid. In 'Against Interpretation' Susan Sontag suggests that: "Real art has the capacity to make us nervous". Referring to Sigmund Freud's phrase that all observable phenomena is manifest content, she argues that manifest content must be probed and pushed aside to find the latent content. The implication is that the true meaning of an art work lurks beneath the surface to be excavated in the way an archaeologist might excavate a found object. Acting as an aesthetic archaeologist has been central to my writing on art.

Yet the market's insatiable appetite for "newness", for an artist to create hallmark "brands" has meant that novelty and irony have become the dominant tropes of contemporary art, overriding all other responses such as compassion, empathy and wonder. But novelty and outrage all too quickly revert to an *à la mode* academicism as in the scatological works of Gilbert and George or the penile-faced dolls of Jake and Dinos Chapman. Like children thumbing their noses at restrictive and boring parents, their main concern has been *épater le bourgeois*. While the work of Francisco de Goya (which the Chapman brothers often appropriate for their own ends), Chaïm Soutine or Francis Bacon may be considered shocking by some, it is also raw and authentic, and expresses something of the poignancy and the pity of what it means to live in a troubled Godless world. The existential nihilism of Alberto Giacometti or Samuel Beckett was bleak, but never cynical. It spoke of the impossibility of hope, whilst understanding that hope is a human imperative. In the last sentences of 'The Unnameable', Beckett reveals this paradox at the centre of modernity with the words: "You must go on. I can't go on. I'll go on". This Sisyphean circularity of the seemingly fruitless search for self, and the apparent impotence felt at finding an appropriate language or a means of expression, is central to any meaningful contemporary artistic enterprise. The fragile choice must always be "to go on." Postmodern irony all too often leads us into a cul-de-sac, leaving no place to go other than staring solipsistically at our own endlessly repeated reflection in a hall of mirrors.

Making decisions about what to include and what to leave out of this book was extremely hard. In the end I chose work by artists who have lived during the last 50 years, which meant, reluctantly, abandoning pieces on the likes of Edvard

Munch and Frida Kahlo, Edouard Manet and Titian. Deciding on the order was equally difficult when groupings such as "painters" and "installation artists" – with so many working across a number of media – created strange bedfellows. Finally, I divided the book's contents into two sections. The first, short, section is made up of essays written largely for magazines and catalogues. These are not sequenced in order of first publication, but organised to exemplify some of my main themes and concerns, which are to do with going beyond the easy clichés of Postmodernism to reach toward new meanings and insights.

The second section consists mostly of reviews; it includes two short commentaries written for 'The Independent' on paintings by Anslem Keifer and Francis Bacon, and is arranged chronologically. Although I may not always agree completely with my younger self, what I have written reveals my growing sensibility to aesthetic issues. Shifts have occurred in my perception of art over 20 years although, basically, I still search for the same things. For if art is to have any purpose beyond entertainment or investment within our contemporary consumerist society, it has to enhance our awareness of ourselves and the world we inhabit.

The point of art is not to be beautiful (though it might be) for, as John Keats noted, beauty and truth can be synonymous. Its role is, rather, to seek out, illuminate and grapple with what is authentic, what is difficult and what is real. As Albert Einstein said, "The most beautiful thing we can experience is the mysterious. It is the source of all fine art and science". Through an experience of art we can, if we choose, become in these anguished times the best of ourselves: perceptive, aware, compassionate, but above all, endlessly questioning.

County Kerry

Contents

Adventures in Art
Section I

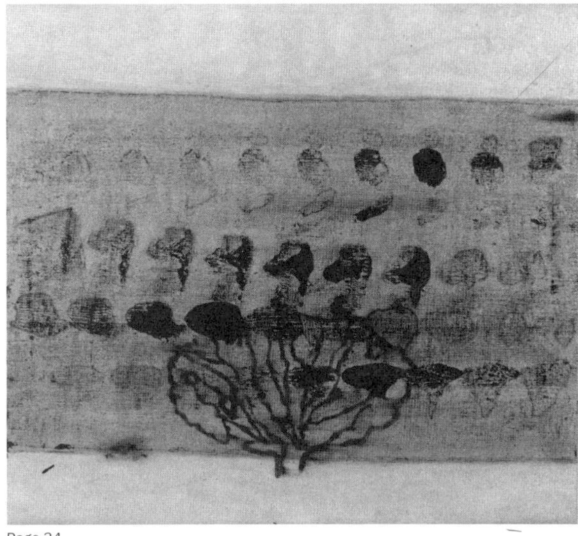
Page 10

Page 34

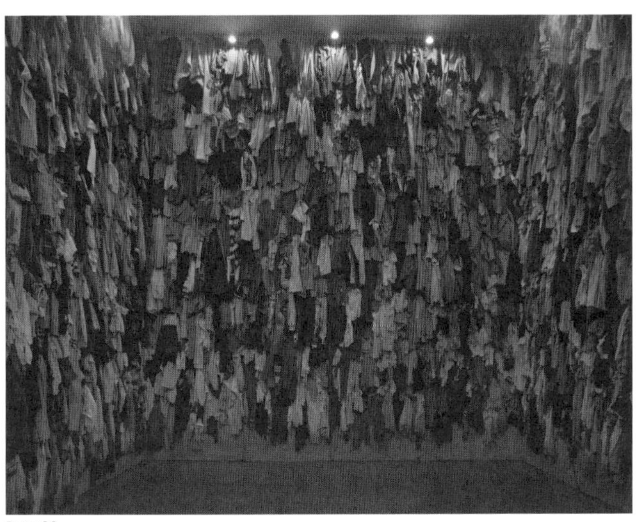
Page 22

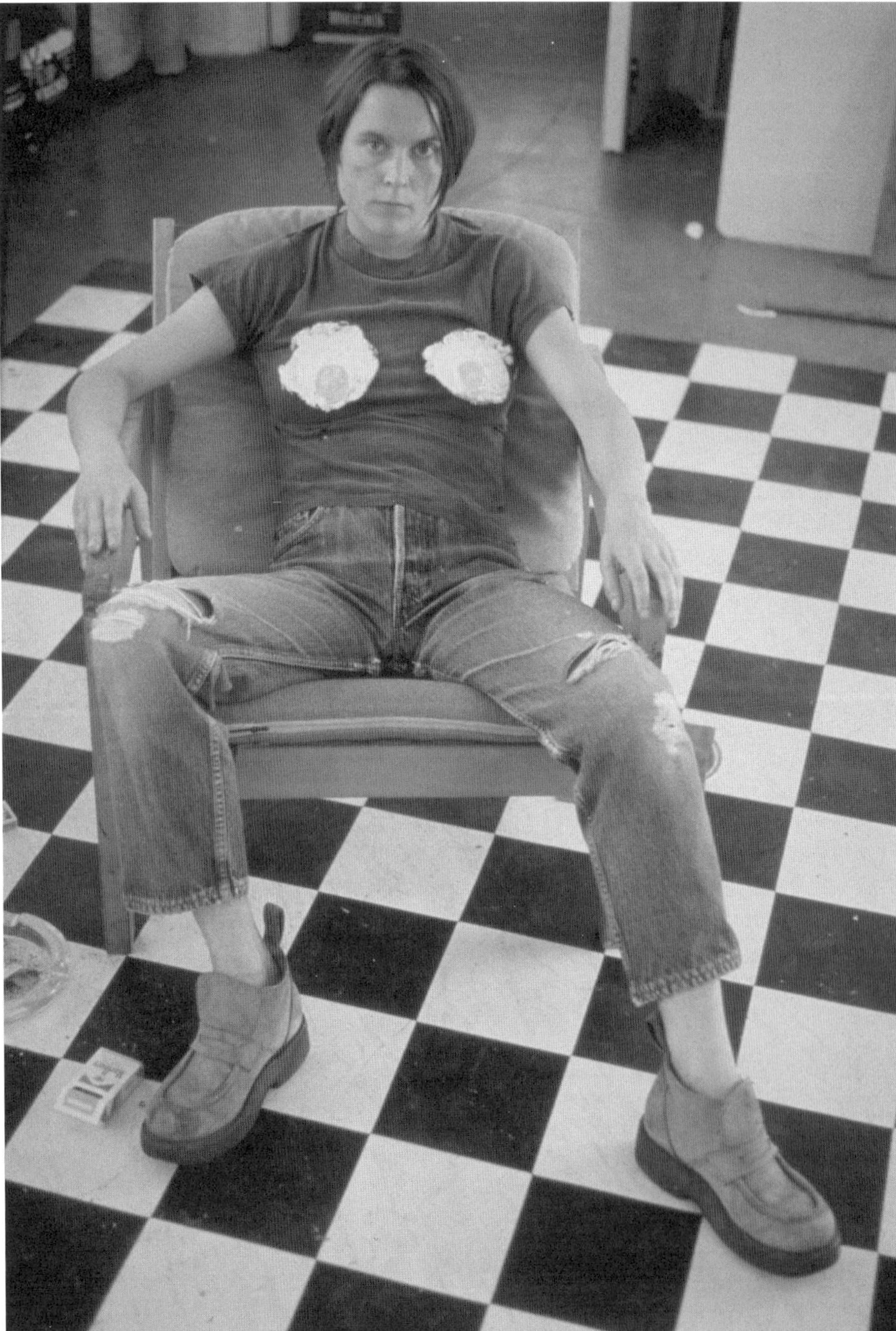

Sarah Lucas, 'Self-Portrait with Fried Eggs', *1996*

Out of the Void

In the early 60s, Bob Dylan wrote that battle cry of the young liberal Vietnam-protesting westerner: "aThe Times They Are A-changin". This was the great humanist decade, the last moment when the modernist sensibility believed that the collective mattered, that it could – indeed would – change the world. In the 19th century (with its passion for scholarship and systematisation, and its emphasis on the role of scientific enquiry and investigation), philosophical thought sought to replace God – now declared dead by Nietzsche – with the Human and the Social. Among intellectuals, particularly in France, Marxism filled the space left by religion and belief. But in 1968 on the streets of Paris – that seat of contemporary thought – something changed. Something was defeated as we waved goodbye to oppositional socialism. The final death blow came from the lance of Thatcherism. Thatcher may have quoted Francis of Assisi on the steps of Downing Street upon her election as Prime Minister, but she was soon proclaiming there was no such thing as society.

We find ourselves nearing the end of a century, a millennium, staring into the void, at a point of philosophical stasis. For the best part of two decades, we have lived on the edge of that psychological wasteland symbolised by the French philosopher Jean Baudrillard as both the empty space of the desert and the American freeway, with its plethora of circular intersections leading somewhere, but going nowhere in particular.

The current renaissance of British art started in the 80s. While Jon Thompson and Michael Craig-Martin at Goldsmiths were blurring the boundaries of painting, sculpture and drawing, and training young artists in the wiles of marketing, Charles Saatchi was buying up and helping to establish an art that had *death of society* written through it like *Blackpool* in a stick of rock. The penile-nosed mannequins of Jake and Dinos Chapman, the "laddish" installations of Sarah Lucas and the shiny hermetic paintings of Gary Hume – all bursting at the seams with insouciant irony – seem like a collective psychological denial of the real. Ironic art is all glittering surface. It fears depth. In the reflective gloss of Hume's paintings, every trace of alterity is elided. While Andy Warhol used similar techniques to emphasise the brittle, self-reflexive, consumerist nature of society, these works function like Ecstasy at a rave, making palatable the endless emptiness of the present.

It is difficult to find suitable terminology to describe an opposition to this cool, satiated position without resorting to cliché or remembrance of things past. The available vocabulary is weighted down by accumulated associations. Words such as "spirit", "sublime" and "transcendent" have all been debased, hijacked by the touchy-feely school of self-expression. It is from philosophy's peripheries that other possibilities arise – from investigations of the feminine and the body by such writers as Julia Kristeva and Luce Irigaray, from places outside the centrality of western thought, such as Buddhism.

In her essay on 'Woman and Space', the cultural critic Philippa Berry argues that "as postmodern thinkers, we have observed the entropic collapse of the supposedly centred "humanist" subjectivity that took, however improbably, the heliocentric Copernican system as its "ground"… [This] new… spatiality… can, perhaps, best be defined as a space of meditation: that is, as a place of articulation between a variety of different versions of space". As the cultural critic Rosi Braidotti has suggested, the void is the space that is created by "the crisis of the master's discourse". The willingness of writers such as these to look at "an in-between space which undoes differences, while it reasserts them, and which veils as well as reveals the production of meanings through opposition", means that we can begin to envisage a place in which art can function in a mode that is offered neither as irony, defence, sound bite, nor the re-establishment of false sentiment or nostalgia.

Writers like Kristeva suggest that a possible arena for a renaissance of "authentic" art is the space left by the death of the human subject. She proposes a return to the Platonic *chora* with its resonance of emptiness and absence. "The *chora* is the *locus* of a *chaos* which *is* and which *becomes*…." It is a place that exists in the space between idealism and materialism, the sacred and profane, between silence and language, the male and female, between being and nothing. It is here that new possibilities of expression may be found – at this point of stillness and meditation, of layered semantic, in this essentially feminine space (according to Luce Irigaray) – where metaphor acts as palimpsest, slowly revealing meaning. Such

work is not simply confined to a singular form such as painting. It exists as installation and sculpture through to photography.

Susan Hiller is an artist of integrity. Excavating the spaces between forms, her art is infused with issues that concern language, gender, desire and death, and is informed by her empathy with "the other". "By dreaming", she suggests, "creatively and in an aware sense", she is able to investigate the possibility of a langue in the interstices between the microcosm and the macrocosm, between the everyday and the spiritual. Her 1995 show at the Freud Museum used the vocabulary of archaeology and psychoanalysis – in a series of boxes presented in a museum case – to investigate dream and memory. Amongst the items contained were divining rods and water from sacred streams. Meaning was not singular, but revealed slowly like an archaeologist's brushed fragments.

Maria Chevska also employs different media. Sometimes beautiful, sometimes unbearably raw, her work uses embroidery, fabric, canvas and paint. In her show 'Weight' at 33 Great Sutton Street, London, 1996, five sets of seven small panels were hung high on a wall to resemble an architectural frieze. Three of these – the same dimensions as Hans Holbein's depiction of the dead Christ in Basle – were made of white quilted fabric, stretched like canvas and fixed to the wall. Another was freestanding. Paint had been dripped onto the back and seeped through the fabric like a stain. Other panels were rubbed with graphite and sand to give the appearance of lead. In one corner, a pile of folded clothes set in kaolin looked liked a heap of discarded bandages. The piece alluded to the great religious works of the past, to the traces left on the Turin shroud, whilst also making oblique reference to Joseph Beuys, Alberto Burri and the *arte povera* movement.

Callum Innes's alchemical works with their dripped gold paint and wax suggest intergalactic explosions and imply change, chance and transformation. Looking towards the extending horizons of nuclear physics, they explore the desire to explain human existence. The bled, pigmented surfaces of Jane Bustin, which echo the "sacred" spaces of Barnett Newman and Mark Rothko, become a visual equivalent of the Baudrillardian void, filled with the quietude of contemplation and meditation. The sculpture of Rachel Whiteread consistently manages to adopt both an iconoclastic position and one of articulate integrity. Her castings of negative space not only challenge our notions of sculpture (as monolithic and phallic, heroically placed on a plinth), but investigate personal and social issues surrounding memory and loss. 'House' (a concrete cast of a Victorian terraced house, completed in autumn 1993 and exhibited at the original location – 193 Grove Road – in East London, where all the other houses in the street had been knocked down by the council) was an illustration of how the avant-garde can touch even the "uninformed" passer-by in the street.

Kathy Prendergast's graphite maps – fragile webs that transform poetic descriptions of locality into explorations of the human imagination – become meditative mazes and maps of the unconscious. That many of them look like livers, lungs or brains is no accident; it connects these places to the body. As in Italo Calvino's 'Invisible Cities', they become the sites of our dreams.

History and the striations left by human development are charted in Maria Lalic's systematic paintings. Using the self-limiting structure of the colour chart found in a *Windsor and Newton* manual, which organises the development of pigments into six historical periods – cave (4 colours), Egyptian (7), Greek (5), Italian (7), 18th and 19th centuries (18) and 20th century (12) – she creates series of monochrome paintings

in which the layering mimics the expansion of the artist's palette through the centuries. The works created not only find a way of making sense of the activity of painting within a contemporary context, but also chart humanity's continuing desire to establish meaning through mark-making.

Science and the natural world collide in the photographs of Helen Sear to create small mystical epiphanies. In 'Divided Ground', a 1996 series of photographs, she uses images of brushwood and gorse set in stony locations such as Delphi – a place of oracular mystery – through which to flood light. Each is abutted, to form a diptych, against a second image of a spiral or diamond of light photographed through a dispersive medium such as water. Found, rather than constructed, these images remain ambiguous, ethereal, rendering indistinct the boundaries between dream and reality in a re-figured state of consciousness.

The Irish sculptor Eilís O'Connell takes as her starting point a vision of Ireland based on its people, landscape and history. Her spare works – employing stretched canvas, bronze and painted birch – resonate (though fully contemporary in their making) with Celtic history. Sculptures of bent and curved wood resemble iron-age musical instruments, while others are reminiscent of domestic and agricultural implements. The small painted steel dome of 'Steel Swelling', *1992*, capped by the lip-shaped opening of a shell can be read as both areola and nipple, and might have been the breastplate of some Amazonian warrior. Full of clarity and light, these works are both sensuous and rooted, whilst also being fully aware of the architectural possibilities of space.

That the tide may be shifting towards a more authentic engagement is demonstrated by two of the women artists nominated for the recent Turner Prize. In her 'From Life', Berlin, *1996* – included in 'Material Culture'

at the Hayward last year – Christine
Borland installed a high glass shelf below
a spotlight in the gallery. Bones, part
of a complete human skeleton, were placed
on each shelf, then dust was sifted lightly
over the whole, and the bones removed.
The faint traces left, projected onto the
gallery wall, spoke poignantly of the death
and war that have dominated this violent
century. The philosophical basis of Cornelia
Parker's work is transformation. Objects
transform into evocative "symbolic
representations" – metaphors for change.
To this end, she has thrown objects off the
White Cliffs of Dover and then run them
over with a steamroller, understanding that
unless things evolve, they die.

At this point, on the edge of the millennium,
we can stare into the great void ahead and
turn away from its vastness, have another
fix, another "sensation" and fall deeper
into self-destructive nihilism, or we can –
as Berry suggests – use "the potential of
this awareness of emptiness to create
a new capacity for genuine dialogue and
communication". I am not advocating
nostalgic kitsch or mawkish sentimentality,
but rather something visceral, powerful
and rooted. As Luce Irigaray insists, "The
transition to a new age in turn necessitates
a new perception and a new conception
of time and space, our occupation of place,
the different envelopes known as identity".

Out of the Void

Contemporary Visual Arts
Issue 17, 1997

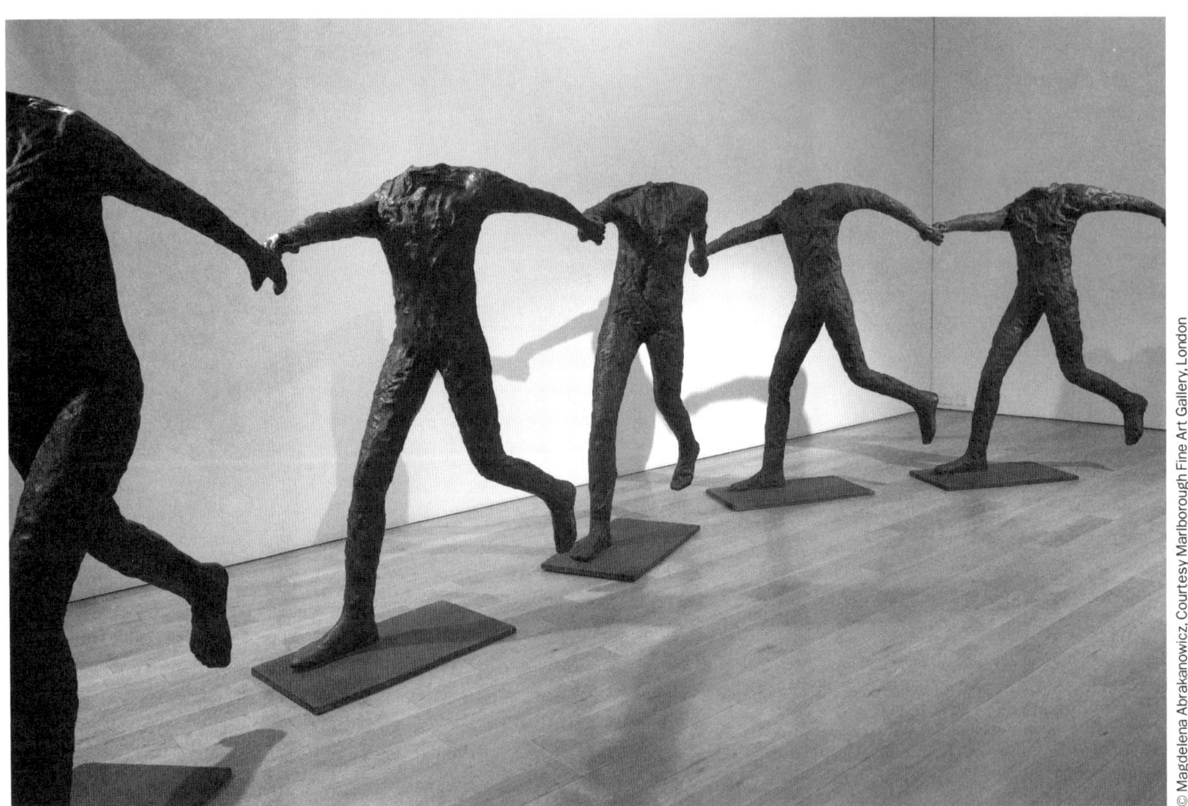

Magdelena Abakanowicz, '7 Dancing Figures,' *2001*

Out with the Old,
In with the New

Is late 20th-century culture ending in crisis? And, if so, is this due to the gradual breakdown of any consensual system of belief that allows for allegiance to anything beyond the self? Secularism, individualism, bureaucracy, pluralism and the market all sit at modernity's core. The increasing western (and possibly global) embrace of these values has, it might be argued, led to a (late) modernist refusal of the "sacred", to an "emptying out" of 20th-century culture. In the first half of the century, poets such as T.S. Eliot wrote that "we are the hollow men", and W.B. Yeats declared that "things fall apart; the centre cannot hold" – but little could they have known how much they were signposting the state of contemporary culture and its values.

The history of (post)modernism embraces the collapse of both the Marxist and the Romantic vision. The Marxist position held that all art should function as a social force. This demanded wide audiences and an integration of the aesthetic into common signs and meanings. The Romantic position placed at its centre the individual psyche and the expression of its drives and desires. This turning inwards – away from the growing pragmatism and materialism of the early 20th century – by artists such as Wassily Kandinsky or Kasimir Malevich – grew from a belief that art should be a form of "pure creation" with its own "spiritual essence". "Art no longer cares to serve the state or religion", Malevich announced.

Art thus became self-sufficient, an aesthetic experience that was an end in itself. Purity was all, and this could only be achieved through a formalism unsullied by the uncomfortable questions thrown up by capitalism and totalitarianism.

Even by the century's halfway mark, the Abstract Expressionists were still adhering to this heroic "spiritual" tradition. "So long as modern society is dominated by the love of property", Robert Motherwell announced in 1944, "the artist has no alternative to formalism... Modern artists have had to replace other social values with the strictly aesthetic". But by the 60s, this idealistic view was already being diluted. Clement Greenberg in particular promulgated the notion that art had no higher purpose than itself – that art simply did what art did. Finally, we had arrived at the *sine qua non* of 20th-century art: the dictum of "art for art's sake". And with its embrace, the notion that the artist stood outside of society, resisting its bourgeois demands through the avant-garde, began to falter. As Andy Warhol claimed: "Being good in business is the most fascinating kind of art. Making money is art and working is art and good business is the best art". Marcel Duchamp understood that once art is shaped by the market, it sets itself up to be appropriated and refigured in a hall of distorting mirrors. His form of resistance was to give up art for chess.

Art as a commodity is, by definition, malleable, open to the dictates of the gallery, dealer and collector. Success becomes a Faustian pact whereby the artist sells his/her soul for the chance of 15 minutes of fame. But artists must now suffer a new anxiety – not whether they have anything to communicate, but whether they are "fashionable". For a suddenly "unfashionable" artist can be as easily discarded as last year's embarrassing fashions. We may have arrived at a token pluralism, but we need to face the fact that when everything becomes art, art very easily becomes nothing, as Alice found whilst staring at the Cheshire cat's grin. In a society where "success" and "visibility" are the ultimate grails, artists are in danger of being sucked into a system whereby they are simply the producers of another commodity – of what the critic Suzi Gablik calls "aesthetic goods". As Warhol so astutely predicted, art then simply becomes a means of production to achieve "fame". And if fame is the ultimate goal, being an artist is easily interchangeable with being a rock star or a chic restaurateur. Artists, as Gablik attests, "now want art to serve their careers rather than seeing themselves as serving art". Soul searching, suffering and meaning are all optional (and largely unfashionable) extras. The question here is whether art, today, is doomed to become just another token of economic exchange, or whether it can find a new way to attempt to be autonomous, questioning and subversive – to examine, to use Yeats' phrase, "the deep heart's core".

The artists who seem to be engaged with these deeper issues are linked by a willingness to look into what Rainer Maria Rilke called "ancient terrors". They turn away from the easy gratification of one-line, one-idea art. The "post-war" generation of artists such as Jannis Kounellis, Anselm Kiefer, Christian Boltanski and Joseph Beuys did this. Rather than accept the philosopher Theodor Adorno's testament that there could not be poetry (or art) after the Holocaust, they looked deep into that dark and "ancient terror" created by the void of war to ask questions about nationalism, guilt, memory, time, mortality and loss. These are artists who have understood the power of archetypes, those symbols that run like underground rivers in the depths of the psyche to re-emerge, again and again, in overground streams of human consciousness and thought.

Another such artist is the Polish sculptor Magdalena Abakanowicz. In 1987 she wrote: "My sculpture is free of the function of glorifying any doctrine, any religion, any individual. It is not décor for an interior, a garden or a palace, or a housing development. It is neither a formal aesthetic experiment nor an interpretation of reality... I transmit my experience of existential problems, embedded in my forms built in space". Her work owes something to the edgy post-war figures of Alberto Giacometti. The bronze crowds 'Puella', *1991* and 'Standing Figures', *1994-95* – made up of armies of spindly headless bodies ranged in rows – speak with bathetic, poetic eloquence and a minimum of melodrama, of the loss, suffering and displacement of this century.

For a long time now, the narrative and the political have been given little houseroom in contemporary art. As a white South African living through apartheid, William Kentridge had plenty of time to witness its disastrous effects. Not since Max Beckmann, George Grosz, or the political theatre of Bertolt Brecht has an artist dealt so savagely with the result of political devastation. Kentridge asks uncomfortable questions, not only about guilt and culpability, but also about what we choose to remember, what we choose to forget. His short animated "films", drawn in nervy smudged charcoal, are surreal accretions built from the haunting landscapes of memory and the nightmares of South Africa's damaged past. The process of continuous drawing and erasure mimics that of psychological denial. Kentridge puts South Africa's past on the couch. In 'Felix in Exile', Felix sits in a seedy hotel room like the lonely protagonist in Samuel Beckett's 'Krapp's Last Tape'. His suitcase is filled with images of the broken, bloodied bodies of African workers scattered in a devastated landscape of abandoned mines. Soho Eckstein, a wealthy white industrialist, lies in a hospital bed in a coma wearing his pinstripe suit as if it were armour. Within his body, the trappings of power, like cancerous growths, are depicted: telephone, typewriters and adding machines. Interspersed between these are the dead bodies of black men. Kentridge's work is raw and uncomfortable, for it demands that we do not slip into a veiling amnesia, that we do not erase memory, and that the personal is still the political.

British artist John Goto is likewise unafraid of big issues. Since 1987, he has been working on a series of interrelated exhibitions concerning the history of the century. In his serious and far-reaching work 'Five Tales from the Twentieth Century' (which includes 'Terezin', *1987-98,* 'The Atomic Yard', *1988-90;* 'The Scar', *1990-93;* 'The Commissar of Space', *1993-97* and 'The Framer's Collection', *1995-97),* Goto explores our experience of history through notions of identity and collective memory. Employing an ambitious palimpsest of imagery, this vast project attempts to make sense of the 20th century through the use of poetic fiction, narrative and visual images. Goto engages with issues of high ethical seriousness: World War II, the Holocaust, the collapse of Eastern Europe, and our post-socialist, consumerist society. Whilst Goto's earlier works looked at the redemptive power of art, at memory and the collapse of social systems, 'Capital Arcade' – his new work and the last in the series – examines the vacuum left by the collapse of socialism. Using a computer, he "idealises" the visual signs in a fictional

shopping mall, and renders them anodyne with the smoothing out of all ethnic and social difference. With deadpan satire, Goto presents a post-socialist Brave New World where "I shop therefore I am".

"The struggle we are witnessing today is not between conflicting moral beliefs, between nature and human technology: it is between our inner and our outer lives," Bill Viola has claimed. Viola creates meditations on the human condition. In the 'Nantes Triptych', *1992,* the viewer is confronted by a larger-than-life, slow-motion image of a woman (the artist's wife) giving birth, while in the far panel we are asked to bear witness to the death of Viola's mother. In 'Arc of Ascent', *1992,* a vast figure is submerged in water on a giant screen, apparently suspended somewhere between life and Earth. With his uncompromising images, Viola reminds us that these states are inexorably intertwined. What does it mean to us in this sanitised, commodified world to be forced to witness life's natural cycle, when the only pornography left to us in a consumer society is the pornography of death with its insulting refusal to be bought? By confronting our own transience, Viola invites us to embrace the fundamental humanity of others, and to see in these images, as John Donne claimed nearly three centuries ago, that "No man is an island, entire of itself... Any man's death diminishes me because I am involved in Mankind".

At the beginning of the century, F.T. Marinetti declared that artists had to free themselves from "the stinking gangrene of... professors, archaeologists, touring guides and antique dealers". Art had to be severed from the past in order to become free. But, like all licence, absolute freedom becomes a value of diminishing returns, and we are left with the question: freedom from whom, to do what? For a society to sustain itself, to avoid wallowing in either false nostalgia or gross narcissism, its members have to hold certain values in common.

Undoubtedly the great achievement
of modernism has been the development
of individual freedom; but Thatcher was,
perhaps, right in ways she little understood,
when she claimed that there is no such thing
as society. For art to be more than another
investment, another diversion, it needs
to reconnect itself to its transformative
potential. Artists such as Beuys and Kiefer
have pointed the way. Yet the revolution of
Modernism has been in danger of throwing
out the baby with the bathwater. This is
the law of history that Heraclitus called
enantiodromia, which claims that once one
state reaches its zenith, it then collapses into
its opposite. Modernism set out to escape
the clutches of tradition and the academy.
But a new conservatism of weary cynicism
is in danger of taking its place. As we are
left holding the shards, of not only this
century but also the millennium, the words
of Beckett are left ringing in our ears: "Fail
again. Fail better".

Out with the Old,
In with the New

Contemporary Visual Arts
Issue 26, 1999

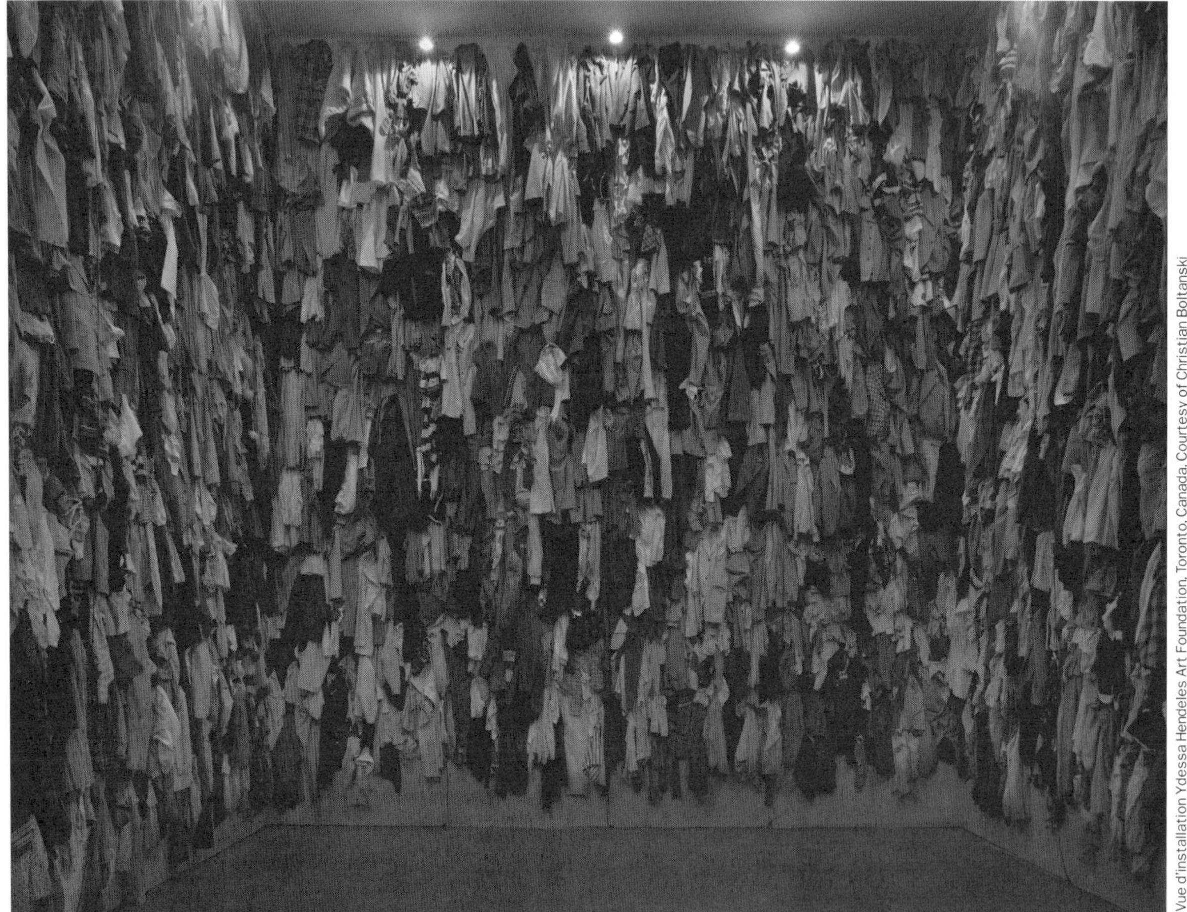

Christian Boltanski, 'Canada', *1988*

Christian Boltanski

In 'Language and Silence', George Steiner talks of being a "kind of survivor". There is a way that I, even born some years after the war, am still implicated by the might-have-beens that link me, as someone who was born Jewish, by an invisible thread to others who were less lucky. Like Boltanski, I do not really know anything of Judaism's festivals, orthodoxies or theology but know that like him, for the Nazis, I would have been defined as such. And because of that label history places on us, I and he are inextricably united to that past.

Boltanski's work is much more subtle than simply being about Jewish history, the Holocaust, or even guilt and survival. Yet it is the fact of this cataclysmic event that gives colour and shade to his work. As the French philosopher Jean-François Lyotard said, "We are all Jews after the Holocaust". By this he meant that we are all capable of being caught up in atrocities, in the events of Bosnia and Rwanda, in the conflict in the Middle East. More than anything, Boltanski's work is about the fact of dying. In his work, death becomes an aspect of life. When we meet he reminds me of Christ's last words, "Father why have you forsaken me?... It is finished". He finds it both incredible and beautiful that a whole religion should have been built on a moment of weakness and despair. Christian narratives are embedded in his work as much as Jewish history, he explains. If he had to choose a religion, it would

be Christianity. This, I believe, is because his work is also about redemption and love.

"I am nobody. The more I work, the more I disappear", he reflects. We are sitting talking amid thousands of telephone directories in the South London Gallery, where he is installing his new show. With his shaved head and unshaven face, this small nervy Frenchman in a grubby black jumper, obsessively poking strands of tobacco into his pipe with stubby stained fingers, is the epitome of Gallic Existentialism – an escapee from a Camus novel. Boltanski is a bundle of paradoxes, a quintessentially 20th-century artist working in the 21st century, a Judeo-Christian artist who has no belief in God, a man who describes himself as a painter, yet who makes installations, a Communist sympathiser who was never a Communist but rather a romantic sceptic.

He first came to prominence with major exhibitions in the mid 80s and early 90s at the Georges Pompidou Centre, Paris and at the Whitechapel Gallery, where he created magical installations using personal objects presented as archival artefacts, which acquired an iconic status. His use of non-art materials – school photos, family albums, rusty archives and biscuit tins, along with piles of old clothes – memorialises the unnamed and unknown: the dead citizens of a Swiss town, the workers of a Halifax carpet factory, as well as the erased children of the Holocaust. These are the traces left by individual, yet anonymous, lives. Beneath flickering shadows and bare light bulbs, the spaces in which he works take on something of the hushed reverence of a church or theatre to generate poignant evocations of loss. He prefers factories and churches to galleries, and has made work in Grand Central Station, New York and La Chapelle de l'Hôpital de la Salpêtrière, Paris. He creates, he says, "small memories" that give substance to the unofficial histories of the ordinary. It is as if this collection of ephemera might ward off death, keep its final, all-encompassing anonymity at bay. Like the makeshift shrines at the site of a crash, these works ritualise grieving and create ways of coming to terms with the most modern of taboos, death.

All work, he claims, begins with a kind of trauma. Child psychotherapist Melanie Klein talks about art being a form of reparation for infantile rage at the abandoning mother. She describes how, out of the smithereens of anger, something new can be reconstructed. Born in France in 1944, the son of a Jewish father and a Catholic mother, Boltanski experienced a childhood that was coloured by experiences of anti-Semitism. His father had spent much of the war hiding in basements. His is the enduring angst of the outsider. Early on, he pretended to speak of his childhood, though the reality disappeared in a construct of false mythologising. He cannot now remember what was true and what a fabrication, having created a kind of universal childhood that binds him to the mass of humanity. This humanistic web is central to his vision.

Whilst he implicitly deals with big themes such as the Holocaust, his art can also be read as a psychoanalytic journey; a process of mourning, not only for the victims of the Shoa, but for the death of his own childhood or, maybe, for the lost child within us all. His is a search for self-forgiveness. It is no

coincidence that Freud was also a Jew. Western culture is, for Boltanski, about stories. We create our own myths. Stories are attached to objects and to the small moments and memories that, like Marcel Proust's madeleine, they yield. A photograph, an old dress – each detonates its hidden histories. These are traces not only of something lost, but also of something shed. This shedding implies transformation; a movement from state to state, from unconsciousness to some greater consciousness.

For Boltanski, who is not conventionally religious, art is the religion of our day. And art, like religion, is a form of ritual, a way of ordering and making sense of the world. It is, he says, about recognition. That's why he uses familiar objects such as biscuit tins. There is always a moment when something clicks in the mind or the heart. What philosopher and writer Roland Barthes called the *punctum,* that "Ah yes, that's it!" moment that pierces the consciousness. Boltanski also works within the tradition of Christian art using the icon, and the sense of mystery, theatre and kitsch so beloved by the Catholic Church. He has said he no longer knows what it means to be an artist. Since the collapse of the Berlin wall, we have lost all sense of utopias. For him, art either works or it doesn't. Aesthetics no longer mean anything. It is not a question of good or bad. "What I make, is something different to art", he says. He tells a story of setting up an installation in Santiago de Compostela when an old lady asked what he was doing. "Commemorating the dead Swiss", he said, and she seemed quite happy. If he had told her he was making a piece of conceptual art, she might have felt he was defiling the place.

A child of the 60s, he was part of that decade's radical *zeitgeist,* influenced by the magical, priestly rituals of Joseph Beuys and the mutely enigmatic silences of the Catholic Andy Warhol. In the late 1960s and early 70s, he made little balls of modelled clay, along with small makeshift knives and roughly carved lumps of sugar, which he exhibited with bits of recycled string. This essentially non-hierarchical and democratic art followed the anthropologist Claude Levi-Strauss's model of *bricolage:* art made from the *ad hoc*. Art, he feels, has to struggle against what is established. For many years, he was a member of a lose network of Parisian artists that included his partner Annette Messager, for whom art was a form of resistance against the strictures of bourgeois society. In 1970, invited to illustrate the cover of an American poetry magazine, 'Blue Pig', devoted to the poet George Tysh, he supplied a photo of a single, bare, electric light bulb and a few balls of earth. Tysh gave the issue the title 'Cheapness means forgiveness', an apt epigram for Boltanski's work. There is a lack of preciousness about what he does and the objects he uses. If he had been an Italian, he might easily have been part of the *arte povera* movement. In a way, he is a deeply unfashionable artist. Committed and involved, he believes in issues.

He has claimed that the displays of inconsequential little objects – their use and function now long forgotten – in the big metal cases of the Parisian anthropological Musée de l'Homme were a major influence on his work. In 1973, he began a 15-year series, 'Inventories', which involved displaying all the household objects of a deceased person, without any commentary. In another work, using the archives of Michel Durand-Dessert – Durand being the most common French surname – he placed photos from the family album in a plausible chronological order, which, of course, was different from the narrative attributed to them by their owners. Photographs, with their implicit associations with loss, absence and death, have become a potent vehicle in Boltanski's work. For memory is fragile, dependent on the icon and the relic. We need evidence, such as The Mandylion of Byzantium or The Veronica of Rome,

it seems: rational explanations for the mysterious. Boltanski never takes photographs himself, and claims to feel more like a recycler than a photographer.

In 1988, he was invited to make an installation in Toronto. He called it 'Canada'. The name not only referred to the host country, but also to the euphemism used by the Nazis for the depot where the effects – clothes, shoes, spectacles, even hair – of their victims were deposited before recycling. The piece consisted of thousands of articles of clothing acquired in flea markets, and was followed, at the end of the 80s, by other works such as 'Reserves: The Purim Holiday'. In the vocabulary of psychoanalysis, the word "phantom" describes the secret pain passed from generation to generation without ever being made explicit. Boltanski refutes Theodor Adorno's claim that it is not possible to make art after Auschwitz. These works represent the slow labour of mourning, the coming to terms with guilt and the secrets buried, not only at the heart of nations, but of families.

His 1991 installation, using photographs of dead Swiss (a people who have never been involved in war), poses questions about the uniqueness of suffering. Photos of Nazis, photos of Jews, of dead Swiss, they are all, he claims, just people. As viewers, we cannot assess who is a victim, who a torturer. All of us have the capacity to be both. He photocopies the photographs again and again, so that they become reproductions of reproductions and individuality becomes lost in a sea of humanity. What these works force us to do is face the mechanisms that made the Holocaust possible – misanthropy, abstraction, self-loathing, objectification. These things do not just belong to history. They are with us every day: now. He claims that he finds it hard to accept that dying is part of life. He acknowledges that we are each unique, yet but a speck in the flow of history. He quotes Napoleon's infamous remark as he looked down on the carnage of Austerlitz – both shocked at its cold-blooded callousness, whilst also acknowledging its truth – that "A night of love in Paris will replace everybody".

When the Tate Gallery bought 'Dead Swiss on Shelves with White Cotton', they amused him by asking what they should do if the cotton went yellow after a few years. He told them to change it. When asked what to do if the photos faded, he replied that there were always more dead Swiss. Then when they complained that the shelves would not fit, as they had been made for a different room, he told them to get more shelves. When a slightly exasperated curator asked just what it was that the gallery had actually bought, Boltanski responded that they had bought photos of dead Swiss, and shelves with white cotton: an idea not an object.

When he first introduced biscuit tins into his work, he peed on them to make them rust. But he used so many tins that he had to switch to *Coca Cola*. When they were exhibited in Hamburg and Oslo, the curators unpacked them wearing white gloves. This was ridiculous as the gloves immediately became rusty and red. The biscuit tins weren't precious and should never have been treated as such. They could easily have been replaced. Boltanski's work is about relics. In fact, it shares a similarity with the art of other cultures, such as Africa, where religious or ritual masks have no financial or material value and, when no longer used ceremonially, are, often, left to rot.

He views his work as a musical score. Akin to a musical composition, the piece he creates has no real existence until it is brought into life by a new performance or installation. It is, in a way, about reincarnation. For when a pianist plays a work of Bach, it is always Bach, though it might be Bach interpreted by Artur Rubinstein or Daniel Barenboim, just as a Boltanski might be interpreted by curator "Mr. Jones". His work is unlike, say, a Willem

de Kooning or a Mark Rothko, where the autograph of the artist is paramount. He also sees himself as closer to the geometrical abstraction of Piet Mondrian and Kasimir Malevich than to the emptied Modernism of Donald Judd and Carl Andre. Like the 19th-century French writer Gabriel-Desire Laverdant, he believes that avant-garde art is an "attempt to lay bare… all the brutalities, the filth, which are at the base of our society". It seems impossible now to imagine an artist of a younger generation having such a politically engaged response to art.

This new installation, 'Les Abonnés du Téléphone', transforms the space into a huge reference library with some 3000 telephone directories collected from around the world. Visitors can sit at tables and browse through the directories beneath the stark light bulbs, searching for lost friends abroad or trying to interpret the arcane listings in a language such as Japanese. Accompanying this is a sound piece in which the names of 12,000 registered voters living within a 10-minute radius of the gallery are emitted from shelves around the space. Central to this work are the implicit tensions between the global and the local, the individual and society, the included and the dispossessed. For, like all archives, this, by definition, is incomplete and flawed. How many of those whose names appear in the directories have died since their printing, and how many disappeared? In the theatrical semi-darkness a number of other more disturbing resonances are suggested: the efficient lists of the Nazi exterminators, of psychiatric patients and prisoners.

As Boltanski fiddles with his pipe, he emphasises that his work is a resistance to what he calls the "post-human". I ask what he means, and he says cloning, genetic engineering, science that takes away our individuality and uniqueness. This piece, he says, nodding at the telephone directories, is a very Christian work. It is about community. These people are his brothers and sisters,

just like the dead Swiss, the children of
the Holocaust, and even the Nazis. He
never, he says, suggests answers, only poses
questions. Like Janus, he manages to look
in two directions at once, turning to history
whilst trying to make sense of the present.

Christian Boltanski

Compiled from: The Independent
6th April, 2002 and a talk at
the South London Gallery, 2003

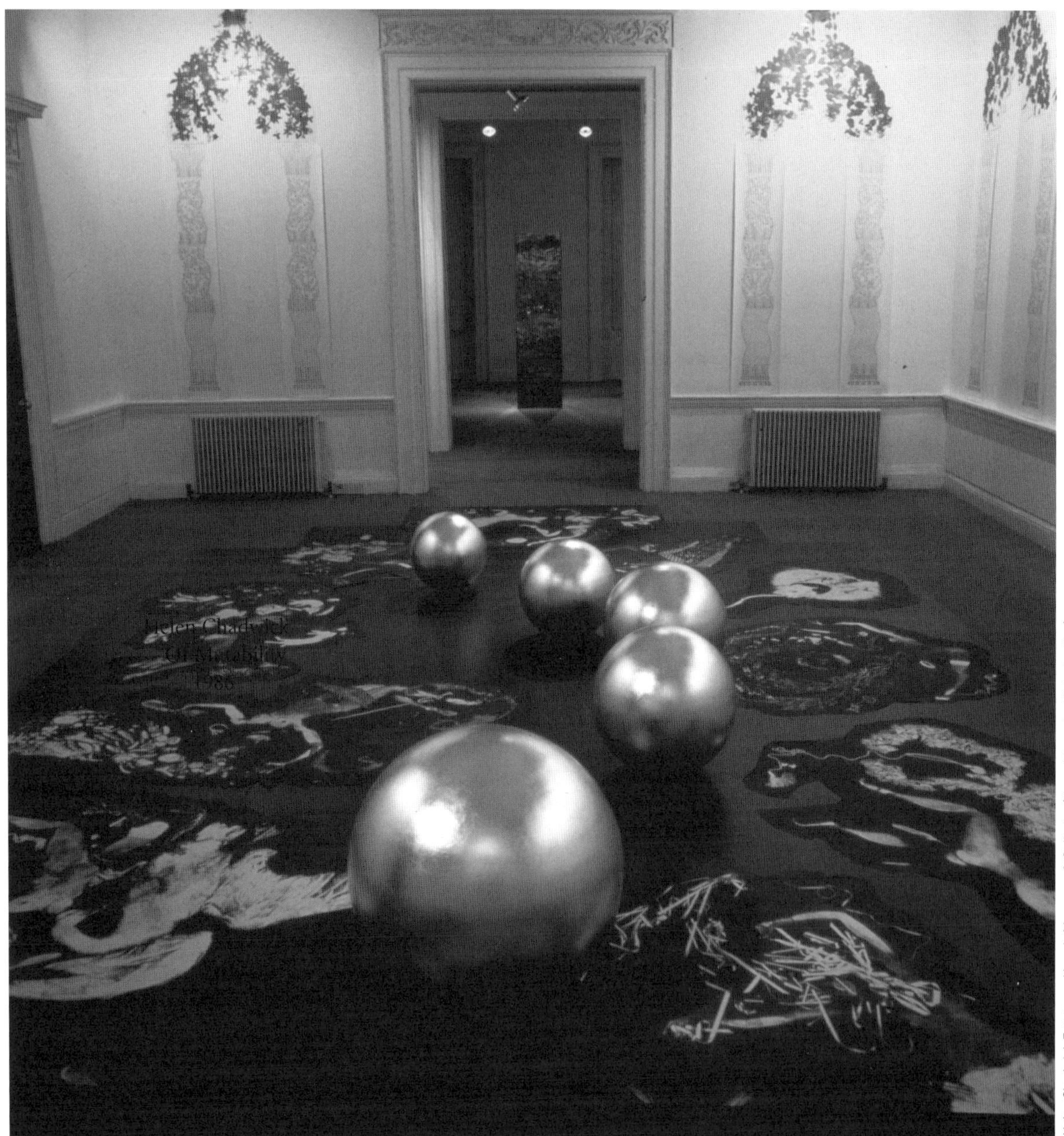

Helen Chadwick, 'Of Mutability', 1986

Helen Chadwick
Changing the Landscape
of Sculpture

It is said that those whom the gods favour die young. Sylvia Plath, Anne Sexton, Frida Kahlo, Jackson Pollock and James Dean have all achieved iconic status. But would this have been assured if we had had to witness their dull levelling into middle age? Does untimely death – the erasure of the still-nubile body, the restless imagination brimming with unfulfilled promise – ensure, certain artistic canonisation?

It is only months since the artist Helen Chadwick died unexpectedly on Friday 15th March 1996, at the age of 42. The art world was reduced to a state of shock that one so apparently energetic and youthful, "with her smooth, light, bendy epicene body and her signature Louise Brooks haircut", as her friend Marina Warner described her, should have been so tragically snatched from their midst. She was described in 'The Sunday Telegraph' as "one of Britain's leading modern artists", and in 'The Independent' as "one of contemporary art's most provocative and profound figures". Though she appears to have had a heart attack or some rare virus, the notion is fermenting that she died of overwork, of dedication to her art. Friends were grief-stricken. Her funeral, according to Judy Collins, curator of 20th-century art at the Tate, and one of the organisers, had all the sense of occasion and theatre Helen would have wanted. "It was", she says, "a bit like a Greek drama".

To write about an artist's work so soon after her death is a delicate affair. Those who loved her – and there are many, both men and women, who talk of her generosity of spirit, and her influence as a teacher – naturally want to ensure her place within the pantheon of art history, and some have written passionately and eloquently about her work as a result. I hardly knew her. I met her only twice, briefly, at private views, and was struck by her immaculate, boyish, Peter Pan elegance and her small stubby artisan's hands bedecked with silver rings. But we only exchanged social niceties. So it is to her work that I must turn in trying to evaluate this all-too-brief life.

In the early 80s, Helen Chadwick turned away from agit-prop to portrayals of the body, which became the main site for her investigations of the self. In her 'Soliloquy to Flesh', written in 1989, she claimed – with what, in hindsight, now seems like devastating irony in view of her early demise – that "my apparatus is a body of sensory systems with which to correlate experience. Not exactly real, I am none the less conscious, via physicality, of duration, of passing through".

The first work of hers I saw and wrote about was 'Ego Geometria Sum', *1982-84*. Titles were important to her. She valued erudition and read widely. Here, as she was to do again and again, she confronted the mysteries of the life-cycle. The Pythagorean thesis that a number of regular geometric solids could account for all nature's constructions was the central tenet of this installation. Ten sculptural polyhedra treated with photo-emulsion bore the imprinted image of her naked body. Each object – an incubator, a font, a pram, boat, wigwam and bed – acted as a Proustian trigger, stimulating memories and sensations from her childhood. Around these hung ten photographs showing her as the naked Atlas bearing the heavy sculptural forms, while in 'Labours' she appeared to be struggling with the weight of accumulated memory or, curled in a foetal shape, about to give birth to her own image. It was as if she were striving to find some mathematical formula to synthesise loss with her self-fashioning as an artist.

Her *opus magnum* was the ambitious installation created for the ICA, 'Of Mutability', *1984-86.* Made of two parts, 'The Oval Court' and 'Carcass', it extended her preoccupations with the body and mortality. 'The Oval Court' consisted of 12 naked women – made from photocopies of her own body laid on a Canon photocopier – floating and twisting within a pool of amniotic blue. A marine version of an 18th-century painted ceiling, it illustrated her fascination with the fantastical interiors of Austrian and German Rococo churches. Where 'Ego Geometria Sum' contained, these swimmers broke free from the remembered restrictions of childhood into the limpid waters of post-pubescent pleasure in an aqueous "Garden of Delights". Literally bathing in a "stream of consciousness", they produced a dance of carnal desire, a cornucopia of forbidden pleasures. For floating beside the artist were the forms of a skate, a lamb, a goose, a crab and rabbit. Chadwick's lost innocence and androgynous eroticism were highlighted by a pair of white school-girl socks and frothy trails of ribbon and lace. Like some macabre Ophelia she floated, a string of pearls about her neck, bubbles billowing from her mouth, surrounded by animal forms representing her various alter egos. Having washed,

groomed and cleaned these torpid carcasses with a lover's attention, she created a necrophilic bond. She spoke lovingly of the monkfish's mouth and the skate's ample genitals. Her body cascading towards the lamb proffered it her lips, while the goose's head reached towards her breast, its webbed feet brushing her stomach in a simulacrum of Leda and the Swan. In a virtual act of sympathetic magic she ate, after the completion of the work, those carcasses still fresh enough to be consumed. In the original installation, photocopied images of undulating columns formed a colonnade around the periphery of the pool. At their apex was the artist's weeping face, her apparent grief at being driven from this paradisal space made all the more poignant with the knowledge of her untimely death.

And, as if in counterpoint to the idealised body of 'The Oval Court', a large vitrine filled with fermenting waste matter stood in an adjacent room. The glass column of 'Carcass' functioned as a metaphor for bodily process and acquired a strange beauty during the transformation from wholeness to putrefaction as the bubbling concoction slowly turned to a noxious mulch: daily acquisitions of rubbish recorded like the strata of rock, the unique history of the work within real time. Whereas 'The Oval Court' presented the playground of an autonomous, sexually potent goddess as an alternative to the predominantly patriarchal, Judaic-Christian myth of the Fall, 'Lofos Nymphon', *1987* used a more Kleinian schema. Here, in a series of photographic projections, Chadwick appeared on the balcony of the family home with her Greek mother, set against a backdrop of Athens. Both women were naked, the small, boyish body of Chadwick clinging to her ageing mother's sagging flesh in an apparent desire for reunification with the denied utopian space of the nursing breast.

Chadwick moved beyond the female body with 'Meat Abstract' and 'Meat Lamps',

1989. Here she transcended gender to discuss inner and outer and the androgyny of sexuality, which denied the western philosophical view, held from Aristotle to Freud, that woman is synonymous with nature. Within these works, Chadwick rejected an Apollonian vision of beauty for the Dionysian. As Camille Paglia claims in 'Sexual Personae: Art and Decadence from Nefertiti to Emily Dickinson', "Dionysus was identified with liquids – blood, sap, milk, wine. The Dionysian is nature's chthonian fluidity". Essentially pagan, the chthonic is where sex and sado-masochism meet. The hourglass form of 'The Philosopher's Fear of Flesh', with its slippage between the human and animal – two tear-shaped pendants enclosing a male stomach and a plucked chicken's breast – were reminiscent of a *momento mori* or reliquary enshrining the desiccated bones or foreskin of a saint. In 'Glossolai' Chadwick created a cruelly revengeful, "below the belt" attack on the linguistic dominance of patriarchy, spending two days stitching together fleshy lamb's tongues, which she referred to as "a hundred tiny penises", thus endorsing Nietzsche's claimed in 'Beyond Good and Evil' that "almost everything we call 'higher culture' is based on the spiritualisation of cruelty".

And no doubt she knew, when making 'Nostalgie de la Boue', *1990* with its hairy anal orifice and circle of entwined earthworms, of Georges Bataille's claim in 'The Solar Anus' that "the world is purely parodic, in other words, that each thing seen is the parody of another, or is the same thing in a deceptive form". In 'Bad Blooms' this imagery is extended, albeit more playfully, with her *Cibachrome* photographs of floral wreaths and various viscous fluids. In these exotic nosegays, strange matings of buttercup and orchid, Swarfega and Germolene – with their fleshy plum and oyster centres, their phallic stamens and cunts of white fur – she played games with traditional sexual signifiers, delighting in images of bisexuality.

Chadwick's most notorious work was her 'Piss Flowers', made with her partner David Notarius during a residency in Alberta. She peed in the snow, the flow of her urine making, when caste, an erect penile shape, in antithesis to the softer pistillate forms created by Notarius: an inversion of human genitalia. But this game of icy sexual politics failed to produce objects with the equivalent impact of her earlier work, whilst the literary and psychoanalytic associations of her chocolate fountain 'Cacao' – earth, shit, coprophilia – were fairly obvious, creating a suspicion that the main purpose of these pieces was a desire to shock.

Last year Chadwick worked in the Hunterian Museum and the Wellcome Pathology Room at the Royal College of Surgeons. There, in an echo of the carnivalesque bestiary she'd employed in 'The Oval Court', she photographed medical specimens – infants and pickled foetuses beyond the outer reaches of what passes for normality – for her series 'Cameos'. Selecting a Cyclops baby, chimpanzee and pygmy, she was, according to Marina Warner, in her element. "She found no revulsion to overcome, but found her imagination began instantly to play on [the Cyclops'] features with a kind of passionate sympathy like love". For Chadwick, these discards of human reproduction were reminiscent of the hybrids of myth – dragons or three-headed Chimera – onto which humanity projects its fear of difference and otherness. Like Beauty towards the Beast, she felt both moved and titillated by their difference, by the very qualities that made them repellent to others. These unformed faces with their soft spongy flesh, these "monsters" to whom every mother fears giving birth, floated in their formaldehyde in a suspended state of becoming. With her images of these grotesque forms, she touched upon the Darwinian paradigm of the survival of the fittest and on 19th-century fears of miscegenation, not to mention late 20th-century debates surrounding abortion rights and our preoccupations with genetic manipulation and bodily perfection.

There is a great irony that just before her death, she was investigating the very beginning of life, having been given permission to work in King's College Hospital's Assisted Conception Unit, where she was drawn by the parallels between "artificially" creating *in vitro* eggs for fertility programmes, and the manipulations involved in making art. This continued her preoccupation with mapping the self through the cartography of the body, and echoed her use of internal organs in earlier works such as 'Self Portrait', *1991*. There, her small stubby hands framed a human brain, echoing Hamlet holding Yorick's skull. Implicit are all those fundamental questions about the nature of individuality. What is the essence of *me* as opposed to *you*? 'Unnatural Selection' pushes these questions back to the moment of conception. As she wrote in 'Lofos Nymphon', "as a Modern, with no centre, no core of belief, it is possible to encounter the void of Origin, to give it form and a body, and so return to the site of beginning". This was her preoccupation when she photographed human pre-embryos that would otherwise have been left to perish. Within these images, the maternal body is ever absent, raising one of the most disquieting questions of our age about the cultivation of foetuses outside the womb.

In these final works, she created a vision of the pre-embryo's interdependency, whilst presenting it as a valued jewel. The lozenge of 'Monstrance' is reminiscent of a *momento mori* ring in which the plaited hair of the dead is set with tiny seed pearls beneath a dome of glass; the pearl string of 'Nebula' and the cluster of 'Opal' all make reference to the scientist's grading and selection of viable cell clusters, done with the naked eye in the manner of a jeweller selecting flawless gems. In Christian ritual, the "Monstrance" is also the chalice in which

the host – the body of Christ, present but not actual – is venerated. In 'Nebula' the transparent beads, containing both cells and fragile dandelion heads, glimmer in the surrounding blue, like the Pleiades floating in the emptiness of cosmic space, while the soap-bubble forms recall the *vanitas* tradition that emphasised the transience and fragility of earthly life, and stress, with a poignant irony, that these last works, made just before Chadwick's death, involved looking at the moment of creation.

Now that she has gone, it is too soon to say how her work will stand up over time. Some of it was beautiful, intelligent, daring and iconoclastic; sometimes it seemed thinner, narcissistic, less sure of its intellectual footholds. As a woman artist, working and teaching over the last two decades, she has challenged the way we think and feel about the body, and extended the boundaries in which it is described. Her charismatic presence was felt by all those she taught, and with whom she came into contact, giving permission to many younger women artists to be expansive, bold, dashing and brave.

Helen Chadwick
Changing the Landscape
of Sculpture

Contemporary Art
Issue 13, 1996

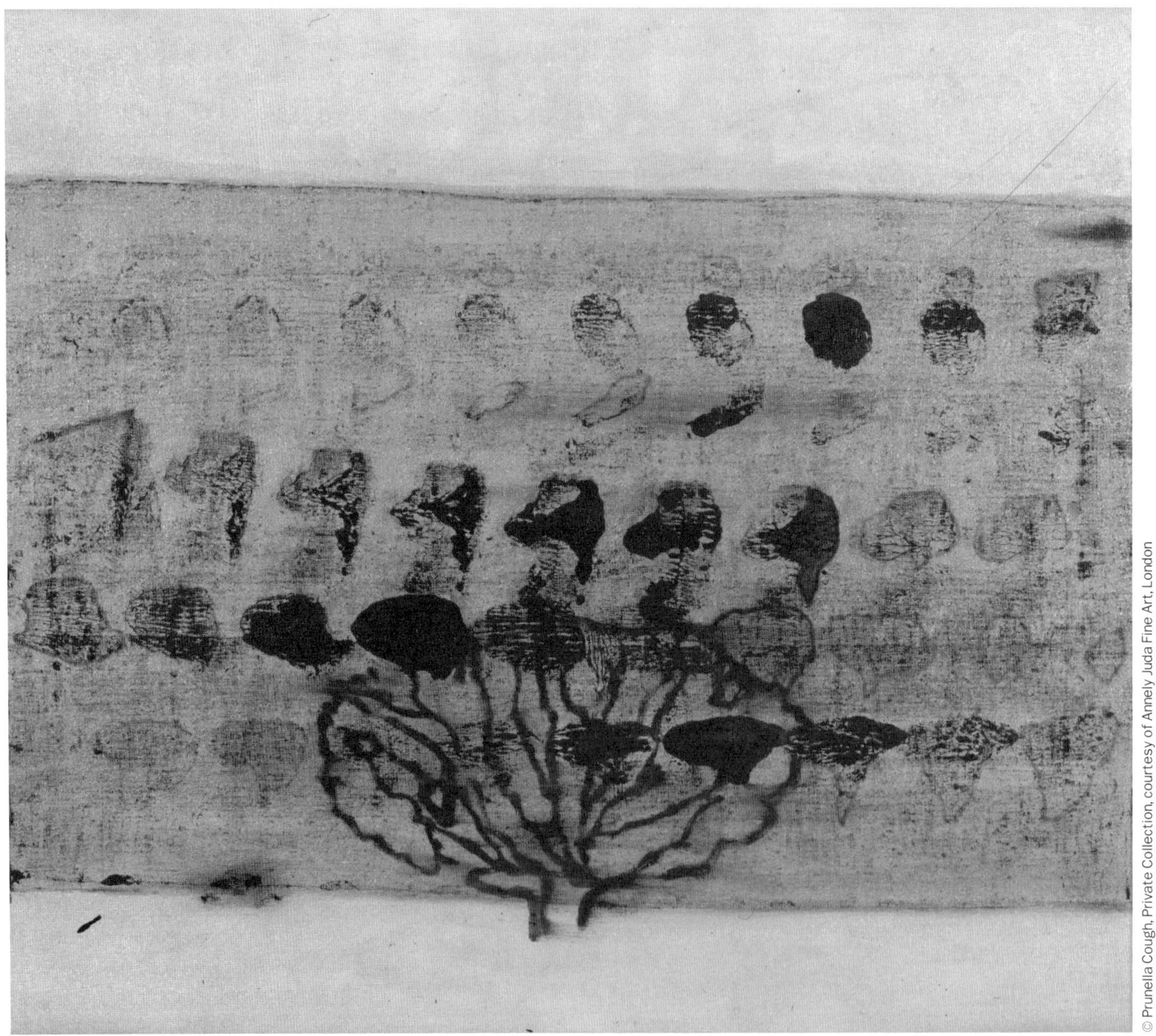

Prunella Clough, 'Trees', *1998*

Prunella Clough
An Artist's Artist

When I contacted Prunella Clough to ask if I might write a feature on her, she replied, with characteristic modesty, "don't you mean on my work?" When I arrived at her Fulham home, she was in the front garden putting out the rubbish. There would be no ceremony here. Despite recently being awarded the prestigious Jerwood prize, she is highly protective of her privacy and notoriously effective at diverting onversation with a quick and subtle intelligence away from herself or the subject of her work. She should have been a politician.

'The Times' rather patronisingly talked of the prize being awarded to a "little-known artist" of 80, as though Clough were some sort of Grandma Moses who had popped out of nowhere, rather than someone who has been a dedicated artist and teacher for more than half a century. Clough has usually been referred to in knowing tones by the *cognoscenti* as an "artist's artist".

This has always seemed like an admission of guilt, an acknowledgement that, within our midst, was a painter of true integrity and originality who was not receiving due recognition. In an era when we like our artists to be instantly recognisable by their aesthetic signature, the daring, inventive eclecticism of Clough's work marks her out as an artist more interested in art's complex process of discovery and revelation than in personal recognition. What she has created over a long career is a body of work that hauntingly insinuates itself into the mind of the viewer. What she paints is a visual articulation of the experience of being alive in this modern industrial world. She is, above all, a painter who has spent a lifetime looking, always interested, not in what is centre stage, but in what lies at the margins. "I am an 'eye' person, totally affected by visual facts", she has said. In this, she reflects the imagist position of the modernist American poet, William Carlos Williams, who insisted that there should be "no ideas but in things".

Urban detritus in the form of modest disposable objects – a tangled scrap of wire, a twist of newspaper blowing along the pavement in the evening wind, a discarded plastic bag or broken packing case left abandoned in a street market – is employed to illuminate something of our complex emotional and physical relationship to the industrial society we inhabit. Clough's severe yet curiously tender abstracts are painterly *haikus*, compressing through their distilled vision, the very experience of memory. Despite the absence of the figure, it is the power of the abandoned traces of a departed human presence that makes her paintings so poignant. Clough's inconsequential objects speak eloquently of both transience and mortality. Yet she sees her diversity of style not as strength but as a sign of intellectual weakness. "I have", she claims with alarming self-effacement, "never made an original mark in my life".

Clough's career spans nearly three quarters of a century and encompasses the major shifts in contemporary art from early Modernism, through Abstract Expressionism to Conceptualism. She first came to public attention as one of the neo-Romantics, along with painters such as John Craxton and John Minton. As we talked, she emphasised her belief that each artist is forged on the anvil of concerns dominating his or her generation. The bookcases in her sitting room are filled with works such as David Jones' 'In Parenthesis', collections of Philip Larkin, and volumes on Gothic architecture and English parish churches. The artists of her youth were Graham Sutherland, Robert Colquhoun, Keith Vaughan and John Piper. The post-war London art world she inhabited was hermetic, innocent, and slightly xenophobic. There were few professional painters, and even fewer galleries and magazines. Internationalism meant, she claimed wryly, 'The Studio', carrying an article on pottery in Korea. In this grey, bomb-damaged London, poets such as Louis MacNeice rubbed shoulders in down-at-heel Soho pubs with artists like Francis Bacon. No one took much notice, because no one was much interested. It was also a politicised generation: Reithian, anti-Fascist, anti-Franco, believing in the possibility of a brighter England exemplified by the ideals of the Festival of Britain. English painting was, then, she says, very muted. London was a dirty, smoggy place. The drabness was reflected in the palette of artists such as Ruskin Spear, and in the grey realities noted by Mass Observation. Even Ben Nicholson was, she claims, "scrubby and subdued" – despite the influence of European ideas.

Clough's work has always been built on a sense of place, unfolding and revealing some hitherto unperceived truth, and unveiling the very "thingness" of things, a process that the poet Gerard Manley Hopkins called "inscape". Running throughout her body of work – from her earliest Social-Realist paintings of Lowestoft through to her formative work inspired by London wasteland and industrial sites – is a quiet, gritty honesty. Her work is always unshowy, intimating a journey of discovery rather than arrival. "At the beginning, a form is almost like an unidentified scent that imposes itself as it reveals itself", wrote the sculptor Eduardo Chillida. The words might almost be Clough's.

Juxtaposed with the precision learnt from her war-time training as a mapping and engineering draughtsman, and her understanding of print and typography (after the war she did graphics for magazines: "we turned our hands to anything"), this desire to journey quietly leads to the creation of the monochromatic spatial surfaces overlaid with more focused marks – a distinctive feature of Clough's work.

When viewing a painting such as 'Plastic Bag', *1988*, one at first senses that it's an entirely abstract work. Yet on closer observation, the rubbed, bleached and erased vertical left-hand third of the painting can be read as a pavement edge. The discarded red-and-white plastic carrier bag lies prone, its right-hand handle reaching forlornly like an arm into the gutter. Whilst it would be wrong to anthropomorphise such an image, the deflated emotions that fill the canvas are utterly human. That Clough has lived all her life in London is important. She feels, she claims, like a tourist in the country, unable to read its signs, to deconstruct its imagery. Hers is an eye grown used to clumps of buddleia sprouting from a site damaged in the Blitz, or the stained concrete wall of a 60s tower block. It is in these images, not in some nostalgic ruralism, that she finds a quiet lyricism. The graphic rhythm of the flowing black lines of 'Wire Landscape', *1985* pulls in the eye like a choreographer orchestrating a dance. 'Emerge', *1996* draws the viewer in by its ambiguous placement of the loosely ovoid, central zebra motif, placed next to a small square and set against a rubbed-slate ground. Though not immediately identifiable as any obvious object, there is the sense, as the title suggests, that something familiar is emerging out of the carefully considered paint. Even though Clough's beautiful painting 'Trees', *1998* appears to be a more naturalistic subject – the unhealthy acid-yellow ground is reminiscent of the colour so often used by Emil Nolde – in fact it evokes something vulnerable growing on a pitted, scarred brown-field site rather than in a rural landscape, with its pockmarks of near black behind the spindly tree.

Clough is of a generation of women artists for whom feminism was neither an issue nor a reality. When I asked if she felt it had been harder for a woman artist when she was starting out, she simply answered: "oh, they all treated me very well". Perhaps it is not irrelevant that she is a niece of the celebrated Modernist furniture designer Eileen Gray, whose interiors, between the wars, were the height of sophisticated chic. Perhaps Gray provided her with some sort of role model. For Clough has always simply been a painter getting on with her work. Gender did not come into it. Yet, though never didactically or sentimentally so, there is, nonetheless, a "female" sensibility about her work. Neither aggrandising nor monumental, her paintings are entirely modest, the scale domestic. Her surfaces feel caressed, loved, touched like skin, the paint applied with a sensibility and delicacy of touch to create a membrane on the surface of the canvas. Her colours, too, are gentle. Not pretty, or necessarily always comfortable, but subdued and modest, exact and true. As she stated in an interview over 40 years ago, "I like paintings that say a small thing rather edgily". Yet in her work all traces of autobiography are veiled, the expressive brush-mark erased. There is intense feeling embedded in her mark-making but it is always discreet, compressed, to be found in the fabric of the paint itself, in the

finely judged combinations of stencil, rubbed drawing and collage.

No two of Clough's works ever look alike because they are ultimately about the very process of painting. Her concerns are born out of the internal language that develops through play and continuing invention. Therefore each painting has its own coherent visual logic, leading to its own series of problems and arguments. None relies on a previously rehearsed formula. Each experience of standing in front of a newly primed canvas is a re-engagement with the problems of how paint should be applied dynamically to a flat surface. Maybe her training as a map-maker led her to internalise the fundamental aspect of the creative process, to understand that it is always a "reaching towards"; and to describe the making of a painting or poem as a "mysterious process". "I still don't know," she said, "why one or two paintings fly and sing when others don't". Half the time, she claimed, one is too "battered by a sense of failure" even to worry about it. A successful painting is, therefore, probably something of an educated accident. Anyway, it's not a huge loss if a painting doesn't sing. There is, in the end, she feels, something really "rather absurd about four sticks with a piece of cloth fixed across them".

Such modesty belies a lifetime's total involvement with the process of painting. Despite her advancing years, her vision is as fresh, inventive and audacious as ever. And it is this apparent lack of ego that allows her to look, to engage with the physical world in all its freshness and originality. She can see a piece of broken packing case in myriad ways. In this, she shares something of the vision of the American poet Wallace Stevens, whose famous poem demonstrates the variety to be found in the ordinary, showing 'Thirteen Ways of Looking at a Blackbird':

 I do not know which to prefer
 The beauty of inflections

Or the beauty of innuendoes
The blackbird whistling
Or just after.

As long as Clough is painting we can be sure that she will draw our attention to the beauty to be found in the unastonishing, that she will find wonder in that which is usually discarded and overlooked. She has the rare ability to illuminate both "the beauty of inflections" and "the beauty of innuendoes" hidden in the forgotten corners of our contemporary world.

Prunella Clough
An Artist's Artist
This interview was the last
given before her death on
26th November 1999

Contemporary Visual Arts
Issue 27, 2000

Edwina Leapman, 'Deep Red on Grey', *1999*

Edwina Leapman
A Dark Light

"Space has always reduced me to silence".
Jules Vallès

How do you paint a breath? How can a painter capture the insubstantiality of air, light and space, or what Gaston Bachelard calls "a phenomenology without phenomena"? His answer would be through daydreaming – what he calls "original contemplation". For the immense, he suggests, is not an object, and can only be arrived at through imagination. Works of art are "by-products" of this imagining: the "real product is consciousness of enlargement".

Edwina Leapman is an artist who understands that to arrive at such a point of "consciousness of enlargement" is about "removing extraneous layers of external experience". Making a painting is like an act of meditation that grows from "the silence of the studio". Working is a ritual that structures her life. She begins by repeating the same thing again and again, but within each painting, shifts and changes occur. Imagine the sky. It is always the sky, but it changes with the weather and nuances of light from deep tones of blue black to veils of almost transparent white. It may appear clear, but looking – real, mindful "seeing" – will reveal infinite levels. The paintings are built by the hand moving across the canvas in a rhythmic flow that will sometimes engage with it and at other moments skim above it. The brush, laden with paint, is gently pulled across the surface and reloaded when necessary to build a shimmer of contrasting tones. It is a felt, intuitive gesture, full of awareness and mindfulness but not "of" the mind, rather like the dance of the whirling Dervish or the light touch of the Zen calligrapher. Her paintings have been described as pulsating, but it is more a quality of stillness that she is after, as Eliot strives to articulate in 'Burnt Norton':

Words, after speech, reach
Into the silence. Only by the form,
the pattern,
Can words or music reach
The stillness, as a Chinese jar still
Moves perpetually in its stillness.

Each painting creates an autonomous atmosphere or emotion. Yet they are never descriptive, revealing their character exclusively through the articulation of the surface. For her "the point of vibration is a point held between two poles". It is important, also, that her paintings feel as though they extend beyond the edge of the canvas, that they parallel infinity. It is as if, as viewers, we are drawn deeper and deeper into a limitless world, losing ourselves in the fluctuations of light and shade, so that we enter what has been called the "psychological transcendent". These spaces have their equivalence in the natural world, as when the light goes down at dusk and objects begin to disappear, but these exterior spaces simply mirror more intimate internal spaces: the poetic space of our imaginations and dreaming.

Edwina Leapman has been painting since childhood. She never had any doubts as to what she wanted to do. In the 70s and 80s, she decided she didn't want to make too many decisions in a work, and realised she was in danger of becoming too knowing, too skilled. Inspired by Chinese landscapes and a Taoist relationship with nature and the natural world, she learnt to let things be, and became more concerned with the process of discovering what was unknown than with the point of arrival. Drawn towards the Eastern mystics, she wanted to allow room for the dictates of the unconscious, to let events, like a stream, simply flow. She is attracted by Herakleition ideas of flux and the cyclical movements of nature such as a river running down from a mountain and returning to the sea. She also wants her work to breathe, for there to be "air and luminosity". Her earlier white paintings were unequivocal in their clarity, brushed over a warm but neutral-coloured ground so they appeared like veils of light. Then came a period of darkly luminous brooding works. But even these paintings were made by the layering of pure colour. They were never, as with black, about the absence of light, for they always harboured nuance and possibility. In these newer paintings, she employs more specific vibrant colours, deep shimmering blues and reds.

Her interests and influences are eclectic, from Piero della Francesca to Turner. The recent exhibition at the Hayward Gallery of photographs of the moon was also significant. She hadn't realised what the edge of the moon looked like. "If I had been on a spacecraft, I would have gone mad. The moon seemed so empty, so dead. If someone died up there, they would just end up going round and round. They wouldn't rot; they wouldn't go back to the Earth. It was so inhuman". Music has always been a more important influence than literature and, recently, she has found herself composing music. Yet in the 60s, when it was too cold to paint in her unheated Parliament Hill studio

in north London, she tended to spend much of the winter months writing poetry. As a poet myself, I find it seductive to read her paintings as the equivalent of visual poems, the lines as obliterated or emerging "stanzas" or "texts". Yet what can be "read" off these works, is, by definition, what cannot be said in words. For it is their sensuous physicality that generates emotion; the feelings come directly out of the language of paint.

Edwina Leapman is an artist who is concerned with the revelation of reality. But that reality is modest, felt and searched for, oblique – like something caught momentarily out of the corner of the eye, which, if one turns around, has already gone. Her art reveals not only something about our visual relationship with the actual, perceived world in all its dynamic flux, but also something of metaphoric space, of the possibility beyond the material. Talking in her studio recently, she suggested that perhaps space, and the concern with the phenomenology of space, is the new Romanticism. That in making art about space – when two kinds of space blend, intimate space and universal space – human solitude deepens into something close to stillness and understanding. In one of Rainer Maria Rilke's letters, we see him straining towards the "something" of the same sensibility: "the unlimited solitude that makes a lifetime of each day, toward communions with the universe, in a word, space, the invisible space that man can live in nevertheless, and which surrounds him with countless presences".

It is amid this coexistence of things, then, to which we try to add our own human consciousness, that Edwina Leapman places her work, giving meaning to Ludwig Wittgenstein's statement: "Our life is endless in the way that our visual field is without limit".

Edwina Leapman
A Dark Light

Annely Juda Fine Art
2002

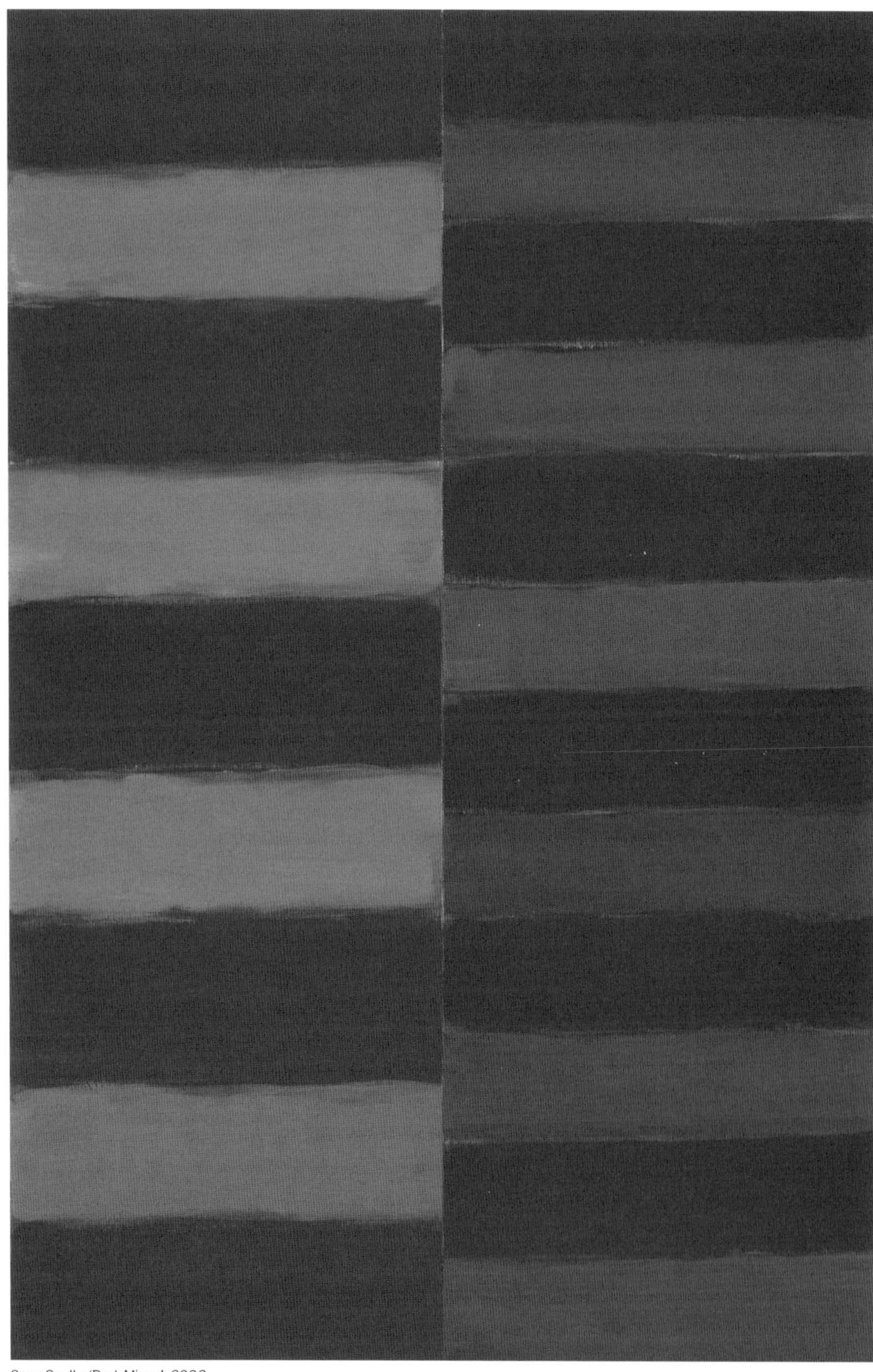

Sean Scully, 'Dark Mirror', *2006*

Sean Scully

"The most important tool the artist fashions through constant practice is faith in his ability to produce miracles when needed."
Mark Rothko

Beginnings: Exile can be a fertile state for an artist, with its sense of not quite belonging, of being "on the edge", of not fitting into the accepted mainstream. Picasso and Modigliani left their homelands for Paris. Vladimir Nabokov and Joseph Conrad adopted new languages. James Joyce and Samuel Beckett, both émigrés, caught the essential Irish soul from a distance. Born in Dublin in 1945, Sean Scully and his family took a boat across the Irish Sea, still filled with wartime mines, to find work in England. What significance, I want to know when we meet, did his Irish background have on his decision to become a painter?

His earliest memories are of living in one room at 82 Highbury Hill, north London. Life revolved around his convent school, St. Joseph's, and the Catholic Church. There is something almost prelapsarian about the description of his "little world" with its intimate backdrop of music, story-telling and Irish craic. His grandmother was a part-time pub-singer at the Highbury Barn, and had a constant stream of itinerant Irish workers lodging in the place she rented for five shillings a week from the butcher in Holloway Road. His mother performed torch songs in the local vaudeville theatre: 'Unchained Melody' was a favourite. Theatre provided glamour in an otherwise bleak and bomb-ravaged London. Vic and Nan, who were also in show business, lived in the room next door. Jewish and childless (he was a transvestite comedian), Vic provided an endless source of good-natured humour for the young Sean. Sean's uncle was a heavyweight boxer who died an untimely death in a gutter outside a pub. His father, as a lad, had been in the Arsenal Junior team and wanted to turn professional, but his mother needed him to go out and work. He became an itinerant barber and worked a seven-day week just to make ends meet. Sean's parents had ambitions for him. He was good at model-making. In the 50s, children made statuettes from rubber moulds filled with plaster of Paris. Sean Scully had two: one of the Virgin Mary and the other of a rabbit. In his games they often dated, and once or twice even got married. When he was six he became a dab hand at making up songs and also thought he might become an architect when he grew up.

Church was home from home. When it rained, you could hear it thundering on the tin roof. Inside it smelt of incense. The walls were decorated with pictures of the Stations of the Cross. This was his first real taste of art.

The nuns did not approve of Scully senior working on Sundays, and told the son that the Devil would move in under his bed. An imaginative child, he was traumatised and

became terrified of the dark. He still is.
He was taken out of his school and sent to
one in Gillespie Road. The Catholic school
had been full of life, love and laughter,
but Gillespie Road was a dead thing. The
difference, he says, between black and white
and red and grey. A woman of extreme
positions, his mother turned against the
Church. The period at 82 Highbury Hill
represents a golden age; he describes it as
if it were a lost Eden. Every day he walked
to school with his two cousins and felt safe
in the locality. Later the family moved to
Sydenham, south London, by the gas works,
and all harmony seemed to break down.
In Islington there had been a wealth of
Irish and Jewish culture. South London
represented the mean streets. It was fight
or be beaten by the older, tougher boys. But
Scully had a strong spirit and wouldn't back
down. Often he came off worst. But he no
longer felt the encompassing warmth of the
Church. He had lost his spiritual matrix.

Reparations: The psychoanalyst Melanie
Klein suggests that the creative process is
a form of reparation for childhood rage
and disappointment – that the shattered
fragments of our early life reconfigured into
art become, for the creative individual, a way
of healing early trauma and transforming
the world. At Scully's school in south
London, there was a cheap reproduction
in the assembly hall of Picasso's 'Child with
a Dove'. It affected the young Sean Scully
deeply. He particularly liked the black
outline. Somehow he turned himself into the
school artist, making puppets and painting
backdrops for the end-of-term play. As he
worked, he realised that he was surrounded
by girls. That, and the encouragement of an
inspired teacher, Mr. Perry, set him on the
road to art, even though he was one of the
toughest kids in school.

So what, I ask him, is he trying to repair,
to reconfigure, in his paintings? Something
profound, human and permanent, he
suggests. He also has an obsession with light.

Perhaps it is not too fanciful to suggest that
the threat of the Devil under his childhood
bed has something to do with it.

The London in which Scully grew up was
full of post-war mess and filth; some of the
streets were still lit by gas lamps so that the
smoggy urban cityscape often seemed to
resemble a Turner or a Monet. His was a
wild youth. He worked as a messenger and
a plasterer, ran a discothèque, sang in a band
with his brother, and got into trouble with
the police for brawling and burglary before
going to Croydon College and then on to
art school in Newcastle. And his boyhood
experiences of the Church left him with
a deep ambivalence for organised religion
along with a hunger, a longing, for
something to take its place. This longing is
embedded in the warp and weft of his art.

Reframing: It is perhaps this quality that
makes him, in this late Postmodern age,
a Modernist. He considers that careerism is
rampant and that much of the art world has
been hijacked by manipulating Sophists. For
him, the bigger picture is, all too often, lost,
and art is in danger of becoming an adjunct
to sociology. He describes idealism and
humanity as having been "parked in a lay-by
with a flat tyre". Everything now is about the
surface. But art that is too directly solipsistic,
he feels, is in danger of becoming self-
indulgent and sentimental.

So can painting still be a meaningful
language? Or has it, as we have been told so
often, run its course? Is there anything left
for a painter to say in this digital age? We live
in a time, he suggests, that sucks the guts out
of everything. When *Coca-Cola* is sung about
in blues form, he says, then you know form
is finished. Yet somehow painting resists. It
has a stubbornness, an impenetrability that
allows for the possibility of regeneration
and renewal.

As a young man, he was influenced by
Clement Greenberg but felt, instinctively,

that such a formalist approach would "crash and burn". He acknowledges, too, a debt to the Abstract Expressionists, to Barnett Newman and Mark Rothko, though he feels there is a gap between him and the Americans. Perhaps, I suggest, he is too European. He agrees. He loves the domesticity of scale of Édouard Vuillard, and there are obvious connections between the two artist's palettes: the beiges and greys, the putty colours. Making small paintings, he says, puts him in touch with the European humanist tradition. Abstract Expressionism was about the heroic. His own work is fundamentally philosophic, metaphorical and romantic. Greenberg came from a metaphysical position but, Scully feels, attempted to turn his ideas into a formula. From Greenberg's perspective, modern art achieved autonomy through a process of abstraction in which there was a gradual removal of all that was regarded as decorative and inessential. But art, Scully suggests, is not that simple. Greenberg's failing was that he tried to take the pain out of it. For Scully, potential failure is built into the process of painting. He might well be echoing the sentiments of the poet Paul Valéry who, when asked how he knew a poem was finished, answered that it was never so much finished as "abandoned". Sean Scully paints, in effect, the same painting again and again because he continually seeks the human, the tender and the poignant. The humanity of imperfection is woven into the painting's fabric. The essence of Modernism lies in the ability of a discipline to criticise itself, to be self-aware. To make work is to go on a voyage of discovery. The journey is more important than any notion of arrival or "success".

Our talk turns to Georgio Morandi, and I say that I have always considered his bottles to be anthropomorphic, to be metaphors for human relationships. I suggest that something similar occurs between Scully's own stripes and rectangles – that these express, in abstract form, something about

human feeling. What he has always wanted to achieve, he says, is a fusion of the classical and the emotional. In his 20s he didn't know how to do it. He wanted, somehow, to combine the qualities of Piet Mondrian and Jackson Pollock. He immersed himself in Zen. He is a karate black belt. Gradually, he began to paint shapes imbued with character and life. In 1969, after a summer of travelling, he made his first true stripe painting, 'Morocco', from glued blue, black and yellow stripes of dyed cloth cut to hang down against the white wall. This "window" was to be the precursor to the inserted panels found in many of his later paintings. Masking tape was used to form taut grids: cages of horizontal and vertical lines that created tight spatial fields of woven colour and complex depths of field. At the time, he felt isolated in the artistic provincialism of London and moved to New York. In the 60s, America seemed to be about the future – it offered hope, a new utopia. He became seduced by the night-time city and its geometry of lights, though now he feels he could not live there full time.

He wanted to make something deeper, less decorative than the complex tartan webs that had been preoccupying him. So he metaphorically "burnt down his own house". What was left was the colour of ash. It was a new beginning. The 70s paintings were, in the strictest sense, classical Minimalism, reminiscent in their stillness and spiritual quietude of the work of Agnes Martin. He used masking tape to create canvases of horizontal and verticals lines of dense dark colour. Everything extraneous was erased. These might have been the paintings of a Buddhist monk. But Scully is a natural colourist. A big man, he might be taken for a boxer or a bouncer rather than a painter. Eventually he rejected these self-imposed constraints. He has talked before of the sensuality of painting, of how his work is imbued with sexual energy, how it is a manifestation of his tactile and physical relationship with the world. He paints with his guts and his heart. There is a visceral quality, a relationship with the glop and stuff of paint that provides its own poetics, its own dialectic, beyond any theories about form. Something of this life force seeps from behind and around the edges of his rectangles. It is as if his grid-like geometric structures had been superimposed on something more profound, something primitive and chthonic. Each block might be interpreted either as a cancellation, a textual erasure or, alternatively, a *tabula rasa*; it is as if in their varying arrangements, meaning is both cancelled and sought in a continuous process of investigation and understanding.

And the size of a painting, I ask – how is that arrived at? He makes different drawings and sketches and then goes with what he feels he can best do at that moment. It depends on whether he wants to reach out with ambition or to be more personal, more introspective. He will then draw, like Matisse, with carbon on the end of a stick so that he can see what he is doing. He works flat, making a proposition and then putting down the colour, which he leaves to dry. At this stage, the work has something of the quality of varnished watercolour. It is then that he can look at it and start to make changes. The form is set, but colour evolves as he goes along. There are always options to be considered. The final layer is painted wet onto wet. As he works, the gaps between the rectangles take on a profound poignancy, emanating emotional vibrations that are at the heart of each painting. Colour is his hallmark, his fingerprint. The relationship to it can't be rushed. You can't force it. It grows out of the experience of both painting and living. There is a moment when you suddenly realise the incredible tenderness of a certain grey against grey. Something has to be built, to be learnt, to express that tenderness. You can, he suggests, have two sorts of career in the art world. An early career, where you burst onto the scene and which might not last, or a long one that unfolds slowly. What interests him is his

relationship not with art magazines or curators but with his work. The worst thing an artist can do is to lose the ability to be profound or noble. The sorrow of things is what touches him. We each pay a price for what we do, for who we are. This is Sean Scully's territory.

Such sentiments are not fashionable in an age of fracture, of instantaneous celebrity where surface matters more than depth. Longing and a sense of something beyond this material world fills these paintings. Sean Scully is a Romantic exile, a Modernist in a Postmodern age. In 'The Postmodern Condition', Jean-François Lyotard writes: I shall call modern the art that devotes its "little technical expertise", as Diderot used to say, to present the fact that the unpresentable exists. To make visible that there is something that can be conceived and that can neither be seen nor made visible: that is what is at stake in modern painting… The postmodern [by contrast] would be that which, in the modern, puts forward the unpresentable in presentation itself; that which denies itself the solace of good forms, the consensus of a state that would make it possible to share the collective nostalgia for the unattainable; that which searches for new presentations, not in order to enjoy them but in order to impart a stronger sense of the unpresentable.

Sean Scully strives for what is authentic, for that which is often unpresentable and cannot be said. He understands that art that can touch and reach out; art that is important – and not simply a fashionable flash-in-the-pan – is not achieved by creating something that is accomplished, beautiful, polished or perfect. On the contrary, it is arrived at by striving for what is true and, in so doing, humbly accepting the inbuilt human failures of such a project. To recognise this is what Roland Barthes referred to as the *punctum*: the wound. Reparation is sought in the tear that cannot ever quite be mended. Its acknowledgement requires that most human of emotions – empathy. The gaps between Sean Scully's forms, as with Barnett Newman's, open up a space for the sublime, a space where that sense of being in the moment is, as in oriental philosophy, understood as the Eternal Now.

Sean Scully

Timothy Taylor Gallery
2006

Rachel Howard, 'Visual Memory', *2006*

Towards Meaning
The Abstract Paintings
of Rachel Howard

If we are what we read, then the titles of the books lying around Rachel Howard's studio give an insight into both her practice as a painter and her underlying philosophical concerns. Tossed among the paint cans and general studio clutter are copies of Bertrand Russell's 'Why I Am Not a Christian', Ernst van Alphen's 'Francis Bacon and the Loss of Self', 'Mere Christianity' by C.S. Lewis and Joseph Albers' thoughts on the 'Interaction of Colour'. Rachel Howard attended a Quaker school and says that from the moment she first walked into church at the age of four, she believed in God. The stories, the concerns and questions posed by religion – although she is now a proclaimed atheist – continue to run through her veins. She still sings hymns in the bath.

A graduate of Goldsmith's, she worked as Damien Hirst's assistant. This exposure to the hard commercialism of the art world appears to have given a toughness to her luscious abstract paintings, which helps to avoid the pitfalls of nostalgia that, inevitably, threaten when flirting with the language of "colour-field" painting. Though Howard is alert to the dangers. For whilst her paintings are often big, and recall the heroic mysticism of Mark Rothko, Barnett Newman or Morris Louis, she undercuts her own tendency to Romanticism with a dose of the vernacular in her choice of medium – household paint.

Not that she is alone in her appropriation of this decorating material in the service of fine art. This particular visual trope dates back to the 50s, and others of her generation such as Ian Davenport, Sarah Morris and Gary Hume have also made it their own. But her canvases make none of the utopian claims of the Modernists, nor are they primarily concerned with structure and space as are Morris's bold geometric paintings, whose architectonic forms derive from urban environments, nor do they indulge in laddish masking of emotion such as we find in Hume's work, where the sealed surface does not allows the viewer penetration of the image. Fashionable art theorising of the last 20 years has involved a sort of endless Postmodern end-game where art – particularly painting – may appropriate from the past, but where it has been powerless either to contribute to, or continue, the tradition. This has arguably led to an era of bleak complacency where the only response has been one of endless irony that has transmuted, over the last two decades, from radicalism to conservatism and stasis. But Howard does not use the shiny, nail-varnish paint either ironically or as a form of emotional armour-plating, but rather as a means of creating a tension between the pedestrian, the utilitarian and the essentially romantic. The mundane material stands in antithesis to the emotional states she wishes to explore. This is spirituality for a postmodern world.

She first used household paint in 1995. Its fluidity was so gorgeous, she felt challenged to conquer and control it. She lets the cans stand, allowing the paint to separate. The top layer is used as the medium to manipulate the pigment, which is taken from the bottom of the tin. It is also used as a varnish to achieve a gloss finish. One of the main differences between her working method and that of the Modernist colour-field painters is her physical relationship to the work. Here, there are no visible brushstrokes, no marks that suggest an intimacy with the movements of the artist's body, or sinewy lines that recall the trace of her hand.

One of the weaknesses of much formalist art criticism is its focus upon the spatial structures of paintings rather than the structure of colour relationships. Abstract painting involves an awareness not only of the formal use of space, but also of the capacity to use colour to suggest a psychological "narrative", to conjure – as do musical notes within a melody – an emotional state. Howard's paintings are built architecturally. The terms she uses are those of the builder: construction, reconstruction, layering and assembling. Gravity is her brush. Layers of paint accrue, built by dripped pathways of paint. While these create the scaffolding of her grids, it is colour that gives them their emotional nuance. She has a love/hate relationship with colour, knowing that certain painterly tricks can create an emotional response as easily as the swelling of violin strings. Although her work is undoubtedly beautiful, she wants us to be pulled into her structures, to experience them as seductive, yet also as places that are somehow difficult and forbidden. Her paintings represent the endless frustration of desire.

Red is one of her prime colours. The colour of birth, of violence and death, of sex and love, it pulsates. It is never static. In these new paintings, she uses it to create a grid over a yellow ground that shimmers from behind like light pouring through a stained-glass window. This distant glow represents

something both seductive, yet unobtainable. It suggests a deep, limitless space, a place of desire and longing, of possibility and promise from which we have been excluded behind the ensnaring architecture of the grid. The Platonic term that the French philosopher Julia Kristeva uses to describe such a locality is the *chora*, a word that loosely suggests a receptacle, or the metaphorical space of the maternal body. It is an image that might, usefully, be applied to the space that hovers behind the grid in Howard's paintings. Kristeva proposes that it is a pre-linguistic space, "where the subject is both generated and negated", broadly the locus of thought, language and creativity. For one educated within the Quaker tradition, in which the divine – sometimes described by Quakers as *the inward light* – is believed to reside within every human being, it is an appropriate conceit.

In a number of these new paintings there is a flat, inert panel of paint that takes up about a third of the canvas. This contrasts with the dynamic space that it abuts. It is, perhaps, not too far-fetched to see this as functioning rather like a proscenium arch within a theatre. For beyond is a space of imagination, drama and dreams. Writing on Roland Barthes, the late Susan Sontag claimed that he asserted that the aim of literature (here one might substitute the word art) was "to put 'meaning' into the world but not 'a meaning'". This description might usefully be applied to Howard's work. Smelted in the emotional forge of Romanticism, Modernism and religious sentiment, she is too much a child of her time to be wholly seduced by art's utopian or didactic possibilities. A fan of Émile Zola, she has a gritty view of reality. She sees beauty as being born out of everyday tragedy. Unusually, she is an accomplished figurative as well as an abstract painter, and these current works stand at the opposite end of the emotional and philosophical spectrum from her recent series of female suicides. Her cruciform paintings and series of colour C-prints shown recently at Anne Faggionato – where she photographed the trellis supports of her studio windows to create dark crosses against the smudged opaline glass, echoing both Kasimir Malevich and Barnett Newman's 'Stations of the Cross' – acted as a formal and emotional link between the figurative and abstract, leading us from the dark pathos of the suicides, to the sublimity of her abstract paintings. These new works stand as affirmations of hope and possibility within the darkness, and seem to imply that there are various kinds of beauty: sensual beauty as well as that of insight and truth. They give meaning to the experience of living in the world, rather than providing explanations.

There are those who see all abstract art as merely mathematical or formalistic, while for others its agenda is fundamentally mystical. But form as a language is insufficient. For where does the instinct to make a particular work come from, and of what is form a revelation – an emotion, a truth, a state? For the Abstract Expressionists, there was a certainty that their painterly language revealed something of the cosmic mysteries of the universe. It was as if they were conduits bringing back meaning from the "realm" beyond. But for a young artist living at the beginning of the 21st century, such certainties are no longer possible. In this cynical postmodern age, where the end of everything from history to painting has become an abiding cultural refrain, it is very much harder to find a painterly vocabulary in which to expresses wonder and hope. Howard understands this dichotomy. This push and pull, this tension between the material and spiritual, the past and the present, surface and depth, is the very fibre of her work. In a world of gloss and surface, her paintings mirror a desire for authenticity whilst acknowledging the complex dilemmas of the times in which we live. No contemporary artist can provide certainties or answers. Indeed, all that they can do is ask insightful questions. For as the

poet Robert Frost once wrote, "Though there is no fixed line between wrong and right/There are roughly zones…"

Towards Meaning
The Abstract Paintings
of Rachel Howard

Gagosian Beverly Hills
2007

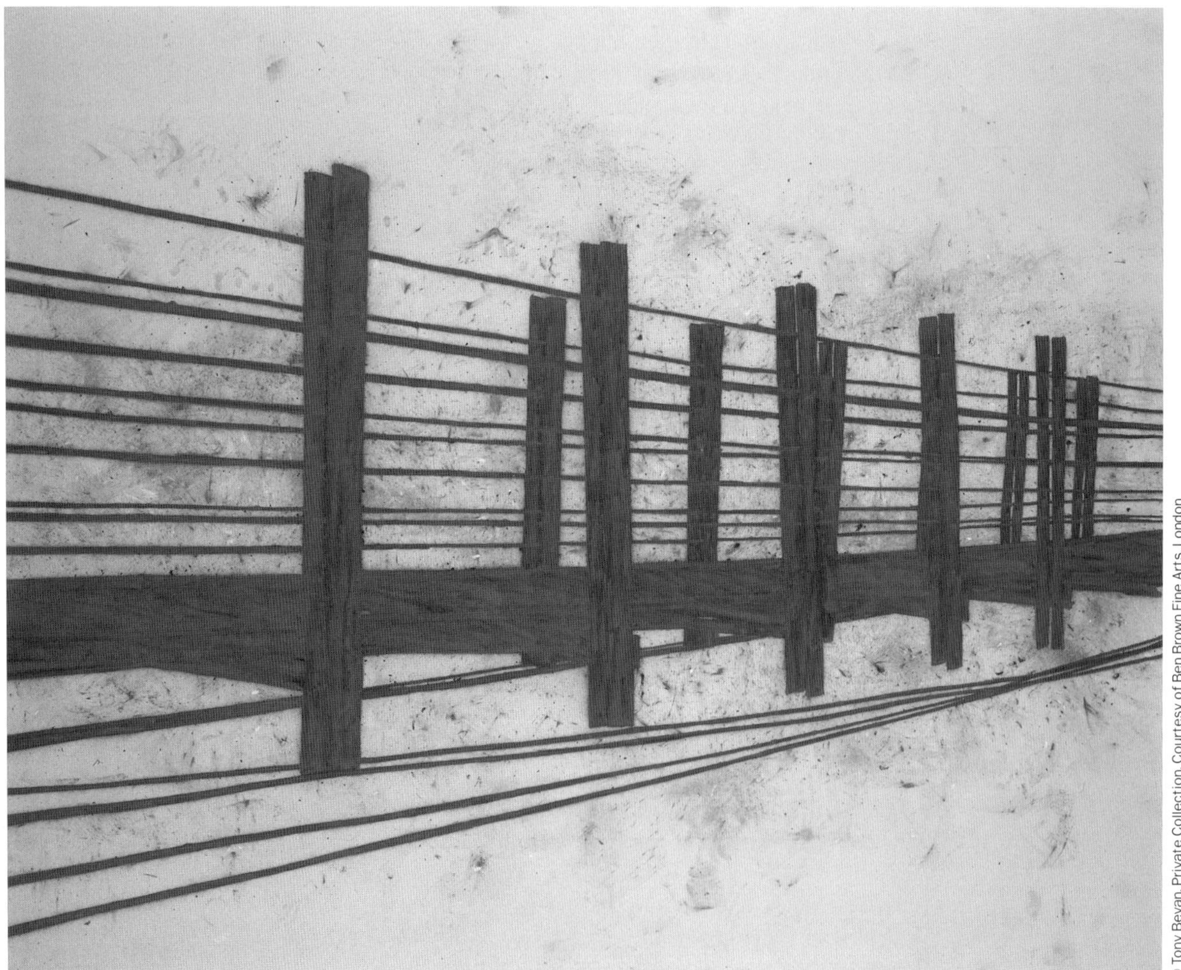

Tony Bevan, 'Crossing', *2007*

Tony Bevan

What does it mean to make a chart or a map? In the conventional sense it is, of course, about topography, and concerns the contours of land, the flow of rivers and the height of mountains. But it can have an altogether more metaphorical meaning, for as Jürgen Habermas writes in 'Modernity – An Incomplete Project': "the avant-garde must find a direction in a landscape into which no one seems to have yet ventured".

Since Modernism, nothing can be taken as given, nothing is fixed. What Habermas calls "these forward gropings" anticipate an undefined future. "The new value placed on the transitory, the elusive and the ephemeral", he argues "… discloses a longing for an undefiled, immaculate and stable present". To "map" in this context, therefore, implies charting the unknowable territory of the psyche, starting out on a journey without a clear sense of direction, or of the final destination. It is an act of faith in a faithless world, for there is no certainty as to where that journey might end. It is propelled only by the desire to find (whilst knowing the impossibility of doing so) something "undefiled" and possibly "immaculate".

Tony Bevan's heads and architectural spaces, along with his newer series of studio furniture, do not fit neatly into any painterly category. They are neither figurative, in the strict sense that they are "copies" of what he has observed in the world, nor are they entirely abstract, in that the imagery has been broken down into a series of painterly gestures divorced from the actual visible world. Born out of the reality of observation, they are a tentative exploration of the one-dimensional space of the canvas, which seems to undergo some sort of transformation so that the paintings open out into a metaphysical space that is experienced as beyond that of the physical picture plane. The canvas becomes an arena in which to act and explore, a space to "express" – to borrow Harold Rosenberg's word used when describing American Abstract Expressionism – an object, actual or imagined. Painting, Rosenberg argues, "is the same metaphysical substance as the artist's existence", a process that reveals the personality of the painter. Through contact with a painting we come to understand something of the artist – not in terms of cod psychology – but rather how he translates his psychological experience into something new, to say what has been previously unsaid. What we witness, if we are mindful, is the creative process enacted.

In Tony Bevan's painting, 'Crossing', a bridge appears to hang in space. Vertical poles are strung out on wires. It is the sort of bridge that might traverse a ravine or a fast river. The structure is similar to that of bridges known from many Japanese paintings and prints beloved by van Gogh. Yet here it is impossible to determine where the bridge begins and ends. No human presence is detectable. There are no scuttling merchants, no horses and carts, no one on a bicycle; it seems simply to be a transitional point linking one unidentified place with another. All that we know is that it connects two spaces. But these spaces remain tantalisingly unknown and inchoate. Like the cartographer travelling in an unfamiliar land, we can only trust, as we make the crossing, and see where we end up. There is a sense that this bridge leads to a different realm, to somewhere deeper and more profound than we are used to on a daily basis. Yes, it is a bridge, but it is a psychological bridge between two states, whilst the fact that it is painted in a sort of rusty ox-blood red suggests a connection with the body, and the possibility of arteries or tendons. This red recurs time and again in Bevan's paintings, along with primal orange and sometimes cobalt blue. With his use of charcoal, it suggests something very ancient, a connection to art's roots, to aboriginal painting made from the earth's pigments or the magical ochre and soot paintings on the walls of the caves at Lascaux in France.

This feeling that there is something important going on beneath the surface of things is integral to all Tony Bevan's work. Blood-red cicatrices run like knife wounds diagonally across the surface of the face and across the neck in 'Head and Neck'. It is impossible not to read these marks as wounds, though Bevan himself talks of them rather as "flow patterns". Yet with their jagged edges, they look like the ragged stitch marks left by some cack-handed surgeon, and suggest that there's been an attempt to peel back the flesh from the bone to reveal what lies beneath. The tendons of the attenuated neck are taut and stretched as if trying to hold up the lacerated head. It is impossible to look at these self-portraits without thinking of Titian's 'The Flaying of Marsyas', where the Phrygian satyr, in a fit of hubristic pride, dared challenge the god Apollo to a musical contest. As punishment for his presumption, Apollo had Marsyas tied to a tree and flayed him alive. And then,

too, there is Rembrandt's 'The Anatomy Lesson of Dr. Nicholaes Tulp', where collective medical students collect around the dissecting table to peer at the sinews of a cadaver, a common criminal hung that very morning. Both these paintings are connected by the revelation of what lies beneath the surface.

In his self-portraits, Tony Bevan lays bare the social face that is presented to the world, peeling it back to reveal an essential essence or fundamental truth. This process is similar to setting out on a journey into the interior, into that heart of darkness that lurks at the centre of all modern individuals. And the place we arrive at? Well, it is one of existential doubt, a place where only more questions can be asked, where all that is discovered is an approximation. That is art's inherent failure. For as Alberto Giacometti said: "All I can do will only ever be a faint image of what I see and my success will always be less than my failure or perhaps equal to the failure".

In 'Head', the image has become even more deconstructed. The top has gone, and the face seems to dissolve and collapse, so that we are reminded of Oscar Wilde's Dorian Gray portrait hidden in the attic, taking on the marks of its subject's lived experience. All that is left behind by the series of lines that run horizontally across the face, like wires holding down Gulliver, or musical staves, is the suggestion of a nose, with its prominent nostrils and a mouth. The whole has been reduced to these basic components, the minimum needed to constitute life; points of inhalation and exhalation thrust up like some animal snout gasping for air. The image conjures, in its isolation and distress, the articulating mouth in Samuel Beckett's 'Not I', which itself was suggested, according to the author in a letter postmarked 30 April 1974, by Caravaggio's 'The Beheading of John the Baptist' in Valletta Cathedral. Bevan has talked of a disembodied sense of existence, which he has experienced several times in the studio – an experience known as "autoscopy", in which a person, while believing himself to be awake, sees his body and the world from a location outside his physical body.

When discussing his work, Bevan gives little away other than talking in terms of form and space. He has said that painting is a silent language that he can't easily talk about. Interpretation is left to others. Yet looking at his piles of rounded stones or boulders, it is not hard to read these painted potato forms as even further-reduced references to the head, by now completely disembodied and featureless – difficult not to see them as oblique references to the skulls found in mass graves. Of course, they are not *about* these things. Bevan talks of them simply as piles of stones, but, as with all good art, they spark the imagination of the viewer and suggest multiple readings.

He likes to work with his drawings and recent paintings all around him, for they act as notes reminding him of particular concerns. To work in an empty studio is uncomfortable. He starts on an unstretched canvas, often working on the floor on his hands and knees. Much comes through the process of drawing, and is suggested by how his material behaves. He tries not to make conscious decisions, but simply to allow a stream of consciousness to flow. Often the material determines what should be a drawing or a painting. Using the physical resistance of the floor, the charcoal splinters and spits, leaving a residue that is locked in with acrylic medium. It is this unpredictability that he cherishes. Marks are also dependent on how paint is loaded onto the brush. The physical quality of his medium is paramount. Yet for such a mild-mannered man, these are violently sensual paintings. It is perhaps for this quality, along with the isolation of the subject within the picture space, as well as the dominance of red and black, that he is so often compared to Francis Bacon.

Following a number of paintings depicting open roofs and rafters, he has taken to painting what he calls studio furniture. The result is a number of horizontal skeletal structures reminiscent of Vladimir Tatlin's famous Modernist tower. With their open lattice-work of girders, they suggest electrical pylons or oil rigs, though on closer observation many of the lines do not connect, and these edifices, as in 'Furniture', seem on the point of disintegration. Again, there are many readings, from the Tower of Babel to the collapse of Modernism. For these images seem to suggest the fragmentation of the holistic grid that was the utopian arena of so much Modernist art. There is a quiet irony to a painting such as 'Monument', where a Piranesian stack stands in isolation on a red ground like an empty symbol of some discredited dogma; for who in the modern world can believe in monuments now?

Tony Bevan

Ben Brown Fine Arts
2008

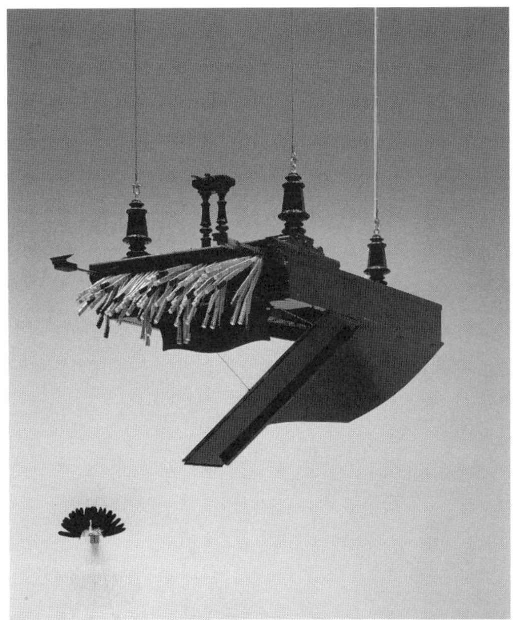

Page 84

Adventures in Art
Section II

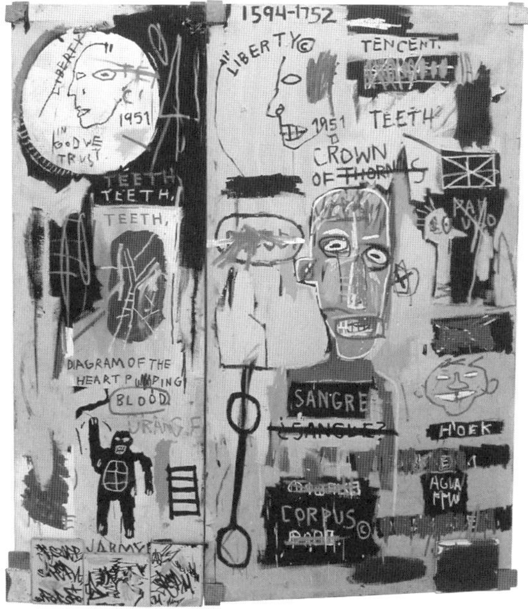

Page 88

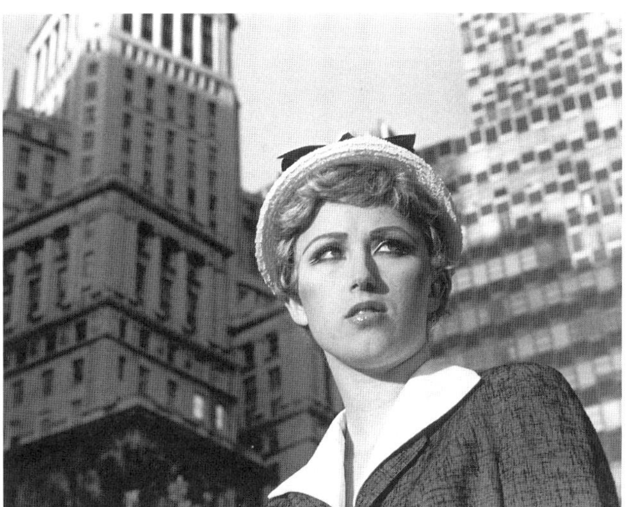

Page 64

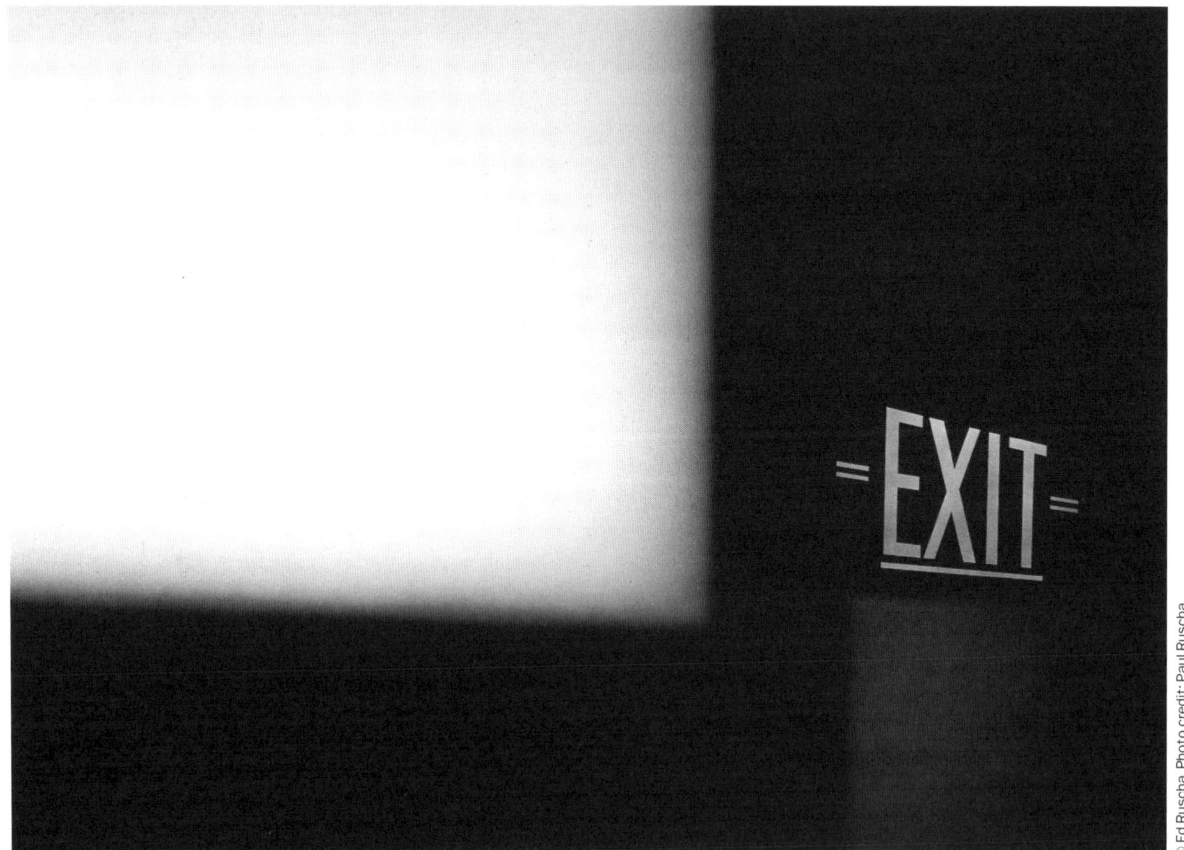

Ed Ruscha, 'Exit', *1990*

Ed Ruscha

America, claims Jean Baudrillard, is "the only remaining primitive society". For it is "neither dream nor reality", but a hyper-real utopia, the stuff that dreams are made of. Americans, he continues, have no sense of simulation, for they are the universal role model, the prototype of all possible variants of the modern world. This chimerical utopia might be described as the American Dream.

Whether or not Baudrillard's assertion that America is the last primitive society holds water, it certainly captures something of the mythical quality of this mercurial continent's multi-faceted reality and ever-shifting quicksilver face: its deserts and wide skies, and unfurling highways, going nowhere, going somewhere, littered with endless dime stores and gas stations. This is the drifter's world of 'Bagdad Café'.

It is also Ed Ruscha's world. His painting of the Stars and Stripes entitled 'Plenty Big Hotel Room (Painting for the American Indian)' assaults us as the symbol of the dream. The emblem, of apple-pie patriotism, and the supposed unifier of diverse and disparate cultures, it flutters against an endless blue sky. Three black rectangles, like supermarket bar codes, censor an implied text. Language, once supposedly present, is being withheld. We can only guess why.

In 1956, Ed Ruscha drove into Los Angeles with his friend Mason Williams, leaving behind his strict Catholic upbringing in Oklahoma to enrol in a commercial arts course at the Chouinard Art Institute. The image of these two young men hitting town has all the potency of a Jack Kerouac novel. An odd job with Plantain Press as a typographer spawned Ruscha's fascination with print and words, along with a developing interest in collage and the European Dadaists, particularly Marcel Duchamp, and Kurt Schwitter's Merz poetry.

His off-beat photographic books of the 1960s and 1970s, particularly 'Every Building on the Sunset Strip', established the tone and milieu of his work, blurring the edges between film, literature and photography. These strips of crude black-and-white snapshots, wordlessly documenting the minutiae of the street – the apartment blocks, the telegraph poles, the diners and the billboards – encapsulate Ruscha's interest in what he calls "the plastic side of life".

A mirror of lower-middle-class realities, he juxtaposes these against the high-class cultural expectations of *beaux-arts* in a way that has often invited comparison with Andy Warhol. The world he offers up is one of images salvaged from drive-in movies and junk culture – the suburbia of 'Blue Velvet', with its continually sprinkled green lawns, or the stark desert of Wim Wender's 'Paris, Texas'. His humour is the deadpan, wise-cracking humour of a Raymond Chandler novel, the landscape he depicts that of the depopulated existential emptiness of Edward Hopper – though Ruscha does not like the comparison – tinged with irony.

The images he creates are as downbeat and spare as those of Raymond Carver. His search in a postmodernist world, where the fallacies of modernist linear cultural growth have crumbled into dust, is for some new iconic definition to fill the void. Yet we live in an era where the very nature of language and meaning is up for grabs. Ruscha's skill is to allow an ambiguous interplay to occur between image and word, between signifier and the signified.

In this space of lateral association lies the paradox – like a modern riddle of the sphinx – describing the absurdity of contemporary life. Because the word is never illustrative of the image, it is subversive. The three letters that spell S E X free-float against a cloud-filled sky. We cannot see this word, this mantra of the 20th century, without a Pavlovian buzz. Yet, at the same time, it recedes into the distance as three separate letters, devoid of any collective meaning, left isolated like a piece of waste linguistic syntax, made "art" by the picture space it inhabits. The sky has become the cinematic screen for the artist's cryptic credits. Like the French Symbolist poets, Ruscha generates meaning by the link between disparate and unlikely concepts.

This multiplicity of meaning, this juxtaposition and layering of references to past, present and future, is further explored in his black-and-grey silhouettes, where picture-book motifs, such as a pair of dark galleons or ticky-tacky houses, their windows twinkling in the twilight, appear like fading negatives. Mysterious and foreboding, they seem to have been drained of all colour and meaning. We are reminded of Plato's assertion that art is but a shadow of an idea, and thus inferior to reality. In

place of text, Ruscha has left empty white strips. With the loss of faith in meaning and language, silence seems preferable.

Paradox and black humour are given further resonance in his drawing 'Exit'. On one level, the image is presented as a beautifully executed piece of kitsch, an illuminated cinema sign glowing in the dark, depicted with all the skill of a sign writer. Yet it has all the pathos and absurdity of a Samuel Beckett play. It is a stark and timely reminder that all human endeavour, all art, points to one end, and that even the artist can hope for no more than a spurious immortality.

Ed Ruscha
Serpentine Gallery
and Karsten Schubert

New Statesman & Society
5th October, 1990

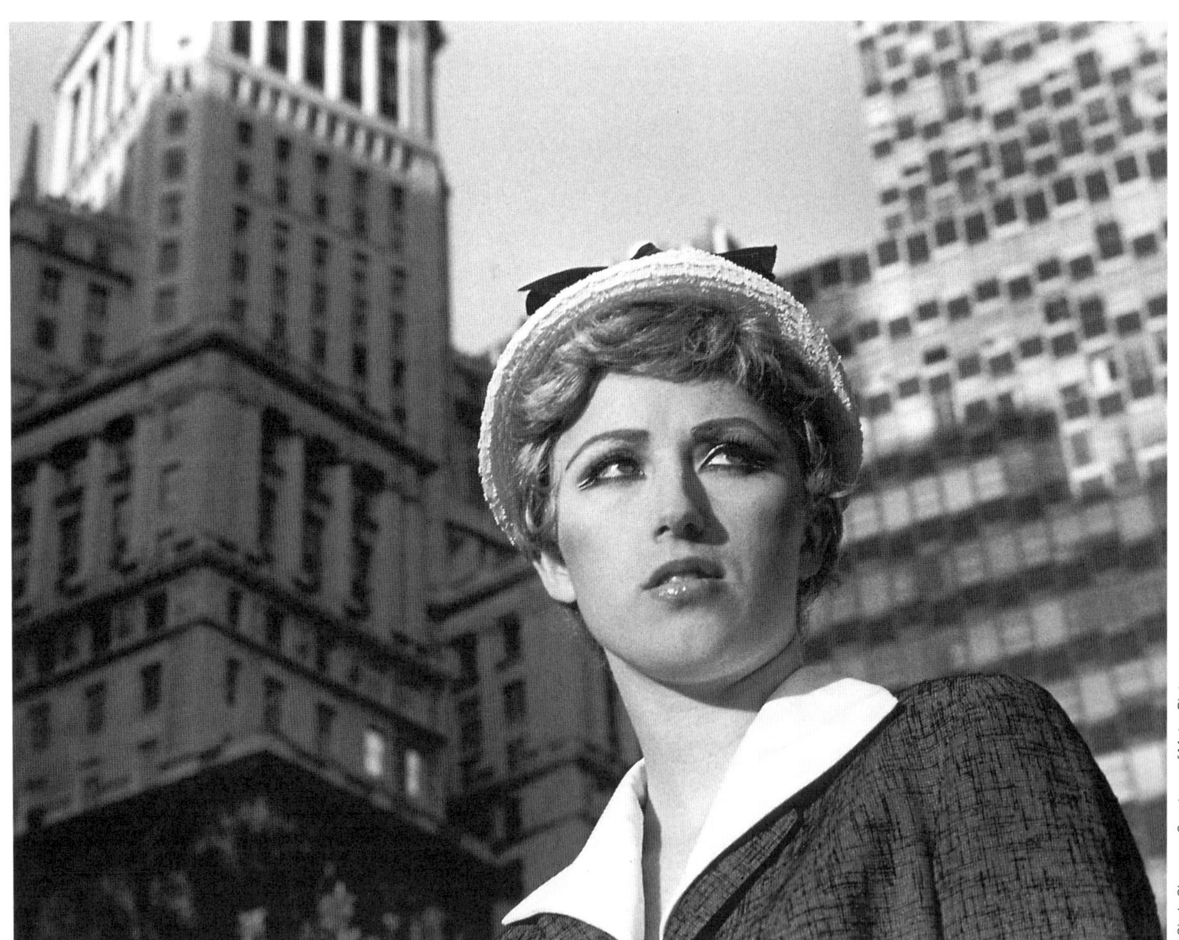

Cindy Sherman, Untitled film still, *1978*

Cindy Sherman

So who is this Cindy Sherman? The Whitechapel Gallery contains more than 40 photographs of the artist using herself as model in various guises: American "nice girl", starlet, victim, even a 17th-century Flemish self-portrait. Yet not one of them expresses anything about her, or even gives a hint of her attitude towards the roles she has chosen to play. Cindy Sherman is the mistress of ambiguity and disguise: her work overturns the statement "the camera never lies".

"To photograph," writes Susan Sontag, "is to appropriate the thing photographed. It means putting oneself into a certain relationship to the world that feels like knowledge – and therefore power". Power games are what interest Cindy Sherman: truth is negotiable. Sherman first received critical acclaim in the late 1970s with her black-and-white series 'Untitled Film Stills'. These evoked scenes from Hollywood 1950s B-movies, whose characters live on as archetypes of American life after the memory of the film itself has faded. In these, she adopts a series of carefully stage-managed poses, from suburban housewife to Marilyn Monroe look-alike and pouting sex kitten. She is both the white-bloused college girl in the library, and the hooker in the window in shorts and décolletage, staring expectantly down the street.

In others, she is the blousy cleaner in an apron and lisle stockings, or the archetypal girl next door mowing the lawn. Sherman forces her audience into a complicity in which we all unwittingly collude, to be judges of the women in her photographs, just as women are judged continually in "real" life by the images they present to the world: "nice girl", "*femme fatale*", "victim", "whore".

Her photographs leave us perplexed, doubting our own responses. She offers herself as apparent vulnerable victim: cowering, knees drawn up under her gingham dress; or tousle-haired, black sheet pulled under her chin as if about to be sexually attacked. In other works there is simply a lifeless hand or a foot covered in dirt, suggesting a recent murder or rape. These images are disquieting, for we do not know how to identify with this photographic victim, aware that she is, at the same time, also the controlling, creative artist.

Sherman confuses because she is both the image and the image-maker. "The determining male gaze", writes Laura Mulvey in 'Visual Pleasure and Narrative Cinema', "projects its fantasy onto the female figure, which is styled accordingly. In their traditional exhibitionist role, women are simultaneously looked at and displayed, with their appearance coded for strong visual and erotic impact so that they can be said to connote "to-be-looked-at-ness". John Berger says much the same in 'Ways of Seeing'.

Sherman is subversive, quietly reclaiming women's power to control their identity. She beckons with a seductive "come-hither" pout, only for us to discover that she is playing, and meant something else. There is no "real" self, no "real" Cindy Sherman offered, only multifarious images onto which we project our collective fantasies. She is what we need her to be.

She keeps up the subversion in a more light-hearted mode in her newer explorations of the iconography of "old masters". "When I was in school", she once said, "I was getting disgusted with the attitude of art being so religious or sacred, so I wanted to make something that people could relate to without having to read about it first... and also make fun of the culture as I was doing it".

In all manner of elaborate disguises, from a Caravaggio Bacchus to an Italian Renaissance Madonna, she queries the "uniqueness" of a work of art and the notion of the "fake". The poses she adopts make no pretence at hiding the props used: huge false breasts strapped to her front (those worn as the Madonna actually spurt holy milk), false noses, wigs and beards.

The conundrums posed by original photographs, made from obviously phoney mock-ups of revered works of art, are both witty and iconoclastic. The irony is further compounded because, in the rejection of conventional easel painting, she has used the criteria of classical portraiture. One can't help but feel a rather gleeful nose-thumbing at centuries of male "high" art.

In her most recent work, she has dispensed with herself as model altogether by using broken children's toys, masks and dismembered dolls to create scenes that suggest death and decay in the aftermath of some terrible unspecified holocaust. These works are less successful than those in which she uses herself, for the double binds and ambiguities, on which her work is so reliant, are lost. For she is dependent on fantasy and collusion, using photography like ancient Greek actors used the mask.

She has been described as a modern-day kabuki performer. No overt message is intended in her work, but there is a subliminal one that many women may choose to read: that if she can constantly remake herself in her own chosen image, why can't we? Will the real Cindy Sherman now please stand up!

Cindy Sherman
Whitechapel Gallery

New Statesman & Society
9th August, 1991

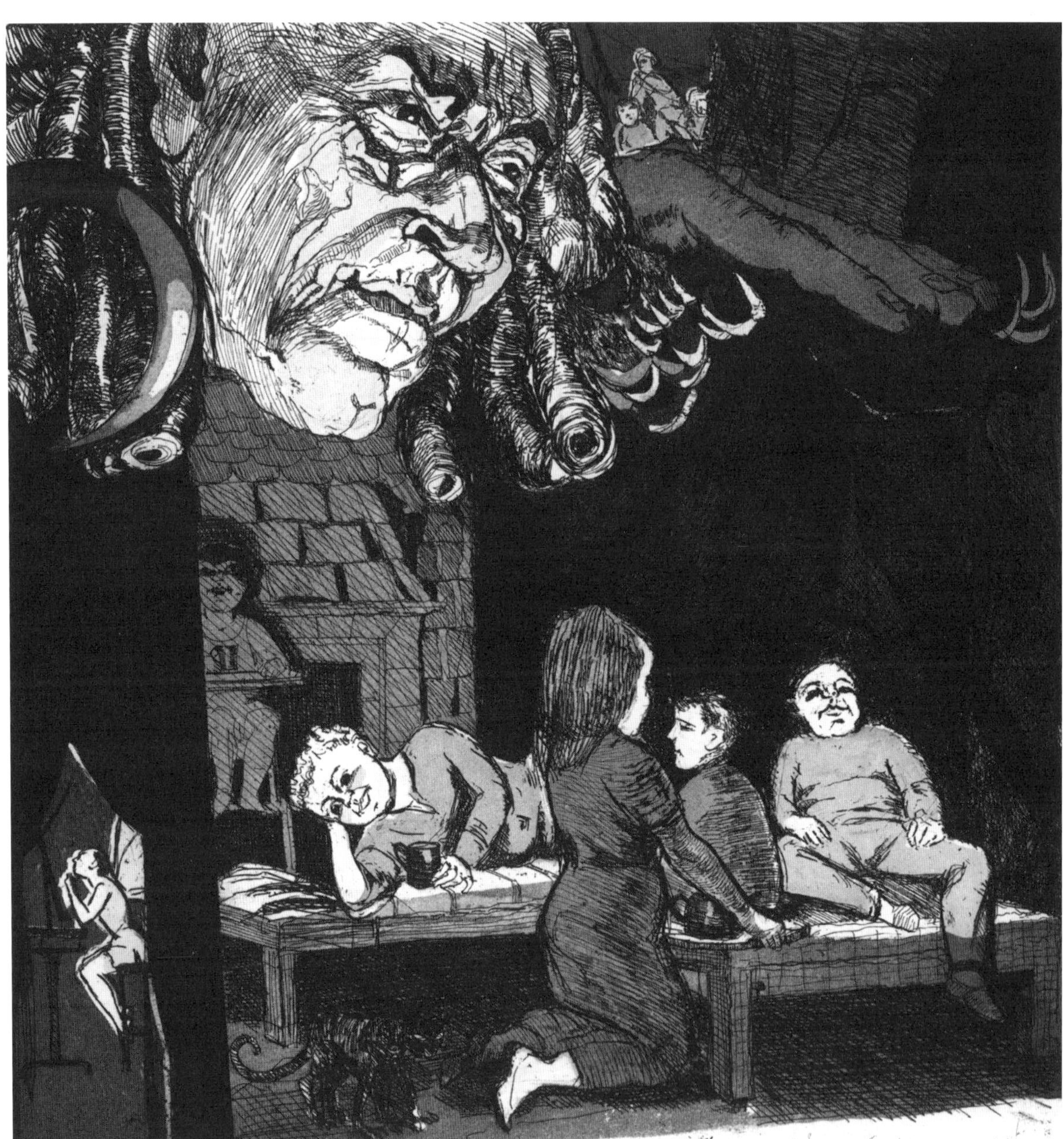

Paula Rego, 'The House Underground', *1992*

Paula Rego

It was an inspired choice of the Folio Society to ask the Portuguese-born Paula Rego to illustrate a new edition of 'Peter Pan' using J.M. Barrie's original text. As it was for Barrie, the world of childhood with its repressions and anxieties has long been a catalyst for Rego's own creativity.

The provenance of 'Peter Pan' is complex. Not originally intended for children, it first appeared as a novel for adults entitled 'The Little White Bird'. Here the novel's narrator, a crusty bachelor who lives close to London's Kensington Gardens, meets a small boy and establishes what, to modern sensibilities, would seem an over-intense relationship with him. This story became the basis of the 1904 children's play. As the critic Jacqueline Rose writes, 'Peter Pan' therefore emerges "out of an unmistakable act of censorship".

The questions raised in 'The Little White Bird' deal with the emotional complexities between adult and child, and the undertones of unconscious sexuality. Rose claims that the rest of 'Peter Pan's history "is an attempt to wipe out the residual signs of the disturbance out of which it was produced".

Just as Barrie was constructing a Never Never Land, based in Kensington Gardens, as a way of coping with his web of repressed desires towards the five Llewelyn Davies boys and their mother Sylvia, around whom the story is built, Freud, in Vienna, was discovering the importance of sexual fantasy.

In dispelling the largely Victorian notions of childhood "innocence", he made it impossible to go on denying the sexuality of children, and our uncomfortable adult responses to it. Despite its status as a classic, 'Peter Pan' is essentially a fantasy of denial. Peter becomes the ultimate childhood fetish: the ever pre-pubescent boy. In the stage version, he is traditionally played by a girl, further compounding the text's latent paedophilia and blurring of sexual boundaries.

For Paula Rego, brought up in post-war Portugal under the twin regimes of Salazar's military dictatorship and the Catholic Church, oppositions such as power and impotence, freedom and repression, are never far away. Hers was a strict childhood. She still paints on the floor as she did when, as a rather reclusive child in her Lisbon nursery, play became her refuge. Her imagery has been inspired by tales heard from her grandmother and aunt.

With her interest in psychoanalysis, Rego has explicitly understood what Barrie could only reach towards implicitly: that the purpose of the fairy-tale, as Bruno Bettelheim suggests, is to ensure that the unconscious fears of the child find a resolution. She is aware that behind the clean, well-mannered little girl playing alone in the nursery, there lurks a disruptive bully, a sneak, a changeling, even a devilish, sexualised Pan. Her late husband, Victor Willing, identified her themes as "domination and rebellion, suffocation and escape". Such a description could equally apply to the story of 'Peter Pan': the boy who wishes for a family but cannot submit to the normal disciplines of childhood, who challenges the father (traditionally Captain Hook and Mr. Darling are played by the same actor) to an oedipal duel, who longs for Wendy's love, yet cannot cope with the implications of adult sexuality.

Rego rescues 'Peter Pan' from the confines of sentiment and nostalgia, giving us not so much a fairyland, as a world of repressed desires. Her dislocations of scale have a surreal quality. The terror she conveys is akin to that of Francisco de Goya. "I paint", she has said, "to give fear a face".

In 'The House Underground', the disembodied head of Hook the pirate/father looms above the lost children like an ogre. The pirates, taking away the lost boys, appear like medieval gargoyles or carnivorous giants. Violation and violence hover close to the surface. The image of the shot Wendy is an inversion of Gulliver in Lilliput – vast, yet helplessly splayed beside the tiny boys, she looks like a victim of gang rape.

The drawing of Wendy together with Hook is both witty and sinister. Wendy is presented as a little Portuguese girl with ribbons in her hair. Yet her face is knowing, with a sexual wisdom that belies her years. Like Lolita or the girls in a Balthus painting, Rego's Wendy is fully aware of her own sexual prowess.

Barrie's 'Peter Pan' is stuck in a Never Never Land of phallic denial. Wendy is destined to become an adult and, as a result, will desert him. But Peter can never follow her to maturity or accept her womanhood. For him, as for Barrie, there is simply no resolution. His tragedy is that he can never grow up. Adulthood is simply too threatening to contemplate. In these powerful drawings, Rego ensures that we never again see this story as a simple children's tale.

Paula Rego
Marlborough Fine Art London

New Statesman & Society
December 14th, 1992

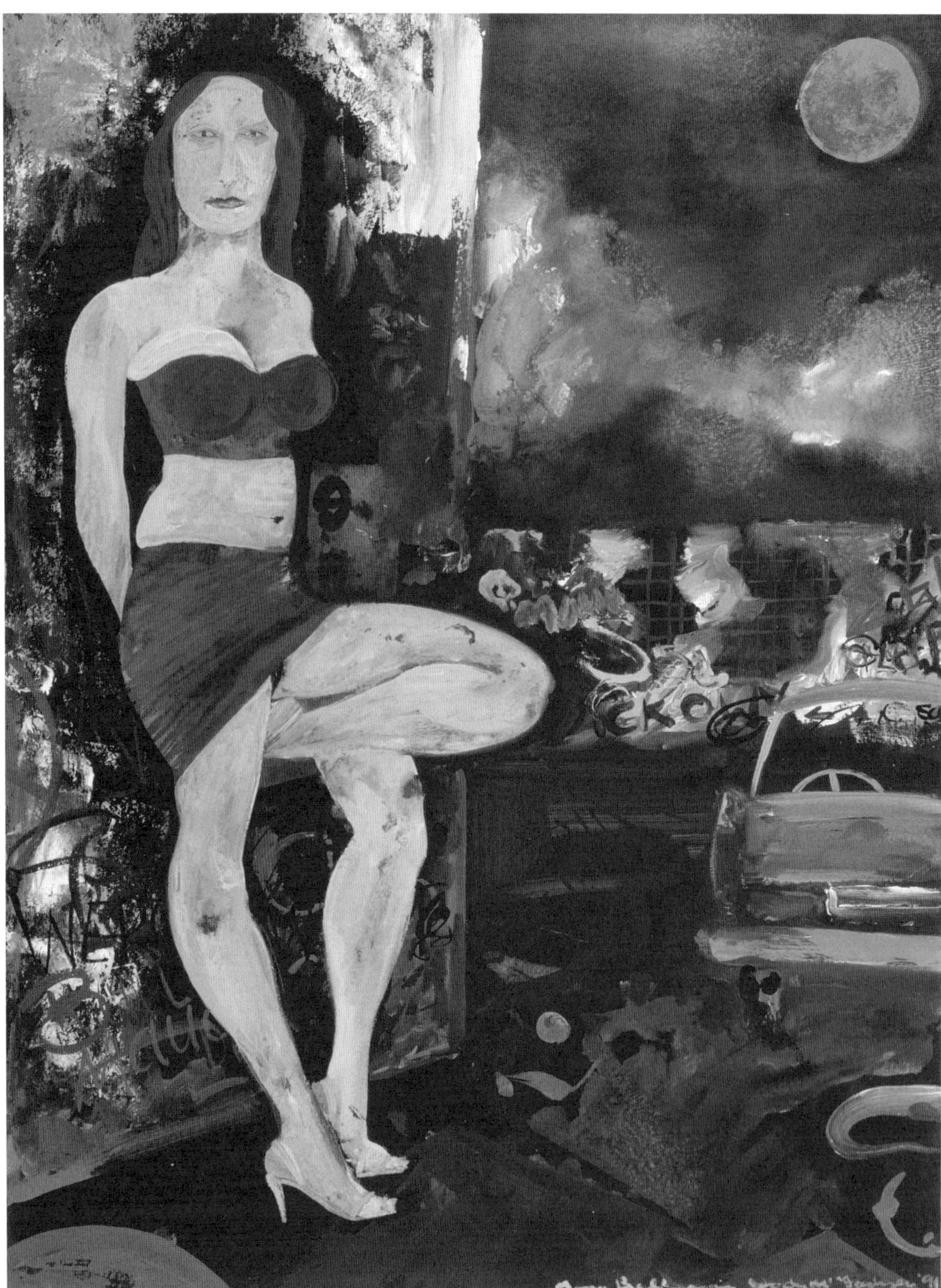

Jock McFadyen, 'Savignyplatz 1', *1991*

Jock McFadyen
Fragments from Berlin

It was the place to be at the end of the 1980s. Anybody who was anybody attended the party the day the Wall came down. A euphoric optimism was in the air. A new era of freedom had dawned. Eastern Europeans flooded into the west in their smoky two-stroke Trabants with little more than a vague hope for a better future, to be greeted with gifts and roses. It seems strange that we were all so naive.

For several years, the Imperial War Museum, keen to rid itself of its bellicose image as an institution eulogising war, has counterbalanced its permanent exhibition of cleansed and sanitised weapons, which fill the main hall like large Dinky toys, with exhibitions by contemporary artists who take a more thoughtful approach to war and its aftermath. The Scottish artist Jock McFadyen, well known for his gritty portraits of the sad, the mad and the bad of the East End of London, was the unanimous choice of the Artistic Records Committee for its commission to record some aspects of Berlin after the Wall came down.

McFadyen is not concerned with apocalyptic historic statements. He adopts no ideological stance. Like all true travellers, he is simply an observer. He is not interested in what he calls, with typical forthrightness, "that wanky, sentimental, political-prisoner kind of art". It is the minutiae of real lives, far odder often than caricature, that fascinate him. During the time he spent in Berlin, he

ensconced himself in the grim eastern suburbs, tramping the wet streets between acres of relentless municipal concrete, to take photographs.

He is insistent that graffiti must be authentically transcribed, that individual creativity and wit cannot be anticipated. In his paintings of the Wall he has deliberately suppressed his own characteristic hand. The result of this non-intervention is that individual voices can be heard crying out in hope, anger and despair.

As with his images of the East End, it is the soft underbelly of the city that McFadyen depicts: the crippled accordion player, the woman in a puppet booth, the apparently three-legged prostitute in 'Savignyplatz' who connects us to the chic decadence of the Berlin of Isherwood in the 1920s. Yet the dreary blocks of flats, still riddled with bullet holes, the cold grey northern skies, and East Berlin's sputnik-style TV tower, along with the city's aura of poverty and downtrodden decay, define East Berlin as the historical accident it is, reminding us that those on the wrong side of the Wall are still suffering, 40-odd years later, from the aftermath of the War.

But it is McFadyen's sculptures that capture this ironic poignancy with the most clarity. That western freedom may amount to no more than the "right to go shopping" is celebrated in the mock-heroic monument

'Born to Shop'. A man stands in a euphoric pose, his arms outstretched, on an ageing Trabant (in fact, a reconstructed Reliant Robin). He is slung about with empty designer carrier bags. His vacuous gesture is that of the innocent Fool. He elicits not only our compassion, but the patronising smile of the well-heeled western cynic. "I consume, therefore, I am" may amount to the new religion, but the cheap goods, affordable by the newly liberated and largely bankrupted east, are tawdry chimeras of a lifestyle to which most of the people can still only aspire.

There is nothing triumphal about the straggling group of figures in 'Procession'. In fact, they are hardly sculptures at all, unconcerned as they are with formal structure. Rather, they are a literal rag-bag of characters made up from the artist's old clothes covered with wax and plaster, and those scavenged from East-End street markets. Slightly smaller than life-size, they amble along like a row of somnambulant dwarfs. The leading figure brandishes a pair of drumsticks, while those following wear paper bags on their heads and ineffectually flap their arms. A woman in improbable stilettos, with a coat over her head, is carried on a makeshift platform. Bringing up the rear is a black-hooded push-chair mounted with the face of a wizened old man.

Who they are and where they are going, we cannot be sure. They are a motley crew, perhaps extras from the cast of 'Mother Courage and Her Children'. But their displacement is implicit; they are, as McFadyen describes, "surplus to requirements". Eleven characters in search of a future walking through rubble with their broken belongings, they progress in the opposite direction to the eleven blinded soldiers in John Singer Sargent's canvas 'Gassed' on the wall behind them. Whether, despite their apparent street-party eccentricity, they are any the less victims than the young soldiers, only history will tell.

Jock McFadyen
Fragments from Berlin
Imperial War Museum

New Statesman & Society
1st November, 1991

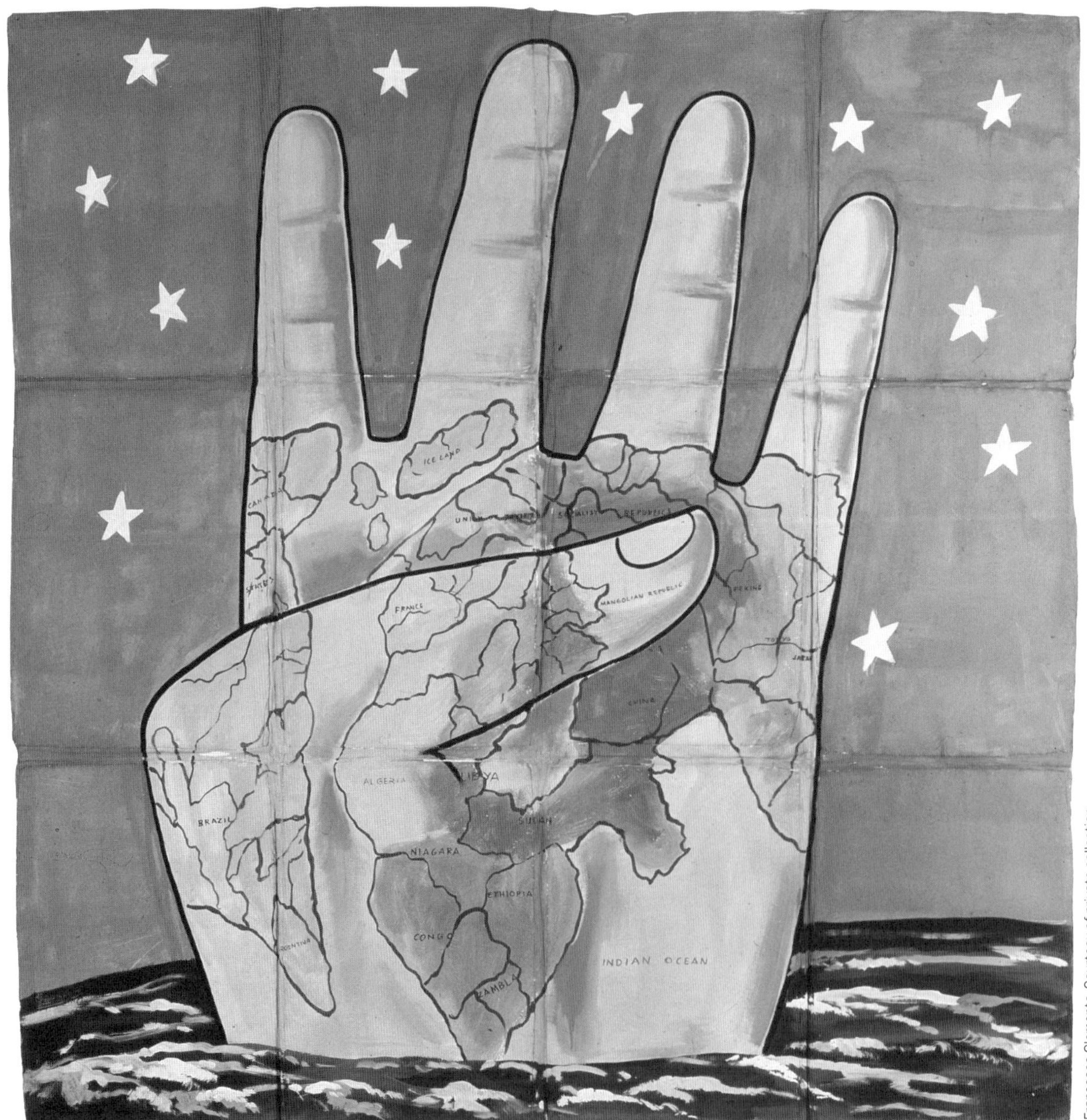

Francesco Clemente, 'The Four Corners', *1985*

Francesco Clemente
Three Worlds

He is probably best known, not as painter, but as the shorn head with designer stubble and dark-lashed eyes staring soulfully from the ad for the designer wear of *Comme des Garcons*. Such a public and commercial act illustrates something of the ambiguity of the artist Francesco Clemente.

Born in Naples in 1952, he has made his home in New York, with long spells spent in Madras. Clemente likes the buzz and the colour these cities offer. Coming from a cultured family – his parents published some of his poetry when he was 12 – he trained as an architect before turning to painting. Clemente has always claimed to be more influenced by poetry than by art. "I am a fan of poets", he says. "I think of all art forms as voice. For me, man's greatest moment must have come before painting, writing or music, when there was only the voice."

For the young Clemente, the poets of the Beat Generation were living symbols of true artists. In them, street credibility and spirituality met. He was drawn to the Beats' rejection of academic values and social structures in favour of the search for the self. Theirs was a path of exploration; the spiritual made flesh in daily repetitive acts.

Clemente also warmed to Jack Kerouac and Allen Ginsberg's interest in Eastern philosophy. Ginsberg, with whom Clemente has on several occasions collaborated, once described him as a "Blake-inspired painter".

For to enter into Clemente's works is to enter an esoteric cosmology of his own making: a world of symbols that appear to be archetypes, but are wholly idiosyncratic and unrelated to any historic imagery.

Clemente's formative years were influenced by the Italian movement of the late 1960s and 1970s known as *arte povera,* which used unorthodox non-art materials borrowed from the scrap heap in a rejection of "high art" and market demands. As a way out of the intellectual closure of much of the period's art, he developed an affinity with the alchemical leanings of Jannis Kounellis and the shamanistic possibilities suggested by Joseph Beuys. With his first trip to India in 1973, Clemente was to find not only "gods who left us a thousand years ago in Naples", but a diversity of spiritual and visual images – temples, beggars, garish film posters and plaster gods: a sensory kaleidoscope that was to revitalise his imagination.

His time in India began a prolific period in which he drew on classical, as well as Indian, mythology. He collaborated with local craftsmen, young miniature painters from Jaipur, Tamil board painters and paper makers from Pondicherry. He was drawn back to the ritualistic possibilities of art and to the body, as if responding with his Italian sensibilities to the eroticism of Hinduism.

Clemente has never been interested in a minimalist honing-down, but rather, like an exotic version of the poet Walt Whitman, to opening himself up to whatever influences assaulted him. One of the most extraordinary works from this period is the series of 24 miniatures 'Francesco Clemente Pinxit', painted in gouache on pages from an antique Persian book, from which the text has been eradicated. Although executed by Indian assistants, the ideograms are entirely Clemente's. Esoteric and hard to read, they constitute a unique microcosm. Maimed and able-bodied youths cavort through formal Indian landscapes, a hermaphrodite lays an egg into a spoon, another excretes turds that turn into delicate decorative flowers, and there is the portentous symbol of a hand with a severed finger.

Insofar as Clemente is ever didactic, this severance serves to remind us of the psychic disasters that can ensue if we cut ourselves off from our physical nature. The image of the hand is recurrent: elsewhere whole and inclusive, it rises like a great colossus from the oceans to hold a map of the world. Clemente is not un-aware that the eroticism inherent in Tantric yoga, from which he draws much of his inspiration, is spiritual.

By contrast to the Indian paintings, those executed in New York are vibrant, edgy and colourfully expressionistic. Self-portraits abound, as if to paint and paint again one's own image is to define existence. A body made of eyes sits on a bandaged head, emphasising that "seeing" is not intellectual but visceral. There is a bringing together of fragments, emphasised in the numerous twins and doubles. Despite his geographical schizophrenia, Clemente knows that, as the poet Robert Creeley said, "The local is not a place but a place in a given man – what part of it he has been compelled or else brought by love to give witness to his own mind. And that is *the* form, that is the whole thing, as whole as it can get".

Francesco Clemente
Three Worlds
Royal Academy of Arts

New Statesman & Society
9th August, 1991

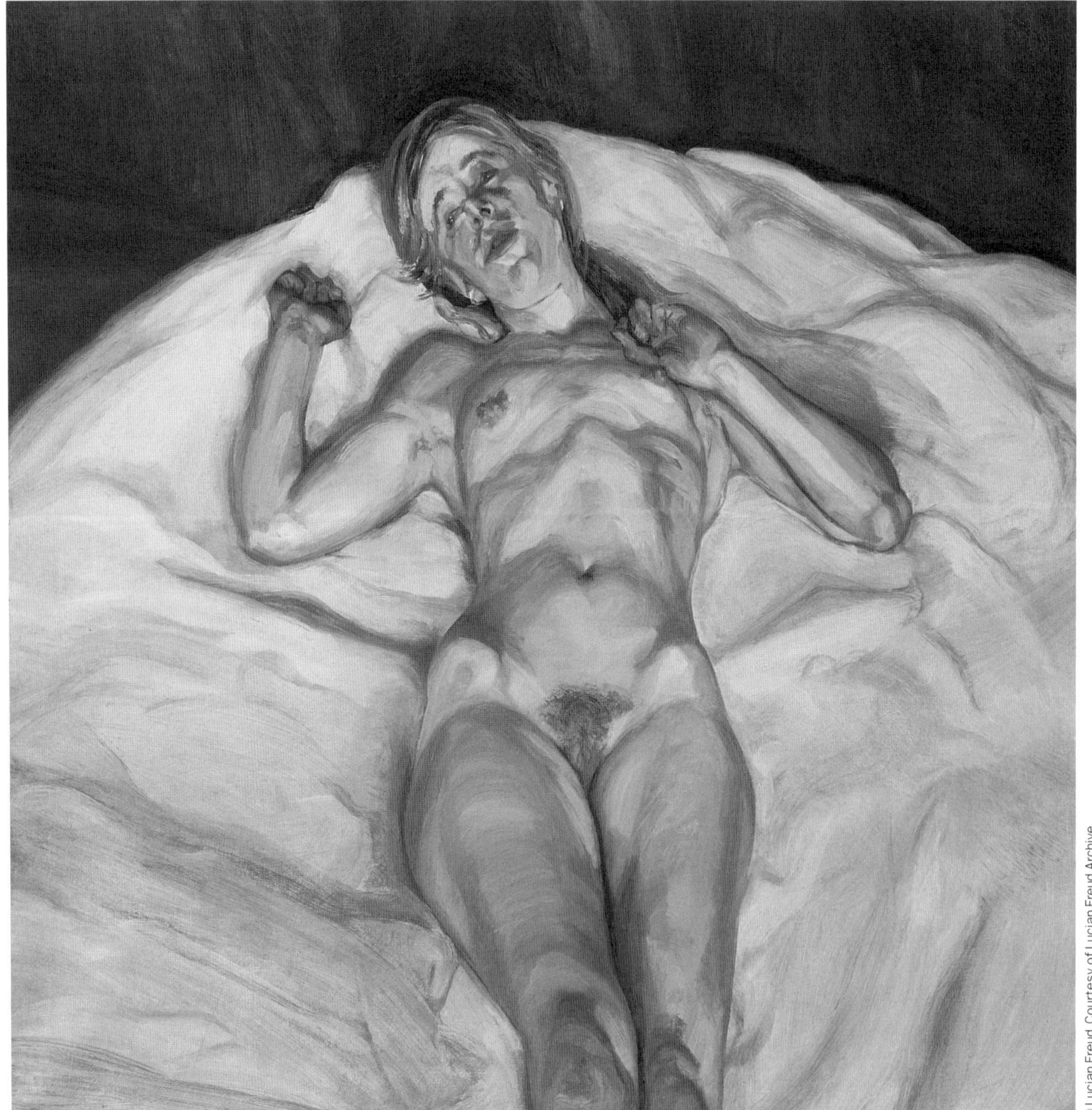

Lucian Freud, 'Naked Girl', *1966*

Lucian Freud

"It looks more like the National Gallery. I can't understand why this show is at the Whitechapel. He's simply not a contemporary painter". "It's such a brave exhibition. Nobody paints seriously anymore. Look at the scale. They look like Rubens."

Both of these contradictory remarks made to me at the private view of Lucian Freud's new exhibition, one by a young artist, the other by Paula Rego, show that this obsessional artist is as provocative as ever. Through the shifting sands of 20th-century fashion – whether Richard Hamilton's Pop Art, Carl Andre's Minimalist bricks or Damien Hirst's flirtations with iconoclasm – Freud has gone on painting, mainly the human figure.

Although London has been his home for much of his life – he was born in Berlin in 1922, the grandson of Sigmund and a member of the talented clan that has spawned numerous writers and "personalities" – he has remained very much the outsider, notorious for his Soho drinking with contemporaries such as Francis Bacon, for his Don Juan love life and for his relentless dedication to work. And through all this, the paintings have changed. Gone are the early, cool Ingres-like surfaces of 'Girl with Leaves', or his famous portrait of Bacon, where the blue-white skin was stretched, translucent and taut, across the base bone structure like a metaphor for angst, and

where the reflections of a room were caught in the iris of an eye around which every lash had been painted with painstaking precision. Now, his vision has mellowed.

It is as if the young existentialist who could only look from a clinical distance, as at "a patient etherised upon a table," has softened to admit not only his sitters' vulnerability, but his own. To compare his 'Naked Girl' of 1966 to his current nudes is to see an artist embracing humanity, much as Rembrandt did towards the end of his life.

"Reality" as photographic likeness does not interest him. Freud has never been touched with the Slade obsession with measuring and putting things in the right place, which emanated from William Coldstream and was passed down through Euan Uglow. What concerns him is essence: to penetrate beneath the surface, to touch (to use his grandfather's terminology) the Id and the Ego of his subject. "I would wish", he has said, "my portraits to be *of* people, not *like* them". He has been criticised for being "too male", for sucking his models dry to serve his own ends. But that is to miss the point. In these paintings there is a complicity between the artist and sitter – a greater equality.

He has said that he wants the paint to "work as flesh". Yet analogies with meat, made by some critics, are misleading. That was Bacon's forte. Whereas Bacon created great archetypes for the 20th century, screaming Popes and faceless victims anguished at the base of the cross – a "theatre" of Euripidean proportions – Freud's work concerns itself with the individual, and faces up, without evasion, to what it means to be vulnerable and mortal.

One of the catalysts for change was his meeting at Anthony D'Offay's gallery with the chubby, outrageously camp performance artist, Leigh Bowery, who had a penchant for sequined masks and furry velcroed female pudenda. Freud did numerous paintings of him: huge full-frontal nudes, a back view reminiscent of Ingres 'Bather of Valpinçon', a close-up genital study and a portrait where Bowery's shaved, fleshy head lolls forward like that of a sleeping pink baby.

Through his candid, tender portraits of Bowery's thick-set body, Freud has subverted the traditional stance of the artist as voyeur who paints the (usually female) nude. These works are reliant on an interplay between watchful artist and watched subject. Freud is no longer the distant scientist of former years. The flesh here is not thin and pale, but doughy and inviting – a landscape of contours and folds. There is volume and a new fullness. At times the paint sags; in other places it is granular. You can feel the artist going beyond the surface, modelling, as a sculptor might, in several dimensions.

Freud's figures, particularly his nudes, are presented without a social background against which they can be defined. Often their only accompaniment is a pile of white rags. The patterning is suggestive of something visceral or flowing. In 'Naked Portrait', *1988*, the female model lies on the bare floorboards in front of the ocean of torn rags, like a beached corpse.

Also startling in their intensity are his portraits of family and friends. The brittleness to be found in the early paintings of his young wife Kitty (the daughter of Jacob Epstein), nervously clutching a rose in

'Girl with Roses', *1947-48*, and Caroline Blackwood, has given way to a greater compassion. More than anywhere this can be seen in the painting of his mother. Tiny, frail and bird-like, she lies, grey haired and dressed in white, her hands folded across her midriff like a chaste nun's, echoing those sleeping effigies found on medieval tombs.

Freud is now approaching his final decades. He is beginning to paint against time. In his nude self-portrait he presents himself as the working artist – literally down to his boots, for they are the only things he is wearing, untied, the tongues flapping open. In his hand he holds the tools of his trade: brushes and a painter's palette. Like the theologian Martin Luther before the Diet of Worms, he seems to be saying that "Here I stand. I can do no other".

"Work", he has said, "is the only way out… the future is the next picture". Labels, schools and fashions have never much interested him. Modernist, Postmodernist, Expressionist: all are inadequate pigeonholes. What he, like his contemporary, Francis Bacon, demonstrates is that whatever the prevailing mode, whatever the claims about the death of painting, there will always be a fundamental need to catch the mysteries of humanity in paint. Freud's isolated figures honour this tradition whilst attempting, in a fractured world, to find a connection not only with the deepest recesses of his own psyche, but also with those of his subjects.

Lucian Freud
Whitechapel Gallery

New Statesman & Society
17th September, 1993

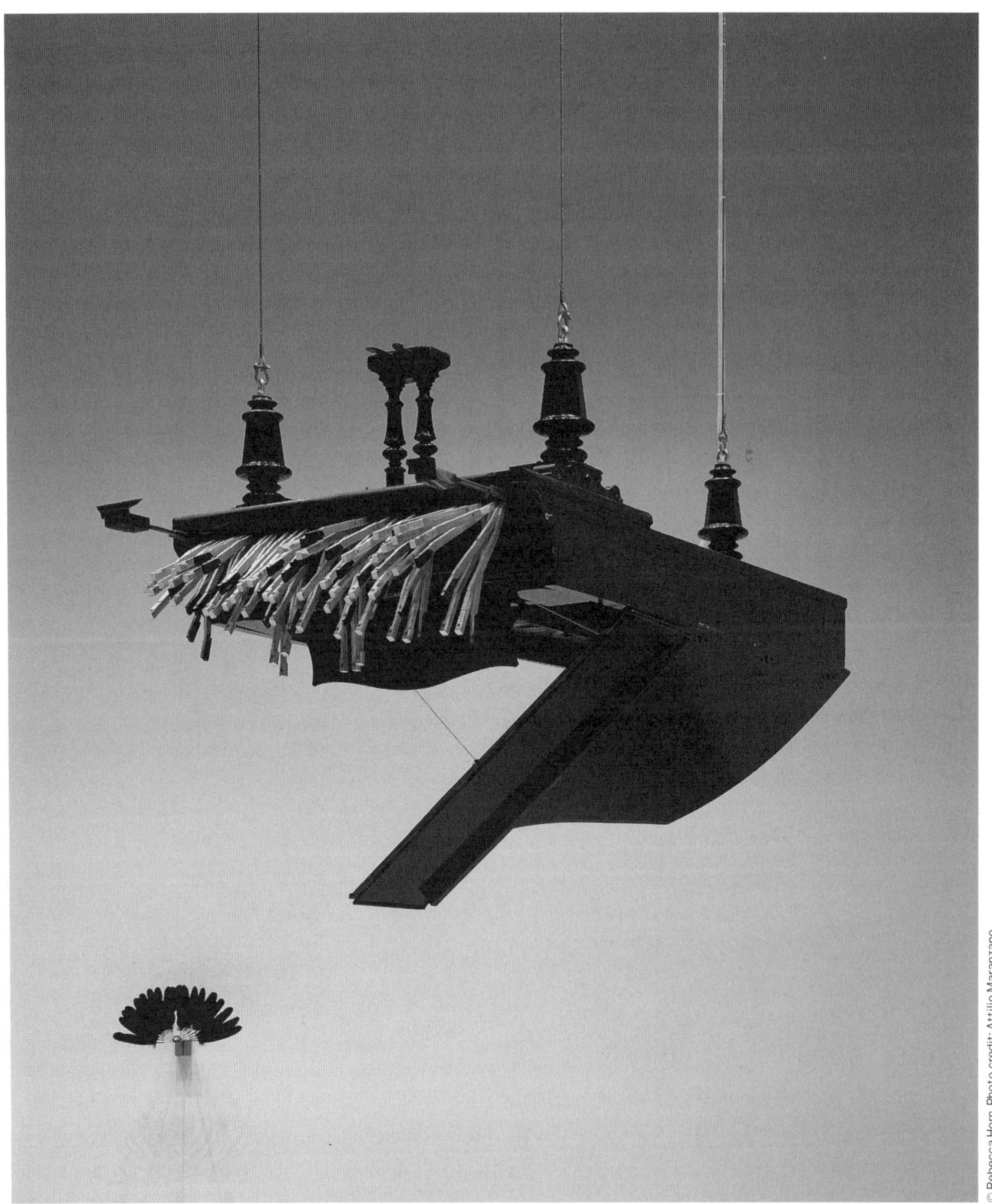

Rebecca Horn, 'Concert of Anarchy', *1990*

Rebecca Horn

Rebecca Horn is something of a sorceress and an alchemist. In the medieval world, alchemy stood in opposition to the dominant strictures of the church. A hermetic system of symbolic language and ritualistic process, it aspired to create both spiritual and material transformation. A "philosophical marriage" of bipolar elements – fire and water, earth and air, male and female – it aimed to mould disparate states into a congruous whole. Mercury (quicksilver) was the crucial transformative element represented by the pagan god Mercurius, the hermaphrodite who embodied the potential for change in his ability to transmute freely between animal, vegetable and mineral forms. Centuries later, alchemy became, for Carl Jung, symbolic of the transformation involved in the analytic quest. As the writer James Hillman describes: "Ore (our common substance) is smelted to yield precious metal; fluids (our vague emotional currents) are distilled for a drop of rare essence; solid masses (our amorphous accumulations) are reduced to their elements. Separation proceeds by discrimination and the dross is discarded."

Enter either the Tate or the Serpentine and you will be drawn into the whirring, spinning world of Rebecca Horn's personal cosmology. Here everything is flux and change. Objects such as feathers, eggs, shoes, mirrors, binoculars, lumps of carbon, mineral powders and stones function as transformative symbols. This shifting instability mirrors not only the fluctuating energies of the body but is also analogous to the delicate changes of mood and emotion.

Suspended from the central cupola in the Tate is an inverted grand piano. Suddenly, without warning, it bursts open: the lid drops down, the keys spew like vomit from the mouth of the keyboard. The atmosphere is one of catastrophic disintegration. Then, within minutes, just as surprisingly, the lid closes and the keys retract and return quietly to the keyboard. The cycle of destruction and renewal is complete. Beside it, a companion piece, 'Little Black Widow', *1988,* made from the feathers of that witches' companion, the black crow, flaps open and closed in eerie silence.

At the entrance to the main hall of both the Tate and the Serpentine, a white baton taps the ground with the motions of a blind man. Like some postmodern Tiresias, it appears to act as a witness to what T.S. Eliot called "the violet hour". Further into the Tate, an *ad hoc* pile of hospital beds is run though by a spasmodic electric charge and a snaking, visceral pipe which, connected to a machine that simulates the pumping of a heart, pulsates with mercury. Elsewhere, two pistols take random pot-shots at the others' image reflected in a pair of opposing mirrors; and a frustrated pendulum swings, forever missing contact with the egg-shaped stone beneath. Mechanical, yet somehow also organic, these machines play out the small psychodramas, the orgasms, rages and inertia of the living. Sexual congress is always a source of potential danger, as in the kiss-of-death charge of the copper tongues of 'Orlando', or the coital encounter in the Serpentine's 'Spoon Sleep'.

Displayed in one of the ante-rooms at the Tate are the body sculptures that Horn has used in her performances. The red coiled bandages and canvas wrappings neatly folded in their boxes suggest the paraphernalia of an orthopedic ward or the dungeon of some dominatrix. Extraordinary head extensions, reminiscent of unicorn horns, along with masks of feathers and others bristling with black pencils, sit alongside winged body extensions. Here we encounter a mind concerned with the limitations of human physicality and dreams of metamorphosis.

As for those other major 20th-century artists, Joseph Beuys and Jannis Kounellis, with whom Horn is spiritually affiliated, her art is, first and foremost, about the act of becoming. Through her sculpture, installations, writing and films she explores subversive landscapes. Like the Romantics, she knows that poetic vision and alchemical knowledge bring us closer to disintegration and death. Her art is never about stasis or arrival but rather, an ingenious and highly articulate manifestation of the search for both universal and self knowledge.

Rebecca Horn
Tate Gallery and Serpentine Gallery

New Statesman & Society
7th October, 1994

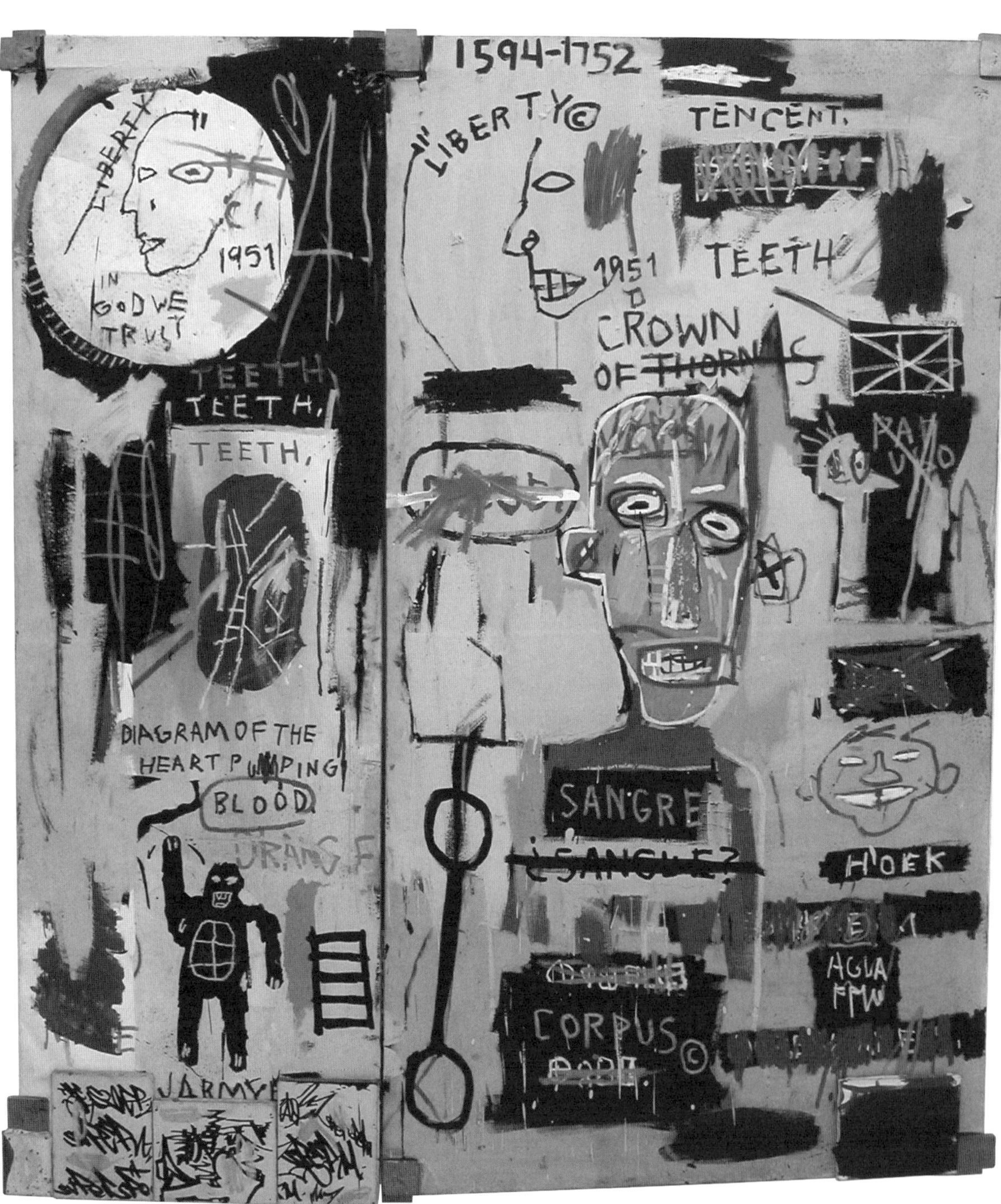

Jean Michel Basquiat, 'In Italian', *1983*

Jean Michel Basquiat

In 'The Painted Word', Tom Wolfe, talking of the glittering spaced-out NY coterie surrounding Andy Warhol, wrote: "The Bohemian was the one who did things the bourgeois didn't dare do". The modern world has always needed its "noble savages", the "primitive" genius onto whom the jaded culturati could project their ideas of a primal sagacity. In Wolfe's cynical critique, he called it the Boho Dance, whereby the culture vultures trawled the lofts and galleries of SoHo in search of original new artists on whom they could shower the rewards of celebrity: fame, money and beautiful lovers.

The pay-off for the Art Benefactor was that without leaving his uptown penthouse, or relinquishing his expense account at Macy's, he could, for a moment, stand aloof from the middle class, feeling that he may be *from it,* but was (thank God) no longer *in* it. Like the poor crowding to touch the hem of a medieval monarch, he could flirt with walking on the wild side, and glow in the reflected chic of the new *wunderkind,* who would, for a price, do his living for him.

In the 1950s, Jackson Pollock wore the mantle donated to him by Clement Greenberg. In the 1980s, the mercurial Jean Michel Basquiat fitted the bill perfectly as Warhol's heir. Black, of Haitian and Puerto Rican extraction, he came not from the slums, but from a comfortable middle-class background – his father was an accountant and his mother encouraged his interest in

art. Basquiat even went to college, but blew it just two months before graduation, becoming, during his teens, with his school friend Al Diaz, the invisible graffiti artists: SAMO – *Same Old Shit.* But he was not to remain invisible for long and, after his first group show at the P.S.1 Contemporary Art Center in 1981, was courted by a panoply of dealers.

A storyteller, a liar, an inventor of tales, he could wear whatever persona happened to suit his present purpose. Insecure, paranoid, despite his celebrity cult status and his friendship with Warhol, he hated being known simply as a "black" painter, despite his homages to heroes such as Charlie Parker and the black boxing champions he canonised in a series of iconic paintings: Joe Louis, Sugar Ray Robinson and Cassius Clay. Though his raw, vigorous work *did* give voice to the marginalised and dispossessed – with its graphic style, its reference to black music and sport, to history and injustice – it was full of signs as to his own sense of omnipotence. In 'Untitled', *1981* he painted an urban jungle, its jagged skyline etched in an energetic scrawl against a raw blue background. Hoardings, TV aerials, cars and planes litter the canvas. But floating in the centre is a three-pointed crown. It is this image that returns again and again, like the base note of an insistent blues chorus, to become Basquiat's hallmark, along with the Notary Public Seal and the © copyright symbol.

Energetic, visceral and inclusive of popular comic forms and street style though it is, his work contains a constant hint of his own perceived greatness. In 'Boy and Dog in Jonnypump', a figure that seems to be a cross between a Mardi Gras carnival skeleton and a black Christ stands, arms outstretched, hands dripping from the wounds of a stigmata, a crimson slash in his side, in front of a violently Expressionist background. With its spiky dreadlocks, it is undeniably a self-portrait.

There is an irony in Basquiat's work that a young urban black should have produced "primitive" images culled from African art, such as the mask-like faces in 'Two Heads in Gold', in much the manner that Picasso and Matisse had appropriated them earlier this century from that unknown "dark continent". For this son of an accountant, with his heroin addiction and his overpowering BO, these images and those of the comic strip and the street provided the ingredients for self-creation as the wild child, the darling of the loft dwellers.

Not only was the three-pointed crown a sign of his own artistic divinity, but so were the references to the great and the good throughout history that litter his work, from Alexander the Great by way of Aristophanes and Socrates, the Punic Wars, to Lincoln A, the names of whom form a scrawled list on the central panel in 'Jawbone of an Ass', 1982. 'In Italian', 1983 is filled with oblique images of Christ. The words "SANGRE" and "CORPUS" are written across the body of a self-portrait. Above are the words "CROWN OF THORNS", with "THORNS" slashed out. Elsewhere in the painting is an image of a King-Kong gorilla beside the image and words of "DIAGRAM OF THE HEART PUMPING BLOOD" and the repeated word "TEETH", as if he were exploring notions of his own evolution and origins.

This hubristic sense of his greatness, along with an obvious death drive, is the central subject of his work, despite its seeming street vitality. When asked during a drug binge in Paris lasting several days whether he could stop, Basquiat answered: "What makes people believe they can say that. They don't know shit. When you say you think I'm going to die, you think I don't know what I am doing. I do. I've been there. I've already OD'd".

Basquiat was driven by an understanding that the best guarantee of iconic status for any artist of the 20th century is his own demise. For all its radical chic, this work is not about life but about Basquiat's own mortality, followed by a resurrection to the pantheon of the great. Basquiat was a child of our times. He knew full well what Jackson Pollock and James Dean had known: that the ultimate career move for a hip artist is death.

Jean Michel Basquiat
Serpentine Gallery

New Statesman & Society
22nd March, 1996

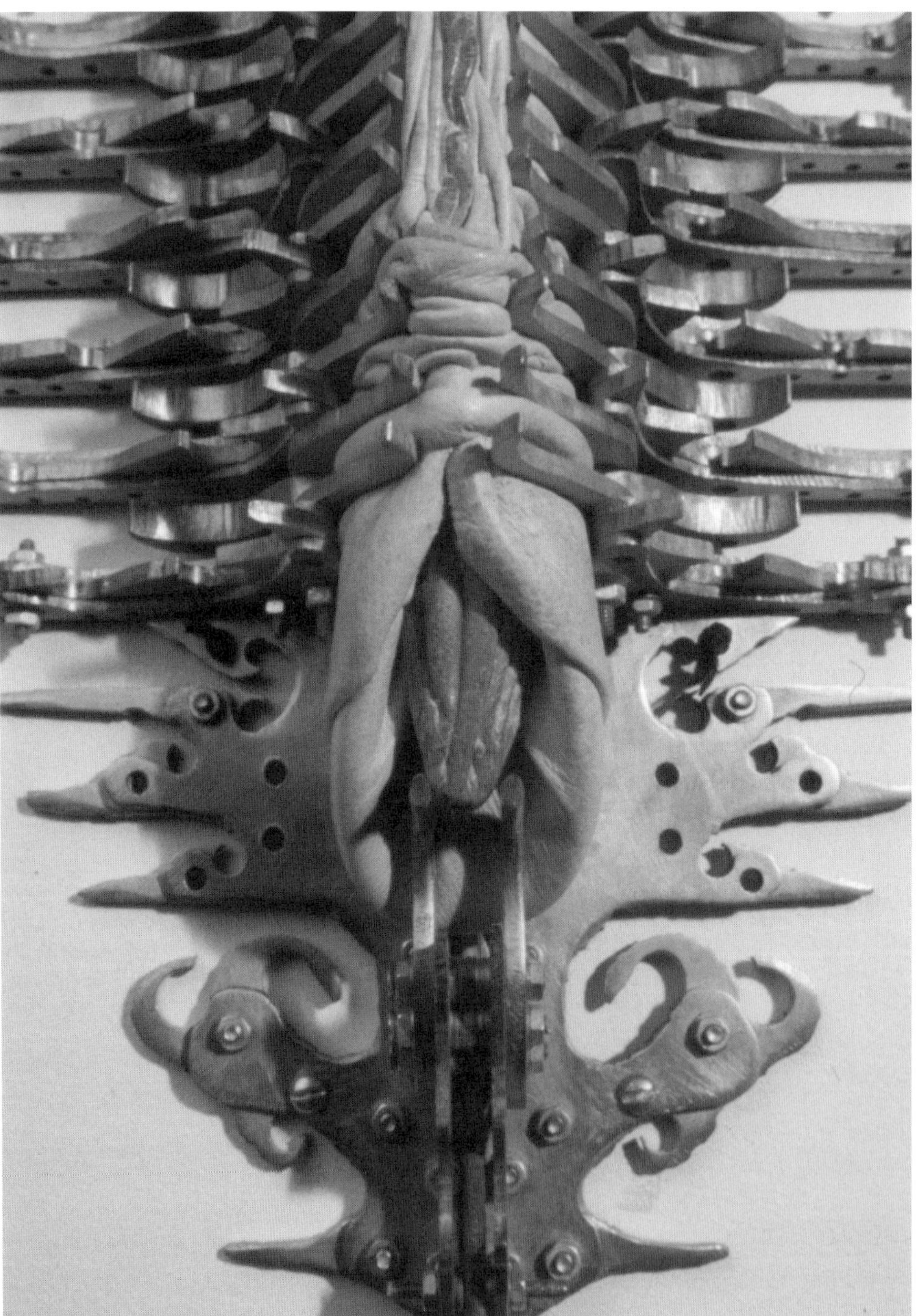

Cathy de Monchaux, 'Evidently Not', *1995*

Cathy de Monchaux

Walking into Cathy de Monchaux's latest show at the Chisenhale Gallery was like entering the boudoir of a successful dominatrix. Byron or Baudelaire might have felt at home in its *fin-de-siècle* Gothic decadence. In her 1993 sculpture 'Scarring the Wound', rich crimson velvet was crushed and folded between ornate ribs of brass, threaded together with ribbons as in some erotic Victorian undergarment. The clamps and baroque leather fastenings in 'Defying Death I Ran Away to the Fucking Circus', *1991*, cut into the lush surface of the fabric – black against red – like restraining stays melting into ample flesh, while in 'Jalousie', *1993*, cool slabs of marble were held by exotic metal grilles resembling screens from the Alhambra. It was difficult to decide whether this was a set for a remake of a Hammer horror movie, or a serious feminist artist at work. Perhaps feminists scholars such as Camille Paglia would claim that such positions are not mutually exclusive, and that this work questioned the nature of desire and power by asking who, in sexual encounters, is the predator, who the victim. In 'Safe 1', two white alabaster balls sat cradled in a small nest of scarlet cloth: cold, "masculine" surfaces juxtaposed with those that were yielding, pliant and "feminine", to create a celebration of androgyny by never exclusively attributing these qualities to either gender.

The leather trusses, the bolts, the fretted sheets of metal, all suggested a taste for the theatrical, as well as a desire to examine the cerebral Apollonian versus the instinctual drives of the Dionysian. This was the visual equivalent of the Super-Ego controlling the lustful greedy Id, an investigation into the nature of female desire and the orthodoxy which states that female sexuality is passive, and conventional psychoanalytic theory that excludes the very possibility of female fetishism.

De Monchaux has talked of her work forming a relationship of "unconsummatable flirtation and desire" with the viewer – which sounds a little like playing a game of artistic prick-tease. Her tough-girl, in-yer-face titles adopt the well-worn Warholian stance that arcane and obfiscatory equals deep and meaningful. This is a pity, for much of the work in the Chisenhale was elegant, sophisticated and witty.

In her new body of work at the Whitechapel, where the irritatingly "cool" titles continue, the work itself has changed. It is less flamboyant and less showy. If the Chisenhale show was about sex, the one at the Whitechapel is about death.

Going to interview Cathy de Monchaux in her spacious, light and extremely tidy studio feels more like visiting an architect's office than that of an artist. Pinned around the walls are meticulous drawings, like details from Victorian pattern books. She keeps little work on the premises. A small mock-up of the Whitechapel illustrates her use of the ground floor for the creation of a massive installation. The immediate contrast to her earlier work is the colour, or rather its absence. Gone are the brothel reds and the polished churchy brass. There is a new stillness, as if the life-blood has literally been drained out. On one wall is a circular work like a tatty ballet tutu. 'Cleaning the Track Before They Appear', *1994* is a negative version of the earlier, corset-like 'Scarring the Wound'. But now the red velvet has been replaced by ragged muslin. The steel ribs are pale and enamelled, the ribbons that thread the layers together dove grey, and the whole covered with a thin layer of powdered chalk like icing sugar. The struts are bolted together, leaving a void at the centre, the interior edges of which are fretted like a savage *vagina dentate* hidden beneath a pale tulle frock. Both beautiful and melancholic, it conjures the decaying wedding dress of Miss Havisham.

The sexual S&M references remain, though they are more subtle. A rusted steel hand holds a flagellatory leather whip like a rat's tail, which ends in a polished blade. Attached to the wall in a corner of the gallery is a work like a flayed spinal column. The exposed soft leather interior, sprinkled with chalk, is pulled open by metal claws to reveal pink labial folds. Yet with its open wounds and splayed struts clamped to the wall, it could, alternatively, be read as a reference to the crucified body of Christ. Here High Baroque meets Jeff Koons. 'Cruising Disaster', *1996* consists of 111 small padded-leather pieces mounted on steel. These prawn-like creatures, stitched onto metal spikes, are fixed to the wall by steel clamps. Half of them are stuffed and trussed like black pods or chrysalides about to split open. Others appear to have already burst, revealing soft pink fleshy orifices, each like the rim of an anus. As in her earlier work, these objects are genderless. The interior is distinctly female, whilst the spikes are aggressively phallic.

In the centre of the gallery is a shrine-like space that can be entered through three separate apertures. Set on low plinths within the enclosed space are 12 lead panels. A central crevasse of pink leather runs between them like an open laceration. The work is finely wrought – much in the mode of a great Victorian craftsman such as Augustus Pugin – though the element of craft is subverted by the implied cruelty in a piece like 'Evidently Not', *1995*, where a pink leather shape, reminiscent of an erect penis, is ensnared by brass clamps. One thinks of Madame de Clairwil in the Marquis de Sade's 'Juliette', who claimed, "torturing males is still my favourite pastime". In 'She Is Not I', *1995/56*, soft down pillows are squeezed beneath panes of white glass by steel claws, like the pale body of a crushed Victorian virgin.

Resembling a small octagonal conservatory, 'Confessional' consists of glass panels, which have been roughly whited out and supported by a verdigris copper frame. The internal space is divided by a brass grille reminiscent of those found in traditional convents or the confessional booths of Catholic churches. The viewer is invited to lie down on the two embryo-shaped pink sofas to discourse with the friend or stranger lying on the opposite couch. Sex and religion, desire and death, voyeurism and art, Id and Super-Ego all merge. Here the Dionysian and the Apollonian meet face to face.

Cathy de Monchaux's Whitechapel exhibition is to the late 20th century what the art of Dante Gabriel Rossetti or Edward Burne-Jones was to the late 19th. Decadent art is ritualistic, with a constant tension between form and moral content, where form always wins. The cruel perfection of its solipsistic beauty says as much about the end of this century as it did about the end of the last. Here we are offered a theatre, a construct where nature and the natural world have been excluded. For as Oscar Wilde once noted, nature is both uncomfortable and inconvenient. The languid participants in de Monchaux's confessional are bound to their alter ego by an endless narcissistic reflection. As in Keats' 'La Belle Dame Sans Merci' – that high priestess of decadent cruelty – the viewer-object is held in thrall by an image of the self as the endless and only subject.

Cathy de Monchaux
Whitechapel Gallery

Contemporary Visual Arts
Issue 15, 1997

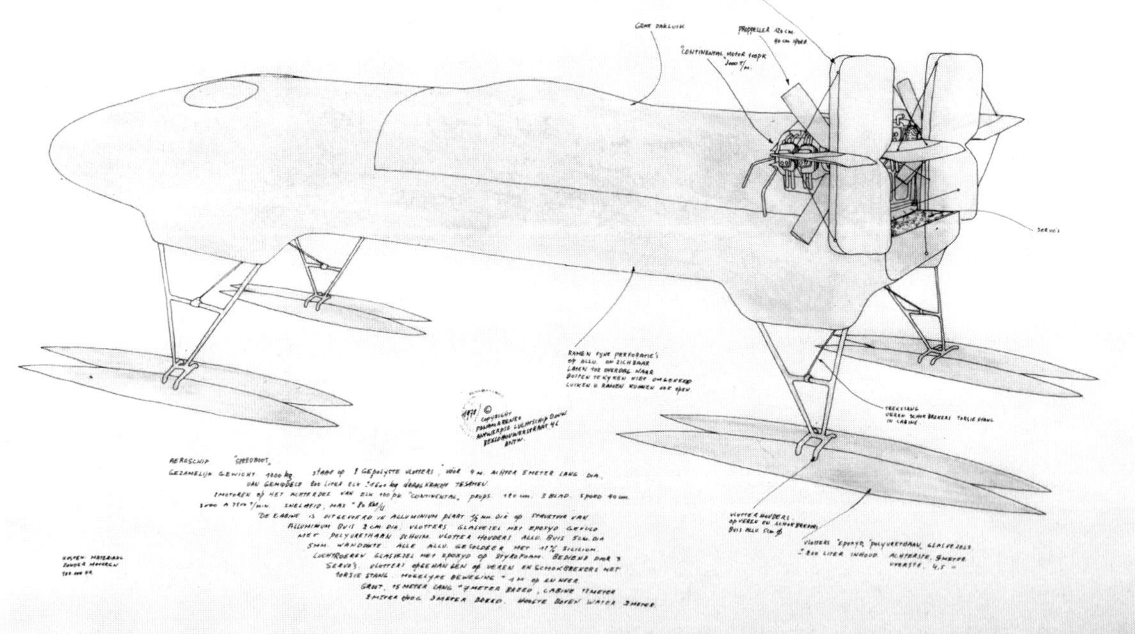

Panamarenko, 'Aeroship Speedboat (Scotch Gambit)', *1970*

Panamarenko

"When will men be most unlike themselves?" mused Aristophanes, who seems to have been fond of asking rhetorical questions and supplying his own answers. "When they learn to fly like birds," he quipped, presumably to a bemused crowd in a sunlit Athenian *agora*. Flight has, since we crawled out of caves, been one of man's most abiding fantasies. The image of Icarus falling from the sky after his father Daedalus's DIY disaster has fascinated artists and writers from Brueghel the Elder to W. H. Auden. Leonardo da Vinci was intrigued with the mechanics of aviation. As both an artist and inventor, he was, no doubt, as much attracted to the metaphorical implications of flight as he was to sorting out the mechanics. The desire for weightlessness, for soaring free unbounded by the Earth's gravitational pull, is atavistic. Dreams of flying are extremely common.

The Belgian artist Panamarenko is a man who has a life-long obsession with flight. Like the Portuguese poet Fernando Pessoa, he has, from the first, adopted a pseudonym to hide from the public gaze. It is not apparent why. In Pessoa's case, it enabled him to live out a creative and emotional Jekyll-and-Hyde existence, to strive for psychological consolidation and completeness. No one seems sure of the genesis of Panamarenko's name. It's been suggested that it refers to the now-defunct Pan Am Airlines, and that the Russian-sounding suffix is a whimsical take on the Cold War that was at its height when he emerged onto the Antwerp art scene in the 1960s. Panamarenko is the Walter Mitty of the art world, a utopian dreamer, an "artist-technologist" who has spent 30 years constructing Heath-Robinson contraptions from an assortment of bicycle peddles, sprockets, rubber bands, wheels, balsa wood (the stuff small boys use to build model aeroplanes) and thingamajigs. What's more, he believes he can make them fly. Looking at some of his machines, I am reminded of those go-carts kids used to drag around the streets made from old pram chassis – bound with tape and string – before the emergence of skateboards. Peter Pan also had a thing about flying. And he never wanted to grow up.

In the 1960s, Antwerp, like Amsterdam, was a haven for alternative lifestyles: American draft-dodgers, hippie dropouts, drifters, would-be artists and poets. It was during this period of social flux that Panamarenko came onto the scene. Like his contemporary Joseph Beuys, he has always been interested in the natural sciences. While the mystical and the Gnostic were to seduce Beuys, Panamarenko claims he has always remained closer to the tradition of hard science. Yet both men share a common desire to expand the definition of what constitutes a work of art. Each began to see the limitations of an art split off from science, where the rigours of Descartian methodology became more concerned with the mechanistic "hows", than the metaphysical "whys". In this sense, Panamarenko is a very European artist, standing apart from the macho heroics of American Expressionism and pop culture that dominated at the time.

At the 1968 Dussoldorf exhibition, Panamarenko's 'Das Flugzeug' formed the central focus of the show. This phantasmagoric pedal-powered helicopter-cum-aeroplane, made from racing-bike parts, rubber driving belts, Styropor wings and occupying a space of 16 x 7 metres, now fills almost an entire upstairs gallery at the Hayward. Its zany inventiveness set the tone for Panamarenko's later work: spaceships, gismos with propellers that can be strapped to the human body and 'Meganeudons' – small flying machines that replicate the wing beats of insects. 'Umbilly I', for example, is a cross between a glider, a toy pedal car and a giant wasp. 'Catapult Max', *1997*, and his 'Super Pepto Bismo', *1966* with its leather straps and outstretched metal arms ending in a mass of small wiring propellers, look like the sort of hybrid contraptions that the baddies in Asterix might have used to make a quick getaway. The first series of drawings and small models for his ongoing project for the flying saucer 'Ferro Lusto X' appeared as early as the 1970s. Once the shell of the spacecraft had been built in 1997, there still remained the problem of getting it off the ground and perfecting the 'Bing Motor's.

Panamarenko sets great store by the notion of "invention". The word, for him, resonates with ideas of adventure and discovery. He eschews the prosaic and actual in preference for the "hardly probable" or "merely possible". As with Voltaire's God, because these artefacts did not already exist, he seems to have needed to invent them. As much as anything, his work is about an act of faith. But a faith in what is not always clear. A clue might be found, whatever his claims about "real" science, in a work made in 1970, entitled 'The Teachings of Don Juan', based on the utterances of that peyote-drinking

hippie guru, Carlos Castaneda. Castaneda, and his shamanistic hero Don Juan were, of course, committed to a voyage of mood enhancement and to fantastic transports of transcendental delight. The food that Panamarenko envisages sustaining his astronauts during their cosmic adventures in 'Ferro Lusto X' is a mixture of crushed peyote washed down with a home-made poteen of potatoes and cactus peel. After that lot, they'd presumably be so spaced out it would hardly matter whether or not the thing actually flew.

Panamarenko has created his own bizarre version of the Theory of Relativity, 'Toy Model of Space (A Mechanical Model Behind Quantum Mechanics)', *1992*. "In the art world", he says, "nobody understands it. In the world of science everybody thinks it is silly, even before they read it". It is hard to assess whether he is simply being disingenuous or is genuinely surprised that this should be the case. Looking at his 'Aeromodeller', *1969-71* – a huge rattan picnic basket of a contraption held together with ropy-looking bolts and suspended beneath a large hot-air balloon – one is inclined to believe that this man is more Jules Verne than latter-day Einstein. The limp, woolly space suits lying on the floor of the craft seem like something from a child's fancy-dress box rather than equipment that would prevent oxygen starvation and weightlessness. Panamarenko also does a good line in ironic Ruritanian peaked caps. 'Kepi', *1997*, an army hat topped with a fish, is "designed to withstand environmental conditions and people". This is a man who has never lost the ability to play.

So should we be flocking to see the work of this obscure 1960s throwback? And is what Panamarenko makes even art? Well, yes. For however 'Boys Own' some of it may appear, there is something rather touching about the obsessive enterprise of this mad visionary and dreamer, this poet-inventor. For unlike so much art that was made during the last

years of the 20th century, and will
presumably go on being made well into
the 21st, this has nothing to do with either
the market, money, investment or even
notions of celebrity. There is no material
gain to be had from this work. It is simply
the culmination of one man's dreams and
reveries: a mad utopian bid for some sort
of transcendence. Like Carlos Castaneda,
Timothy Leary, R. D. Laing, love-ins, and
hippie bells, it all seems to belong to another,
more innocent age. Yet I can't help but feel
that in this mitigated, self-promoting world,
we need all the visionaries and dreamers
we can get.

Panamarenko
Hayward Gallery

The Independent
15th February, 2000

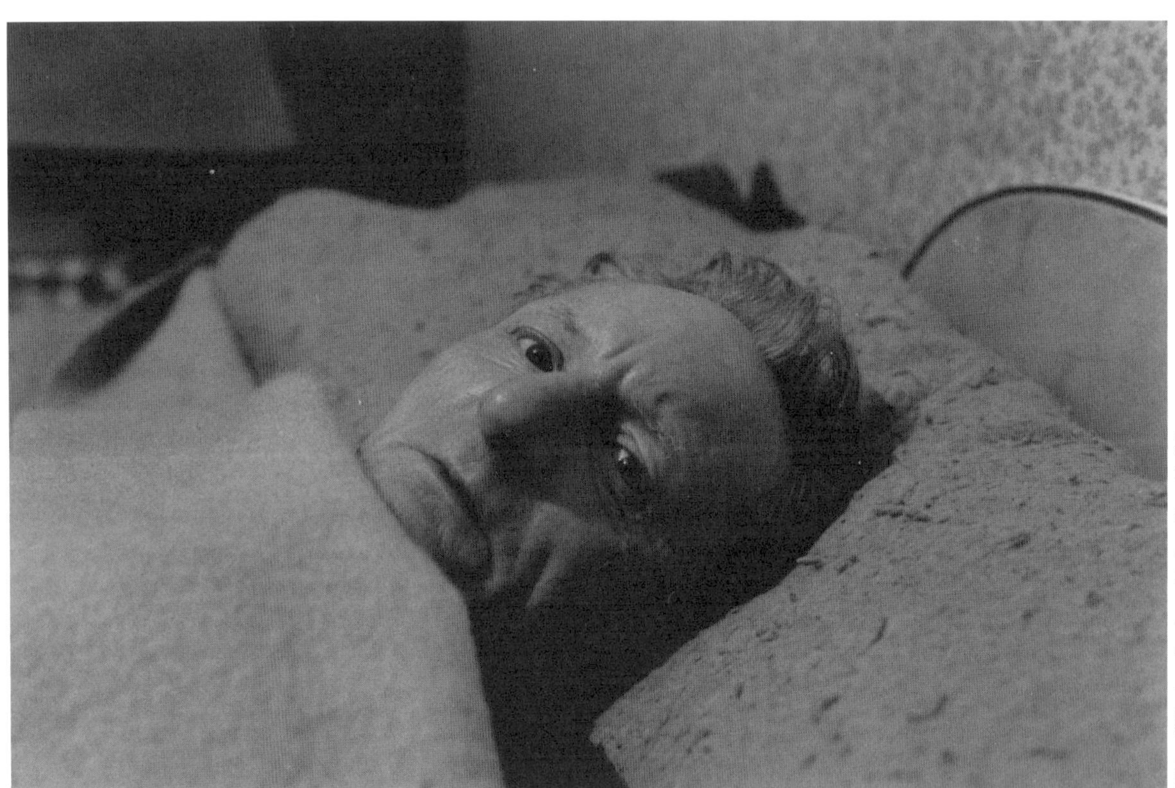

Richard Billingham, Untitled, *1991*

Richard Billingham

"All happy families," wrote Tolstoy, "resemble each other; each unhappy family is unhappy in its own way".

Richard Billingham was born in Birmingham in 1970. Statistically, he should never have made it to college, let alone become one of the hottest photographers around. Brought up on a deprived council estate, he endured home circumstances that make those of the Royle family look truly aristocratic. A loner as a child, he was never encouraged by his apparently feckless parents, but neither was he discouraged. He was always the "best drawer in school" and his talent secured him a place on the art foundation course at the local Bournville College, from where he went on to study fine art – "the drop-outs' course" – at the University of Sunderland. It was there that he began to take photos of his family as source material for his paintings.

Billingham has been accused of exploiting his family. The gritty "memoir" is perhaps a more familiar genre in contemporary literature than in the visual arts. In any creative-writing workshop, the first instruction to young writers is to write about what they know. Think of the novelists Roddy Doyle or Toni Morrison. Yet Billingham claims "it is not my intention to shock, offend, sentimentalise, be political or otherwise – only to make work that is as spiritually meaningful as I can make it, whatever the medium".

The discomfort of many viewers says a good deal about the social divides that still persist under this Blair government. For it is largely a middle-class audience who will look at these photographs in which Ray, Richard's dad, trips blind drunk over the swirling debris of the filthy carpet. They will be forced to confront their barely disguised distaste at his mother Liz standing in her mucky bathroom with the cat, her vast spongy breasts veiled by a torn egg-stained nightie, her tattooed arms like two boiled hams, or fists clenched, yelling at Ray like a fat fishwife, or smiling to reveal her bad teeth. And yet there is something "spiritual" – if that word means revealing some fundamental truth about the human condition – to be found in these works. The smudged black-and-white photos of Ray, bottle in hand, both laughing and comatose, recall the pathos and absurdity of Harold Pinter's dossers in 'The Caretaker' or Samuel Beckett's ever-waiting tramps. For what else can be done when caught in the poverty trap at the bottom of the heap except drink, laugh, or kill oneself?

In the video of 'Ray in Bed', the artist pans the room in which his dishevelled, toothless father sleeps. The beaked nose peering above the bedcovers gives the impression of a death mask. The landscape of Ray's body, the chicken-skin neck, the white hairs poking from his nose and ears, is as poignant an image of impending mortality as any by Rembrandt. For there is something loving in this son's unflinching gaze as he watches over his battered father lying amid the synthetic Arcadia of stained rose-pattern wallpaper and cheap floral sheets, the detritus of his life all around him.

Billingham has an extraordinary eye for colour. A photo of Liz stretched on the sofa, arms raised above her head, a large mound of flesh in a floral tent of a dress against a background of busy wallpaper, has something of the fleshy sensuality of a Matisse odalisque. While in another, where she sits centre frame in the same dress doing a jigsaw, the colours and print echo the swirl of her blue tattoos along with the confusion of loose puzzle pieces in the box on her lap, and the half-finished scene on the table in front of her.

What Billingham reveals is the unbridgeable gaps in human relationships. The bitten fingers of his stoned brother moving obsessively over the mouse buttons of *Play Station* is a despairing image of emotional inarticulation, as is the video of Liz smoking in front of a rain-spattered window. These acts fill the spaces between words, the void between desire and its realisation. Only the gift of two boiled eggs on a plate, from Liz to Ray – who receives them with outstretched hands – demonstrates a love of sorts that cannot be verbally expressed.

 The series of urban landscapes taken around the Black Country are visual barometers of psychological bleakness. These are the places betwixt and between. A fringe of scrub straggles alongside an empty factory, a clump of burdock sprouts on the edge of a rundown estate. Green hangs on by its fingernails. In the no man's land of a litter-strewn recreational ground, a children's roundabout stands unused and rusting. These are the spaces at the edge: at the edge of the city, of society, of culture.

In these funny and moving photos, Billingham makes visible the infinite pathos of life. Fights, playing with video games or pets, drinking and smoking – these are the activities that form the warp and weft that pattern these vivid lives, giving them colour and meaning.

"That passed the time," Vladimir said to Estragon while waiting for Godot. "It would have passed in any case," he replied. "Yes, but not so rapidly".

Richard Billingham
Ikon Gallery Birmingham

The Independent
16th July, 2000

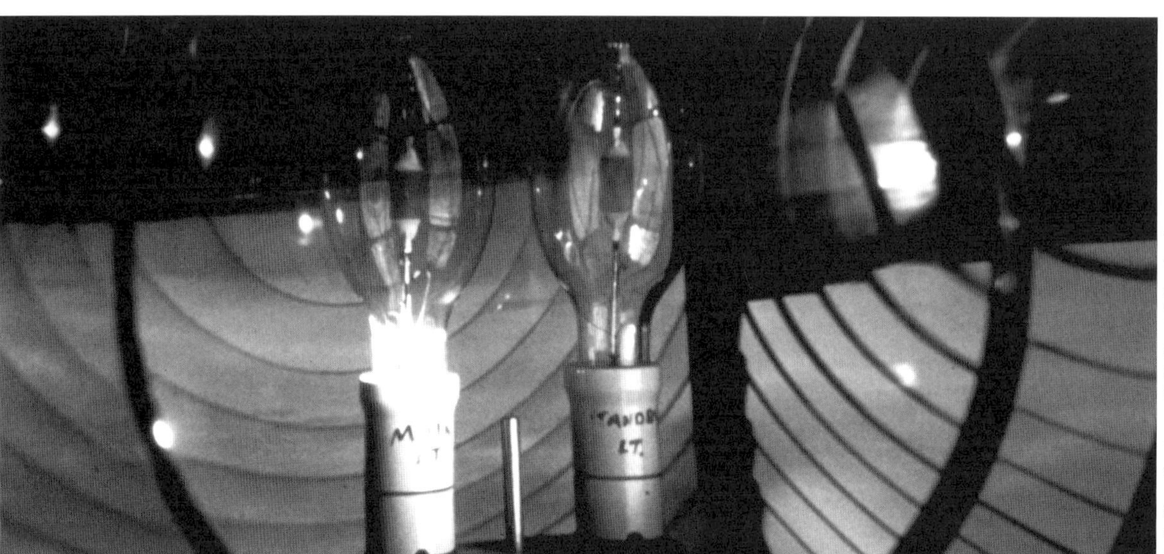

Tacita Dean, 'Disappearance at Sea' (still), *1996*

Tacita Dean

As a metaphor for the unconscious, the sea is hardly original, but in Tacita Dean's hands it becomes revitalised and transformed into a newly potent image. At art school in Falmouth, its tides and rhythms entered her soul. It became a symbol of the edge, where wilderness and culture, fixity and movement meet. Her work is concerned with mapping both the actual physical wilderness and the internal space of unconscious desires. Her journeys, both inner and outer, are a quest for some sort of unnameable and, by definition in this fractured world, unobtainable, Grail. Her work reaches towards the sublime and is full of Caspar David Friedrich sunsets, lighthouses blinking against dappled roseate skies, and endless expanses of blue sea. In 'Banwel', *1999*, shown on an anamorphic (film-format) screen, which frames a herd of gently munching Holstein cows as the sky blackens above a Cornish field during the recent eclipse, Dean makes reference to the tradition of English landscape painting. Other pieces highlight obsolescence, decay and dereliction. Objects – often architectural – and places are charged with the *tristesse* of a failed and abandoned vision. Her work is not, in any usual sense, Postmodern – lacking the brittle irony that has become its hallmark – but its melancholia mirrors the unrealised hopes of the utopian Modernist enterprise, revealing the actual and emotional detritus that those ideologies and dreams have left behind.

Tacita Dean first came to public prominence when, in 1998, she was short-listed for the Turner Prize. Trained as a painter, she now works in a variety of media, including drawing, photography and sound, but is probably best known for her seductive, meditative 16mm films. That she should choose to work in film, whilst so many of her contemporaries work in video, is no accident. Dean is obsessed by the nature of time, and the linearity of film allows her to explore its historic and poetic properties. She has differentiated the use of digital video by describing it as a form of "looking", and the use of film as "seeing".

Her pilgrimages have taken her as far afield as Rozel Point, Utah, in a search for the lost site of Robert Smithson's seminal, but now submerged, Earth Work, 'Spiral Jetty' *1970*; to the Caribbean; to a television tower in Berlin; and to the Cornish coast. Her fascination with the sea has led to an abiding preoccupation with the story of the lone sailor, Donald Crowhurst, who disappeared in his fragile trimaran, the 'Teignmouth Electron', during the Golden Globe Race in 1968. A chancer, desperate to reinvent himself and create a distance from the events of his past life, Crowhurst soon ran into difficulties in his untested vessel. Unable to face failure and withdraw from the race, he faked his navigational records, finally throwing himself overboard with the ship's chronometer, as if he had run out of metaphysical, as well as actual time.

Whilst afloat, Crowhurst retreated into a private world where conventional notions of time and space became blurred. In this liminal state, a sort of madness set in. It was as if he had become pure Id, lost in an amniotic ocean of fantasy and desire. The Crowhurst story has proved the genesis for a number of Dean's works including 'Teignmouth Electron', *1999*, a photograph of Cayman Brac in the Caribbean showing what is believed to be Crowhurst's abandoned trimaran beached amid tropical vegetation next to the abandoned shell of a 1970s "bubble-house"; a failed futuristic structure that was supposed to withstand hurricanes. It also inspired 'Disappearance at Sea', *1996* and 'Disappearance at Sea II (Voyage de Guérison)', *1997*. Filmed at two light houses on St Abbs Head and Longstone Lighthouse on the Farne Islands, the beams of the lonely beacons – flashing a fixed number of times each minute – act as sirens calling lost sailors home across the empty reaches of the sea. Archetypal journeys such as those of Jason and the Argonauts, or Tristan and Isolde are invoked. In fact, the subtitle 'Voyage de Guérison' (journey of healing) refers to the near-mortal wounding of Tristan who, relinquishing himself to the forces of the sea, was washed up on a magical island where supernatural forces healed him.

In 'Sound Mirrors', *1999*, the sense of being on the edge has a particular resonance. The film is haunted by the presence of great concrete dishes that, during the 20s and 30s, formed part of our coastal defence system. An acoustic early-warning system, they were soon discovered to be inaccurate, and supplanted by radar. Left to crack and crumble on the mudflats of the Kent coastline, these lumbering architectural relics, their angles caught against the fading light in Dean's grainy grey film, look like sculptural monoliths. Part Brancussi, part Easter-Island heads, they slowly erode and decay, subjected to time's remorseless melt, as they are absorbed back into the landscape rather like Smithson's 'Spiral Jetty'. The desolation of shingle and shale is interrupted only by the traces of human existence – the barely audible sound of a train, a light aircraft taking off from nearby Lydd airport. Timeless and anachronistic, the film might have been discovered among the archives of Mass Observation.

Tacita Dean's most recent work 'Fernsehturm' (Television Tower) was made in Berlin in October 2000. Having spent time in the city as a student, she remembered the tower on her return as a guest artist of the Berlin Artist's art programme. Built at the height of the Cold War in 1969, the Fernsehturm has dominated the skyline above Alexanderplatz, achieving notoriety through Alfred Döblin's novel 'Berlin Alexanderplatz'. Dean was attracted by the Modernist architecture that seemed to encapsulate a lost historic vision and an optimistic belief in a now-defunct social system. She was drawn particularly to the tower's restaurant poised on a circular revolving platform that turned 360 degrees every half hour, allowing the diners a panoramic view of the city during a full rotation. Using a static camera, she filmed the interior, recording the comings and goings throughout the day. Bathed in daylight, the restaurant gradually metamorphoses into a claustrophobic, womb-like space as the evening draws in and the electric lights are switched on. The tower takes on a mythic quality: the divisions between the windows resembling, in silhouette, the columns of a Greek temple. Light has traditionally played a huge part in painting, from Turner to the Impressionists as, indeed, it does in photography and film. Here, the changing light both emphasises the specificity of each moment – for on any other day the experience would be different – whilst also implying historic change. For this building, once enclosed in East Berlin, now finds itself in a newly democratic world, looking both back to the past and forward to the future.

So much contemporary art is about art
that "life" seldom gets a look-in. What Tacita
Dean does is restore us to the world, and
to the experiences of looking and being,
reconnecting us to our deepest emotions
of longing and desire.

Tacita Dean
Tate Britain

The Independent
17th February, 2001

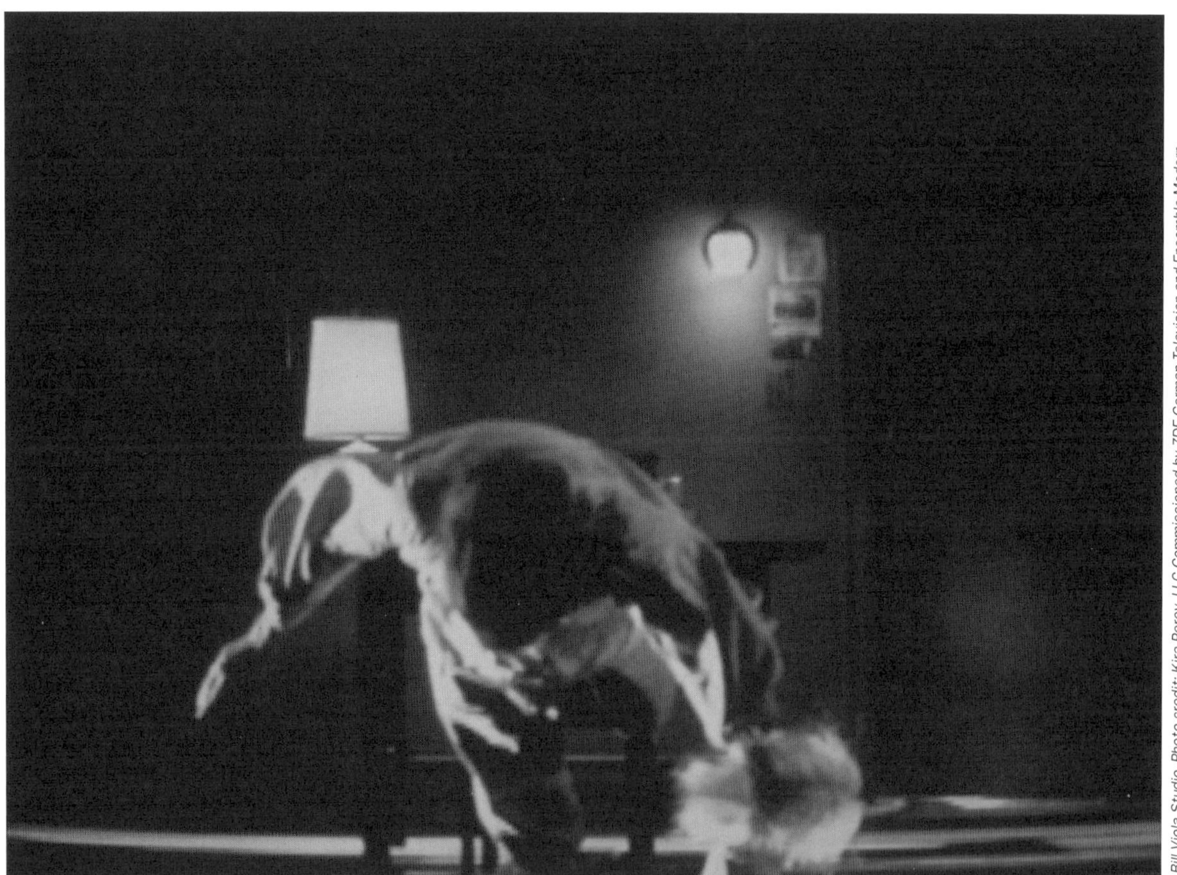

Bill Viola, 'Déserts', (still), *1994*

Déserts
Music by Edgard Varèse
Video by Bill Viola

Early in his career, the French-born composer Edgard Varèse befriended Claude Debussy, became a student of Ferruccio Busoni's, and was championed by Richard Strauss. Born in 1883 (three weeks after Anton Webern) he studied Mathematics and Engineering before turning to music. As a young composer, he sought an ever-more-expansive musical language, feeling his vision hampered by the inadequacy of available resources. Later in his career he claimed, "I am not a musician: I work with rhythms, frequencies and intensities".

In 1915 he set sail, Columbus-like, for New York, which he saw as his own New World. After his departure, his Berlin warehouse burnt down destroying his store of manuscripts, further severing his ties with Europe. His first massive orchestral work, 'Amériques', premiered by Leopold Stokowiski in 1926, marked his renaissance as a composer. Characterised by astringent masses of sound, his work came to represent anti-Romanticism at its most uncompromising. An unabashed Modernist, he wrote dissonant music that, nonetheless, had an optimistic utopian quality. Although he employed electric tone generators, he felt that current technology could not adequately describe the sounds of his imagination and, as a result, he wrote almost no music between 1936 and 1954.

In 1953, when already working on the score of 'Déserts', he acquired a two-track tape recorder and new vistas began to open. He started to record in the factories of Philadelphia, ending by juxtaposing "three interpolations of electronically organised sound" and four purely orchestral sections. 'Déserts' is, therefore, the first work to combine live orchestra and tape, though never simultaneously. Although already in his 70s, he had a profound influence on serialists such as Pierre Boulez and Karlheinz Stockhausen. Boulez wrote on his death in 1965, "Varèse, your time is over, and is just beginning". For Varèse the title 'Déserts' evoked "that distant inner space that no telescope can reach, where Man is alone in a world of mystery and essential solitude".

"Mystery and essential solitude" are the terrain of Bill Viola's work. The accompanying video to Varèse's music, made in 1994 and premiered at the Hollywood Bowl in August 1999 with the Los Angeles Philharmonic, follows the score only in as much as Viola alternates images of a lone man in a room with those of "an expansive external world devoid of people". This echoes the manner in which Varèse juxtaposes periods of orchestral composition with intervals of tape to imply both internal and external space. Since the early 70s, Viola has used video to explore perception as a route to self-knowledge. His celebrated 'Nantes Triptych', which drew strongly on traditional religious art, presented the cycle of birth and death in real time, with the left "panel" showing a young woman giving birth, whilst in the right an old woman (his mother) lay dying. With his roots in Eastern mysticism and Christian iconography, Viola creates archetypal, loosely spiritual works that are at odds with the cool cynicism of much contemporary art, and sit comfortably with the utopian vision implied by Varèse's charismatic music.

The first shots in black and white sweep through unidentified terrains. All are empty. What we see might be the surface of the moon or the bottom of the ocean. It is an apparently timeless space, a space "beyond" time. Viola's iconography is elemental: fire, air, water. There are moments of colour: orange balls of fire, lightening striking an empty landscape as if it were a bolt from God. A man dressed in white enters a room and walks around a laid table, sits down and eats, pours water into a glass from a jug. The gesture is ritualistic. There are other images of emptiness – rock faces, empty car parks lit by unnatural light, Baudrillardian highways – spaces of perpetual and depersonalised motion. Periodically we return to the man and his Zen-like meal. Then with a sweep of the arm, he upturns the table and the jug shatters. Water drips from the glass as if from sheets of ice before he throws himself into the gathering stream, merging with it as if returning to some elemental state.

There are those who accuse Bill Viola of being portentous, of taking himself too seriously, but his poetic quest stands in opposition to the brittle closure of much current artwork. In writing about Friedrich Nietzsche, Maurice Blanchot emphasized Zarathustra's distress when he understood that he would never be able to go beyond man's inadequacies, or that he would only be able to do so in some form of paradoxical return: "It affirms that the extreme point of nihilism is precisely where it is reversed, that nihilism is reversal itself: it is the affirmation that, in passing from the *no* to the *yes,* refutes nihilism."

It is in this affirmation implied in the marriage between Varèse's score composed in the early 20th century, and Viola's video created near the end of the millennium, that the power of this collaboration lies. We are drawn into their shared vision, staring out into the void of the 21st century to murmur a tentative *yes.*

Déserts
Music by Edgard Varèse
Video by Bill Viola
Queen Elizabeth Hall
Part of Related Rocks:
The World of Magnus Lindberg

9th December 2001

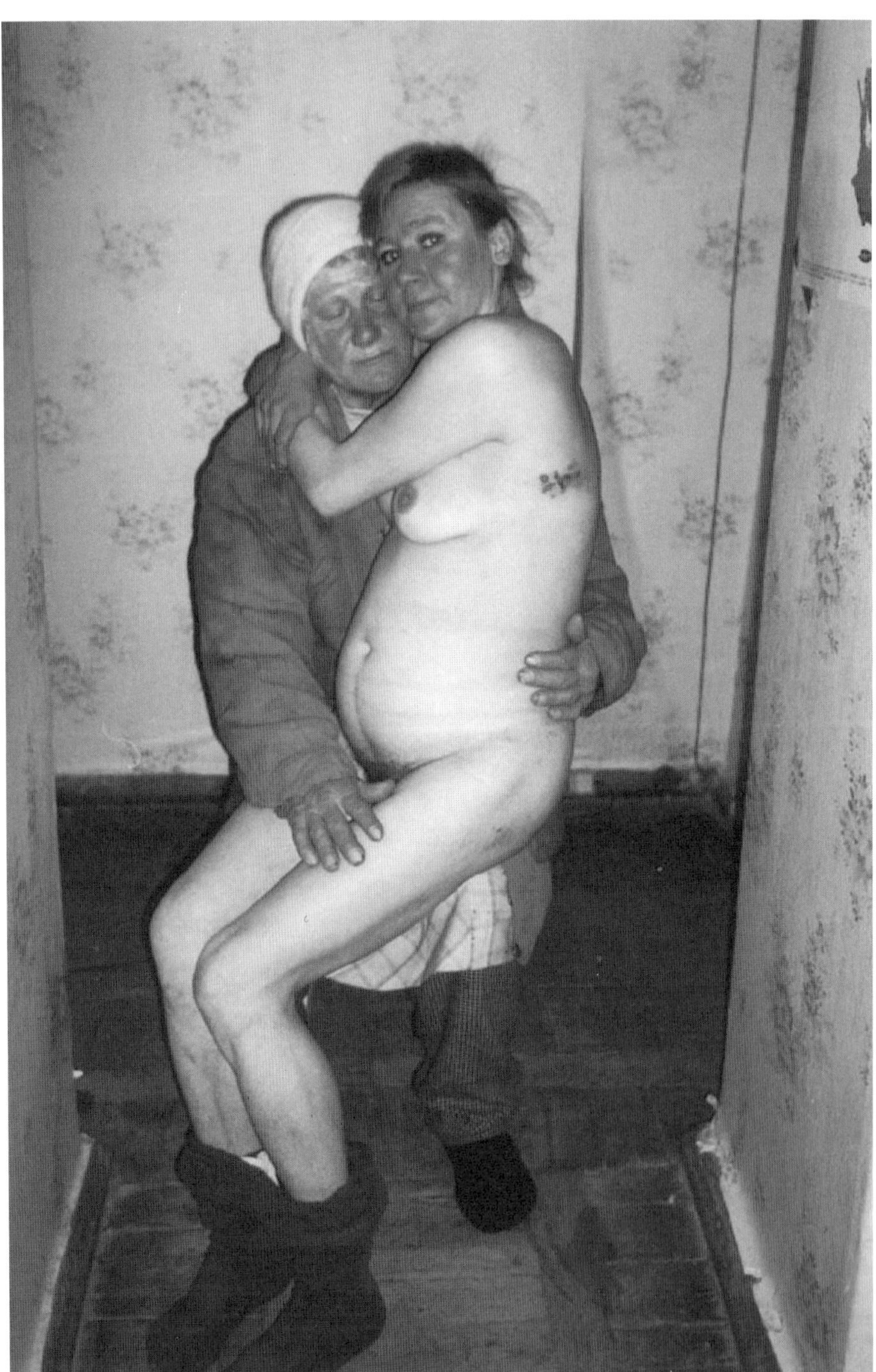

Boris Mikhailov: Case History, illustrated selection, *1999*

Boris Mikhailov
Case History

Boris Mikhailov is 63, has dyed black hair, a white moustache and a young wife. Born in Kharkov in the Ukraine, he has recently exhibited at the Photographers' Gallery, just been awarded the Citibank Photography Prize and is now showing his work, 'Case History', which consists of over 400 photographs taken in the Ukraine, at the Saatchi Gallery. For anyone with a taste in Postmodern irony, there is plenty to be found here.

Mikhailov takes pictures of the *bomzhes,* the homeless down-and-outs, victims of the economic and social collapse in the former USSR. But he is no Bill Brandt or Don McCullen, capturing life's gritty realities with a clear humanist agenda; nor is he an objective eye simply documenting what he sees from behind his lens. Rather he is a director, a creator of *mise en scènes,* who seeks out the alcoholic, the drug addict, the ill and the dispossessed, and pays them not only to pose for him, but to expose themselves – genitals, scars, menstrual blood and hernias – to his scrutinising gaze. This is the ultimate market exchange, the sale, for a few kopeks, of these people's only resource: their bodies. Like all capitalists and entrepreneurs, they sell what they have for the best offer, in this case to a photographer who takes their picture, which will then be consumed by the international art world. The irony is brought full circle, in a game of signifiers and signs, by the fact that it is Saatchi, the advertising guru who anticipated

18 years of Thatcherism, who is playing host to these photos of some of the world's most abject. What, I kept wondering, would these subjects make of the private view, where the likes of Tracey Emin quaff champagne in her latest *Agnès B*, surrounded by exposed and blistered penises, black eyes and filthy bodies; and what does it say about those of us who look at them?

When I met Mikhailov, he insisted his aim was to act as a witness to a particular moment in history, that he wanted to show the *bomzhes* as "normal" people, as a "class", a "clan", with its own structures and psychology, before its members became what he called "hardened". But unlike the work of, say, Diane Arbus, who came upon her subjects in all their weird and idiosyncratic individuality, Mikailov encourages (he says facilitates) those he photographs to act in ways that turn them into objects. The Diane Arbus "freaks" were simply being themselves – however odd – and did not act for the camera. The same is true of the photographs of the young British photographer Richard Billingham, who takes pictures of his tattooed and drunken parents in the domestic squalor of their northern tower block. For Billingham documents what he actually sees, and though it is often shocking, there is a sense that it has been recorded with a sort of love. But one cannot escape the fact that many of Mikahilov's subjects seem to be "performing". Perhaps for a new coat, a few coins, for their 15 minutes of fame, who knows? He claimed, when I asked, that he had their consent, but just what it was they thought they were consenting to is impossible to know. Tom Wolfe once famously wrote of the symbiosis between the bankers and glitterati of New York, and Jackson Pollock. Cash was exchanged, not just for a painting, but also for an appropriated slice of life in the fast lane. Pollock had the street cred and they had the money, and the contract allowed the well-fed and the well-bred to go back to their bourgeois apartments, their maids and their offices in Wall Street, feeling oh-so-very hip for having purchased such a cutting-edge artist.

And yet it is not easy simply to dismiss all of Mikhailov's work as opportunistic or voyeuristic, for there is a huge charge to many of these life-sized coloured photographs – even an unsentimental pathos. The images of street children glue-sniffing have a raw and terrible beauty. The inflated pink plastic bags from which they inhale noxious fumes echo, with a shocking aestheticism, the pink of one of the young girl's T-shirts. Many of the children, most no more than 10 or 12, are blond and beautiful, if somewhat scruffy, and pose and smile, half out of their minds with booze and cigarettes. As with so many street children, the pathos and the pity lie in the hope and innocence still visible behind the world-weary and brutalised faces. These children sleep, eat and rob in gangs, which is the nearest many of them will ever know to a family, and their early sexualisation is not only a way of earning cash, but all too often a substitute for other forms of communication and warmth. The images of crumbling, rusting factories, of a new *Coca Cola* sign poking out of a drift of dirty snow in front of an old Soviet building, of men carting filthy animal ribs flapping with a few ribbons of meat through the pot-holed streets, and the broken and bruised faces of the drunks and the drugged, all speak of social disintegration, anarchy and decay.

And it is perhaps this that gives a clue as to how we might read the seemingly amoral positioning of Mikhailov towards his subjects. When I tried to push him on the issue of ethics, he was evasive, and talked only of making work that was new, of showing things in a way that had not been seen before. For him, ethics were "not special"; anything that was legal was "OK". He did claim to be concerned about what his subjects felt, though it was hard to establish whether this stemmed from compassion or a desire to create a photographic charge. Yet maybe it is this very lack of empathy, this amorality, that most truly reflects the condition of social breakdown that has resulted from the break-up of the Soviet Union. Perhaps it is this harsh. For whatever we feel about the injustices of the old structures and systems, this exchange between the have-nots and the photographer-who-has, has come about as a result of capitalism, not communism. The shocking truth implied by these photographs is that compassion itself is a liberal luxury.

Boris Mikhailov
Case History
Saatchi Gallery

New Statesman
15th September, 2001

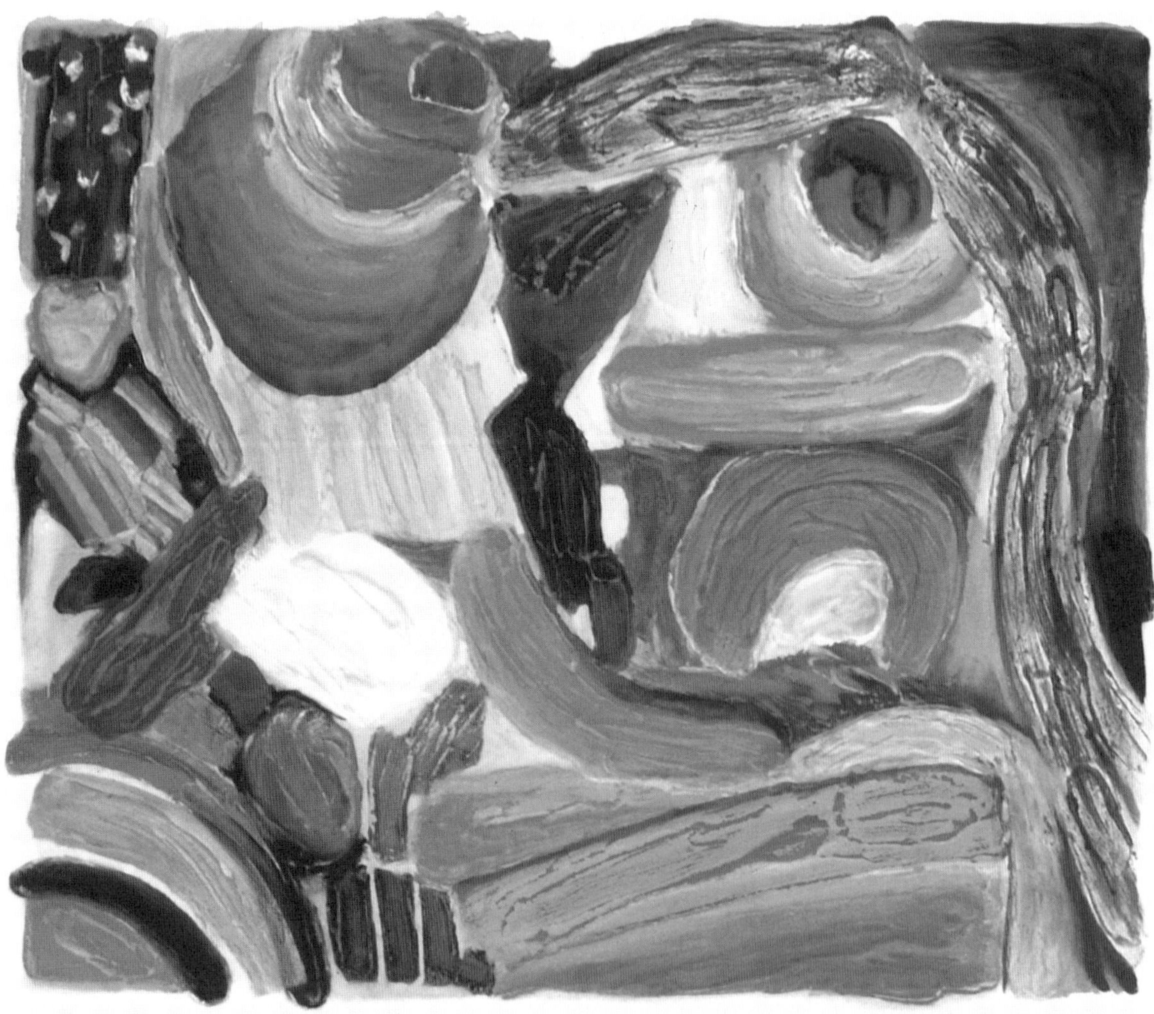

Gillian Ayres, 'Matuka', *2001*, Edition of 35

Gillian Ayres

When I last stayed with Gillian Ayres at her home in Cornwall, one of her dogs peed on the carpet before dinner and then died in the night. When I came down in the morning, it was lying in the wheelbarrow, in her pretty three-bears cottage garden, stiff with rigor mortis. It is sometimes hard to believe that some of the best-loved contemporary British paintings have been produced at the end of a wooded lane in this warmly chaotic milieu full of books and pets. Now there are fewer animals and there is a cleaner, who also happens to be a painter, controlling some of the domestic muddle. And there are no more cigarettes. It used to be 40 a day untipped *Senior Service*. But then there was the heart attack and Ayres was forced to be sensible and moderate.

Moderation is not an Ayres characteristic. Even as a child growing up in bourgeois Barnes she was, by her own admission, "a brat". When she was ten she rode round on her bike collecting bomb cartridges, walking back, one day, through Barnes High Street with an unexploded shell. In her early teens she announced to the headmistress at St. Paul's Girls' School, where Shirley Williams was among her best friends, that she didn't believe in God and would no longer be going to prayers. At 16, she walked out of her exams and threatened that if she weren't allowed to go to art school she would run away to Scotland. Her kindly, but slightly bemused, parents agreed. Maybe, she says, they thought it would help her choose nice curtain fabrics. Though her headmistress warned of "the sort of men you get in art schools", she enrolled at Camberwell. To begin with, her mother took her on the bus. It might, she thinks, have been different if she'd been a boy. Born in 1930, she is today one of the *grandes dames* of British painting. Highly intelligent, feisty and fiercely independent, she has a compulsive creative energy and a generosity that are reflected in her lyrical yet muscular works. Staying with her in 1997 at the British School at Rome when she held the Sargent Fellowship, I was struck not only by her knowledge of art history, but also by the breadth of her reading. She is a committed modernist, part of a generation that, after the war, subscribed to the possibility of a "brave new world", to the affirming power of a creativity based on a restless and vigorous questioning. She has always eschewed fashion and "followed her nose", believing in the humanistic value of painting, and deeply committed to the intellectual and emotional freedoms – a legacy perhaps of 50s Existentialism inherent in abstraction. Having a conversation with her is like inhabiting one of her canvases. Ideas and words flow and swirl in all directions. You think you are in the equivalent of a red square, only to find she has plopped you down in a blue arc.

In 1943, while still at school, she discovered monographs on van Gogh, Cézanne and Monet and thought, "my God, so this is what painting can do". In those days there was huge suspicion of "modern art" and she was desperate to find people who shared her interest. This she did at Camberwell, where demobbed servicemen such as Terry Frost and Henry Mundy (later her husband), were studying as mature students. Ayres' temperament soon led her to reject the muddy English colours and "the measuring thing" of the dominant Euston Road School aesthetic. When Sir William Coldstream one day remarked in her presence that "Matisse can pass me by" she answered, with characteristic brio that, "he may pass you by, but he won't pass me by". As she says, she could be an argumentative brat. But it was her involvement with the AIA Gallery in London, which in 1951 mounted the first post-war exhibition devoted to abstraction with artists such as Barbara Hepworth, Roger Hilton and Victor Pasmore, along with her discovery of American Abstract Expressionism including Jackson Pollock and Mark Rothko, that was to define her own idiosyncratic visual language.

She experimented with *Ripolin*, a household paint, and other "non-art" materials, working on hardboard to create an abstraction where not only the visible traces of her actions, but the characteristics of the material itself, were apparent. It was around the time she was commissioned to make a mural for South Hampstead High School for Girls that she began to paint on the floor, pouring and tipping paint in pools of colour. She had seen Hans Namuth's famous photo of Jackson Pollock dripping paint but was, at this point, not familiar with Pollock's work. But Ayres was interested in something deeper than mere experimentation. She was concerned with visual truth, though she is not an intellectual aesthetician. Her influences are other painters such as Titian, Rubens and Turner; and her love of colour and light, which she appropriates from the natural world to create works full of movement and energy like polychromatic jewels.

Elements in her paintings – she later returned to oils – often resemble natural objects such as stars, leaves, petals and moons. But it is not nature she is attempting to paint, but a comparable feeling of pleasure and awe evoked through the paint itself. She works intuitively, creating arcs with the sweep of an arm, pulling her fingers through the thick paint. She spends a great deal of time looking, and this visual intelligence is translated into the variations of light and colour, and the vitality of movement, that characterise her work. Despite ill health, she paints ceaselessly, when not rushing around making wonderful meals for family and friends. While I was with her, the papers were full of the New York twin-towers disaster and talk of impending war, and there was much discussion about moral certainties and the role and value of art. Yet, for her, painting is about the fact of being alive. The very act of "doing", the endless intuitive creative search, the "condensation of sensation to perception" that can be shared between artist and viewer, is utterly life affirming. Her work is, like her, vital, anarchic, bold and generous spirited. In the end, she says, "the act of painting is an act of belief".

Gillian Ayres
Gimpel Fils and
Alan Cristea Gallery

Independent on Sunday
30th September, 2001

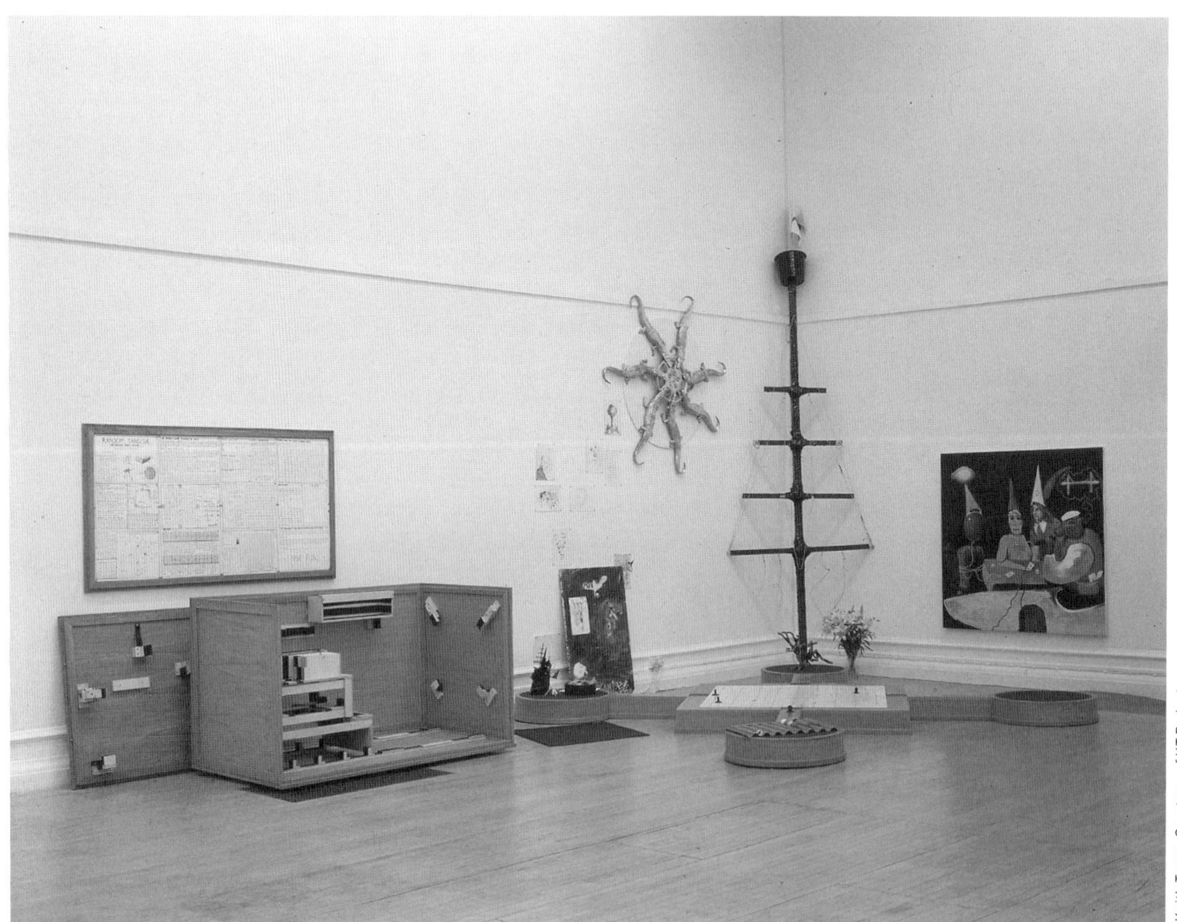

Keith Tyson, 'Random Tangler (A Recursive Transition Knot) Played Version', *2001*

Keith Tyson
'Supercollider'

What do you get if you put Panamarenko, Duchamp and 'The Hitch Hiker's Guide to the Galaxy' in a pot and boil? Answer: Keith Tyson. To walk into the South London Gallery at the moment is a bit like entering the set for 'Doctor Who'. You expect to find a Dalek or a waiting Tardis. For all the sophistication of Tyson's ideas about scientific determinism, he still retains something of the curiosity of the small boy who grew up in Cumbria fascinated by ideas of infinity, devouring 50s sci-fi films. All his models, charts and games, with their cogs and sprockets, are real 'Boy's Own' stuff; *Meccano* with a philosophical twist. His work is, he claims, fundamentally a kind of research, a non-scientist's investigation into the mysteries of the universe.

He first came to prominence with his Artmachine, a Dadaesque tool for obliterating the "authorial voice". A complex algorithm, it generates proposals for an infinite number of artworks over which Tyson has no control. Its random decisions demonstrate something of the arbitrary nature of chaos theory. Amoral and lacking in critical judgement, incapable of making either "good" or "bad" art, its sole purpose is simply art production. It is an ingenious philosophical concept that illustrates the fine line between chance, chaos and organisation that is at the core of all scientific and artistic creativity. He's stopped using the machine, but his passions remain pretty much the same. 'Supercollider', a huge nine-section

drawing describes, through a series of poetic aphorisms, the complex matrix that is the universe at any moment in time. As Tyson walked me around the exhibition, he explained how he always carries a notebook to jot down images – such as "two little old ladies crossing the road". Phrases like: "a poppy seed head"; "the heat fluctuations inside a frying sausage"; "a damp field at 5.30 am in Yorkshire", have been used to construct a yellow cartoon-like map or chart. It's as if by obsessively and inclusively listing the microcosmic, some understanding of the macrocosmic might be achieved.

He took an almost childlike delight in explaining that 'A Night in a Billion', a drawing in 12 parts of stars in space, comes in a box, and that the pieces can be arranged in 479,001,600 ways, and that each sheet can then be re-orientated to give a further 7,961,990,600,000 possible arrangements. With odds like this, it's surprising to learn he's a keen gambler. On the back wall is 'Nature – Window on an Infinite Cellular Blanket': what Tyson calls a "landscape painting", only there is no landscape, just 565 square feet of aluminium in eight panels painted with a cellular design in black and white and shades of grey, where the labyrinthine cells (he's a great fan of Jorge Luis Borges) become smaller and smaller. Looking at it is like being drawn into a black hole where at any moment one might be sucked into another dimension. Most dotty of all is his 'Random Tangler', a boxed game with pieces and printed instructions for its installation. Made from a series of tiles that form a circuit, like the Artmachine it gives instructions on what to make. If you follow the rules, you still end up constructing whatever you want. With Wonderland logic, whatever you do is correct.

Tyson would not deny that his work is hubristic, but the potential bombast is undercut by his infectious humour. By deconstructing the very notion of an artwork, by leaving aside autobiography and ego, by drawing on the eclecticism and diversification of the universe and investigating how all events cause chain reactions, he invites us to ponder on the interconnectedness of all things, thereby giving sense to the momentary specks in time that are our lives.

Keith Tyson
'Supercollider'
South London Gallery

Contemporary 2002

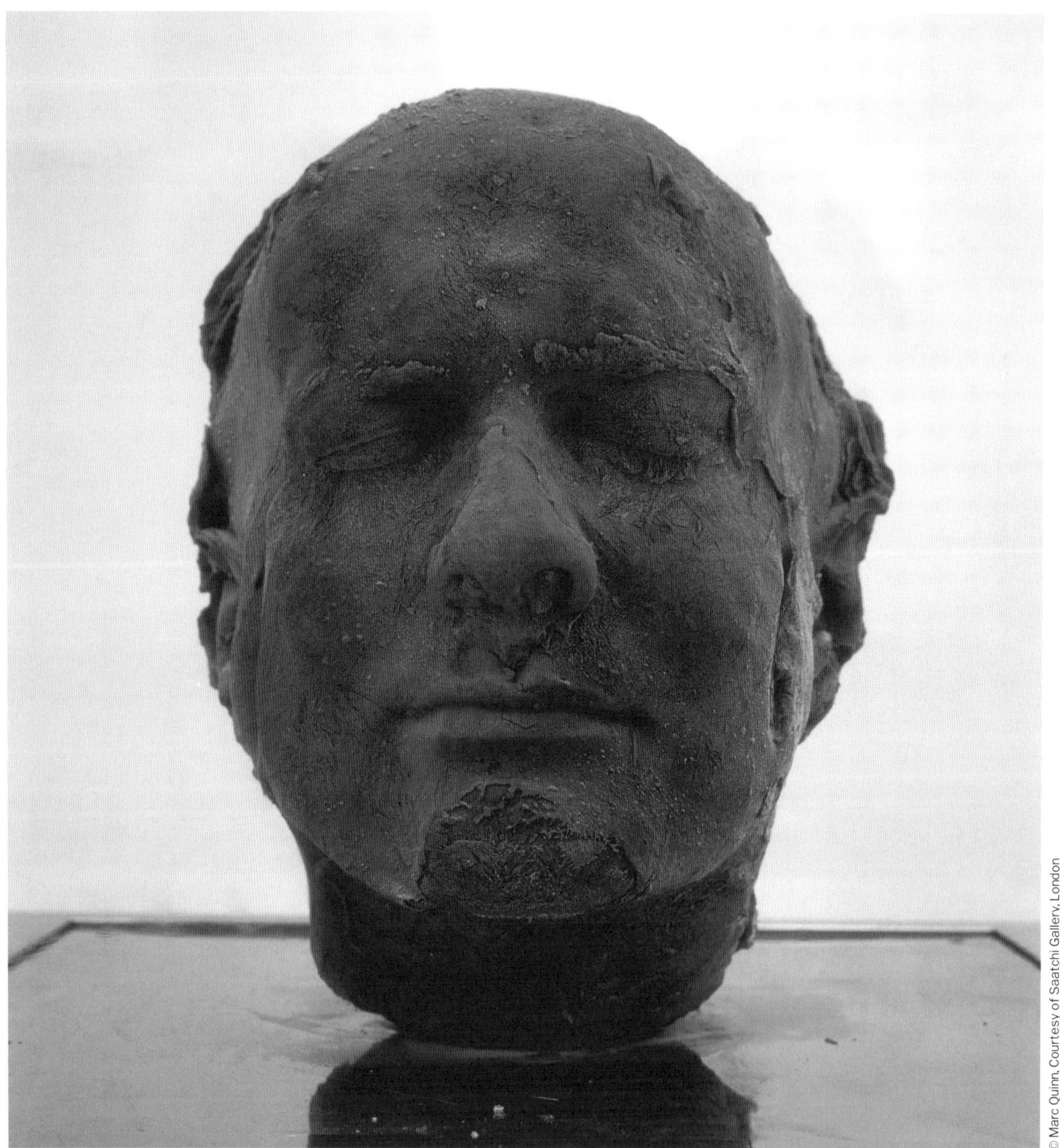

Marc Quinn, 'Self', *2001*

Marc Quinn

For a member of the brat pack of Young British Artists, someone who uses blood, shit and his new son's placenta to make art, Marc Quinn is surprisingly quiet and serious when we meet on a rain-lashed day at Tate Liverpool to discuss his new exhibition. Outside the gallery window the Mersey forms a grey backdrop of storm-tossed waves. It's an image he likes – a vast amniotic soup slurping around as we talk about what he calls the age-old themes of art: life, birth and death. "After all, we all come from water", he says. Indeed he might be a junior philosophy lecturer at some former poly rather than an artist. So it's no surprise to learn that he never went to art school, but studied art history at Cambridge. Somehow this fact changes a lot. He can't be naive, then, I suggest, to the references that abound in his work. The blood, the pregnant women, and the family draw on traditional Christian iconography. "Of course", he mutters enigmatically.

He first gained recognition in 1991 with his provocative sculpture, 'Self', a life-size caste of his head made from his own frozen blood. This was followed by the flayed bodies at the South London Gallery: part torture victims, part saints hanging from the ceiling, their skins peeled back like unzipped bananas. I kept thinking of a small boy looking inside a torch and taking it to bits to see how it works. Quinn's interest in science, in how things are made – in their intrinsic nature – is a legacy, no doubt, of having a physicist as a father and an artist mother. Although the work at Tate Liverpool includes a wide range of forms – drawing, sculpture, painting, photographs and installation – it is all of a piece, exploring issues of procreation, perfection, decay and mortality. When his son Lucas was born he puréed the frozen placenta and poured it into a mould he'd modelled of the baby's head. It sits in its refrigerated unit like a religious reliquary or one of Francis Bacon's grizzled Pope's heads. "You couldn't *not* be thinking of Bacon," I suggest. "Of course," he admits.

Genetic and generational bonds are also explored in the photograph of Quinn's son and his own grandmother, but less conventionally in 'DNA Garden' and 'Family Portrait (Cloned DNA)'. Here, apparently empty stainless steel frames – which conjure those Byzantine icons imbedded in silver, or Christian Boltanski's photographic installations – actually hold polycarbonate agar jelly, bacteria colonies and cloned DNA (both plant and human). Virtually invisible, they act like biological photos (or rather negatives) – portraits of possibilities. He is, he tells me, really interested in material and in the material world, for we are the first generation able to see the instructions for making ourselves.

He also freezes flowers. 'Eternal Spring' consists of a bunch of frozen lilies. These draw on the tradition of 17th-century Dutch flower painting, when the loss of perfection and subsequent decay were reminders of our mortality. But they also make oblique references to the work of the late Helen Chadwick, who explored similar territory. He likes the fact that these pieces can only exist in a society with an infrastructure where refrigeration is possible. That, of course, is also true of that wish-fulfilment technology, cryogenics, where the rich and the batty are frozen after death "just in case".

One day, when he was in the British Museum, it suddenly occurred to him that the visitors looking at the fragmented limbless sculptures – ideals of classical beauty – would react very differently if they were looking at real people who were thus "disfigured". Both traditional and contemporary ideals of perfection are explored in his white marble sculptures. Using disabled models as subjects, he challenges viewers' preconceived notions of what constitutes beauty and "appropriate" eroticism. Approaching the athletic male figure in Quinn's marble 'Kiss' from behind, the torso looks like an example of heroic perfection. But his arms have, in fact, been deformed by thalidomide and his female partner has lost one of hers. This is Rodin's 'The Kiss' for a Postmodern age.

Probably the piece that will provoke the most predictable outcry is his 'Shit Painting', made from his own excrement. Actually it looks like an American Abstract Expressionist painting of the 50s and he won't be the first artist to use his own faeces to make art: Piero Manzoni displayed his shit in small paint tins in the 60s. Bodily fluids have always formed part of Quinn's work: metaphors for our humanity, materiality and flux. It is our material make-up, the physical components that make us unique, that fascinate him. His most enigmatic piece is 'Mirror Self Portrait', *2000*, a looking-glass he stood in front of every day for 12 months. A mirror is, he says, "the ultimate indifferent object. It celebrates you while you are there and then, when you are gone, it forgets you immediately". No traditional *vanitas* painting could illuminate the fleeting nature of our material existence with greater potency.

Marc Quinn
Tate Liverpool

New Statesman
4th March, 2002

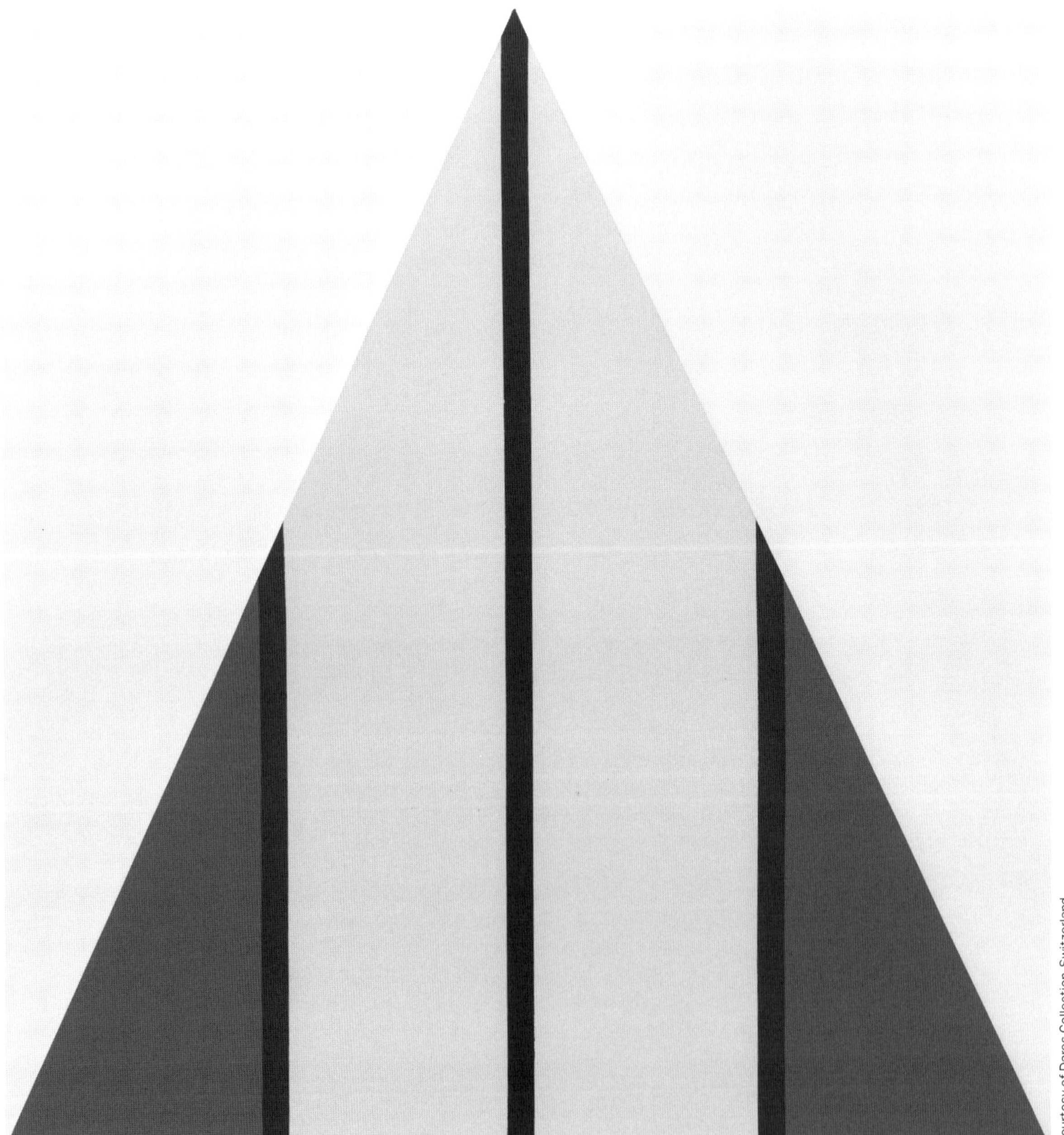

Barnett Newman, 'Chartrés', *1969*

Barnett Newman

In his great poem 'Song to Myself', Walt Whitman turned from the hegemony of a European literary tradition to create, in his heroic Everyman, the voice of a burgeoning, uniquely American culture. In late 1942, a group of artists organised a protest against an exhibition planned at the Metropolitan Museum of Art, sponsored by a conservative wartime coalition of American arts organisations. The group, which included Adolph Gottleib, Mark Rothko and Milton Avery, elected the painter Barnett Newman to lead their publicity campaign. Newman announced that their intention was to create "a body of art that will adequately reflect the new America that is taking shape today and the kind of America that will, it is hoped, become the cultural centre of the world". Thus Newman became unofficial spokesman for an art that was to be "an adventure into an unknown world which can only be explored by those willing to take risks".

The exhibition at Tate Modern is the first full-scale retrospective of Barnett Newman's work since 1972. Among the 50 paintings included is the series 'The Stations of the Cross', *1958-66*, which has never before left Washington's National Gallery of Art. Also returned to London is the large-scale 'Uriel' of 1955. This is being shown along with the magnificent late painting, 'Anna's Light', *1968*, while the two late-60s triangular paintings, 'Chartres' and 'Jericho', rarely seen together, have been reunited. Five sculptures, around 30 drawings and two portfolios of prints are also included in this exhibition.

Like many of the first generation Abstract Expressionists, Newman was born to immigrant parents – on Manhattan's Lower East Side. His father was to climb to middle-class respectability through his clothing business. Attending the city college, the young Newman studied philosophy before becoming a painter. An anarchist by temperament, he became steeped in American Transcendentalism and the writings of Ralph Emerson and Henry Thoreau that espoused a life of personal liberty. Along with a growing interest in pre-Columbian art, this gave Newman the intellectual ammunition to turn from a European culture blighted by holocaust and war, and to free himself from "the impediments of memory, association, nostalgia, legend and myth, or what have you, that have been the devices of Western European painting". Above all, he wanted to create an art of human impulse rather than one of luxurious commoditisation. That it should also embody a sense of self-definition was paramount, as it was to many of his fellow artists, whose nationality, as first-generation Americans, differentiated them from both their artistic and biological parents.

Abstraction seemed to be the only viable route for this new art. Struggling for originality, Newman grappled with the legacies of both Miró and Mondrian before, in 1948, finally declaring independence in the painting later known as 'Ornament I'. Here, for the first time, Newman introduces his characteristic "zip" – a vertical band that spans the full height of the painting and simultaneously unites and divides the composition. The work, he insisted, was a "painting", not a "picture". These paintings are not "abstractions" but "specific and separate embodiments of feeling, to be experienced, each picture for itself". This was a painting that could be made over and over again, repeated in varying forms. For Newman, it was not just a statement, but also a language. This and subsequent paintings, he instructed, had to be experienced close up. Their large scale, in fact, made them more intimate, enveloping the viewer in a direct physical encounter. The exchange between observer and object was implicitly democratic compared with looking from afar at a fresco or an altarpiece in a church.

Newman's use of colour was also uniquely his own. "Colours", he argued, are what is squeezed from tubes; "colour" is what is created by the artist. His focus on white was a legible sign of his preoccupation with purity and newness. Its silent emptiness was both awesome and sublime. Herman Melville, in that great American novel 'Moby Dick', referred to it as a "symbol of spiritual things", as "the intensifying agent in things the most appalling to mankind". For Newman, it embodied "silence, simplicity, eternity", providing a *tabula rasa* that functioned as a metaphor for the transformative experiences of this new American art.

Barnett Newman
Tate Modern

RA Magazine
Autumn, 2002

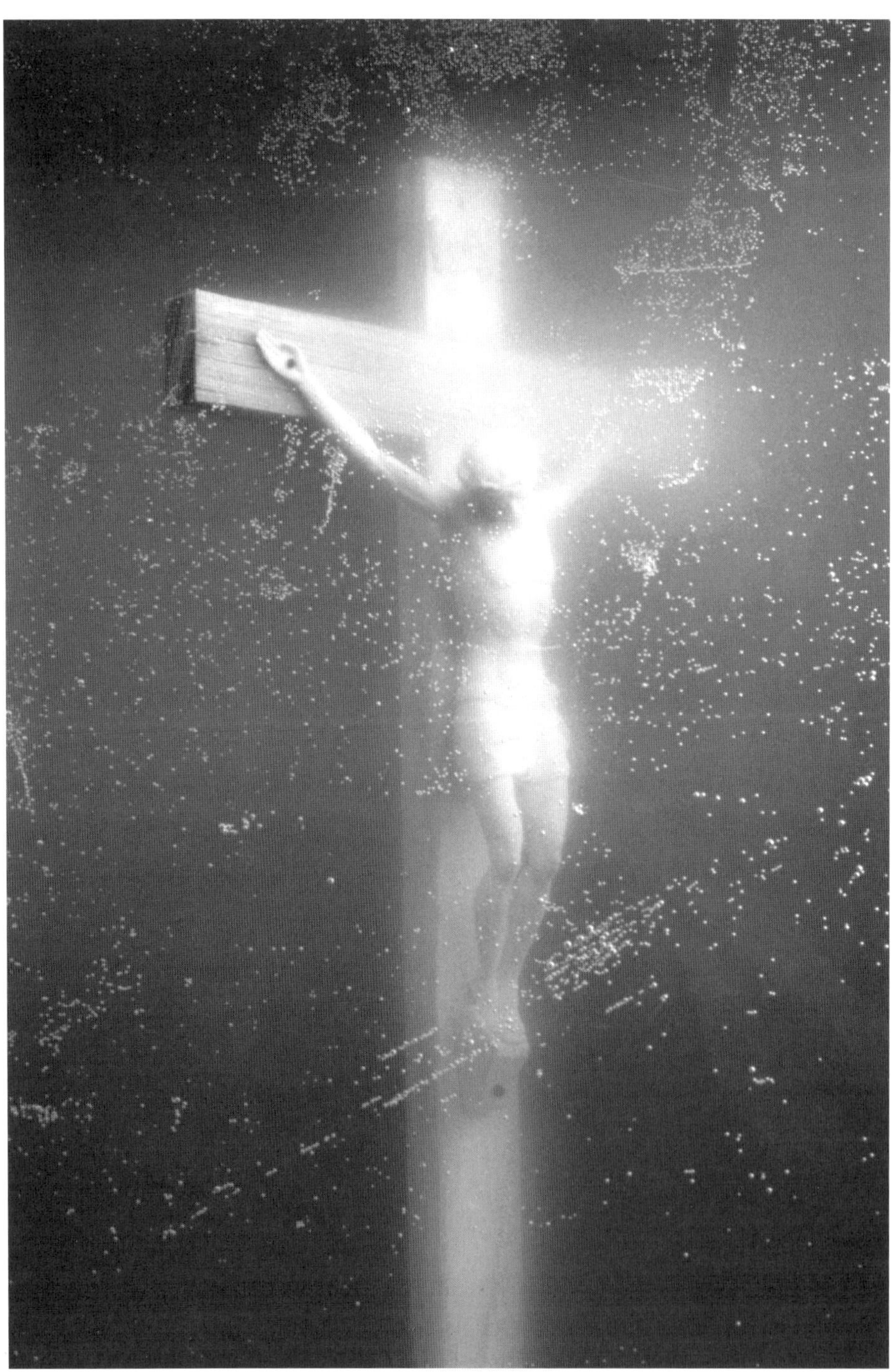

Andres Serrano, 'Immersions (Piss Christ)', *1987*

Andres Serrano
American Pieties

"Sometimes people call me an idealist," declared President Woodrow Wilson on 8th September 1919, in an address at Sioux Falls, South Dakota. "Well, that is the way I know I am an American," and "America", he continued, "is the only idealistic nation in the world". More than 90 Septembers later, a very different group of idealists flew into the World Trade Center in New York City ending, with their audacious act of terrorism, America's sense of itself as inviolate. For many, the American dream was over. From a nation that had flung open its doors to the poor and persecuted from the four corners of the globe, that prided itself on being an ethnic melting pot, America has become paranoid and distrustful, a nation in the grip of an identity crisis.

In 1988, the Latino artist Andres Serrano caused a sensation with his notorious (and actually rather beautiful) image 'Piss Christ', a photograph of a cheap crucifix submerged in his own urine. Since he is a gay Hispanic, this work, made during the high point of the AIDS epidemic, caused some ruffled feathers. Never mind that for centuries the Catholic Church has carved and painted images of Christ dripping in blood, or that they claim to own sacred relics of the Christ child's foreskin, NY Senator Alphonse D'Amato announced that Serrano's art not only dishonored God, but also "the American people". In this exhibition, Serrano has taken as his starting point this very

concept of "the American people" and returned it from homogenous WASP mass to that of a rainbow nation.

Like most of his compatriots, Serrano was touched by the events of 9/11. A few nights before the attack he had been at a party at the New York Armory on 26th Street given by the designer Emanuel Ungaro. Four days later, it had become a mass grave. Since then, Serrano, the bad-boy of the 1980s and 90s, has, rather like a Catholic penitent, expressed nostalgia for the 1960s and 70s, decades in which he feels ideals and aspirations still mattered. He certainly now seems less inclined to shock. For these works are subtler, less in-your-face. This is, after all, the artist who has given us images of fist-fucking, a woman masturbating a pony, and a female dwarf having sex with a full-sized man.

On entering the gallery, the viewer is confronted by a small blond, blue-eyed boy in Cub-Scout uniform. All dimples and chubby cheeks, he is as wholesome as apple pie, proof that cleanliness is, indeed, next to godliness. But there is something disturbing about his well-nourished smile, his clean-cut innocence. Other images are evoked, other blond-haired, blue-eyed boys in uniform – the Hitler youth. The same disquiet can be felt in front of the photograph of the actress Chloe Sevigny. A confection in white lace, her blonde hair coiffed into Goldilocks curls, she is the epitome of an Aryan Heidi. This comes as an uncomfortable reminder that the Right is alive and kicking in the midst of American life. Yet Serrano avoids the temptation to be didactic. He simply shows, in these diverse images, that there is no such thing as a *single* America, as "*the* American people". His powerful portrait of the sneering black rapper Snoop Dogg also illustrates that antipathy and hate are no respecters of race. While the photograph of Yi Hong Zheng, a Chinese cook in a chip-fryer's hat, set against a pink-and-yellow sunset like some figure from a Caspar David Friedrich painting, shows how deeply held is the belief that America is the land of milk and honey, that anyone, however humble, can dream of being president or a Hollywood star. Perhaps that is what the homeless Lucas Suarez is contemplating as he stares into the middle distance beneath grey bouffant hair, his torso naked, an American flag knotted around his throat.

Serrano's images are set up to resemble Renaissance portraits. Bishop Mercurius of the Russian Orthodox Church in NY in his golden robes might be posing for a Velázquez painting, while the scarlet of Rodeo Queen Jennifer Ridgely's red-spangled poncho and of bunny-girl Deanna Brooks' red bustier and long ears, is reminiscent of papal silk. At once both stereotypes and individuals, these images portray a bunch of people who often seem, quite frankly, pretty deluded and dysfunctional. Having come from a strict Catholic background via art school in Brooklyn and a spell in advertising – with a dash of wild sex and drugs thrown in along the way – Serrano produced early work that explored the margins of sexuality, and felt like that of a naughty rebel. With 'America', he seems to have come of age. Less flamboyant and less narcissistic, he gives us images that pose real questions about what it means to be a citizen of the world's largest superpower. Though we might conclude that, if this is the cast of characters that makes up Woodrow Wilson's nation of

idealists, we are rather better off stuck on this side of the pond.

Andres Serrano
American Pieties
Gimpel Fils

Art Review
December, 2002

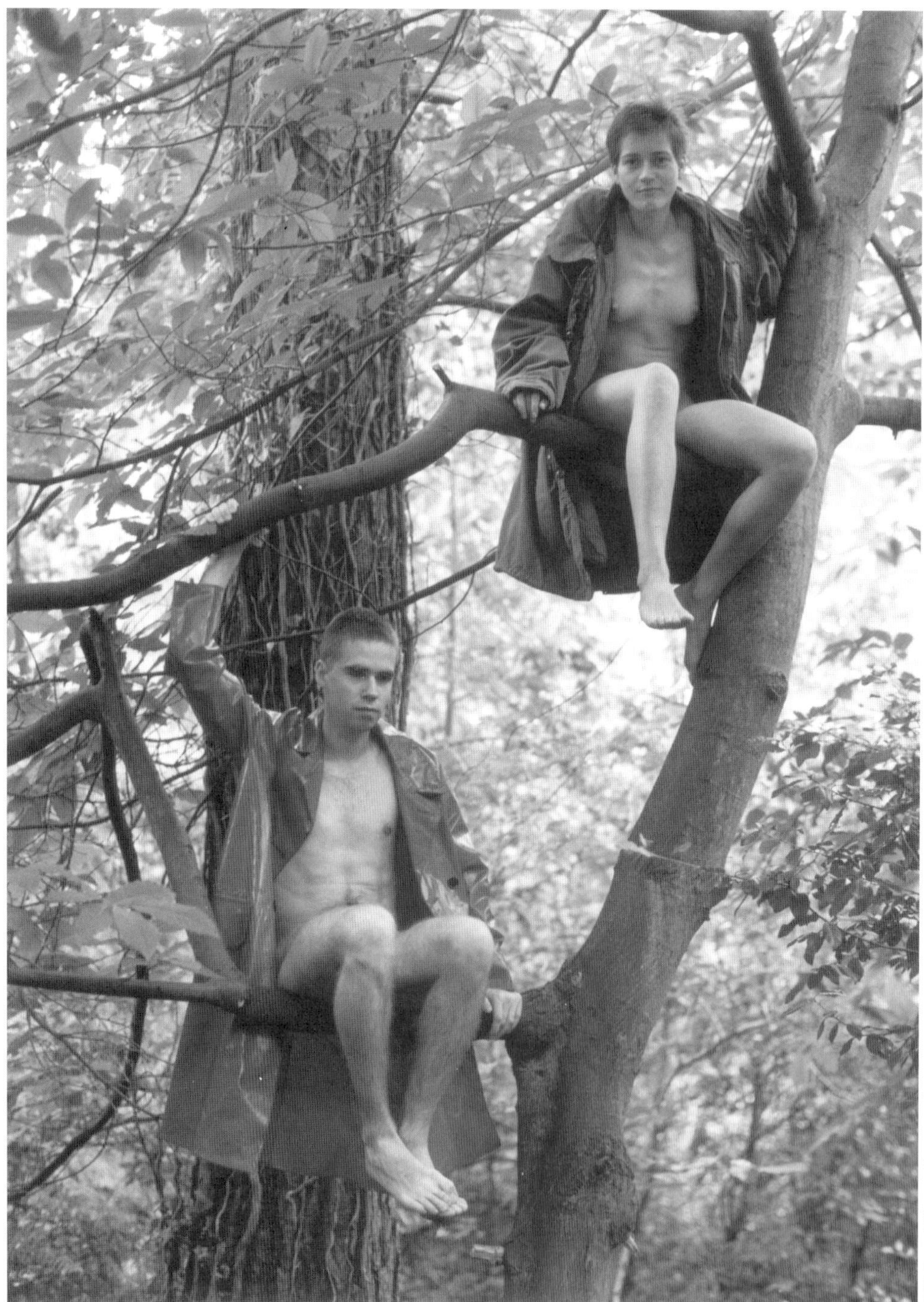

Wolfgang Tillmans, 'Lutz and Alex Sitting in the Trees', *1992*

Wolfgang Tillmans
if one thing matters,
everything matters

In the second half of the 19th century, the great American poet Walt Whitman wrote his huge poem 'Leaves of Grass'. People never before associated with poetry made their debut into literature: drovers, peddlers, brides, opium-eaters, prostitutes were all jumbled up pell-mell. It was as if this inclusiveness echoed something of the structure of the idealised democratic society, released from the hierarchies and restraints of the Old World, that Whitman dreamt of for the new America. The poem is an anthem-song of early Modernism – value-laden, forward-looking, utopian.

Fast forward a century and a half to Tate Britain to the exhibition of the young German artist Wolfgang Tillmans, born in 1968 in Remscheid, Germany, educated and living in England and a former Turner prize winner. His first one-person show in Britain, 'if one thing matters, everything matters', is a highly inclusive affair. Shot to fame in the late 80s and early 90s at an early age by his photographs – for magazines such as 'i-D' and 'The Face', and of gay-pride activists, eco-warriors and clubbers – Tillmans was dubbed by some a chronicler of his generation. Seven rooms of the Tate are filled with his photographs, many of them reflecting his relationship to London. None have labels (though there's a map for those who insist on titles) and they are grouped together in no apparent thematic order. His friends Alex and Lutz sitting naked, except for raincoats, in the branches of a tree, jostle

for space with a classic still-life shot of a vase of pink roses and a mess of roadworks in some undisclosed location. There are lots of friends, lots of parties, a lot of erect penises and copious masturbation. All the works are pinned to the wall, none are framed. The effect is that of a student bedroom collaged with posters, photos of friends and reminders of nights on the razzle. A beautiful Rothko-like sunset – a brooding black sea beneath an orange horizon-line and navy sky – is placed next to a photograph of a pile of black rubbish sacks being investigated by a rat. An overhead source of light illuminates the surfaces of the sacks so they appear as luminous as the sunset. There is no hierarchy to these images. All are presented as having equal value. But unlike Whitman's vision in the 19th century, there is no utopia here, no sense of democratic inclusivity. This is a Postmodern mix. If one thing matters, everything matters. Or alternatively, nothing really matters very much so why select, why choose? And anyway, on what basis could any rational choice be made? What belief system could be employed in such an editing process? As in the newly published book of Tillmans' work, the exhibition comprises a personal choice containing most of the images that he has released to date, and many others that he feels "are or were at some point in the past of relevance to me".

Tillmans claims he wanted to avoid being seen as overly art historical, or relying on "worthy" categories such as "portraiture" and "still life". For they are, he claims, not part of the way we live our lives. "When we see a person, we don't think 'portrait'; when I look at my window sill I see fruit in a bowl and light and respond to them, I don't see a 'still life'. That's how I want to convey my subject matter to the viewer, not through the recognition of predetermined art historical/image categories, but through enabling them to see with the immediacy that I felt in that situation."

It has been argued that he subverts our ideas of conventional beauty, and who is to say that his painterly colour-field photographs of the Arctic or of blush-like "skin" are any more beautiful than the semi-erect cock held in the hand of one young breakfaster, which seems to be intruding into the fast-food tray on his lap like a pink German sausage? Is it only outdated Kantian notions of the sublime that lead us to believe that one is a more beautiful, more uplifting (so to speak) image than the other? In a world where we have been told *ad nauseam* that history is dead, that ideology crumbled along with the Berlin Wall, where all is now fracture and surface, is not Tillmans' anarchic view of beauty as valid as any other? And if we don't like it, if we regret the passing of art that uplifts and vivifies, should we perhaps be careful not to shoot the messenger for delivering what, to some of us, may seem like an unpalatable message?

Although some of the photographs, such as the gnarled trunk of 'Shaker Tree', *1995* or the 'Conquistador' sunsets, have a slick, crafted quality and are obviously the work of a professional photographer, many of the smaller images are not any different to the snaps you and I might take on holiday or at a friend's birthday party. So why then are they art? Because Tillmans has decided they are, because they are in the Tate, because they are grouped together for public display. Because they are of as much value as anything else we might term art in a society

that no longer wishes its artists to edify and instruct, or even to anger and deconstruct, but rather to entertain, to shock on the ersatz level of 'Big Brother'. Why bother to make choices, to spoil the fun, the night out clubbing with the gang, when it's easier to shrug nonchalantly if asked for an opinion, and answer: *whatever*. This is a world of single-issue politics – gay-pride marches and eco-conflicts – where spectacle is as important as vision. Being seen is the new caring.

Yet the fact that this work is photography means that by its very nature it is about the passing of time, about nostalgia and memory. In 10 or 20 years we may look back on these images and say of the computerised base-line amplifier lying in the grass, "How funny, how old fashioned, did we really use such stone-age equipment?" Or: "My god, did people really dress like that?" By photographing everything – the down-and-out lying on the pavement that has special bumps to prevent him sleeping on the hot air ducts, the concrete pylons of Macau Bridge that have not yet been joined together, an ashtray of fag ends, or a supermarket shelf rowed with soap powder – Tillmans, consciously or otherwise, does become a chronicler of contemporary life. These images, whether we like it or not, reflect something of our 21st-century world. In 1995, Tillmans took a photograph of a young man approaching a deer on a beach. It is impossible to tell whether this deer, which looks so out of place, has been imported especially for the photograph, whether it is alive or stuffed. How are we to read this image and does it matter anyway if it succeeds in perplexing us or making us smile? Who cares about messages and truths?

'Image 35' shows his studio after a party. All that can be seen are two big mirrors leaning against the wall like a diptych. They reflect back the studio, empty now except for the detritus of beer cans, fag ends, paper cups and bottles. These fragments are all that is left when everyone has packed up and gone home. The overriding feeling is one of satiated despondency and emptiness. But there is also another photograph of his studio. A close-up of the window and sill. On it is a carefully arranged collection of postcards, showing paintings by Caravaggio. Perhaps, as in 'Animal Farm' when all the animals were declared equal some turned out to be rather more equal than others, Tillmans is (unconsciously?) acknowledging that even in a culture where image *appears* to be the great homogeniser and equaliser and surface is all, if one thing matters, there will always be another thing that matters just that bit more.

Wolfgang Tillmans
if one thing matters,
everything matters
Tate Britain

The Independent
10th June, 2003

Ian Hamilton Finlay, 'Les Femmes de la Révolution', *2003*

Ian Hamilton Finlay
Idylls and Interventions

On the right-hand side of the gallery is a dining table – a rather nice one made from cherry wood – the sort you might buy from Habitat. It is laid with 12 place settings: 24 tasteful white porcelain plates and dishes decorated with small flowers. It might be laid for a dinner party. The flower on each dish has a name beside it: Albertine Marat, Charlotte Corday, Madame Roland. The place at the head of the table has been designated for Marie-Antoinette. Twelve places. A Last Supper of sorts, for the piece is called 'Les Femmes de la Revolution' and is the newest work by the Scottish artist Ian Hamilton Finlay. Close by on the wall is a floral lithograph. The flowers look like illustrations from the 'Collins Book of Wild Flowers'. They too are labelled with the names of women from the French Revolution. The sweetly anodyne sprigs sanitise, or at least stand in juxtaposition to, the brutality of Robespierre's Terror. Nearby are a couple of shelves. Each one holds four ceramic vases containing wild flowers. Inscribed on the jars are aphorisms, like phrases plucked from some Victorian book of moral improvement. "A bank of wild flowers is like a page of the bible." "A wild flower is a garden flower permeated by morality and poetry." "The rationale of a wild flower, its governing principle, is always distinct."

Born in 1925, in Nassau in the Bahamas, where his father was a bootlegger, Finlay returned to Scotland as a child, where his education consisted, after the age of 13, of a single year at Glasgow School of Art before moving down to London. After military service he went back to Scotland where, for a time, he was a shepherd. His life and work are full of contradictions and enigmas. He is an autodidact, a poet and philosopher who works largely as an artist: an anarchist revolutionary who seems to find no problem in appropriating Nazi insignia for his own ends; a man preoccupied with the tensions between culture and nature, liberty and control. He is obsessed with the classical world and mythology, which he plunders to make contemporary art, while his pusillanimous reputation has attracted almost as much attention as his poetry. He has a profound love of the sea, yet has spent half a lifetime building a garden.

As a young man, Finlay saw himself as a painter rather than a poet. Then, in 1958, he published his first literary work, 'The Sea-Bed and Other Short Stories', with an obscure publisher. Encased in a cheap card cover, it was clipped together with staples. "I write poems that demand that people know what has been done in the literature and the art of the past and present", he once said. One senses he does not suffer fools gladly, for there are few concessions or signposts in his complex and, at times, gnomic works. In Edinburgh in the 1960s, he established, with Jessie McGuffie, the Wild Hawthorn Press, which published the work of the American Black Mountain poets (then little known in Britain) who gathered around the poet Robert Creeley. Finlay has always been rather at odds with his compatriots, for he felt the Americans appreciated him, whilst his fellow Scots did not. When interviewed for BBC radio in 1972 he said, "I feel on the edge as regards the Scottish scene, but as regards the world I feel in the centre. I seem on the edge *because* I am the centre".

Finlay is a poet – if poet he can truly be called, for he employs few of poetry's disciplines such as form, metre or rhyme – of aphorisms and lists. His 12 ceramic candlesticks placed on a row of wooden stools each bears the name of a French revolutionary: Robespierre, Saint-Just, and Hérault de Séchelles. It is largely left to the viewer to construct a meaning. For meaning is revealed – though never stated – in the juxtapositions between word and image, the interstices between signifier and sign. War and peace, violence and freedom, past and present, are the binaries he employs to reach towards some approximation of what he considers to be the truth. This dichotomy can be found in the four classical bronze figures, 'Apollo/Saint Just', *2003*, where each small figure wields a machine gun, revolver or grenade rather than a lyre or a laurel.

Work in the upper gallery continues Finlay's revolutionary theme. Finlay has never been the fabricator of his work, but rather the ideas man, a fact that irritates some critics. He collaborates with stonecutters, carvers and ceramicists who execute his ideas. A wooden guillotine block inscribed 'La Revolution est un Bloc' was made in collaboration with hand lettercutter Nicholas Sloan, while the two pillars in red sandstone segments entitled 'Classical' and 'Neoclassical' – one in the shape of drums, which makes reference to a small drummer boy who beat out his deadly rhythms to accompany the tumbrels on the way to the Bastille – were made with the sculptor John Sellman.

Trying to fathom Finlay's central philosophical premise is not easy. Is he being ironic or deadly serious? What are his politics? Is he a supporter of the idealistic but, finally, murderous Robespierre? One senses he would have sympathy with his remark: "What does this mysterious science of government and legislation amount to? Putting into law the moral truths culled from the works of the philosophers", or does he mourn the passing of those pampered French aristos? What is the link between the horrors of the French Revolution and his work about the sea?

The final room is dedicated to his maritime concerns. Many of the works here were shown in his recent show at Tate, St. Ives, and evoke an apparently gentler, lyrical side than that displayed in the lower gallery and in many of the sculptures that dot his famous Scottish garden, created on five acres of farmland bought during the 60s, in the Pentland Hills near Edinburgh. A small wooden sailing dinghy sits on the gallery floor looking even more beached and bewildered in this Islington ex-warehouse than it did in the Tate where it was still within a sniff of the sea. Inscribed on the wall is a text: "one bow curves, two bow cleaves, three sail powers". The corresponding numbers are marked on the boat so that we are invited to think about the force of the verbs – curves, cleaves, and powers – that describe the actions of the boat cutting through the water. Nearby, on the wall, like some Duchampian readymade, is a rudder. It is rather beautiful and bears the words "a last word rudder". Names hold a fascination for Finlay, as if their correct usage denotes a particular knowledge and intimacy. His 'Reef-Points' screen prints appropriate the names of different classes of vessel – 'Yarmouth Lugger', 'Mount's Bay Pilchard Boat', 'Campbeltown Zulu Skiff' – and use the individual knot patterns of the sails to locate the marks on the orange, brown and blue/green prints. The sea he evokes is not the sea of Romanticism – you can't imagine Finlay lashing himself, like Turner did, to a mast in order to experience the force of a storm – but one of workaday operations. Boats are for fishing, conquest and war.

But Finlay's most enduring legacy will be his Scottish garden, Little Sparta (in contrast, perhaps, to nearby Edinburgh, which is known as the Athens of the North), which many consider to be the most important garden to have been created in Scotland in the present century, and one of the most distinctive in Europe. The Spartans were a war-like people and battles have literally been fought over the place, famously when a band of supporters saw off the bailiffs after Finlay was refused permission to reclassify a barn as a temple to Apollo. It is this garden that shows him at his most enigmatic. Set amid rolling hills and filled with ponds, sundials and other sculptural objects, it also contains something uncomfortable in his appropriation of Nazi signs and language – the model fighter planes, the SS lightning bolts, the engraved stone that warns *Achtung Minen!* (Beware of Mines). It was after correspondence with Albert Speer about the garden he created at Spandau that Finlay made his 'Third Reich Revisited' series (1982), which includes 'Hitler's Column' and 'Little Fields at Nuremberg'. But Finlay refuses either to explain or excuse. And we are left asking if he is a sympathiser or a mirror? Maybe, in the end, what he shows us are the dichotomies within ourselves and society: the polarities between culture and nature, between liberty and hatred, violence and beauty. It may be an uncomfortable message but one, perhaps, we need to heed.

Ian Hamilton Finlay
Idylls and Interventions
Victoria Miro Gallery

The Independent
8th July, 2003

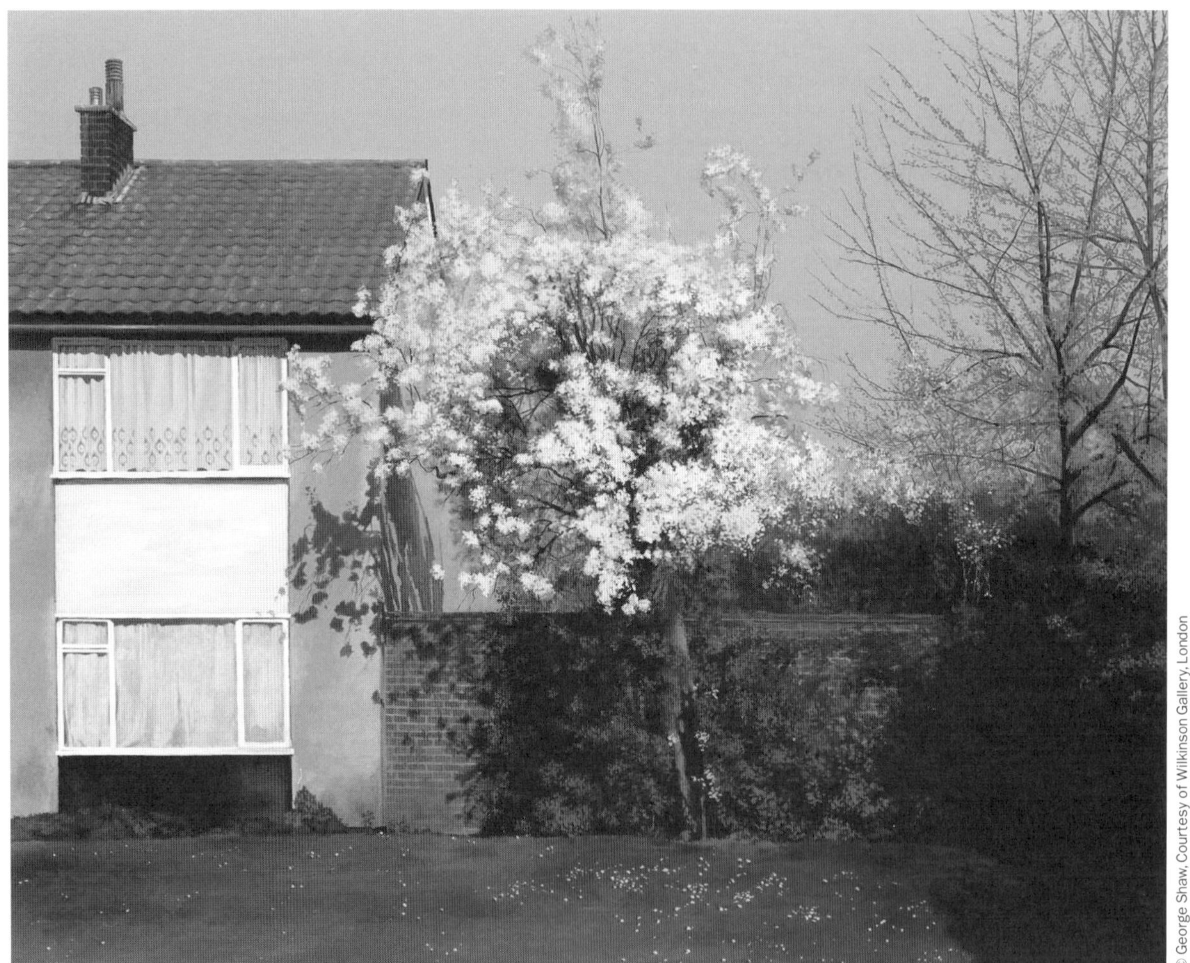

George Shaw, 'Scenes from the Passion: The Blossomiest Blossom', *2001*

George Shaw
What i did this summer

It is always late afternoon in George Shaw's world, a wet afternoon on a small provincial English housing estate – November, perhaps, or February. Everywhere there's a smell of damp – in the small rain-soaked gardens of the hunkered bungalows that line the silent streets, in the empty blue bus shelter outside the run-down flats. The tarmac glistens. Green mould stains the concrete walls. Dampness seems to seep from the fabric of things. There is no one about. Children, home from school, lie sprawled in front of the TV, the dog snoring by the grate. This is the landscape of a lived life. If Edward Hopper were English this is what he might have painted, these suburban streets, their windows blanked by net curtains, the dripping back gardens divided by a grid of fences and corrugated sheds, the rundown breeze-block garages where weeds sprout through the cracks of the concrete forecourts among the wind-strewn chip papers and photos ripped from pornographic magazines.

The trees are bare. The pigeon-coloured skies lour with rain clouds. At any minute there might be another downpour. Here, it is always twilight and teatime. "Four o'clock: wedge-shadowed gardens lie/Under a cavernous, a wind-picked sky", as Philip Larkin wrote. It is a world that is quintessentially provincial, lower middle class and English, where the slow erasure of the pastoral dream has gone almost unnoticed as new council estates have encroached on what must once have been open fields and woods. Now it is a hinterland between two forms of existence – then and now – where children ride bikes and make camps away from adult eyes, where dogs are walked and men expose themselves to the unwary. In the summer children might even pick a few blackberries among the tangled brambles, staining their mouths purple as if in remembrance of some lost rural past.

Then and now: this is the theme that underlies George Shaw's work. Not a soft-focused nostalgia, but a mirror held up to the smallness of most lives. Though this is not quite despair, for it is redeemed by love – a love of the actual and the real, of a life remembered and lived. This has nothing to do with the oversaturated technicolour of American suburbia, of the well-watered lawns of 'Blue Velvet'. No severed ears lurk in the long grass here. The deserted municipal playgrounds with their slides and swings streaked with rain contain nothing more than the memory of a scraped knee, a first kiss, or a bullying pinch. The church echoes with the remembrance of past weddings full of girls in Larkinesque lilacs and yellows, or the Cub Scouts' Christmas concert. And the war memorial? That's where you hung around when you bunked off school, a can of illicit beer and a cheap packet of fags in your pocket.

This is a world of margins, perimeters, and places in between. Where the path that runs across the scrubland is known as "behind the shops" and forms a short cut through the new estate, once known as Ten Shilling Wood, to the new surgery or the bus stop into town. Every corner reverberates with the sounds of childhood: an Action-Man game down behind the swings, the chatter of the gang that met in the abandoned garage.

And now, seen again through different, adult, eyes – eyes that have taken in a wider world – what is there? The smallness of home and a tree: a cherry tree extravagant as a bridal gown, like a small epiphany in the fading evening light, shimmering against a house that looks pretty much like all the others houses in the street. That is what happens when you go back. What once seemed like the whole world now looks tiny, run down, and dowdy. What must have seemed like a smart new pub, a forbidden adult zone, 'The New Star' (the very name is redolent with touching optimism) now has as all the conviviality of a DHSS office.

This is George Shaw's past. Born in 1966, he grew up on a council housing estate in Tile Hill, Coventry before leaving for an MA at the Royal College of Art via Sheffield Poly. These empty playing fields, peeling comprehensives and run-down housing estates are the land of his childhood. Here mothers marry young and many of the men are unemployed. The title of the show, 'What I did this summer' reads like the essay title given to young children on return to school in the autumn term. It implies a remembrance of things past, that moment of "splendour in the grass" which, despite the actual, mundane, reality seems, on reflection, like an endless summer, a lost land on the other side of adulthood.

Shaw has written that "for me, time has… become diagrammatic around certain points in my childhood". So he makes paintings – always devoid of people – that function as archetypal scenes rather than being located in specific moments. To this end, he takes

long rambling walks around Tile Hill, taking hundreds of photographs along the route. These are simply snaps, developed at the local chemist. But among them may be one with that special quality he's looking for – some mood, some trigger of a memory. Then he makes a drawing, which he describes as being similar to something copied from a 'How To Draw' textbook. This is coated on the back with charcoal dust, then pinned to a piece of previously primed white MDF, on which he traces the outline with a fine pencil before beginning to block in areas of colour. All his paintings are made with *Humbrol* enamel paints – the kind used by small boys to paint *Airfix* models – which he builds layer upon painstaking layer, so that the trees, say, resemble the fine detail of an early Dutch landscape or the highly polished finish of a Pre-Raphaelite painting. It's a lengthy, painstaking process. The model paint is important, forming a bridge between his boyhood and his later, adult, awareness of art history. His influences are broad, from the chiaroscuro of the Victorian painter John Atkinson Grimshaw to Modernist architecture. Many of his earlier drawings and installations rely on dark figures from popular culture such as Peter Sutcliffe, mythologised in the sensational pages of the tabloids. In his studio are books ranging from the poems of T. S. Eliot and Hilaire Belloc, to those on Caspar David Friedrich and Picasso, and a 'Look-In Television Annual'. Interspersed among photos of Tony Hancock, astronauts and museum postcards of paintings are those he's taken of Tile Hill.

There is a strong desire to create narratives from Shaw's work. Each painting conjures a possible story, so it is not surprising to learn that he is also interested in writing. But most of all what these paintings evoke is a tenderness towards something lost that can never quite be regained, because what is being portrayed can no longer be experienced from the inside but is seen with the eyes of someone who has left –

someone who has been changed by a
wider perspective.

Yet there is nothing haughty or patronising
about these works. In the shadows of these
wet gardens, these recreational grounds
and community halls, these hinterlands of
suburban banality, Shaw discovers a kind of
poignancy. Larkin said of this encroaching
suburbanisation, "And that will be England
gone/The shadows, the meadows, the lanes/
The guildhalls, the carved choirs". Though
"there'll be books", he said. And also, one
might add, paintings that show us in the
microcosm of these slumbering estates who
we are and where we came from.

George Shaw
What I did this summer
Ikon Gallery Birmingham

The Independent
5th August, 2003

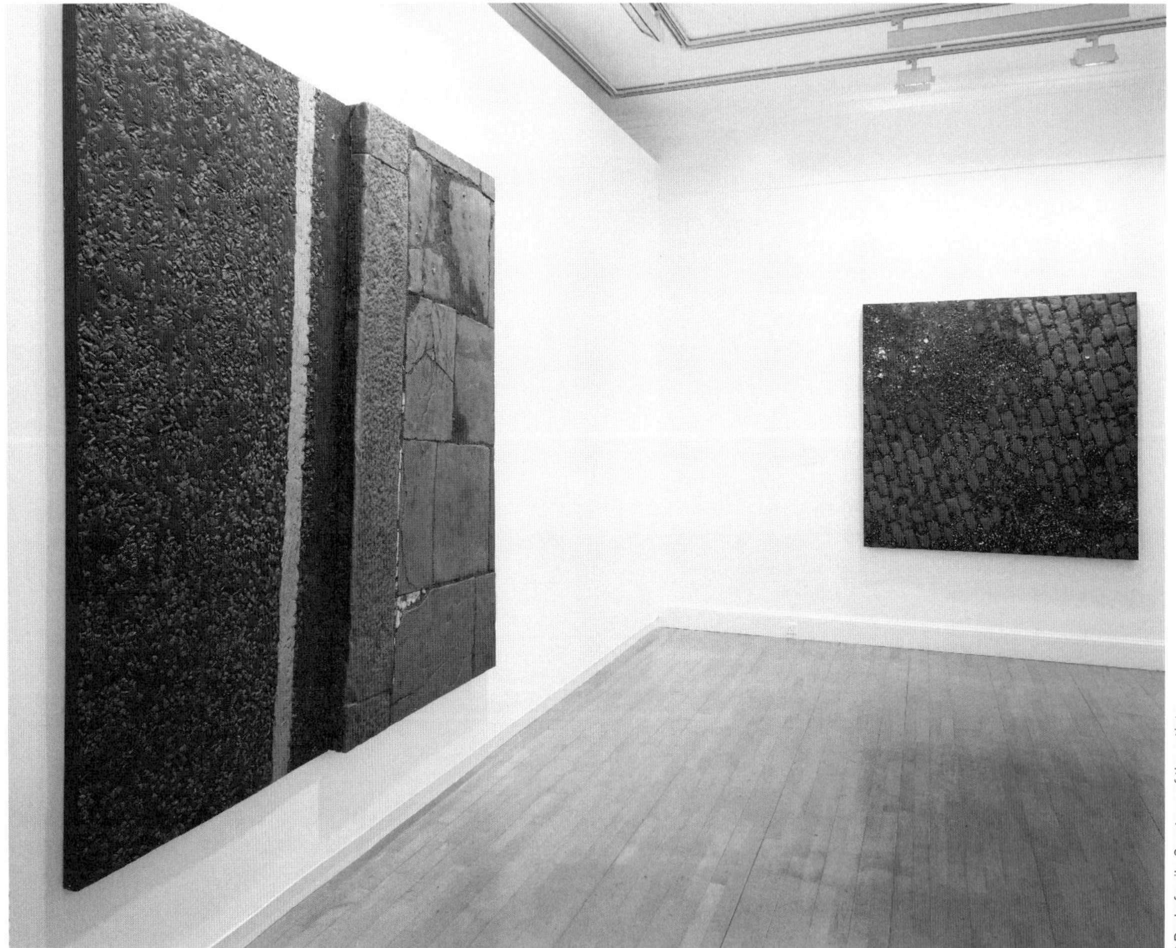

Boyle family, 'L, Holland Park Avenue Study, London Series', *1967*, 'R, Cobbles Study, Lorrypark Series', *1976*

Boyle Family

According to Philip Larkin, the 60s did not really start until 1963, around the time of The Beatles first LP. Before that, the world had been different: hierarchical, class ridden, culturally conservative and circumscribed. Slowly the old order had begun to crumble. Politicians were found sleeping with call girls who were considered a threat to national security; Kenneth Tynan said "fuck" on TV; censorship was abolished; Jimmy Porter got angry; and respectable students at the LSE grew their hair long. Welcome to the permissive society.

In the mid-50s Mark Boyle, son of a Scottish lawyer, enrolled at the University of Glasgow to study law, leaving the following year to join the Scots Guards. Meanwhile, Joan Hills had just left her course in architecture at Edinburgh College of Art to get married, set up a beauty parlour and paint on the side. When Joan and her husband split up, she went to live in Harrogate in a small flat above a café, where the young Boyle, who organised supplies for the Royal Army Ordnance Corps, went to write poetry. Thus was born an artistic collaboration that has lasted until the present day and now includes the couple's two children, Sebastian and Georgia. In his first published statement in 1965 concerning his artistic practice, Mark Boyle said, "My ultimate object is to include everything in a single work… In the end the only medium in which it will be possible to say everything will be reality".

In 1964 Boyle and Hill invited an audience to an event at a venue in London where they were led through an entrance marked *Theatre* and seated in front of a curtain. When the curtain was raised the audience found themselves looking through a shop window at passers by who, in turn, stared back at them. Thus the boundaries between viewer, actor and event were erased and the hierarchy of looking broken down. This "performance" followed on the heels of the first "Happening" in Britain on the final day of the International Drama Conference at the Edinburgh Festival in September 1963. The conference had been turned into a spontaneously anarchic event during which, rather than "discuss" drama, a drama had been "created" and the "actual" material of the world presented as "art". Such subversive action grew out of the Dadaist philosophy that saw the world and humanity as nihilistic and without purpose – a position that accorded with the 60s *zeitgeist* and the desire to break down old taboos and constraints. This "total action" was to become very much part of Boyle and Hill's aesthetic. Art was to include everything and avoid any form of preferential selection. The artist had to become as objective as the scientist in order to portray "reality".

After spending time in Paris, the Boyles returned to London. In the summer of 1962, they had already started to make a series of assemblages. Without funds or conventional art training they pillaged the demolition sites

– the results of bombing and slum clearance – that covered swathes of west London. This use of detritus fitted with their "inclusion-of-everything" aesthetic. It also acted as a potent anti-art, anti-establishment metaphor. Assemblages that included bedsprings, doors from old wardrobes, shoes and rusting paint cans needed no special skill or equipment to put together. This methodology owed much to Kurt Schwitters and paralleled the spirit of other artists working with non-art materials – those within the *arte povera* movement in Italy, and Rauschenberg and Jasper Johns in America.

When the Boyles chanced upon a discarded grey television surround, it was radically to alter their working methods. Throwing it like a die they decided that whatever portion of a site was framed would became the subject of their next work, even if it fell on a patch of bare earth. Chance – that element which had so appealed to the Dadaists and Surrealists – was to become a major component in their work. Collected surface material was pressed into resin. But, beyond saying that, it is impossible to explain how they make their "paintings", for they resolutely refuse to discuss their working methods. It is probable that they make some sort of cast – so that the subject is both real and replicated. Their first experiments were made in Camber Sands, East Sussex in the late 60s where they recreated the tidal patterns left on the beach over seven days. Sites for subsequent works in London, around Notting Hill where they lived, were chosen by throwing darts into a map. The darts would select sites in a way that was entirely random. A carpenter's right angle was then thrown into the air to delineate the bottom edge. A series of printed cards claiming that they were members of the Institute of Contemporary Archaeology usually prevented any unnecessary official interference. In 1968 they took the project to its natural conclusion and invited friends to throw

darts at a map of the world. The aim was to "take the actual surface coating of earth, dust, sand, mud, stone, pebbles, snow, grass or whatever, hold it in the shape it was in on the site, fix it. Make it permanent". So huge was the project that it is still unfinished.

From their early childhood, the Boyle offspring Sebastian and Georgia have been involved in the making of work, accompanying their parents on all their trips. It has taken the family to Norway to create snow pieces, to a German coalmine, to stony escarpments in Sardinia, and to Israeli and Australian deserts. Unlike Christo, that wrapper of buildings and landscapes who seeks the permission of officials and dignitaries, the Boyles tend to work in secret.

And what is it they have ended up making? Are they paintings or sculptures? Well they are, I think, closer to painting than sculpture, for primarily they are about surface: the surface as earth, the surface as skin, the surface of a mundane object that was once horizontal but which now hangs vertically on the wall as an art object. They have made work that replicates potato fields and paths – the sort that lead to countless London houses, complete with intricate Victorian mosaic – and fabricated gutters and pavements where the yellow stripes painted on the road read like the zips in a Barnett Newman painting, or where the regular concrete slabs of a sidewalk look like a Minimalist Carl Andre. They have taken sections of Mark's magnified skin and blown it up so that it has the appearance of cracked mud or a lunar landscape. Like magicians, they have produced a series of stunning tricks – illusions that ape reality. It is as if by collecting numerous specimens of the actual, material world, that they can, like crazy Victorian fossil hunters or palaeontologists, somehow make sense of it. Despite the fact that their work is composed of fragments, it has little to do with Postmodern sensibilities. There is no irony here, nor is their work a metaphor for anything other than itself.

Art made by committee raises all sorts of questions and hackles. There are Gilbert and George, of course, that Darby and Joan of Brit Art, and Art and Language. But a family? Artistic endeavour is historically seen as male and heroic and involves the struggle of an individual psyche to create a unique aesthetic. The Boyles describe themselves as four argumentative individuals, but mostly it is Mark who talks on video about the work. So do they divvy out the tasks? Do they all work on the same piece at the same time, and do the younger Boyles have any life of their own? Didn't they ever want to run away to become accountants? Perhaps these questions are not pertinent to the work, but they are the ones everyone wants to know.

Mark and Joan are now in their 70s and this is largest show ever mounted of their work – a retrospective spanning 40 years. Comparisons have been made with photography – with that eternal frozen moment when the shutter closes. Yet it is more visceral than that: its physical presence, the memory of its previous state, more insistent. What grew out of the alternative counterculture of the 60s – the ideology that nothing was of greater value than anything else, that chance was as good a belief system as any other on which to base human destiny – has evolved into a unique way of seeing the world. Such a vision has its limitations. For it accepts as axiomatic that art is always amoral and objective. Yet, despite this insistence on objectivity, something else happens – perhaps something over which they have no control – a form of transformation of the mundane into the aesthetic. The ordinary suddenly becomes elevated to the extraordinary. Our eyes are opened to the world: to a world we largely take for granted or ignore. As Francis Bacon – a friend and a fan of the Boyles – said, "If only people were free enough to let everything in, something extraordinary might come of it".

Boyle Family
Scottish National
Gallery of Modern Art The

The Independent
19th August, 2003

Hiroshi Sugimoto, 'Ionian Sea – Santa Cesarea', *1993*

Hiroshi Sugimoto

"There has," said John Constable in 1836, "never been an age, however rude or uncultivated, in which the love of landscape has not in some way been manifest. And how could it be otherwise? For man is the sole intellectual inhabitant of one vast natural landscape. His nature is congenial with the elements of the planet itself, and he cannot but sympathise with its features, its various aspects, and its phenomena in all situations…" Such sentiments reveal the core beliefs at the heart of western Romanticism, which perceived nature to be the revelation of the infinite within the finite. G. W. F. Hegel maintained that art was one of the forms in which "divine nature" and the "deepest interests of humanity" might be revealed, while Caspar David Friedrich painted canvases where man, solitary and alone, was dwarfed by the infinity of the untamed wilderness. For art, Friedrich believed, "occupied the role of mediator between nature and man", for "the original is too great and too sublime for the majority to be able to grasp". At around the same time, Schopenhauer was constructing a metaphysical system in which art was the only medium through which it was possible to achieve release from the endless cycle of desire and suffering constitutive of the human condition.

Now we live in an age where, as the poet Geoffrey Hill writes, "God is distant, difficult". Can we still look to the natural world to act as a palliative to our bruised spirits or as a phenomenon that symbolises our metaphysical desires – that sense of awe (or more conventionally religion) that Freud described as the oceanic feeling that washes over us when faced with what we perceive to be the unsayable and unknowable? Not since Mark Rothko, Barnett Newman *et al*, who strove to give expression to such spiritual feelings in a secular, disillusioned, post-war world, have visual artists really attempted to occupy this territory. Postmodernism has been predominantly preoccupied with simulacrum and surface, with fracture and fame, with deconstruction and daring. But the human heart is still hungry for meaning, for something beyond the limitations of human strife.

Born in Tokyo in 1948, Hiroshi Sugimoto studied at the conceptually based LA Art Center in California, before moving to New York. Drawing not only on western notions of the sublime and Modernist references to Minimalism and Conceptualism, he is also influenced by his contemporaries Carl Andre, Donald Judd and Dan Flavin, as well as traditional Japanese imagery and Noh theatre. To this mix, he adds something of the Shintoist belief that objects embody the souls of deities.

Inspired by classical photography, and using a specially designed wooden box camera and large format 8x10-inch film, along with traditional techniques such as the gelatin silver process, he creates spare black-and-white images of profound meditative stillness and stark Zen-like beauty. Over his 30-year career, he has consistently worked in series, photographing a limited number of subjects, including modern architecture, wax figures and cinemas, in which all extraneous detail is eliminated. His large-format 'Seascapes', photographed in remote locations around the world, are both timeless and elemental. Here, water and sky meet and merge. Purplish black melds into bleached grey, silver into pearl. This is an archetypal vision of the world, a world that might be imaged as a place before history or language: amniotic, healing, and primordial, where sea and sky have been untouched by human intervention for millennia. This vision accords with the theories of the French feminist philosopher, Julia Kristeva, following on from Plato's 'Timaeus', and refers to the *chora*: that nourishing "womb-like", pre-linguistic space of instinctual drives and desires. In these oceanic images, the variations in time of day and weather, with their subtle changes of wave patterns and starlight, or the moon cradled like an embryo picked out by the rays of ultrasound on the sea's dark skin, are all that differentiate individual works one from another.

To enter the cathedral calm of the central gallery created by the frieze-like installation of 'Pine Landscapes' is to encounter a stillness that demands the lowering of voices, the slowing of movement and quiet gestures. The feeling is similar to the awe experienced on encountering Rothko's Seagram paintings for the first time. Here, using deliberately underexposed film, Sugimoto has created a series of six soft-focus nocturnal images of pine trees, a symbol that is revered in Japan as one associated with age and permanence. The pine, along with the bamboo, is also the only image used as a stage prop in Noh drama. Taking his inspiration from an ink painting of a pine landscape by the 16th-century artist Hasegawa Tohaku, Sugimoto has created a visual metaphor for the fleeting

shadows of memory, for the traces of things once seen and experienced, then imprinted on the mind's eye like a negative. But his vista is also, implicitly, an image of redemption and renewal, for we know that soon the inky darkness will dissolve into cold grey dawn and the silenced birds will once again sing.

Created originally in 1998 during a residency in Kitakyushu, Japan, this version of 'In Praise of Shadows' has been specially devised for the Serpentine. A traditional Japanese candle was left to burn over the course of an evening beside an open window that caused the flame to stutter and flicker. Sugimoto exposed his film for the duration so that every nuance of the flame and every movement of the air were recorded. As part of the gallery installation, a real candle has been set in front of the photographic image to create a recurring hall of mirrors, for the flame seems to recede backwards into time itself. The image of the candle appears on a black-and-white positive where it has been produced using a separate negative. This too relates to the passage of time, to a nostalgia for the first photographic procedure that Sugimoto was introduced to at primary school. For it was there that he was taught the photogram technique, which exposes photosensitive paper to light so objects placed on it leave their ectoplasmic impressions.

"All that photography's program of realism actually implies", writes Susan Sontag in her seminal 'On Photography', "is the belief that reality is hidden. And, being hidden, is something to be unveiled. Whatever the camera records is a disclosure – whether it is imperceptible, fleeting parts of movement, an order that natural vision is incapable of perceiving or a 'heightened reality'". "Just to show something", she argues, "in the photographic view is to show that it is hidden". But more than that, it is to show what, by definition, has passed. For photography reveals, printed in black and white, our histories. To photograph something is to understand the very nature of passing time – to face death. For when the shutter falls, that particular moment is trapped forever, shut in a lost domain that can never be revisited except as a simulacrum of itself. The "now" and the "future" can never be photographed, for when the button is pressed, the moment has already elapsed. As Sontag says, "Photographs depict realities that already exist, though only the camera can disclose them". The power of Sugimoto's sublime sea and landscapes is not simply that they record with great exactitude the actual, physical world, but that they acquire the power of icons in a secular age. A psychological transformation occurs: they become images not just of the perceived world, but of our "inner" landscapes.

To stand in front of one of these spare, sublime works is an act of self-effacement similar to that achieved through meditation. The body slows; the breath quietens as we enter the deep spaces, the bleached whites, the inky blacks of these seascapes and pine glades, so that with the glow of a flickering candle we are brought back to the minute shifts and changes of each moment. This experience reconnects us to wilderness and nature so that we are able to establish, for a moment, a small oasis in the neon glitz and flashing simulacra of contemporary life.

Hiroshi Sugimoto
Serpentine Gallery

The Independent
23rd November, 2003

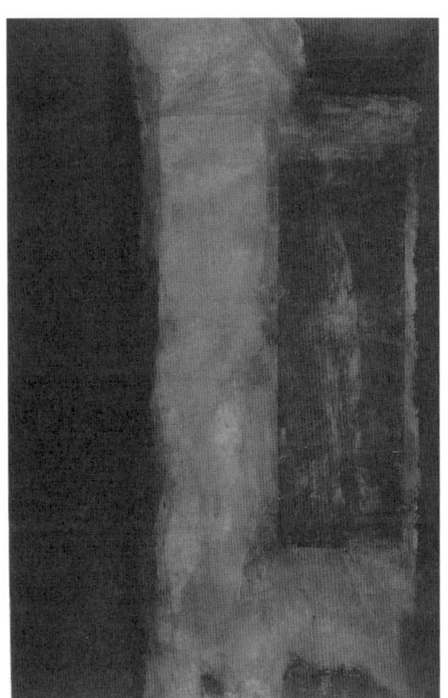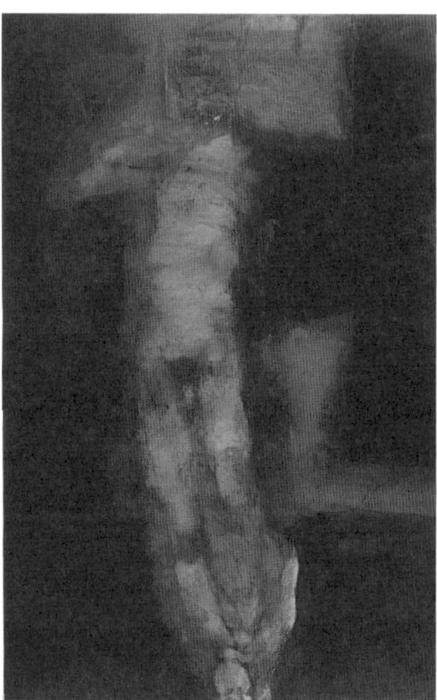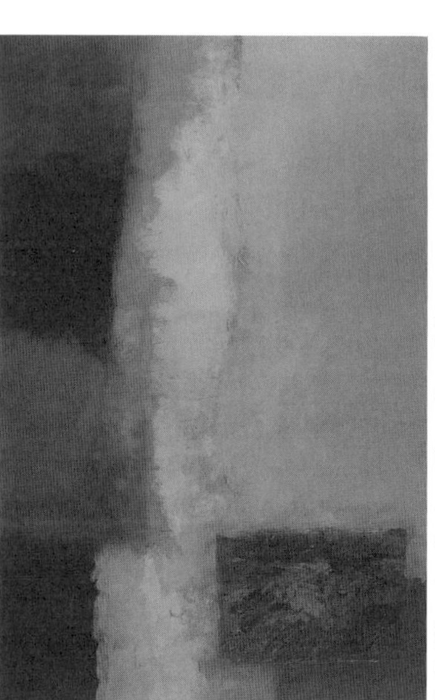

Hughie O'Donoghue, 'Crossing the Rapido IV', *1999-2000*

Hughie O'Donoghue
Painting Caserta Red

Hughie O'Donoghue paints very big paintings. During the opening of his exhibition at the Imperial War Museum, one critic was heard to mutter "hubris". But that is completely to miss the point of these brave, expansive works that deal with memory and myth, the epic and the personal. Complex, forceful and moving, these ambitious paintings – in oil on linen canvas, often incorporating inkjet on gampi tissue to entrap a photographic image beneath – attempt to grapple with birth, life, death and redemption in a way few contemporary artists – except perhaps the German painter Anselm Kiefer – would dare. Homer, Titian, Goya, even Michelangelo, are the sources that inspire, and against whom O'Donoghue pits himself. Despite an MA from Goldsmiths in the early 80s, he displays no fashionable insouciance here, or discourses on art about art. For early on O'Donoghue eschewed formalism for the supremacy of the image and its metaphorical resonance. War, in this exhibition, is his theme – one that runs like a subterranean river leaving behind its mineral traces, rather than advertising itself with shock and gore. He draws parallels with the "classic epic poem, with the individual pictures functioning like chapters, verses or lines".

As did the poets Wilfred Owen and Siegfried Sassoon, he universalises from the particular. The particular here is his father, Daniel O'Donoghue. Born in Manchester of Irish descent, he served as an infantryman in the Second World War, chronicling his experiences in letters home to his wife. It is these eye-witness accounts – along with the artefacts Daniel carried with him: his flute, goggles, sheet music, a camera and books – plus material Hughie O'Donoghue gleaned from the archives of the museum, that act as a catalyst for the son's visual meditation on what Owen called "the pity of war". Yet this exhibition is not a sentimental homage to a father by a son. For as O'Donoghue says "we disapproved of each other most of our lives". Rather, it acts as a passing-bell "for these who die[d] as cattle", as Owen described the invisible young men, the Unknown Soldiers sent from every corner of Suffolk and Somerset, Cornwall and County Durham to fight in the Great War. Or, for that matter, for all those sent since, to the front lines of some foreign field, who have ever been sold "the old lie" of "*dulce et decorum est pro patria mori*".

O'Donoghue has built this body of work around these found images in order to describe the wanderings of a soldier in retreat during the fall of France in 1940, and the experience of crossing the Rapido in southern Italy in 1944. Among Daniel's effects were snapshots and postcards sent from Italy and Greece. These included a photo of a 1930s bronze diver, and a postcard of the ancient Greek sculpture of Marsyas (the satyr flayed for challenging Apollo to a musical contest, famously painted by Titian). O'Donoghue has long admired Titian's late, edgy work and its many sculptural variants. When Marsyas lost against the god, he was not only brutally flayed, but also silenced. O' Donoghue draws a poetic parallel with his father Daniel, who lost his flute as he, and his fellow soldiers, crossed the Rapido. These imaginative coincidences are further woven into the paintings, for among Daniel's papers were widely reproduced newspaper clippings of the executed corpses of Mussolini and his collaborators, hanging by their ankles from the roof of a Milanese garage in 1945. The parallels between this gruesome image and the Marsyas are unmistakable. During the painting process, the appropriated photograph became buried in 'Rapido VI', while in 'Rapido IV' it is juxtaposed with a photograph of a badly burnt German soldier. Thus ancient and modern are fused. Echoes of mythic cruelty and modern brutality intertwine, reverberating like the lost notes of Marsyas's pipes.

Photographs of Grauballe and Tollund Man, discovered during the 1970s excavations of Danish peat bogs, along with a shocking newspaper clipping pinned to the studio wall of a figure plunging head first from the sky in New York City on 9/11, also contribute to the palimpsest of O'Donoghue's imagery. The central motif of a falling or diving figure has haunted his large canvases for many years. The 'Sleeper' series of the 1980s and the later 'Red Earth' paintings are precursors to his recent 'Diver' paintings, where the central figure, in all its naked vulnerability, makes implicit reference to the Crucifixion. These, often S-bend, bodies serve as reminders of the ancient mummified "bog figures" preserved in Irish peat that inspired Seamus Heaney, with whom O'Donoghue has, on occasion, worked. A sense of melancholy for something unnameable, something lost, permeates these paintings. Like suppressed memories – both collective and individual – of famine and war, of trauma and decimation, these shadowy figures act as signs for what is buried deep

in the bog of the unconscious. Expression is given to the regenerative power of nature and the ancient cyclical myths of birth, death and resurrection. As Heaney wrote in 'Kinship': "Quagmire, swampland, morass…. Ground that will strip/its dark side/nesting ground/outback of the mind".

It is these metaphors of journeys and suffering that O'Donoghue weaves into his paintings to form complex psychological maps. At once both gorgeous and lush – with their deep blues, ochres and ox-blood reds, and their glazed surfaces – they are, in the true sense, awe inspiring. There is no postmodern amorality here, no hedging of bets, only an unapologetic view as to the pain, but value, of life, and the enormity, yet prosaic nature, of death. Images rise to the surface like divers slipping through dark water. Like ghosts, like memories, or photographs finding form in developing solution, they slowly emerge from the murk.

There has always been a tragic quality to Hughie O'Donoghue's work, a sense of the fatality of history. His paintings of the late 1980s, 'Fires', revealed an awareness of nature's ruthlessness, along with the fragility of human endeavour. He has never been attracted to making coded or elitist work full of in-jokes, but has sought to create visual equivalents for sensations and emotions that have the visceral appeal of music.

Born in 1953, too young to remember the war and the urbane voices of BBC announcers emanating from the mesh grills of Bakelite wireless sets in the corner of front rooms across the land announcing yet another Allied defeat or victory, O'Donoghue does not create works drawn from reclaimed memories. Rather they are an imaginative leap – an emotional and psychological re-enactment of what it must have been like for his father and those other bewildered young men of his generation to be sent off to war. Like Pat Barker's

wonderful novelistic trilogy, they could
best be described as aesthetic acts of
empathy. For empathy, like all serious art,
is a creative act requiring not only humanity,
but imagination. It is this quality that
prevents these paintings from becoming,
as that misguided critic at the private
view suggested, hubristic. The scale of
O'Donoghue's work has long placed him
firmly in the Grand Tradition. Whilst the
turbulent surfaces suggest the influence
of Abstract Expressionism, these are by no
means, either in their conception or their
making, gestural paintings; rather they rely
on Old-Masterly patience. For O'Donoghue
builds his surfaces in thin layers of paint and
varnish, a technique that owes a great deal
more to the traditional craft of painting than
is met with by most modern painters. These
works speak to all those who believe in the
regenerative power of art, who believe its
themes remain the universal ones that T. S.
Eliot once described as birth, copulation and
death. In a secular age, O'Donoghue dares
to make art that deals with the bits of the
psyche that religion once nurtured and are,
so often, now left out in the cold.

These paintings assert that art matters,
that life matters, that history is not dead
and that we are part of its continuing warp
and weft. War and its devastation are likened
to archaeological fragments. Only through
a gradual sifting, through a voyage into
our own depths and those of the past, can
we begin to fathom something of the
complexity of human nature. "History and
painting," O'Donoghue asserts, "have the
same goal… truth".

Hughie O'Donoghue
Painting Ca
Imperial War Museum

The Independent
15th July, 2003

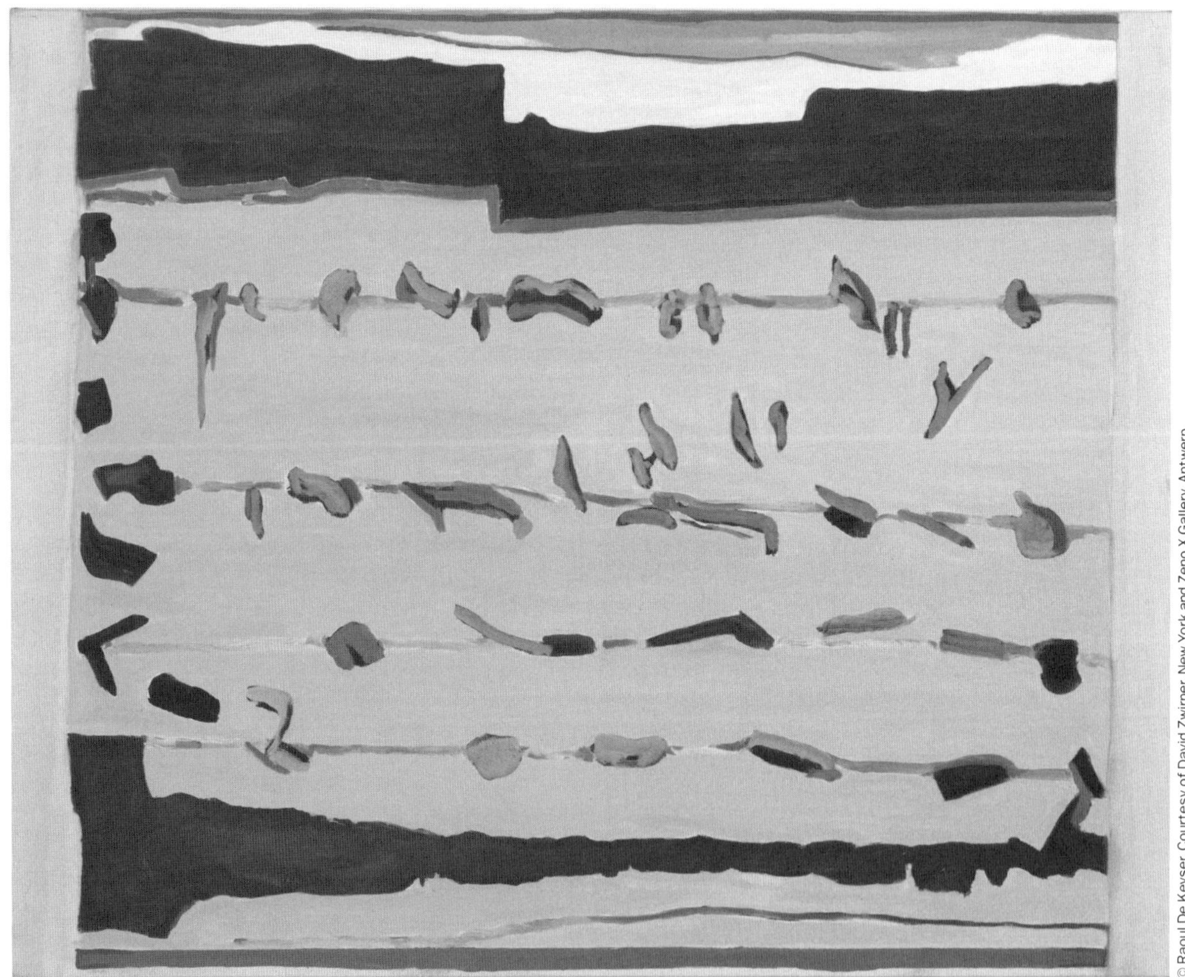

Raoul De Keyser, 'Defile', *2002*

Raoul De Keyser

The change from sports columnist to painter is hardly a conventional trajectory for an artist. But in 1963, the Belgian painter Raoul De Keyser gave up his journalistic career to pick up the brush. Barely known in this country, he has lived and worked all his life in the same small Belgian town in which he was born. Is this, perhaps, why he shares a characteristic unfussy quietness with Giorgio Morandi, another painter who remained rooted to his home base? And why should we, here in London, amid the razzmatazz and arrogance of much of the current art scene, be looking at the work of this provincial artist in his 70s, and is it important? Well, yes, it is. Not in an earth-shattering, name-up-in-neon-lights sort of way, but for anyone who is remotely interested in the possibility of making paintings in an age when the "end of painting" has been endlessly predicted, the issues addressed by De Keyser have to be of interest.

It is hard to put labels on him. He is not a Postmodernist, but then neither is he, strictly speaking, a Modernist. Rather, what he seems to be is a late Modernist, a painter who is trying to take the last possible vestiges of a purely painterly language, one not skewed by quotes from art history, popular culture, ironic pastiche, or even art theory, and seeing what he can make of it. For, as Frank Stella understood, there are "two problems in painting. One is to find out what painting is, while the other is to find

out how to make a painting". This is exactly what De Keyser does. The exhibition at the Whitechapel of 75 of his key works from 1963 to the present day – the first major survey of his work in this country – charts this development.

The language of Modernist criticism firmly rebuffs discussing painting in terms of its associative elements, its possible relationship to the seen, felt and experienced world beyond the illusionistic space of the flat surface, the stretched canvas held between four strips of wood. But this is not a useful way of trying to make sense of De Keyser's work. On the face of it, he is an old-fashioned abstract painter. The colours and tones have that slightly dirty, dry, modest look of many post-war painters. There is nothing glossy or flashy here. Yet his work is referential, taking its inspiration from the real, mundane world around him: a flight of birds or the monkey-puzzle tree in his neighbour's next-door garden. His linen boxes and paintings of the late 60s and 70s isolate objects from the ordinary day-to-day environment in which he lives: a door handle, or the white lines chalked onto the local football pitch, about which he has made a number of paintings.

But more than anything, his work exemplifies the "point" of painting, which is probably why he has been referred to as a "painter's painter". It was the poet Paul Valéry who once claimed that a poem is not so much finished as abandoned. I take this to mean that the process of making the poem, the search for a satisfactory synthesis of form and content, is what ultimately matters, and that it is an enterprise which, by definition, can never be arrived at entirely satisfactorily, but has to be revisited and rehearsed again and again. For the resulting poem – or in this case painting – can only ever be an approximation of what has been intended. This is the crux of De Keyser's painterly project.

The collective title for his most recent group of works is 'Remnants'. It is as if he is saying that, at this point in our cultural history, we can assert nothing absolute – that each and every work can only ever be partial, a borrowing, and a reworking of that which has gone before, albeit in a marginally new way. The canvas that starts his latest series, the aptly named 'Starter', *2003* (should we view this as an appetiser to the main course?), is a white upright painting of two vertical rectangles delineated by yellow lines, which sit on a third horizontal rectangle to create sections of a grid, or even what could be read as separate pages. Filling each "page" are dark jagged shapes that might be some sort of mutating organic cells or, stretching the imagination, some primitive form of hieroglyph (the fantasy "writing" of Henri Michaux springs to mind). The impetus for this series was a rediscovered linocut print that De Keyser found lying around forgotten after many years.

This linear notation is, again, present in 'Defile', *2002,* a quietly beautiful painting where the violety pink marks are strung out like washing on a line, or migrating birds perched along a telegraph wire. Another way of looking at it is as a form of visual shorthand, a way of describing the process of painting in note form that charts the painter's thinking: thinking that can be erased, changed or corrected, as if an attempt to say anything more definite would simply be too insistent for such a fragile

medium as painting has now become. A further image that springs to mind is more contemporary – the digital marks on a computer screen: marks that can be electronically erased, cut up, edited or replayed again and again like a sports video. Returning to the original linocut for inspiration seems similar. For within the new works there is a rehearsing of the problems thrown up by the old, a recycling of the memory of the previous struggles of production encountered in yet another form. Often, in fact, De Keyser discards, then reworks, paintings, sometimes cutting them up, sometimes re-stretching them or working with the fragments.

There is a bewildering array of styles here, yet a thread links them all. In a way these are paintings that insist on the question, "what is painting for?" For contemporary painting can no longer be seen as a faithfully reproduced image of the "actual" world or even, to use the Renaissance metaphor, a window onto it. Some of the works here are quite simply beautiful, though it is hard to say why. A sensitivity to colour, perhaps, such as in the gentle monochromatic painting 'Grenier 7', *1991,* where an under-painting of Minimalist bands has been cancelled by a veil of bluey grey paint, scribbled across the surface in hurried up and down strokes, as if to quote the poet T. S. Eliot, "That is not what I meant at all/ That is not it, at all". These are not, in any conventional sense, Expressionistic paintings. Rather, to use a psychoanalytic term, they are visual screens of subtle colour and fragile marks onto which the viewer is invited to project an emotional response about what it means to inhabit the physical world. It might be a slightly melodramatic overstatement to refer here to Kandinsky's notion that "the psychological power of colour… call[s] forth a vibration from the soul", as there is nothing I have read that leads me to believe that De Keyser shares such a blatantly "spiritual" view. Yet it is hard to give any other reason why a painting like

'Lok', *1995,* with its trellis of smudged ox-blood-red painted against a dun ground, is so emotionally charged.

'Reply', 'Recover', 'Residue', 'Resume', 'Reserve', 'Resonant'. These titles of De Keyser's paintings read like a mantra from a self-help manual for the dedicated contemporary painter who understands that it is the body of work – the journey towards something both elusive and ineffable – that counts every bit as much as an individual work within that body. Ulrich Loock, the one-time director of the Kunsthalle Bern and the Kunstmuseum Luzern, who has worked extensively with De Keyser, has described his paintings as an expression of "grief" for Modernism. It is as if, with the end of the possibility of describing what the camera, since the 19th century, has done so much better, contemporary painting is committed "to bring to an end, in every respect, time after time, stroke after stroke, that which once distinguished painting from the industrial production of images (photography)".

The position that De Keyser seems to inhabit is a rather small space left at the end of Modernism, a place where the quest for the "masterpiece" or the ultimate picture is bound to fail. Yet what this body of work seems, rather modestly, to be suggesting is that through a process of recycling, a reworking of what has gone before, we have a chance to see, as Eliot once suggested, that "the pattern is new in every moment/ And every moment is a new and shocking/ Valuation of all we have been". Only by arriving "where we first started" can we have any possibility of knowing "the place for the first time". As Raoul De Keyser's most recent body of work suggests, remnants are now all we have – whether they are the grand aesthetic theories of the past, our own private memories of the neighbour's monkey-puzzle tree in the next-door garden, the bark of a silver birch, or the scuffed chalk markings on the local football pitch.

Raoul De Keyser
Whitechapel Gallery

The Independent
13th April, 2004

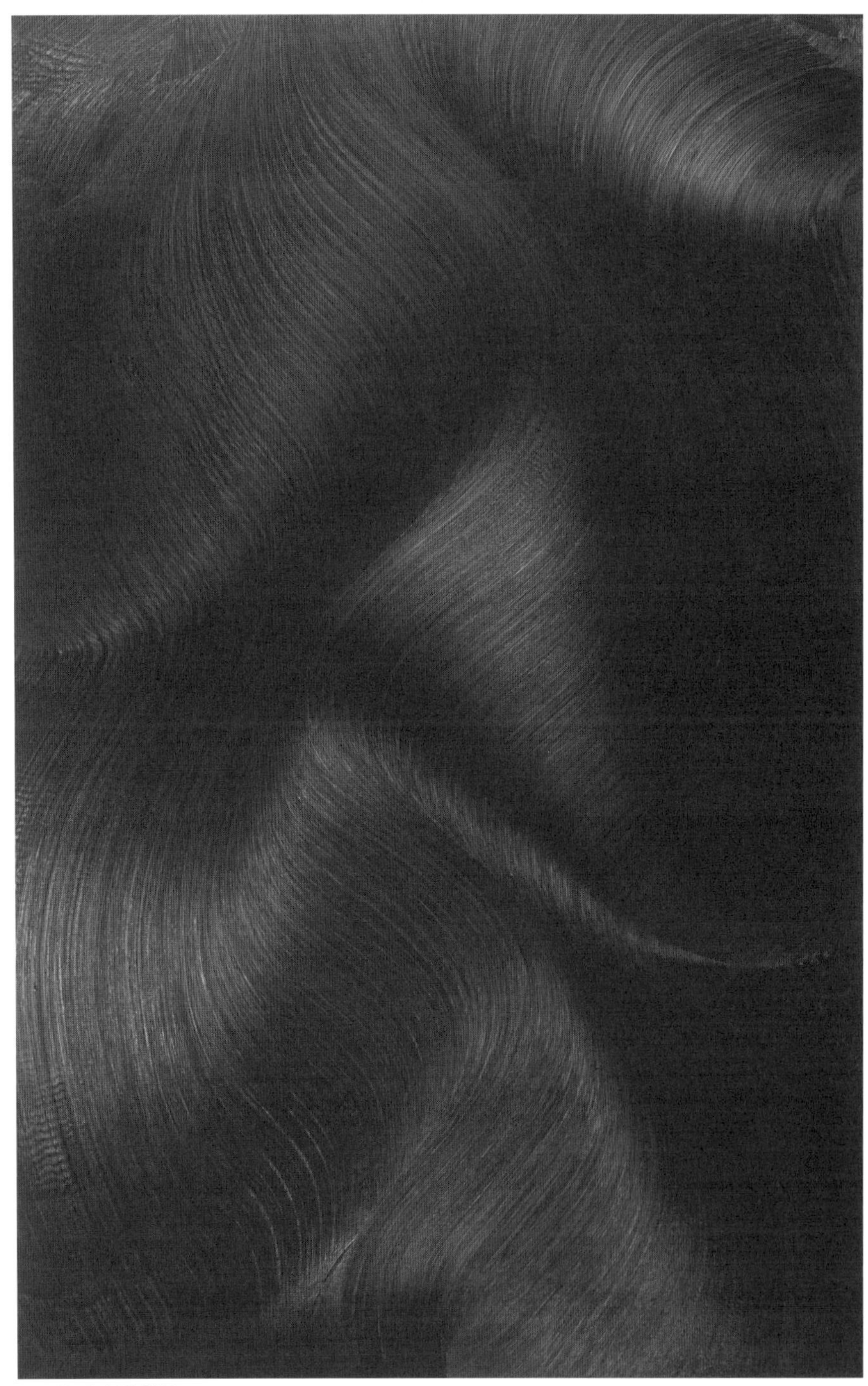

Jason Martin, 'Fell', *2006*

Jason Martin
Day Paintings

"To make visible that there is something which can be conceived and which can neither be seen nor made visible: this is what is at stake in modern painting," suggests the French philosopher Jean-François Lyotard. He proposes two distinctions in contemporary art: those forms that cater to the nostalgia for an unattainable "wholeness", and those "ingenious" forms – to which he gives the name "Postmodern" – through which the very impossibility of this attachment is what is presented by the artist. It is this dialectic – rather than the easy acceptance of one position over the other – that Jason Martin makes his territory. For in the light of such thinking, it is well nigh impossible for the young painter today any longer to make the romantic, heroic gesture. Perhaps the American Expressionists – Mark Rothko with his sublime saturated canvases, Jackson Pollock with his visceral viscous lines – were the last for whom this was possible with any degree of certainty or innocence. Now the Postmodern artist (and it might be argued that because of the accidents of history, we are all Postmoderns now) is in the position of the philosopher. The work he makes is not governed by pre-established rules and cannot be judged by familiar categories, for it is these very rules and categories for which the art is searching.

Jason Martin, a one-time graduate of Goldsmith's, has limited the possibility of the "gesture" within his painting to create a level of detachment and objectivity, though he has not erased it completely. Each painting begins as an entirely zinc-white surface over which he lays subtle layers of pigment to create "a floating transparent veil of colour", which he then "rakes" with either a section of draft excluder or a comb-like piece of metal or board. This is an act of faith, a journey across the panorama of the surface in which the history of the painting's making, the trace left by his chosen implement, is integral to its "meaning" and "interpretation". For these are not the cathartic, expressive, calligraphic marks of the Modernist, rather they seem to be asking: where now with painting? What is still possible within its narrow confines?

Martin's work commands the gallery space. It is architectural – painting as sculpture – and has a self-confident, even arrogant, sense of its own presence, opening up the volume of the surface to the viewer. While his language is entirely abstract, his work is made in the world and therefore refers, obliquely, to it – to the body, to the movement of light, to organic forms, to the processes of making that can still be seen retained at the painting's edges, where the history of the layers that have gone into constructing the surface are still visible like the striations in rock.

And there is, of course, colour – monochromatic colour – that is at once subtle and complex: fan-like arcs and loops of black on black, organic feathers of blood red in 'Fecund' and shifting tones of white that undulate across the surface of the large horizontal panorama 'Untitled', *2004*. This is slashed by two diagonal flashes of creamy yellow that run from top to bottom, attracting and refracting light in balletic shafts that shimmer and glimmer and move. In the front gallery are two works that have been made *in situ*. A large tondo and a third of a circle covered in what looks like molten gold, which has dripped and collected on the floor. Abstract they may be, but they appropriate some of the drama and dynamism, some of the luxury and self-assertion, of Aztec images of the sun. Within all these works Martin acknowledges a dichotomy: the desire to find a reductive, purely painterly language alongside the human imperative to make work that "speaks" on a more visceral level. But these paintings insist that there is no going back to the discredited utopianism of Modernism. For as Jürgen Habermas wrote in 'Modernity – An Incomplete Project', "the avant-garde must find a direction in a landscape into which no one seems to have yet ventured".

Jason Martin
Day Paintings
Lisson Gallery

The Independent
26th April, 2004

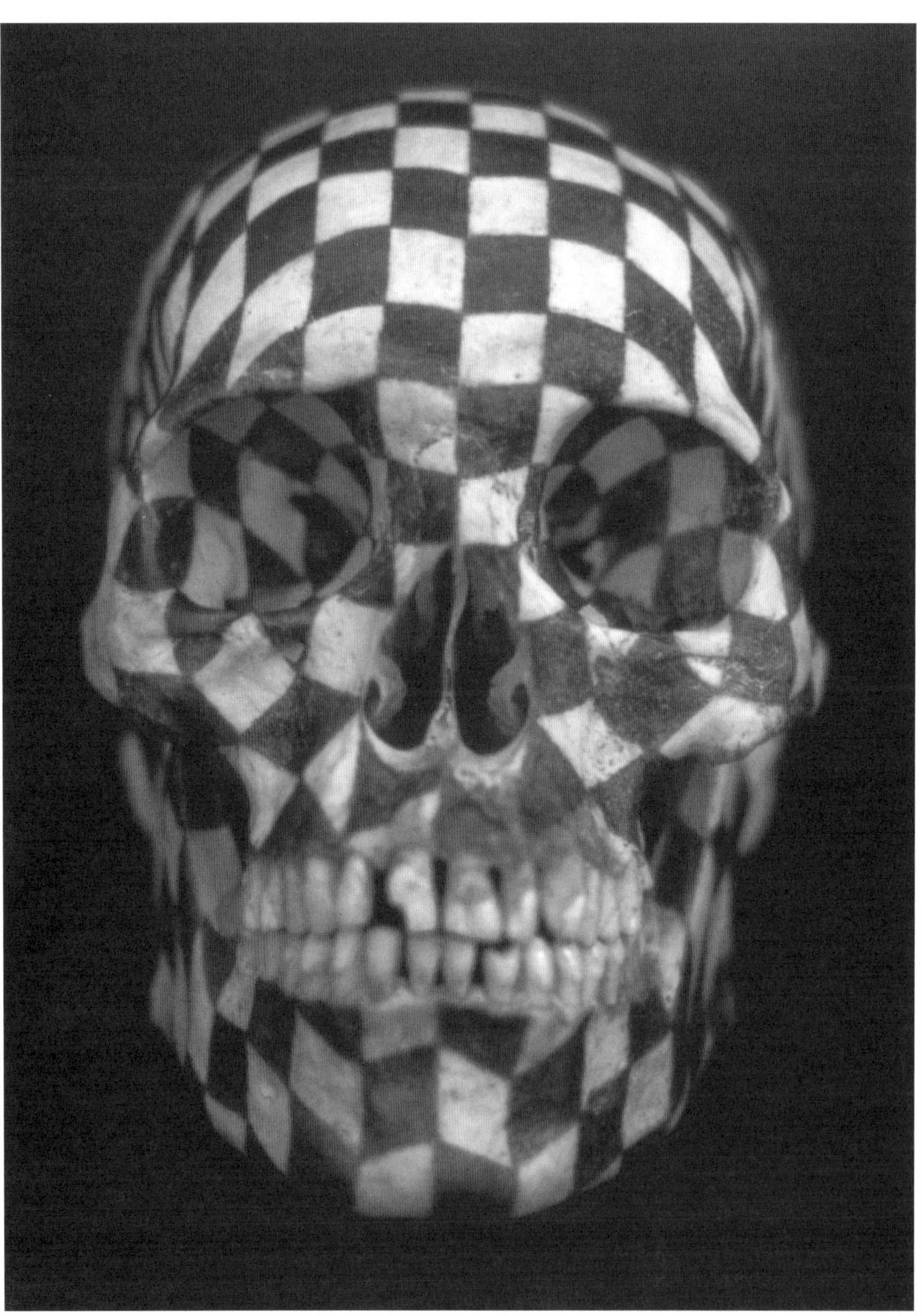

Gabriel Orozco, 'Black Kites', *1997*

Gabriel Orozco

If you enjoy playing chess or the oriental game of Go, if you are an enthusiast for deciphering cryptic crosswords or a fan of the short stories of Jorge Luis Borges, then you will enjoy the work of the Mexican artist Gabriel Orozco. I use the word "artist" advisedly, for Orozco is a conceptualist who employs whatever medium happens to seem appropriate – paint, photography, sculpture, collage – to explore his obsessions. Skill, as such, is not the point, as say with a painter, who may have spent years trying to master how pigments react one with another on canvas. Rather his is a Duchampian investigation into the nature of the physical universe – its oddness, coincidental similarities and idiosyncrasies – with whatever materials happen to be at hand or capture his imagination. For Orozco seems not so much to be searching for "the meaning of life" but trying instead to establish a series of self-constructed systems to impose on the random chaos of the material world, and incidentally to highlight some of its small beauties, banalities, synchronicities and discrepancies.

Born in 1962 in Jalapa, Veracruz, into an intellectual left-wing family, he was encouraged, early, to eschew all forms of Americanism, including the English language. As a teenager he spent summers in the Soviet Union and Cuba and, as a student in the late 1980s, he led a group of radical young artists who rejected the predominance of *neo-mexicanismo* – art that dealt in gaudy commercial Neoexpressionism and cultural stereotypes of a nationalistic sub-Kahloesque nature.

At first the work at the Serpentine all seems rather arbitrary, inchoate even – a bit of painting here, a collage or sculpture there – until one realises that there is a conceptual and intellectual thread that links one work to another. Grids and formal structures are obviously important, and slowly, if one concentrates – for Orozco is an intellectual artist who demands attention from his viewer – it becomes apparent that there is an interplay between the rational and organic, the structured and the intuitive; if you like, between the Cartesian mind and the sentient body, though it seems to me that in Orozco's universe, the mind always wins.

'Black Kites', *1997*, his most arresting and seminal work, graphically embodies these concerns. Over a period of six months, he meticulously worked out how to create a seamless graphite grid across the surface of a human skull. Here the organic object – the skull – is overlaid with a geometric pattern that metaphorically suggests the structures of logical thought. Coincidentally, it also seems to display a very Mexican concern with images of death, and looks as if it might have been dug up on some ancient Aztec site. But then that too would be appropriate to Orozco's thinking, for the found object or "readymade" is a dominant motif in his work.

On entering the gallery, one is confronted by his 'Mixiotes', *1999* sculptures (the term refers to a traditional Mexican dish in which rabbit is cooked wrapped in cactus leaves) at the other end of his creative spectrum from 'Black Kites', but which also uses "found" objects – small coloured rubber balls, clear plastic bags and dried transparent cactus leaves – which float suspended from the ceiling like sea birds or fish, the flimsy ephemera of leaf and plastic held in place by the weight of the rubber balls. This is echoed elsewhere by 'Delta Tail', 'Double Cut' and 'Spume Fin', *2003*, whose anthropomorphised forms were created by pouring liquid polyurethane foam onto a tilted rubber sheet so that when the rubber was stripped away, the smooth surfaces of the shark-like objects, which now hang from the gallery ceiling, were revealed.

Among the oddest suspended objects are 'Lintels'. Strung on wires suspended across the gallery like surreal washing are swaths of fluffy grey lint collected from New York laundromats. Joseph Beuys, of course, comes to mind, but this lint has not been imbued with any magical or mystical properties. Rather, through this display of human detritus such as skin and hair that form the lint, Orozco invites us to see its possibilities as sculptural material, and to note what we might very well not otherwise see – its varying textures and subtle vestigial colour. The verbal word-play around something as insubstantial as washing machine effluvia is typical of his games-playing inclinations. The soft ground etchings made from pressing the lint onto printing plates in 'Polvo Impreso' (Lint Book), *2002* are surprisingly beautiful; with their subtle grey-black tones, they might be describing the surface of the moon or the bark of a tree. But they also demonstrate Orozco's predisposition for non-art materials, linking him strongly with the mood of the Italian *arte povera* movement. This eye for the incidentals of the world is very much part of his art. 'Havre-Caumartin', *1999*, a set of three graphite drawings, was made from rubbings taken of the circular mosaics on the wall of the Parisian metro station of the same name. These apparently classic abstract drawings vary in density due to the bodily pressure exerted.

Geometric patterns, particularly circles, are revisited and repeated within Orozco's work. The formal patterns of 'Blackboards', *1998*, a series of ten classroom boards silk-screened with computer-generated designs reminiscent of electronic circuitry boards, also form the basis of a number of drawings that he has filled in with colour, working out from the centre like a model of the expanding universe. Since 1994, he has been dividing circles and ovals into two and four quadrants with perpendicular lines, and then filling in the sections with primary colours. The placing of the colours and their relationships are based on the moves made by the knight on the chessboard. The results look like molecular structures – 3D models of DNA or proteins – depicted on a flat surface. He has used this same intersecting devise with collected ephemera – from airline tickets to paper currency – to create works influenced by that master of detritus, Kurt Schwitters. Circles, drawn and incised with a compass, dominate his 'Atomist' series. These are the only works to include the human form, if one excludes the two rather beautiful series of his own handprints. The spheres are superimposed on images gleaned from the sports pages of newspapers and thus relate to the analysis of movement and the desire to formulate a system that describes the human body in motion, in the manner of Eadweard Muybridge.

Games are at the heart of much of Orozco's work. Often they are displayed on "working tables", a field of action that functions rather like a blank sheet of paper on which new scenarios can occur. His 'Game Boxes', *1998*, are constructed of *Plasticine* "pieces" – balls and "submarine-like" shapes – fitted into "found" boxes that once contained educational film material, and therefore dictate the shape and size of the *Plasticine* objects placed in them. The games invite the viewer to pick up the pieces and engage in a match without any apparent rules, where the system and methodology can be constructed by the players, and either brought to an abrupt end or continued indefinitely. These 'Game Boxes', which have never before been shown, were made around the time of the 'Penske Work Project'. For this, Orozco drove around SoHo and the West Village in New York collecting whatever detritus turned up, arranging and photographing it on the street, and then transporting it to the next site in a removal truck rented from the Penske Automotive Group. The vehicle thus became a sort of mobile studio, allowing serendipity to play its part within the tightly constructed framework that defined the "rules" of the project.

Perhaps Orozco could best be described as a Postmodern Surrealist – for in his work chance, beloved by the Surrealists, meets the mood of eclecticism that is so much a feature of Postmodernism. He is an artist who not only lets happenstance play its role, but one who knowingly sets up well-defined systems, only to allow them to be subverted by accident, experiment and chance. For him, art can be anything – a photograph of a mosque made from sacking and timber poles set up in the scrubland of Timbuktu, Mali, which seems to have attracted his attention because of the pattern of circles cut into the fabric to let in light, or a series of found yoghurt cartons with circular holes, or the endless lines drawn on a scroll of paper with a ruler, where an "accidental" bulge has developed because his projecting finger disrupted the flow. In fact, anything that fits with his obsessions and intellectual investigations.

An appropriate image for his corpus of work might be that of the *Meccano* set where bits are bolted on, one to another, to make a complete structure. It is almost impossible to think of the pieces singly, for individually they don't add up to anything. What he has created is an idiosyncratic schema of the world, one that asks questions about the nature of art, about how we see the everyday and the marginalised, and about the differing values we place on what is "found" compared to that which is made, manufactured, discovered or simply "seen".

The catalogue essay quotes the French Structuralist Claude Lévi-Strauss: "If I may be allowed the expression, it is not the resemblances, but the differences, which resemble each other". It is this sentiment that is at the heart of Orozco's work. But Orozco is not some neo-Romantic making a new organic whole out of the shards of Postmodernism; rather he is an artist who simply gives another twist to the kaleidoscope in order to see those shards in a different format and experience them from a different perspective. This is not art that delves into deep emotion or talks of grief, loss or love but, as in a Borgesian short story, suggests that there are always more labyrinths along which we have not yet been, and new ways of seeing.

Gabriel Orozco
Serpentine Gallery

The Independent
6th July, 2004

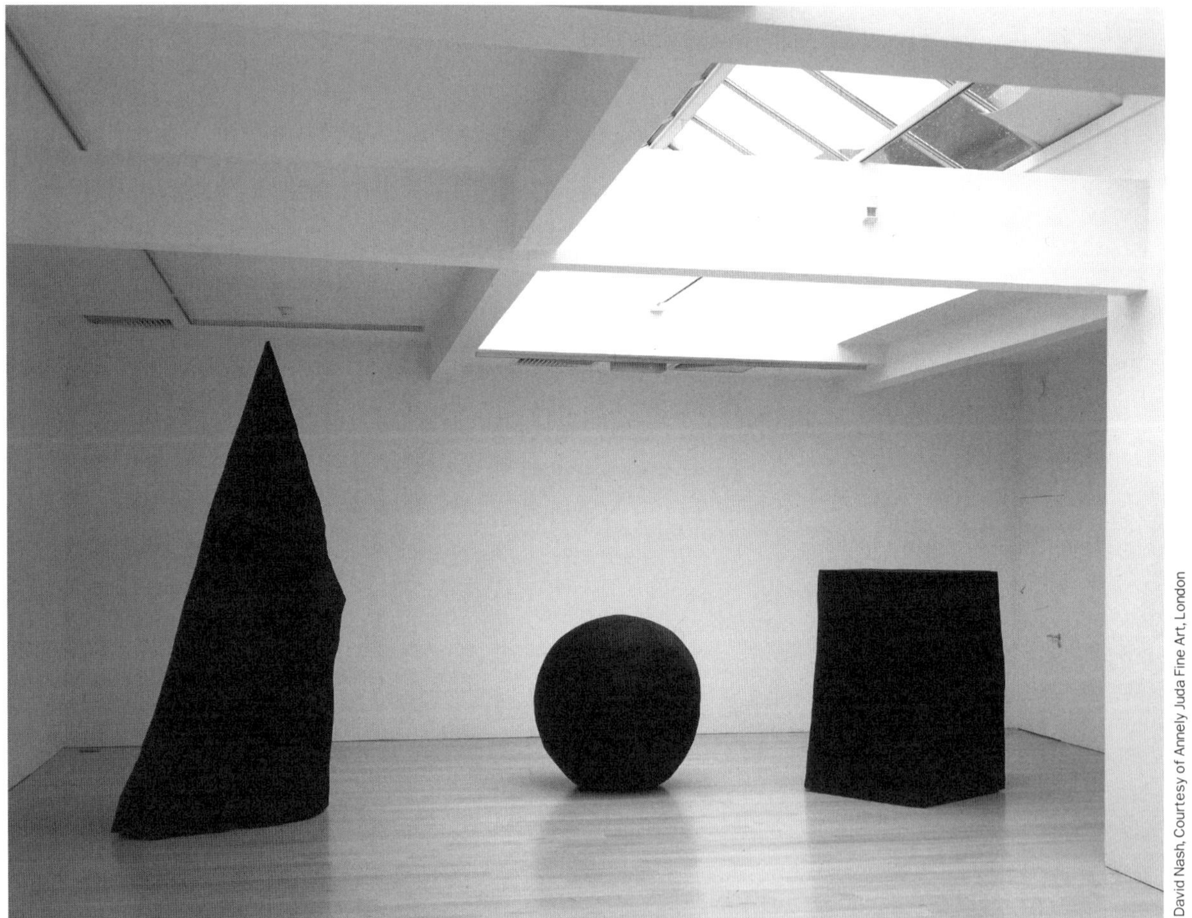

David Nash, 'Three Forms, Cube, Sphere, Pyramid', *2003-2004*

David Nash
Making and Placing Abstract Sculpture 1978–2004

Years ago, when writing another piece on the sculptor David Nash, I went to visit him at Capel Rhiw, his home and studio in a converted Methodist Chapel in Blaenau Ffestiniog, a dour village set high in the Welsh hills, surrounded by slag heaps of slate. It has been his home since 1968, when he left what he felt to be the materialistic southeast of England where he had been born and bred. He had fallen in love with the valley after spending holidays there, roaming with his brother as a boy. The place is very important to him and to his work. It takes a long time to get there. On the last lap, you have to take a tiny train that winds up through the folded hills like Thomas the Tank Engine beside tumbling waterfalls and streams. But the slowing of pace, this sense of going on a journey, is an appropriate mindset through which to view David Nash's work.

One of the first things he did was to take me to a stream in the Cynfal Valley where he had pushed a rough-hewn wooden boulder over a waterfall into a stream. Black and water-logged, it had become stuck below a bridge and had been there for months. It looked just like another dark rock. From 1978 to 2004, Nash visited his wooden boulder regularly, documenting its progress. It has been covered in snow and ice, and remained in one place for years at a time washed by the icy stream and baked in the occasional sun, before one day being swept away by floods to rest on a sand bank in the Dwyryd

Estuary. In 2003, the tide floated it out to a salt marsh where it lurked like some dark lake monster in the shallows until, suddenly, it disappeared, no doubt washed out into the Irish Sea. Nash does not consider his boulder lost. "It is wherever it is," he says philosophically, though he still hunts for it. "My search is part of the work."

The film 'Boulder' by Pete Telfer forms the centrepiece to this exhibition of Nash's work at Tate, St. Ives, and includes documentary footage charting the progress of this large wooden sphere over 20 years. It encapsulates many of Nash's most important themes: the notions of time, evolution and life's natural cycles, as well as the nature of transformation, change and chance that evoke the Greek philosopher Heraclitus's famous remark that we cannot step into the same river twice; that life is, in essence, a continuing journey.

David Nash has been working in wood for 30 years, mainly with broadleaf trees such as oak, beach, ash, lime, cherry, elm and birch, choosing each for its unique properties. Birch, for example, he describes as benign, feminine, yielding, a loving wood, while oak is very male, hard and resistant. It's like carving stone in that, when he hits it with an axe, it answers back. The sound of the blow keeps him attuned to the correctness of the cut. Lime is one of the best carving woods. It is slow growing with a purity of whiteness, and has fantastic warping and cracking potential. These processes of chance are intrinsic tools in Nash's sculptural repertoire.

For Nash, context is all. He has made work especially to be sited outside – as can be seen in many of the sculpture parks around the country – as well as work for public and commercial spaces where he has to take into account the immediate architectural environment. Here he has found a sympathetic milieu among the St. Ives Modernists whose work is on show in a new hang in the first gallery. When Ben Nicholson and Barbara Hepworth moved to Cornwall, they were exploring the possibilities of non-representational art, which by the 1930s had been stripped of all unnecessary decorative elements. Hepworth described herself as "absorbed in the relationship in space, in size and texture and weight, as well as in the tension between forms". Such sentiments could well describe David Nash's work nearly 80 years later. Again and again, he returns to the pared purity of the pyramid, the cube and the sphere: universal forms that belong to all cultures and are owned by no one. His large, charred and blackened 'Three Forms, Cube, Sphere, Pyramid', *2003/04* has an atavistic presence that dominates the small gallery and contains echoes of the ancient henges scattered across the surrounding Cornish landscape.

'Three Charred Panels' of beech have been hung like a triptych. The cuts in each are vertical, diagonal and horizontal. Against the white wall, they have a severe Minimalist beauty, for black absorbs light rather than giving it back. Scorching has long been an important process for Nash. It has a practical as well as a semi-mystical purpose. Fire both cauterises and purifies. For despite the earthy muscularity of his work Nash has, over the years, been much influenced by the philosophy of Rudolph Steiner, by Plato's vision of reincarnation, and by Tao Te Ching, a form of Buddhism. Charring removes the narrative history of the living

wood, erasing what he considers to be the aesthetic distraction of the grain. As carbon, the sculptural form can be viewed with greater clarity. Charring is also associated with the transformations of mediaeval alchemy that occurred when two opposing elements were heated in a crucible to produce a new synthesis. The phoenix rising from the ashes was an alchemical symbol of renewal and rebirth – themes that occur subtly but insistently throughout Nash's work. For as the French philosopher Gaston Bachelard wrote in 'The Psychoanalysis of Fire', "Fire is the ultra-living element. It is intimate and it is universal… Among all phenomena, it is really the only one to which there can be so definitely attributed the opposing values of good and evil".

The cuts and tools Nash uses are also crucial. His preferred implement is the electric chain saw, which he wields with the fluency of the painter's brush. The scores he leaves on the raw wood evoke the painter's marks. In his totemic 'Crack and Warp Column', *2002*, he has very nearly sliced through the thick trunk of lime to form thin leaves or sheets that, as they dry, buckle and warp. The splits, knots and cracks in the unseasoned wood, and the slips of the saw, are all left visible. As a young man, Nash was deeply influenced by the simplicity of Constantin Brancusi's forms. He likes to quote one of his aphorisms that in art, the "simple" is very "complex". He also has a respect for his peers who work within the environment: Richard Long, Hamish Fulton and Andy Goldsworthy – artists who, in another age, might have become landscape painters, but who wanted to be absorbed in the actual physical world.

In the 70s, Nash saw how David Smith had developed a fluency of language using metal, and wanted to do the same with wood. He insists, though, he is not a wood "craftsman", though a "truth to materials" is essential. He likes his wood raw, unpolished and pure. It is the poetry and geometry of movement that is of interest. "Geometry represents an order in nature or a path for me," he has said, "like my line of cut". It is both human order and a process of understanding. Works such as 'Capped Block', *1998* and 'Extended Cube' *1996* expand our concept and understanding of universal forms. The wood is cut away and the cubes dismantled and extended into space, rather like the segments of a telescope. Volume is dramatically increased. He is, he says, very satisfied – as Moore and Hepworth discovered – when he can see through, in and around a form. Beauty exists in that simple rightness, the truth of things. Although such a sentiment smacks of a Keatsian Romanticism, Nash somehow manages to meld this vision with the more conceptual elements of a work like 'Wooden Boulder'. That is his skill. He may be a Romantic at heart, but his head is that of a Modernist.

Even though the sculptures in the curved, sea-facing gallery – which include the vertical 'Sheaves', 'Elm Frame, Fourteen Cuts' and the powerful yet maternally enfolding 'Coil' – seem a little squashed in the comparatively small space, there is a certain rightness to their placement in relationship to the sea; like great logs of driftwood or planks from wrecked ships, they feel as if they could have been washed up on Porthmeor Beach just outside the window. Earth, air, fire and water – all these four basic elements exist in Nash's work.

Working away from the metropolis in his remote Welsh chapel amid the slate slag heaps of the Ffestiniog Valley, David Nash has been able to hold onto that rare commodity, integrity. It may be unfashionable, but he believes there is a moral requirement involved in the practice of art, a necessary level of consciousness as to how what an artist makes affects the world. He speaks of his own feelings when he came across Richard Serra's great big torque pieces for the first time: the tenderness he felt. In the end, that is what

he wants to transmit through these great chunks of hacked, sawn, cut and burnt wood, wood that, like us, has lived and died: a certain tenderness.

David Nash
Making and Placing Abstract
Sculpture 1978-2004
Tate St. Ives

The Independent
31st August, 2004

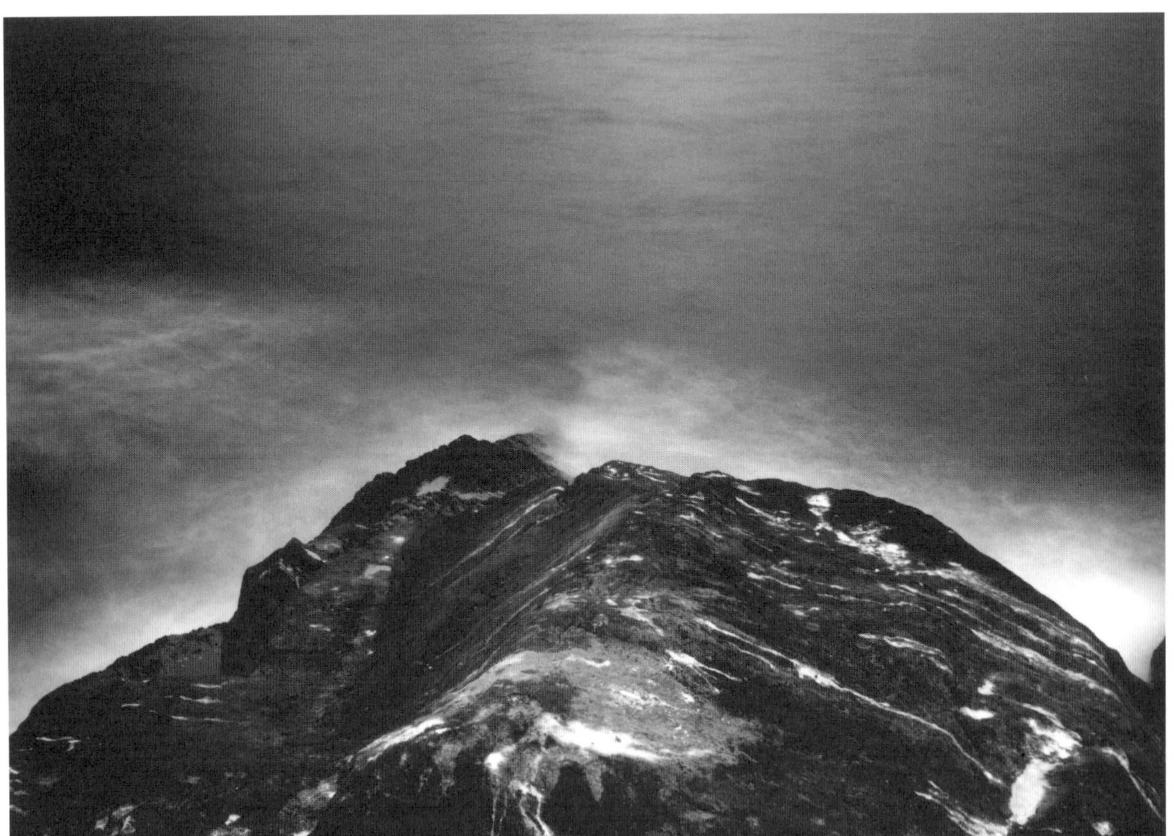

Thomas Joshua Cooper, 'Furthest North – The Barents Sea – 71° 11' 08" Knivskjelodden, Norway, 2003-2004 The North-Most Point of Continental Europe', *2003-2004*

Thomas Joshua Cooper
Point of No Return

What does it mean to be a cartographer, to go on a circumnavigation? In the Renaissance these things were symbols of adventure, of the imagination, and of the global exploration that pushed out the boundaries of the known world. With modernity they have come to mean something rather different. We go on journeys, not so much to make sense of our external environment, but to explore our internal worlds. The word "journey" has become synonymous with personal exploration. Maybe in the process of discovering who we are, we might come to find our place in the physical universe, and relinquish the hubris that is fast destroying the actual planet, thus learning a little modesty in the face of the disappearing wilderness.

From 1969, Thomas Joshua Cooper, who was born in California in 1946 and is now Professor and Senior Researcher for Fine Art at Glasgow School of Art, has worked with a 19th-century field camera, mapping the landscape with his lyrical black-and-white photographs. His grandiose and insanely Romantic project entitled 'The Atlantic Basin Project – The World's Edge', stemmed from his reading of 'A World Lit Only by Fire' by the American historian William Manchester, in which the latter postulates that the greatest achievements of the Renaissance were not those of Leonardo or Michelangelo, but of Ferdinand Magellan. Not only did Magellan's circumnavigations

confirm the world to be round, but they were the catalyst for the process of globalisation in which we are still involved. Cooper has set out on an epic venture, begun in 1990, to map the extremities of the land and islands that surround the entire Atlantic Ocean. This exhibition contains more than 30 works made in over ten countries, including Morocco, Senegal, South Africa, Spain and Norway.

Starting in the Old World, Cooper is slowly moving to the New in an attempt to make sense of "why our culture has become what it has become". With this aim, he has literally gone to the ends of the earth to stand in the lonely places where our forebears stood before setting out on their migrations. But there is a dichotomy here, for although he is concerned with the growing homogenisation of culture, he only makes pictures of the sea. Yet what we learn from his beautiful photographs is something not only of the awe and sublimity of nature, but also of its uniqueness. Wave patterns and ocean currents may appear superficially the same, but they are as individual as fingerprints, influenced by complex dynamics and underwater swells. To see the difference takes awareness and concentration. It takes time – something that is in short supply within contemporary society. For such subtleties only reveal themselves in quietness, stillness and meditation. Yet the sea continues to draw us – amniotic and huge, its continuous sound like the inrush of blood. Cooper's

titles read like haikus: 'Clouded Moonlight
– South, South West – The Mid North
Atlantic Ocean' or 'Unexpected Nightfall –
The Mid North Atlantic Ocean'.

His series of the Barents Sea, taken on
three different days, charts the visual changes
in one location, the difference of moods
induced by dark corrugated waves or the
bleaching sky fading into the horizon. The
varying densities of white and black might
come from the brush of an Abstract
Expressionist though they are, in fact, the
differences between freezing rain, freezing
fog and the midnight sun. Though these are
photographs of the natural world, it is a
highly selective vision. Cooper's camera
catches the light on the crest of a wave,
the white swell breaking over black rocks,
the glisten of wet seaweed or the lime
bird droppings against granite that are
highlighted to resemble the brush marks left
by a painter. His very dark grey, almost black
'Sudden Nightfall – Comet Trail, The Mid
North Atlantic Ocean, Cabo Girău, The Isle
of Madeira', might be made of graphite it is
so dense. Painting is evoked over and over
again with oblique references to Turner, to
Monet, to Robert Ryman.

These are wonderful, poetic evocations to
be making in cynical times that have little
patience with the Romantic gesture. These
works are about our relationship to the tides,
to the moon and the world's gravitational
pull. Cooper manages to encompass the
sensibility of oriental Minimalism with
western Romanticism. In these images,
the artist stands alone, heroic as a figure in
a Caspar David Friedrich painting. On the
edge of the world looking out across the vast
and lonely ocean, we can only ask existential
questions about who we are and what is next.

Thomas Joshua Cooper
Point of No Return
Haunch of Venison, London

The Independent
13th October, 2004

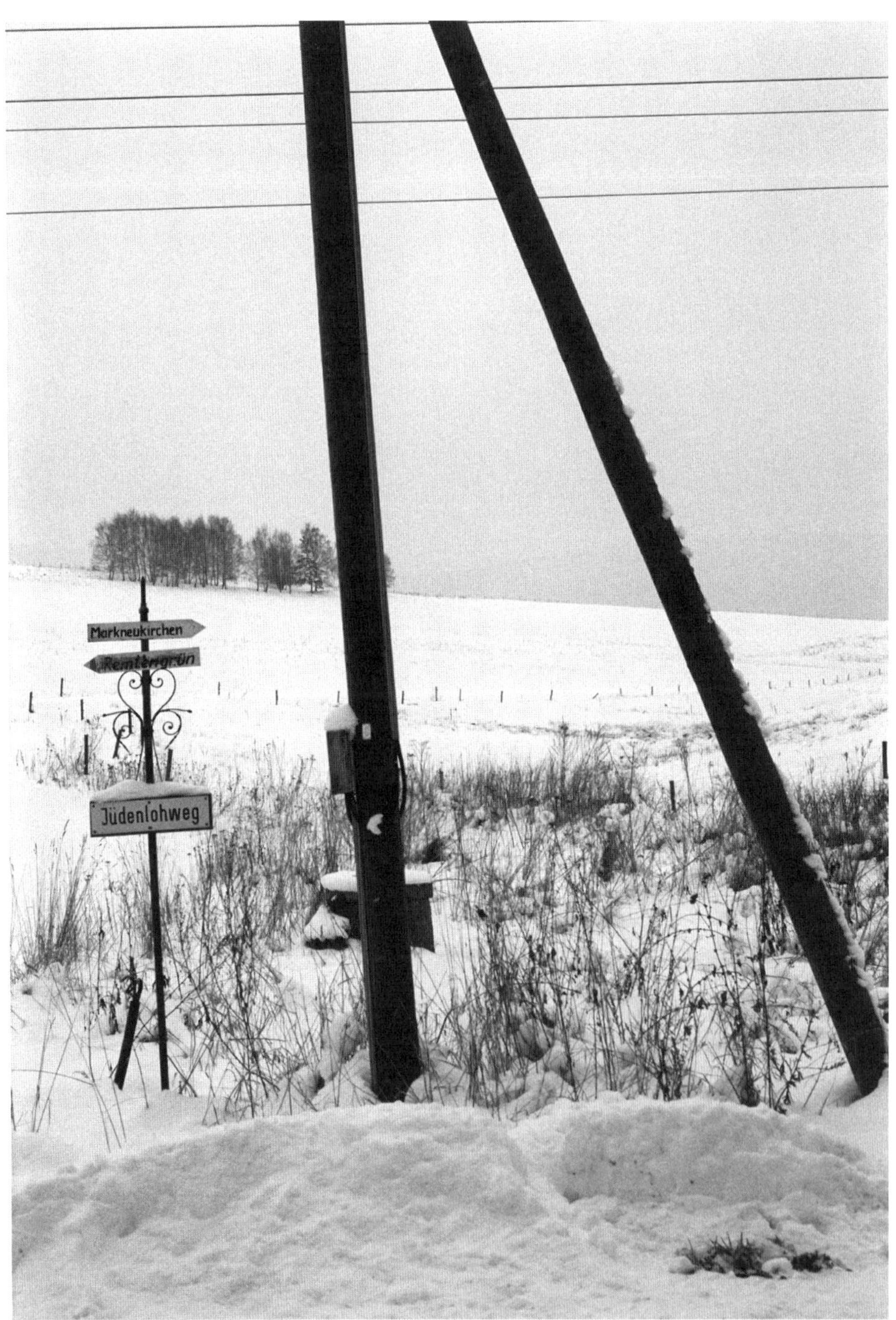

Susan Hiller, 'The J Street Project (Snow Scenes / Schneeszenen)', *2003*

Susan Hiller
The J Street Project

Myth, claims Roland Barthes, is "a system of communication… it is a message". "Every object in the world can pass from a closed, silent existence to an oral state… for nothing constructed in the world today escapes meaning… Myth can be defined neither by its object nor by its material, for any material can arbitrarily be endowed with meaning…" Pictures and images, he suggests, are more imperative than writing – they "impose meaning at a stroke". Signs cannot be dissociated from the messages they carry. They become a kind of writing, a language that discloses layers of often unintentional and unconscious meaning. The role of the artist is to look, to make connections, to see the world afresh, to fill in the gaps between the signifier and what is signified, to remember. This is very much the territory of Susan Hiller's art. She has in her drawings, her installations and videos – whether they are about memory and Freud, or investigations into the paranormal – been involved in an excavation of what is usually overlooked and ignored: what is rejected, silenced or marginalised.

When Hiller moved to Berlin to take up a residency in 2003, she was taken aback by the chance discovery of a street in Berlin Mitte called Judenstrasse (Jews' Street). This stirred mixed emotions. There seemed to be a strange ambiguity in the retention of a place name that evoked such a strong sense of absence. For what was actually being commemorated by such a sign if not the ghosts of those obliterated by racism, segregation and violence? Extensive research disclosed over 300 roads, streets and paths both in the West and former East Germany that referred to a Jewish presence.

Hiller embarked on a three-year project charting these hitherto undocumented locations from Flensburg in the north to Munich in the south, from Bonn in the west to Passau in the east, all of which included the prefix "Juden". Some of the densest areas were around Mainz, Mannheim and Würzburg. Numerous trips were made, criss-crossing the country to photograph and video city streets and shopping precincts, cobbled alleyways and woodland tracks, paths that cut through parks or ran along the edge of railway tracks. There are photographs of yellow street signs set on poles against the whiteness of a snowy suburban street that evoke the yellow badges Jews were forced to wear for identification; others seem odd simply because of the incongruity of the street name placed beside an ordinary looking garden or an uninteresting stretch of pavement. But, like a child's dot-to-dot drawing, this series of physical journeys has created a web that connects these erasures and silences into a complex cartography of signs.

In the front gallery a wall of photographs and a map document the 330 places visited, along with an index of street names in alphabetical order. What is so striking about these locations is their banality. History has been obliterated, to be replaced by the parked car, the supermarket window, the industrial site and the local café. Time has acted like the sea washing away footprints in sand. Only the street names indicate that these sometimes bland, sometimes picture-postcard locations with their cobbles and timber-clad buildings were once ghettos or bustling commercial centres. The resonances are deeply disquieting, for the names read like prayers to the dead: Judenweg, Judenpfad, Judentenberger Strasse, Judengasse, Judenberg, Judentrappe. What was erased has finally been given visibility through the interconnections and traces of language.

Jews are not usually associated with what is pastoral or rural and so, perhaps, the most uncanny images are those of country roads where an ethereal light shimmers through the canopy of trees or illuminates a grassy glade. Though mentioned on maps, these actual rural locations were often not sign-posted. There is something very German about these woodland paths and forest tracks that connects to the dark imagery and night fears of the folk- and fairy-tale. For the forest, according to psychoanalysts such as Bruno Bettelheim, represents the unconscious, suggesting what is wild, hidden and untamed. There is a connection, too, with German Romanticism and the paintings of Caspar David Friedrich and, by implication, to the whole relationship between German nationalism and land. That these rural locations should have been "cleansed" of their Jewish population speaks implicitly of ideas of racial purity and ethnic cleansing. Blood and soil are linked.

Susan Hiller has said that all her work "deals with ghosts. Ghosts are invisible to most people but visible to a few". Her installation, 'Witness', made originally for an old chapel in west London and later shown at the Tate, consists of earphones hanging from the

ceiling on shimmering silver cords. From out of each of these a voice whispers in a different language telling of an encounter with a UFO. What was secret, hidden, marginalised and incredible is given validity by these "witnesses" through the force of language, by the process of their telling. In Germany there may be more than 300 streets named after their former Jewish residents, but, as Hiller says, "hardly anyone notices them. These street names are ghosts of the past, haunting the present". Part of the project of this voyage into the heart of contemporary Germany involved the making of a video. Scenes move between empty snow-filled landscapes and summer gardens, from early morning to dusk and the setting sun in an endless cycle that implies the movement of seasons. There are groups of old people, of children roller-skating and a shop filled with clocks, but most of the time it feels as if the artist is a fly on the wall, ignored by those going about their business. Few here seem prepared to tell their tales or to bear witness. History and genocide have been reduced to a symphony of street signs.

What this exhibition asks is how art can stand against the facts of history. Even 60 years after the Holocaust, the irresolvable paradox of the Nobel laureate and Holocaust survivor Elie Wiesel is still pertinent. "How is one to speak of it?" he asked of this dark period. "How is one not to speak of it?" Yet it is in the very act of making art, by "speaking of it" that the ghosts of the past are not forgotten. It is all too easy for responses to the Holocaust to become dulled, blunted by the ghastly familiarity of over-used images. Finding a new language, one that ironically uses the "objective" register of categorisation so beloved by the Nazis, ensures that this chapter of German genocide is not simply reduced to a dusty footnote in the annals of history, but continues to reverberate within the present, to touch contemporary lives. These place names not only connect us back to those who once inhabited these streets, but also force us to forge links with, and ask questions of, those who inhabit them now. The past is not simply another country.

"Political art" is not fashionable for this is not, within the west at least, an age of causes. But our ethical sensibilities still have constantly to be renegotiated, not only in the shadow of Europe's darkest decade, but in the context of new terrors, new genocides to which we would, in the hustle and bustle of contemporary life, all too easily turn a blind eye. Such was the scale of the Holocaust that for thinkers like the philosopher Theodor Adorno, to continue to make art seemed impossible. But silence, at this distance in time, merely seems like a form of capitulation. George Steiner wrote "that fear lies near the heart of the way in which I think of myself as a Jew… We do tend to recognise one another wherever we meet, nearly at a glance, by some common trick of feeling, by the darkness we carry". Susan Hiller comes from a secular Jewish background. She was not looking to make "Jewish" work when she arrived in Berlin. But these street names insinuated themselves into her consciousness, drawing her into a Jewish "community" whether she chose it or not. For as Steiner says: "the Nazis made of the mere name necessary and sufficient cause. They did not ask whether one had ever been to synagogue, whether one's children knew any Hebrew". Language and naming can be insidious. Hiller has called this 'The J Street Project', reminding us that a section of humanity can all too easily be reduced to, and then categorised by, a single letter of the alphabet.

Nationalism is the venom of our age. This complex and courageous project not only gives voice to the forgotten dead, but also to all those made outsiders by careless language and zealous fundamentalism, by the rise of neo-fascism and xenophobia in Africa, in Eastern Europe, in Iraq and even – with all the current election talk of mass immigration – on our own doorstep. It could not be more timely.

Susan Hiller
The J Street Project
Timothy Taylor Gallery

The Independent
25th April, 2005

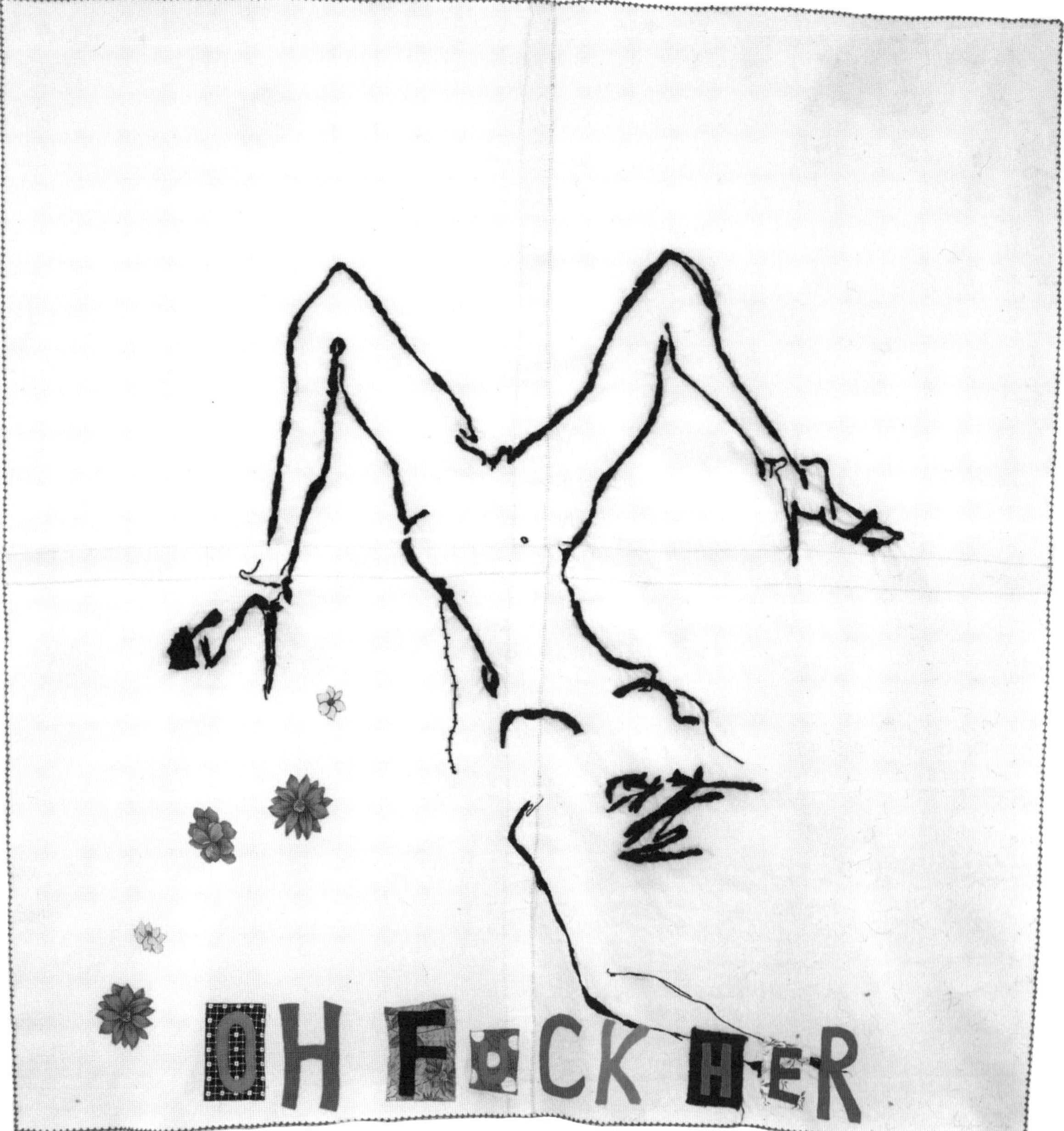

Tracey Emin, 'Oh Fuck...', *2004*

Tracey Emin

She is known for her boob-revealing Vivienne Westwood outfits, for her drunken fits on TV, for her dishevelled bed in the Tate, for her abortions and adolescent sexual fumblings behind the beach huts of her native Margate, for being at every glitzy art opening, for her failed love life and her cat Docket and, now, for writing a column in 'The Independent' opining her lack of an adequately endowed man and espousing her new celibacy. Tracey Emin is the tabloid face of Brit-Art.

But how does she rate as an artist? I first came across her work when she was comparatively unknown and had her "museum" down in Waterloo. She was zany, engaging and irritating in about equal measure. Already a great self-publicist, she produced work that was raw, real, quirky, fresh, in-yer-face and utterly self-obsessed. Now she is rich, with a big 18th-century house in Spitalfields, and London's hippest artist, represented by its hippest gallery, White Cube – that byword for Hoxton chic. Her new exhibition is called, with characteristic brio, 'When I think about sex…'.

It is beautifully installed. In the centre of the gallery is a wooden rollercoaster made from reclaimed wood, inspired by a dream. It is very "arty", very *arte povera*. Everything on the walls is white, beige and cream, in contrast to her earlier colourful tent 'Everyone I Have Ever Slept With 1963-1995'.

There are a number of small gouaches and pencil drawings on canvas of naked, scratchy female figures washed with thin layers of watercolour. The influence of Egon Schiele is obvious, as is that of Edvard Munch, but even more than these there lurks the ghost of Joseph Beuys's fragile drawings. Nervy and edgy, they are mostly rather good.

Then there are the larger works based on her drawings, appliquéd or embroidered onto old off-white blankets and bits of sheet (on the whole, though not always, they are done by others). Visually they are rather pleasing with their black-on-cream stitching, their patched lettering and embroidered sperm. She has a good eye and has, as many other women artists have done, reclaimed the craft of sewing, and placed it within the arena of art. The German Prinzhorn collection, shown at the Hayward Gallery in 1996 – obsessive art made by the inmates of mental hospitals – was an inspiration. Her work is unremittingly autobiographical and confessional. She is her sole subject and has become the face of contemporary art in all its provocative 'Hello'-style popularity. The image of "Mad Tracey from Margate", fucking, bawling and masturbating, may have its roots in lived experience, but her hysterical, wanton self-portraits are as much a self-construct as was the persona of the enigmatic Andy Warhol.

Her aesthetic is entirely of our time. She offers up images of her body and her psycho-sexual fantasies with a passion for self-disclosure worthy of any wannabe 'Big Brother' contestant. This is art as therapy with a commercial twist. She presents herself as vulnerable, but is highly manipulative of her audience's sensibilities. Her aphorisms written in her hallmark mirror writing – phrases such as *Is that why you have no friends; You ruined everything* or *I dream of sitting on your face* – offer up to the viewer/voyeur tear-stained solipsisms worthy of any teenage diary.

Her work is a symptom of, rather than a critique on, contemporary life. She has brilliantly commodified a space between high and low culture where the disclosure of personal "trauma" has become the stuff of soap and tabloid, as well as TV arts programmes and the broadsheets. This is art that, if not exactly "lite", is then at least "low fat". She has likened herself to artists such as Frida Kahlo, Louise Bourgeois and Edvard Munch. But whereas these artists universalised from the particular, revealing the complexities – political, psychological and psychoanalytical – of what it means to live in an alienated modern world, Tracy bullies and cajoles us with her texts, whispering insistantly in our ear and telling us what to think, never allowing us the space to feel for ourselves. These works, for all their visual adroitness, for all their energy and strategic artfulness, do not speak of the human condition, but only, ever, about the condition of Tracey.

Tracey Emin
White Cube, Hoxton

The Independent
2nd June 2005

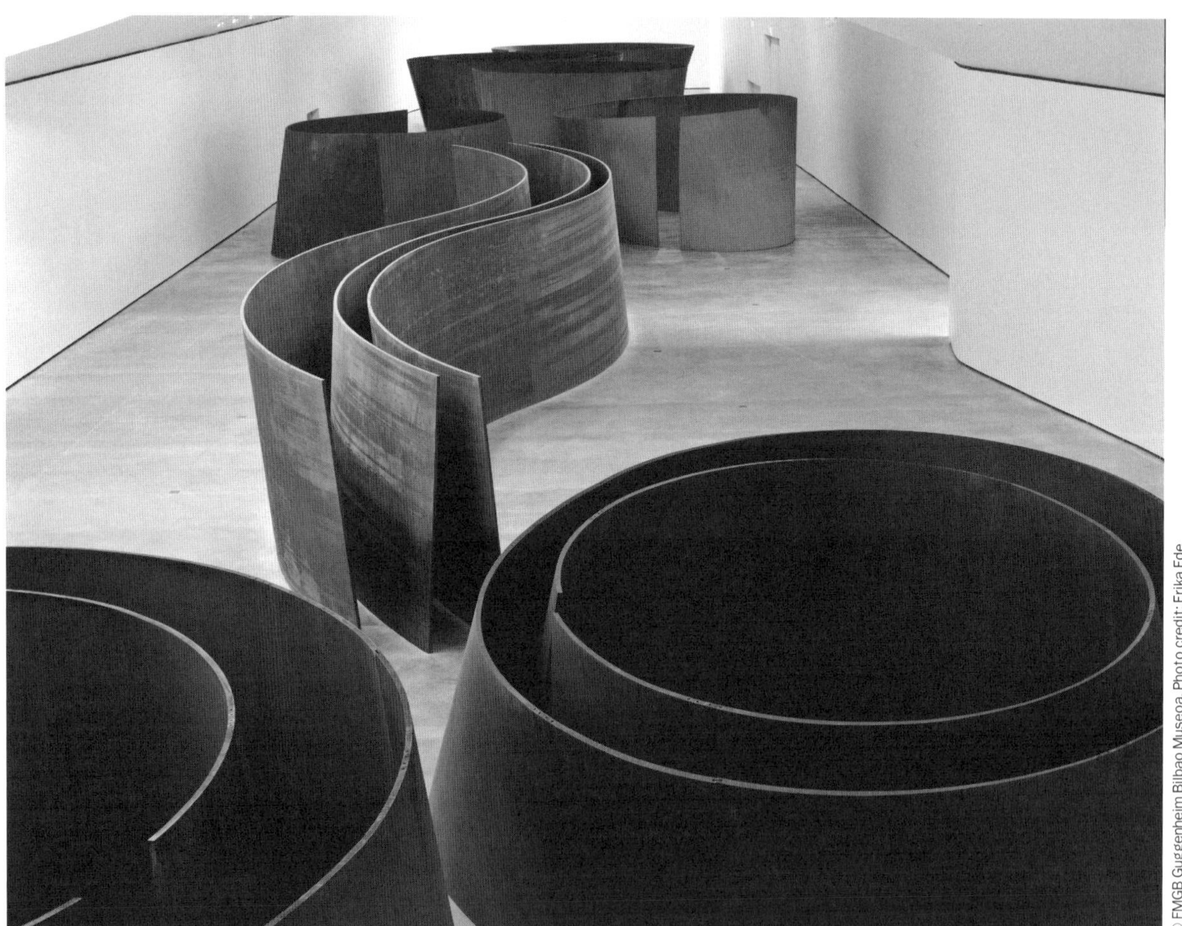

Richard Serra, 'The Matter of Time', installation at Bilbao Guggenheim, *2005*

Richard Serra
The Matter of Time

For the Romantics, wilderness and landscape encapsulated a sense of the Sublime – that mix of terror and wonder at the unpredictability of the natural world. It is not an experience common to most of us within contemporary society. But to walk among the curved and leaning steel walls of Richard Serra's new sculptures at the Guggenheim Museum in Bilbao is to feel something of that sense of atavistic dread and awe – largely excised from modern life – which the 19th-century poets and painters must once have sensed. Perhaps, too, the early 20th-century inhabitants of the great American cities such as New York and Chicago felt something similar amid the new architecture of skyscrapers that so dwarfed the human form.

In the 440-foot-long gallery of Frank Gehry's virtuoso museum, with its shafts of light and titanium "fish-scales", Richard Serra has added seven new large-scale works that join his 'Snake', *1994-1997*, to echo the twists and sinuous curves of the building. The work is of a scale and ambition unrivalled in the history of sculpture. All the pieces share the same vocabulary of topologies. As Serra explains with a series of rapid graphite sketches on his note pad to assembled journalists, the basis of the complicated theory of topology, the mathematical study of surface and direction, is a methodology that creates its own sense of order. Advances in steel making have allowed him to spin out different volumes, voids and passages. The torqued ellipses, spirals and spheres exist in the polarity between the downward forces of gravity. The sculptures are not objects that sit separately in the space, but are interrelated. Though to explain these sculptures in such terms may be of interest to architects or engineers, it gives little idea of the powerful emotional experience they engender in the viewer.

First there is the scale: the sheets of oxidised metal are huge. They bulge, curve and twist to form complex paths, a sort of spiral maze. As you walk between them, they evoke a sense of anxiety. You feel insignificant, lost, disorientated. The walls lean in at unexpected angles and you cannot be sure how long it will take to find the way out as your hollow footfalls echo down the steel passages. Then there is the colour. This is accidental, for Serra does nothing deliberate to the surfaces. But the steel rollers leave abrasions and burnt scars that make the giant metal sheets look like vast abstract paintings. Some are black and coppery, others bright orange, though slowly, over a seven- or eight-year period, they will all oxidise down to a permanent, even, amber.

T. S. Eliot's quotes about time, ends and beginnings come to mind, for 'The Matter of Time' is based on multiple and layered temporalities. It does not suggest a linear narrative; rather it is discontinuous, fragmented, de-centred and disorientating. In this sense, it is a thoroughly Postmodern work, for it does not offer a total vision but perceptual fragments and a multiplicity of views and readings. We can only ever experience it in part. Yet despite its monumental scale, it is neither domineering nor hubristic, and remains open and fluid to interpretation. The discoveries made depend on the time invested in the journey, and on each viewer's emotional and psychological awareness as that journey unfolds.

There is no prescribed way to walk through these pieces. Meaning is activated by the rhythm of the viewer/participator's movements through the space. Each person must negotiate his or her own route, which becomes a metaphysical voyage into the recesses of the self. Serra claims that he can't tell anyone how to look at or experience his work. But moving through these labyrinthine corridors is like entering a cathedral or the chambers of some ancient site such as Knossos. It is as though if one penetrated deep enough, some mystery, something oracular might be revealed.

Richard Serra
The Matter of Time
Guggenheim Museum, Bilbao

The Independent
15th June, 2005

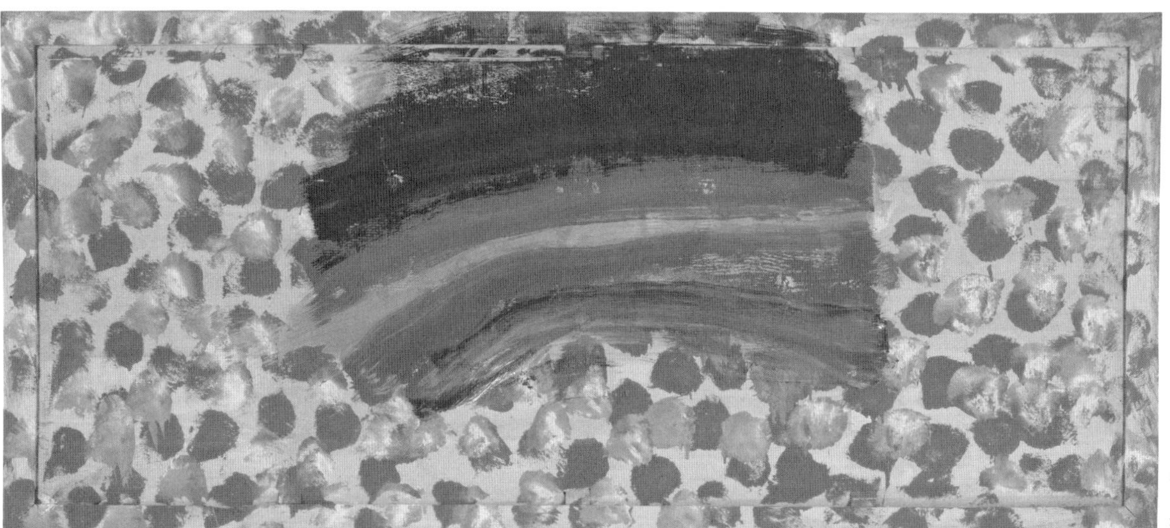

Howard Hodgkin, 'A Rainbow', *2004*

Howard Hodgkin

Of all Charles Baudelaire's poems, it is 'Correspondances', originally published in 'Les Fleurs du Mal' in 1857, that speaks most articulately of what he considered to be the task of the modern painter. It is a poem that particularly illuminates the work of Howard Hodgkin.

Like long-held echoes, blending
  somewhere else
into one deep and shadowy unison
as limitless as darkness and as day
the sounds, the scents, the
  colours correspond.
There are odours succulent as young flesh,
sweet as flutes, and green as any grass
while others – rich, corrupt and masterful –
possess the power of such infinite things
as incense, amber, benjamin and musk,
to praise the senses' raptures and
  the mind's.

I quote the poem at length because it will give those unfamiliar with Hodgkin's paintings an accurate sensual image of his work. The world is both concealed and revealed in his colourful, swooping brush marks, and they show a synaesthetic correspondence between scents, colours, sounds, tastes and tactile sensations.

Tate Britain's landmark Hodgkin retrospective, which opens next month, brings together, for the first time, works spanning his entire career, from the 1950s to the present day. It traces the development of his distinctive visual vocabulary, from early portraits and interiors through to the gradual loosening of his style in recent years. The exhibition offers an insight into the development of his work, demonstrating the qualities that have made him one of the most popular painters of his time with cognoscenti and punters alike.

Hodgkin is a very poetic painter. I do not use the word to mean beautiful, though his paintings, rich in colour as any stained-glass window, are indeed beautiful. He is poetic in that his paintings, like poems, conjure the emotions of a moment, a memory, a place, a smell, even a lover's touch. He paints what eludes verbal expression, concentrating on feelings rather than facts. His paintings are not, however, cathartic outpourings. Only very occasionally in his later work, in a painting such as 'Italy', *1998-2002*, does he come near to true Expressionism. Rather, the residue of feelings is the stuff of his art. Emotion is his fuel but, as Wordsworth remarked of a good poem, it is "emotion recollected in tranquillity".

There are other ways in which these paintings resemble poems. Hodgkin's brush marks have a sense of their own weight and rhythm. His paintings are self-contained worlds; like a poet, he creates framed spaces that are not narratives but where emotion, incident and meaning can occur. In 'Snapshot', *1984-93*, a dark border, which functions like a proscenium arch, directs the eye to a space beyond the picture frame – one that is luminous, pastoral in its suggested forms, yet also inchoate and ecstatic. It conjures many things: a sacred space, a lost domain, a paradise out of reach, or even a mood. All this is articulated with a huge sensual and visual intelligence and an understanding of the materiality of paint. The green here is, as Baudelaire writes, as "green as any grass", while the vibrant yellow orb and the red and purple zones imply the power of "infinite things".

Colour, is, of course, what characterises a Hodgkin painting. Seductive and jewel-like, it is never simply there for its own sake. In this, he belongs to a distinctively European tradition, with the French Post-Impressionists Édouard Vuillard and Pierrre Bonnard, and with Henri Matisse. As Susan Sontag pointed out, he is mindful of the ancient quarrel between Michelangelo's preference for *disegno* over Titian's *colore*. It is as though he wants, she said, "to give *colore* its most sumptuous exclusive victory".

Hodgkin's paintings could not be mistaken for anybody else's. He has created an immediately identifiable choreography of marks, spots and stripes. The harsher, more geometrical forms in his earlier work give way to looser bravura curves and lyrical swirls, which allow him to occupy the border between figuration and abstraction. His titles – 'Haven't We Met?', 'Counting the Days', 'In Central Park' and 'Venice Evening' – read like torch-song titles, and remind us that all his paintings start as an emotional rather than an intellectual response to a situation. There is lovemaking, as depicted in the fecund curve and comma of 'Lovers', *1984-92;* there are dinner parties, India, Italy, gardens and Venetian glass, as well as the small, the incidental and the commonplace, observed in the little grey painting 'Dirty Mirror', *2000.* And there is war.

'Undertones of War', a canvas more than six feet high and eight feet wide, is different from anything else in the exhibition. Bare wood surrounds the painting, as if it had been stripped of all lyricism. The marks are urgent and tortured, truncated rather than flowing; the colours are muted, muddy blues, black and browns with a touch of red. There is an enormous force behind the marks, as if Hodgkin had lost patience with his own visual language. In its looseness and determination to work against his natural virtuosity, it reminds me of late Picasso. It is a potent and tragic statement. There, amid all the brilliant colour, among the sweeping crescendos and diminuendos of red and blue, seems to be Howard Hodgkin's 'Guernica'.

Though 'Undertones of War' suggests a more introverted, questioning and tragic "late" style, the trajectory of the painter's career is not so clear. 'A Rainbow', *2004,* returns us, with its raindrop splodges of green and yellow, to the joy of the sensual.

These paintings speak first to the eye, then to the heart, and finally to the mind. They stir memories of particular times and places, of smells and sounds and emotions. They conjure spring rain, or the partial view of the sea from a window; they suggest rooms where lovers have loved and friends have met. Like poems, they capture the intensity of a moment: what it is to be sentient, erotic, conscious and alive.

Howard Hodgkin
Tate Britain

New Statesman
29th May, 2006

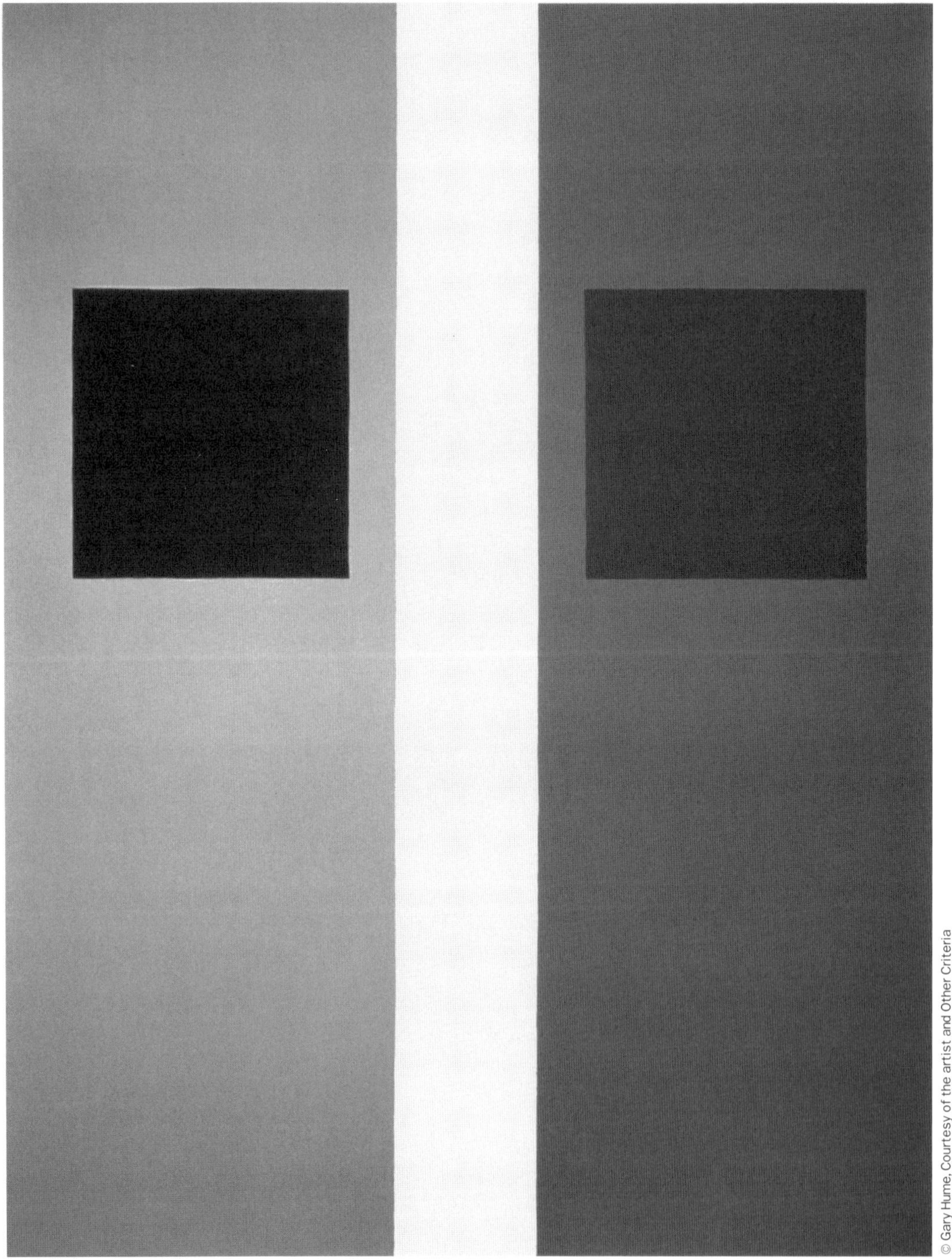

Gary Hume, 'More Fucking Values', *1991*

Dark Matter

In the bright light of the heat wave, amid the sweltering Hoxton streets, the shimmering pavements and the glare of this very un-English summer, I entered White Cube to find, in stark contrast, the cool deep dark of their current exhibition.

The words "black" and "dark" are full of negative connotations. We talk of being in the dark and refer to the Dark Ages and to the Black Death. Darkness is something we fear. For primitive man it was full of dread and terror. The discovery of fire to illuminate the night and throw light on our real and imagined fears was one of humanity's most important achievements. Darkness is not only an absence of light; it also represents a psychic place of non-being and death, and is seen as a symbol of ignorance. We say that we are "blind" to certain facts and that we have "seen the light" when we emerge from a lack of understanding to a place of clarity. We wear funereal black to mark the death of a loved one, while the "dark night of the soul" denotes despair, and mention of the Prince of Darkness evokes Satan.

But the dark carries other meanings. "Dark matter" is the term astronomers came up with to describe invisible expanses between points of visibility. Darkness is enigmatic and ambiguous, a place of deep mystery; it is profound and limitless or, in the words of the poet e e cummings, it is "the wonder that's keeping the stars apart". The primordial point of nothingness, it is also the place out of which being – the Big Bang – emerged and has been described by the theologian Meister Eckhardt as a place of wonder, "the divine dark".

In contemporary art, black has a very particular resonance. In 1915, the Russian painter Kasimir Malevich painted his iconic 'Black Square'. It was a profound and seminal work. The monochromatic surface signified a full stop, for it was a painting that signalled the end of painting, expunging all that was apparently decadent, descriptive and decorative. The ancients so feared God that they were unable to utter his name, and substituted the word *Yahweh*. Malevich's painting suggests that what is truly significant can only be made manifest through the invisible. An over-reliance on sight, on what can be seen and named, the painting implies, will not enlighten us. We have to enter into deeper recesses to achieve understanding. Malevich returns us to the primal dark, to point zero, to the blank sheet at the beginning of time before the manifestation of word and image. Originally hung in the corner of a room like a Russian icon, Malevich's painting suggests polar possibilities – a place of transformation so sacred that it cannot be named, and an emotional emptiness – an incapacity to speak that has come to embody the existential despair of modernity that reflects Estragon's words at the beginning of 'Waiting for Godot': "Nothing to be done".

The American painter Ad Reinhardt saw his own black paintings as apocalyptic. 'Abstract Painting', *1958,* represents the "end of the road", the death of painting. Reinhardt referred to the "dim and dark" Tao, and his painting suggests an internal process of seeing that unfolds slowly in time and demands the kind of focus that changes consciousness.

This deep revealing dark is also present in Hiroshi Sugimoto's luminous black and barely white photograph 'Lake Superior, Cascade River', *1995,* which was taken at night. Here the horizon line is no more than a pale slash shimmering between silky dark water and dark sky. The image carries within its abstract, almost sacred geometry, the implication and possibility of renewal, while the artists who work under the title 'Art and Language' take Malevich's mystical black square and replicate it with their 'Four Suprematist Squares', *1965,* directly onto the wall. Placing it low, near the floor, expunges all sense of mythical presence, and the sublimity of Malevich's painting is reduced to no more than the paint with which the work has been created.

The idea of blank space onto which the imagination or the psyche can project whatever it chooses is suggested in 'Untitled (Party Platform 1980-1992)', *1991.* Here the artist Felix Gonzalez-Torres invites the viewer to remove a sheet of blank black paper from a neat stack. There is a severe puritanical beauty to this Minimal work, which functions as a metaphor for change and loss. Our perceptions are also challenged by Ellsworth Kelly's 'Dark Gray Panel', *1986.* Normally a sublime colourist, Kelly has created a rectangular shape that seems to hover, even to peel, disconcertingly from the wall like a shadow. The physicality of Damian Ortega's formalist construction 'Concrete Cube (black)', *2006,* made up of interlinking blocks, both echoes and recasts the language of Minimalism to speak of the built environment, of construction and architecture. Its separate components suggest the break up and fragmentation of utopian purity.

In contrast, the surface of Damien Hirst's large diamond-shaped painting is anything but still and minimal. Rather, it is as thick and gloopy as tarmac. Move in closer and it turns out to be a graveyard of glued flies trapped in resin. Hirst has always been interested in the cycles of birth and death. 'Infanticide', *2006* reminds us that he is still able to produce visually and philosophically arresting work.

Black's density is emphasised in the velvety matt surface of the German artist Katharina Fritsch's 'St. Katharina'. Reminiscent of that most holy of Roman Catholic icons, the Black Madonna, which has been venerated across Europe for centuries, this tiny plaster cast absorbs the light around it like a Black Hole. Jokingly named after the artist herself, it both wittily and cynically implies that all worship has a solipsistic agenda.

Providing a rare touch of colour, the yellow edges of Gary Hume's painting 'Black Door with Sash', *2006,* come as a surprise within this monochromatic landscape. Based on his earlier hospital-door series, this emblematic and abstract painting with its shiny gloss paint seems to be the antithesis of the healing dark of Malevich's spiritual painting. For Hume's brittle surface and quickly dashed horizontal slash do not so much suggest hidden depths or the darkness of the void, but impenetrability. Whilst Richard Serra's 'Willie Dixon', *1997,* a rough circle of black *PaintStick* suspended on a white paper ground, suggests cosmic explosions and the compression of energy, even dark matter itself. It is both a microcosmic cell and the expanding macrocosmic universe. The radiating fans of black paint, like the folds of some gorgeous Issey Miyake designer dress, recede into deep vanishing points in Mark Grotjahn's 'Untitled (Black Butterfly Dioxide Purple MPG 05)' causing the light to travel over the ridges and indentations of the painting's surface.

Other works, such as Andy Warhol's 'One Gray/Black Marilyn', Cerith Wyn Evans' neon text, and Gavin Turk's painted bronze black bin bag really don't sit so comfortably within the metaphysical context of the show, appearing to have been included only because they refer in some way to darkness or blackness. Their function is that of celebrity guests whom the host has asked along to swell the party (just so long as they wear black).

Summer shows in commercial spaces are all too often made up of old work by gallery artists hauled from the basement. This exhibition makes a refreshing change in its seriousness and exploration of the boundary between the black void as spiritual metaphor, and darkness as a symbol of negativity and death. As Wassily Kandinsky wrote in 'On the Spiritual in Art' in 1912: "black has an inner sound of nothing bereft of possibilities, a dead nothingness as if the sun had become extinct, an eternal silence without future, without hope". Though as Malevich and Reinhardt understood, black can, perhaps, be more usefully seen as a place of ambiguity, a space that symbolises what is both nihilistic and futile, whilst also suggesting the possibility of spiritual purity and renewal.

The void, Mark Levy writes in 'Void in Art', "can be directly experienced in the gap between thoughts". To make a black painting is, therefore, to strive in the Buddhist sense towards nothing; to enter into a luminous darkness, where, if we stand still, what is mysterious might be revealed.

Dark Matter
White Cube

The Independent
7th August, 2006

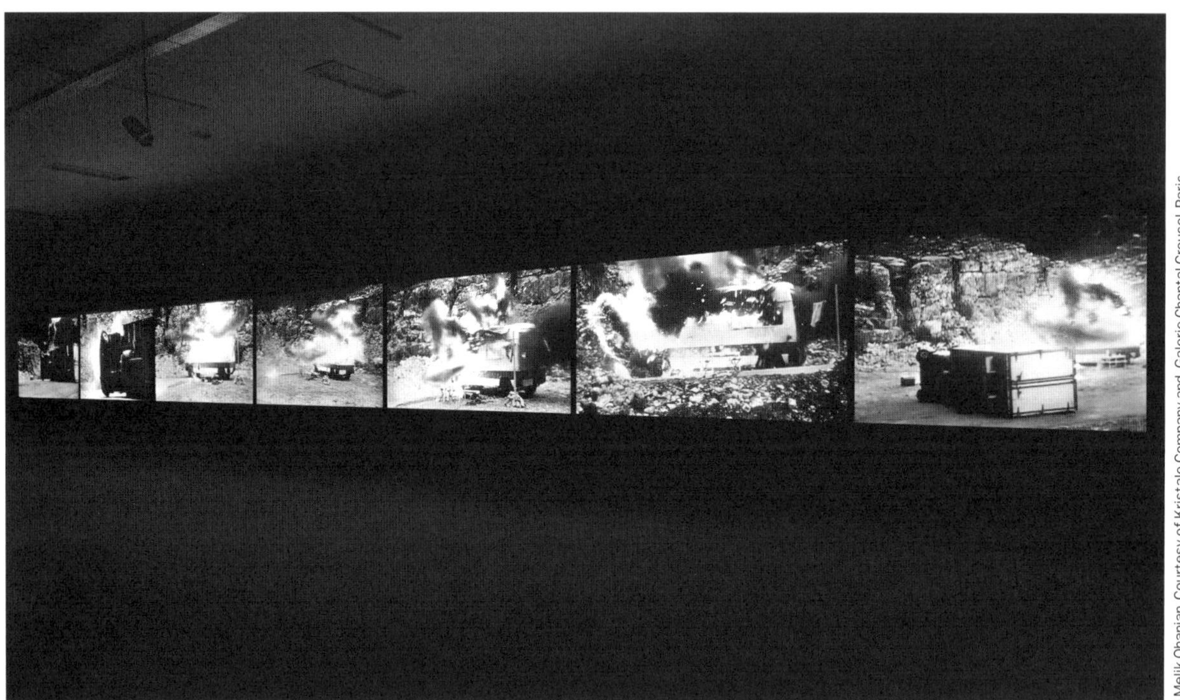

Melik Ohanian, 'Seven Minutes Before', *2004*

Melik Ohanian
Seven Minutes Before

A faint light glimmers at the end of a long tunnel. There is a sense that we are passing through a transformative space as we emerge into a high valley (so the voice-over tells us) in the Vercors Mountains in southern France. A stream babbles over rocks, an oriental girl plays a haunting melody on a stringed *koto*, a lone wolf howls in a cage and a camp-fire burns within the walls of a derelict stone farm building. These are some of the images that appear on the seven screens of the French-Armenian artist Melik Ohanian's epic video installation 'Seven Minutes Before' at the South London Gallery.

With a background in documentary film-making and cinema, Ohanian makes implicit reference to cinema, contemporary art, music and cosmology, attempting to bring together apparently disparate images into a dramatic, cohesive whole. Located in a pristine Alpine landscape, apparently untouched for centuries, the "narrative" is framed by two enigmatic events. The film starts with an account of the death of 43 grazing horses found crushed at the bottom of a steep cliff, while the final sequence presents a double accident: a white van being hit by a motor bike that zooms in from a side turning, and further down the road, a camper van that explodes. There is no explanation for any of this, but the two incidents act as book-ends to the images that arrive and dissolve on the screens in front of us.

'Seven Minutes Before' does not attempt to construct a linear narrative, rather provoking a mood that is both poetic and philosophical, demanding the total involvement of the viewer to construct a meaning. The elemental images that involve fire, water, earth and rock unfold as if in a dream. A lit window shines from a lime-washed sheepfold, a bird of prey sits chained to a falconer's glove, strings of lights twinkle in a field and large white sheets, pinned to a clothes line, stretch across the valley to form a fabric wall. There are fireworks and an Armenian musician dancing in the road.

The road is the spine of the film. Even though events don't happen sequentially, the road provides an implicit structure so that, as viewers, we feel part of some symbolic journey. Perspectives are blurred, as is our sense of time. What seems linear is continuously disrupted to suggest alternative possibilities and roads less taken. The result is a palimpsest woven from a multiplicity of events and elements. The seven trajectories through the valley are all meticulously plotted, but the overall feel is of something fluid and arbitrary. The central thesis emerges as an investigation into time and space, memory and history, which attempts "to map the possible coordinates of the new spatial paradigm that is taking shape before our eyes – and which the film allegorizes". This refers to current debates in physics and information technology that alert us

to the compression and acceleration of time.
The film also acknowledges our desire to
understand the scope of historical time
and grasp something of the life of the
entire universe. The latest thinking in
contemporary astrophysics, along with the
political and socio-anthropological analysis
of globalisation, has led us away from the
idea of the world as a homogeneous, organic
whole. An alternative model is implied in
Ohanian's favoured term "cosmogram",
which suggests a paradoxical idea of the
cosmos, one of different scales, where events
occur, not so much within linear time, but
within the same space.

If modernity is about rupture and endings
– the end of the world and the theme of
endless arrival – as well as about the loss of
unity and signification, then 'Seven Minutes
Before' is a film that debates complex
questions about what it means to exist in
time and space, and asks which story exactly
is the one that should be told.

Melik Ohanian
Seven Minutes Before
South London Gallery

The Independent
1st December, 2006

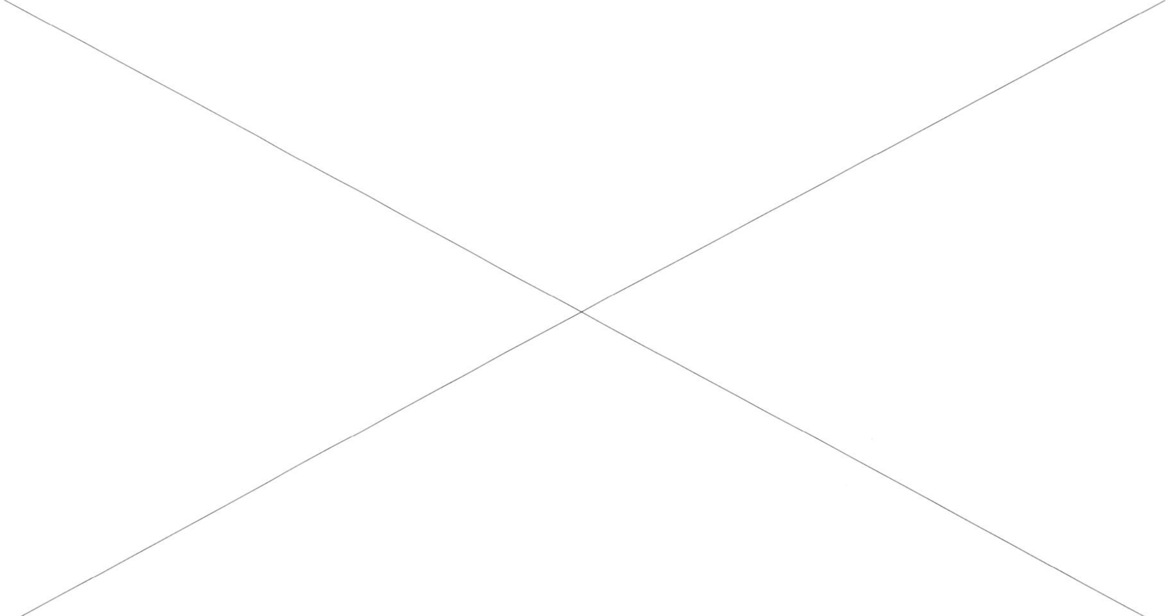

Gilbert & George

Gilbert & George are well known for dressing in suits that make them look like a pair of tailor's dummies from a Burton's shop window display, *circa* 1963 – the year Philip Larkin claimed sexual intercourse was invented. Now I come to think of it, George looks rather *like* Philip Larkin and, no doubt, with their love of Mrs T and all things scatological, they would have got on rather well. Perhaps they could have extended their act to Gilbert & George and Philip – it has a certain ring, I think you'll agree. They are also famous for being gay; for living in an 18th-century house in Fournier Street, Spitalfields, which they moved into as students when the place was a slum and which is now worth mega-bucks; for not having a kitchen and eating the same meals every day in local cafes; for being polite and charming to journalists; and for never saying what they really mean or (probably) ever meaning what they say. But most of all they are known for their relish in *épatent le bourgeois.* It is the armature on which their very lucrative artistic careers have been built.

And now they have a major retrospective at Tate Modern. We know it is a "Major Exhibition" because that is what they have called it. And yes, I did say Tate Modern, for British artists, on the whole, are not meant to show there, but rather at Tate Britain. But Gilbert & George wanted the cathedral halls of Tate Modern and that is what Gilbert & George got: two whole wings of the place. The work goes on for miles.

They have been called fascist and disgusting and many other things besides by those shocked by the vast, stained-glass-window-effect photographs littered with giant turds, sputum, spunk, blood and a smattering of pretty gay boys of various hues. And, of course, that's what they love; because then they can say that the press has it in for them, that they are misunderstood, outsider artists who make "ART FOR ALL", work that can be appreciated by any East-End Tom, Dick or Harry down in the spit-and-sawdust local, and that has nothing to do with the effete, elitist bourgeois art to be found in Cork Street or the Royal Academy. Certainly, the work these two produce shows "everyday" life, including drinking, graffiti and rent boys, as well as a close relationship with their own bums and bodily fluids.

The exhibition begins with a large pastoral five-part "charcoal-on-paper sculpture" (a large drawing to you and me), in mood part Janet-and-John illustration, part Shell-Guide nostalgia, where they have written "WE BELIEVE THAT LOVE is the PATH for a better WORLD of ART in which GOOD & BAD GIVE WAY for GILBERT and GEORGE TO BE". The children of Andy Warhol, they cleverly understand that irony, enigma and self-promotion are the true subjects of late 20th-century art. In 1969, they drew up a manifesto entitled 'The Laws of Sculptors', which reads:

1. Always be smartly dressed, well groomed relaxed and friendly polite

and in complete control.

2. Make the world to believe in you and
   to pay heavily for this privilege.
3. Never worry, assess, discuss or criticise
   but remain quiet respectful and calm.
4. The lord chisels still, so don't leave
   your bench for long.

So how did it all begin? George Passmore
was born in Plymouth in 1942, while Gilbert
Proesch (the short one who doesn't look like
Philip Larkin) was born near Venice in 1943.
Neither came from a privileged background,
though they each managed to get to St.
Martin's College of Art to study sculpture
just at a time when European art was
regaining some parity with the dominant
American scene, and conceptual art was
rearing its head against a background of
political upheaval and ideology. That
high-water mark of change in the late 1960s
saw a re-examination not only of how
society was structured, but a discussion
as to the very purpose and function of art.
Partly due to "French theory", including
writers such as Roland Barthes, everything
from paintings to objects, from creative
practices to sites, and even people
themselves, became legible as "texts". In
short, the practices and philosophy of
Modernism – high minded, spiritual
and utopian – were being filleted on
the surgeon's table. It was against this
background that Gilbert & George presented
themselves as "Living Sculptures" in their
performance – part Flanagan & Allen, part
Vladimir and Estragon – 'Underneath the
Arches'. The photographs taken in Railway
Arch, No. 8, Cable Street, E1 encapsulate
a number of themes: an iconoclastic
identification with the outcast, a linking
with a specific locality of London, and a
particular Englishness that runs through
their work. This joint performance would
provide them with their signature for the
next 30 years. From then on, they would
become the subject of their art, and
drinking, violence, gay culture, racism and
the decayed and graffiti-scrawled East-End

streets around their home would form the
backdrop. They used the building in which
they live and work in Fournier Street to
present themselves in 'Dusty Corners', *1975,*
like characters out of a Sunday-afternoon
black-and-white B movie. The piece is
evocative, even poetic in an 'Old Curiosity
Shop' sort of way. But it was 'Coming', *1975,*
a series of nine black-and white-photos of
them in insouciant poses, their fingers
loosely held in a provocative V, amid pools
of spilt beer (or spunk) that was to point
the direction of their later art.

Since then, straight photographs have given
way to slick, technicolour photomontages
that hover somewhere between cartoons
and Gothic pastiche about copulation,
coprophilia, death and religion, in which
the run-down inner-city urban space
becomes a sort of solipsistic prelapsarian
gay playground in which they feature as the
main players. To some extent, they are the
Joe Ortons of the art world, only without his
wit. For it is hard to take seriously a work
like 'Shitty Naked Human World', *1994,*
showing a crucifix made of four brown
turds, or 'Spit Law', *1997,* where they are
bent over, baggy Y-fronts crumpled around
their ankles, revealing their bum holes to the
viewer, without being reminded of small
boys behind the bike shed who think they
are being ever so smutty when, in fact, they
are being simply boring. Gilbert & George
want us to be shocked, but they'd be rather
less happy if they knew that all some of us
feel is *ennui.*

And then there is God, or the kitschy
trappings of religion, which for them act as
a dressing-up box of signs from crucifix to
blood, from ecstasy to Islam, without a jot
of religion's doubt or philosophical
questioning. Even their recent works about
the London bombings seem like cynical
appropriations, for theirs is solipsistic world
where there are no women, old people or
even children, no one but them and their
cast of beautiful boys. Yet the catalogue

would have us believe that their art is a sort of expansive humanitarian enterprise, one that illustrates human frailty and involves a process of "unremitting self-exploration and self-exposure, not out of self-importance or vanity… but as an example to others of the necessity for a fully examined life".

The case is also made for their multi-cultural inclusivity, evidence of which is cited by the number of black and brown youths used in their photos. But this smacks of the sort of sexual exoticisation and essentialism complained of by critics such as Edward Said (in a slightly different context) in his celebrated work 'Orientalism'. If these were images of women made by heterosexual men, would we react differently? Gilbert & George's work is not objectionable because it is crude, raw, or in our faces. Many paintings by Picasso are cruel and ugly, and Surrealism, demonstrated by the likes of Salvador Dali or Luis Buñuel, frequently relishes what is profane and degraded. For as Georges Bataille wrote: "Intellectual despair culminates neither in cowardice nor in dreaming, but in violence". In Gilbert & George's case, however, there is the suspicion that with their fat bank accounts, their building-society-manager suits, their international reputations supported by the sycophancy of much of the art world, there is nothing real behind these works, no vituperative anger, no despair, no existential doubt, no love or passion – nothing, in fact, that makes art a meaningful and important human activity. That we accept this as great art worthy of half of Tate Modern shows how lacking in confidence we have become about insisting that art *should* actually show what is painful, true and meaningful, and that we should not simply be fobbed off by these ersatz commodified versions. Oddly, it is the sealed, glossy sanitisation of these works that makes them objectionable, and not their supposed iconoclastic content, so that walking through room after room of this hubristic stuff I was reminded of W. B. Yeats' famous lines:

"The best lack all conviction, while the worst Are full of passionate intensity".

Gilbert & George
Tate Modern

The New Statesman
26th February, 2007

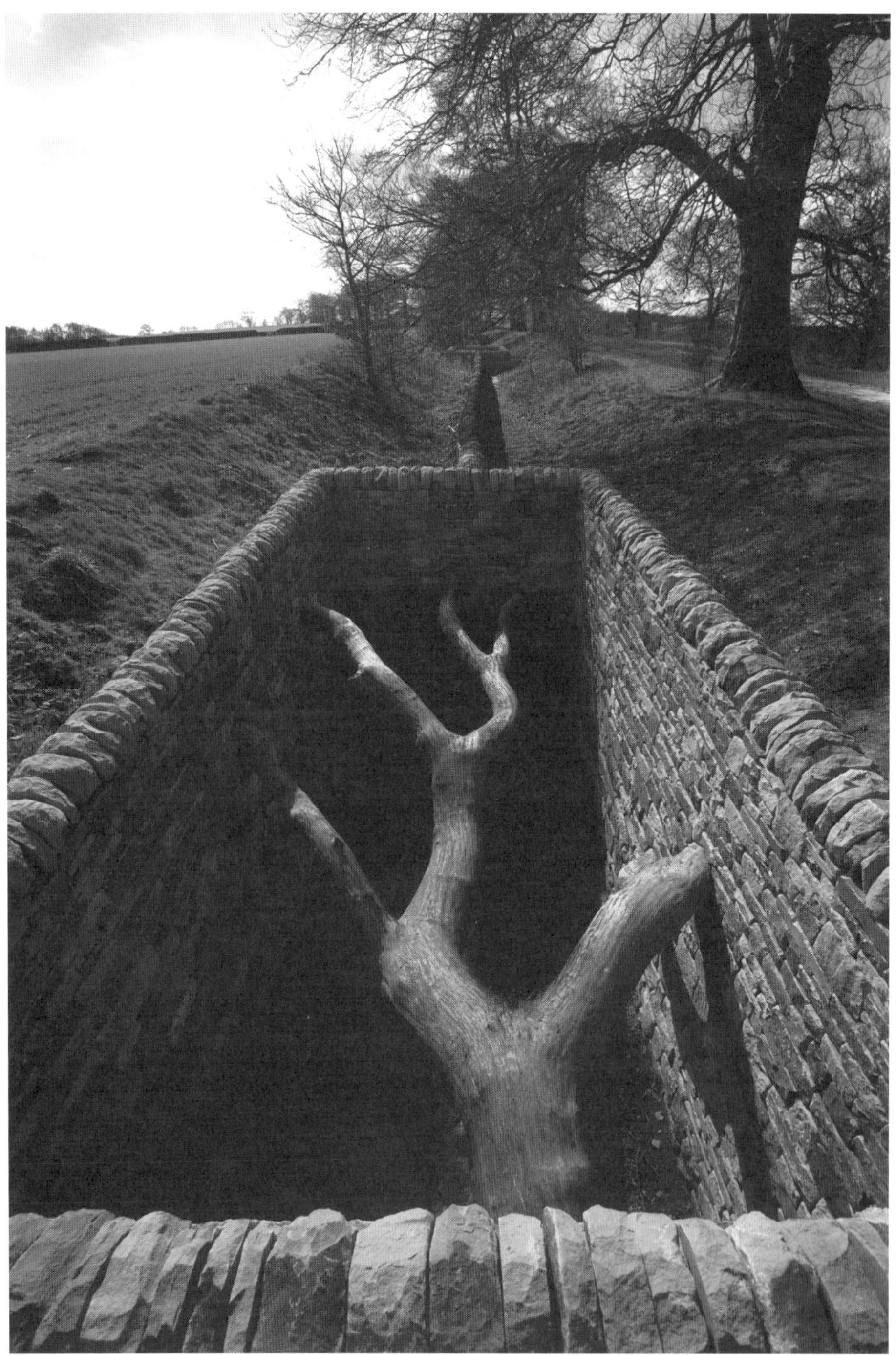

Andy Goldsworthy, 'Hanging Trees', *2006*

Andy Goldsworthy

The rural landscape has a deep hold on the English psyche; in some profound way it defines who we are. In Yorkshire, the field formations and patterns of drystone walling reveal generations of human intervention, of working and husbanding the land. What to the uninitiated urban eye may seem merely picturesque has evolved through years of toil. Forestry has shaped the woodland, while the hooves of grazing sheep, or those corralled for dipping and shearing, have sculpted the contours. Drovers' roads and footpaths crisscross the dales and hills to leave their trace of historic activity. The cycles of birth, copulation and death are the very mulch of this terrain.

Mud, stone, wood, clay, hair and blood – these are the elements used by the artist Andy Goldsworthy in the works that form the most ambitious project ever curated by Yorkshire Sculpture Park, to celebrate its 30th anniversary. Best known for the photographs of his ephemeral constructs made from snow and ice, leaves and twigs, that some have criticised for their seductive decorative qualities, these new works underline his chthonic relationship with the landscape. This is no idealised tea-towel imagery of the countryside. The work is harsh and raw. It speaks of the violence of nature, of the cycles of death, putrefaction and renewal, with an uncompromising elemental beauty. For Goldsworthy is to environmental art what Ted Hughes is to poetry.

I find him, when I visit, high on a platform in one of the Underground Galleries. His first comment on spotting me is "bollocks". This does not denote rudeness, indicating rather the degree of physical involvement he has in the construction of his work. For, with an assistant, he is lifting a heavy pole, a length of coppiced sweet chestnut cropped from a Kent woodland, to finish the roof of his yurt-like structure, 'Wood Room', where the smell of newly cut chestnut is all pervasive. Standing inside is like being in a dark womb. This forms part of a series of installations that move from darkness to light. On entering the galleries, I have to squeeze past 'Stacked Oak', a cone-shaped stack made from locally felled branches, which have been interlaced so they are held up by their own weight and bulk. Next is 'Stone Room', filled with 11 Yorkshire sandstone domes (apart from the coppiced chestnut, all materials for the exhibition have been sourced locally). The low beehive forms, constructed by the same method used to build drystone walls, have had holes cut in the centre to reveal dark circular voids. Cones and holes are a recurrent theme, as are the concepts of inside and outside, with all their attendant metaphorical resonances. To stand amid this stony hush is like being in a burial chamber for the ancient dead.

For 'Clay Room', tonnes of clay were dug from the grounds of the sculpture park, then dried, sieved and mixed with human hair and applied to the walls by a mass of volunteers. Andy Goldsworthy tells me that some of the volunteers felt quite threatened by the hair. "Though the piece was driven, not by metaphor, but by physical demands", he adds. The fine filaments, just visible in the cracks, are revealed like the secrets of an archaeological dig, and bind the mud as it splits to leave an intricate crazed pattern. Powerfully evocative in its Minimal elegance, the work suggests timelines and maps, human craft and endeavour, death and renewal. There is a potent melancholy to the piece, which is in complete contrast to the atmosphere of light and air in the final work, 'Leaf Stalk Room'. Here, horse-chestnut leaf stalks gathered from trees around the park have been pinned together with blackthorns to create what looks like an ethereal ecclesiastical screen. Constructed to form a central void – a void that tacitly poses any number of philosophical and theological questions – the slender twigs seem to float in a weightless evocation of Zen calligraphy.

When Andy Goldsworthy finally climbs off his platform, we meet in the project room, where by a happy accident the "paintings" I most want to see, but that have not yet been installed in the gallery, are leaning against the walls in their bubble wrap. These "blood drawings", 'Hare, Blood and Snow', form a triptych. Driving home one night in the twilight, he hit a hare. Upset, he went back to collect it with a view to cooking it for his supper. "When I skinned it I was surprised by the amount of blood – after all it's the blood that gives the richness to that traditional dish of jugged hair". Later he mixed the blood with snow, which he stuffed into the hare's stomach, hanging it in the pantry where the melting liquid dripped from the mouth and nostrils onto sheets of paper. The subsequent trail suggests sanguineous droplets of newly shot game in fresh snow, while, on another sheet, a dark pooled mess leaches from the central stain with the pale ethereality of the Turin Shroud.

Conceptually and visually powerful, these are modern-day versions of 17th-century Dutch *vanitas* paintings, which remind us of our mortality. When I suggest the piece resonates with religious references – death, blood and renewal – Goldsworthy does not demur. But he is not happy giving interpretations of his work. A smallish, wiry man in his 50s with thick grey hair and a tattoo on his arm, he looks more like a gardener than an artist, and prefers, he says, to let his images speak for themselves. What is important is to reclaim the landscape from the sentimental and the pastoral. The countryside is not an idyll – a backdrop for the weekend activities of jaded urbanites – but a harsh and brutal place formed by a working relationship with the land.

The cycles and uses of a working landscape are reflected in 'Sheep Paintings', some of which were made in Dumfriesshire, where he lives. They look like classic Minimalist pieces, although they were made entirely from the hoof prints and sheep droppings of animals moving across the surface of the spread canvas to reach a central salt-lick, which, on its removal, created a clear circular void. When I entered the gallery, I was assaulted by the stink of cow dung being enthusiastically painted by students in a serpentine coil onto the large window that looks over the fields – fields that, Goldsworthy points out, would not be so luxuriant without the cows' excrement.

Goldsworthy's work has its roots in "land art", that genre which began in 1960s America, challenging the supremacy of the museum and gallery along with the prevailing hegemony of Abstract Expressionism. It was the riposte of artists such as Robert Smithson and Nancy Holt to the anodyne decorum of the gallery and the growing commodification of art. Land art was democratic as well as hands-on, and fitted Goldsworthy's temperament exactly, for although he studied art, he had beem a farm labourer since he was 13.

In the grounds of the park, he has made a number of pieces that feel as if they are hardly "art" at all. In the centre of a newly constructed stone sheep pen is another enclosure containing a huge flat wedge of sandstone. Visitors are encouraged to spreadeagle on the block in the rain to create "rain shadows" – transitory imprints of the human form, which are then photographed. As with the new commission 'Hanging Trees', a triptych of walled enclosures created from the original ha-ha in the park's landscaped gardens where three felled oaks stripped of their bark have been suspended like the bleached bones of skeletons, these works suggest ancient burial chambers and the relationship of the human body to the landscape. Archaeology, local history, the ethic of work, all are implied in these powerful, yet surprisingly modest, interventions. "A good piece of work has intense clarity and truth and somehow makes sense of why you are here", says Goldsworthy. "You must never lose sight of that. The work is a journey, a reflection about your life and its connections. I think of Matisse in old age, with his brush on a stick, and Rembrandt's late self-portraits".

British landscape artists such as Andy Goldsworthy, David Nash and Richard Long tend to be seen – despite their obvious wide appeal and international success – as some sort of latter-day 60s renegades working on the parochial margins far from the cynical chic of the London art scene. Yet never has there been a time when their work was more resonant, as the planet warms and traditional landscapes are destroyed. There is something inspirational in this Ruskinian devotion to the skills of handling wood and stone, to the crafts of stone walling and forestry that are fast dying out in rural life. There is the suspicion, too, that among the art establishment, Goldsworthy's work is viewed as too metaphysical, too lyrical and unapologetically moral, for this is not an age that feels comfortable with truth and the stench of dung and death, but is happier

with the ersatz and the simulacrum. After all, he deals with the big questions: those of mortality, memory, history and our place in the fast-disappearing natural world.

Andy Goldsworthy
Yorkshire Sculpture Park

New Statesman
2nd April, 2007

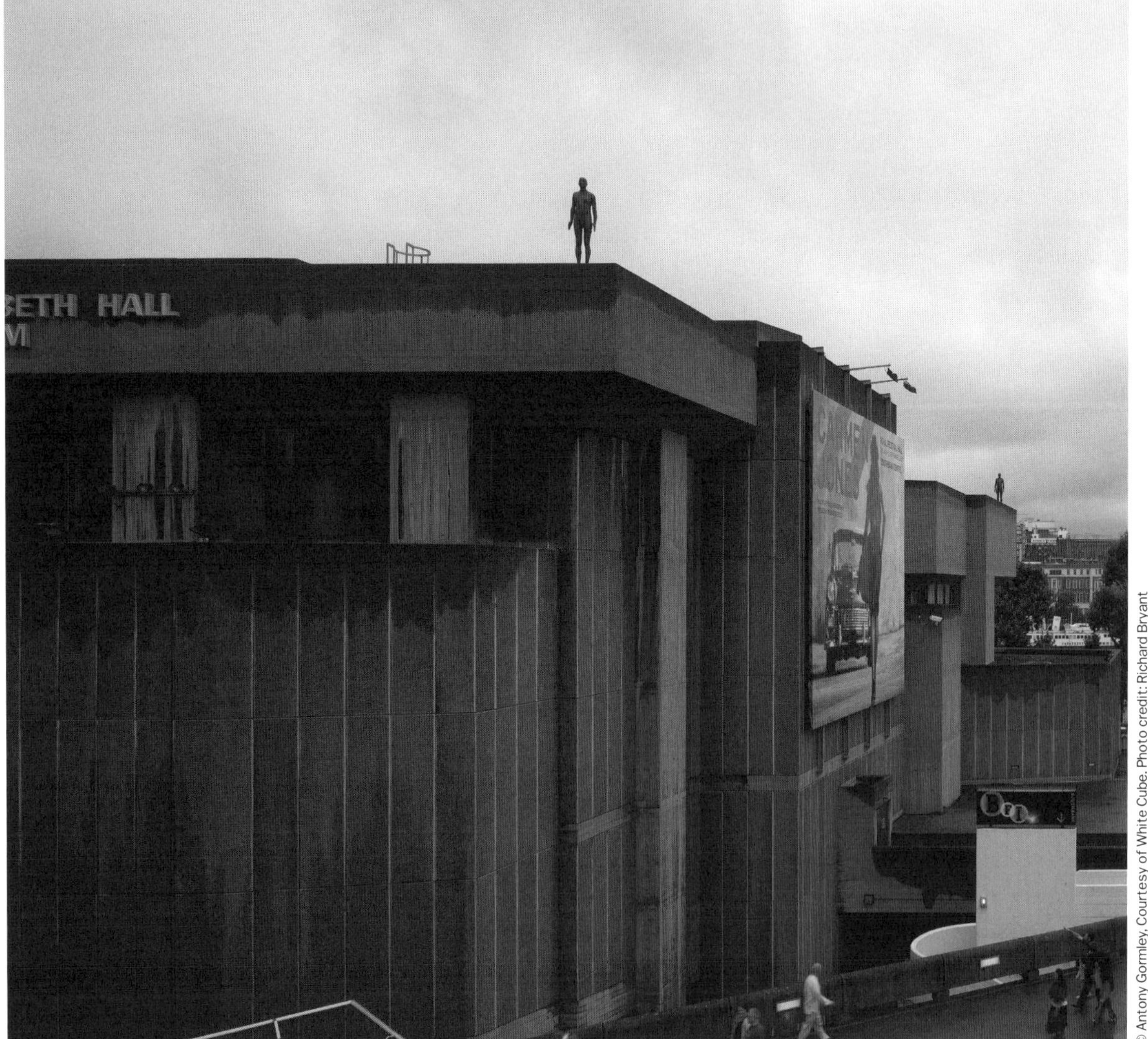

Antony Gormley, 'Event Horizon', *2007*

Antony Gormley
Blind Light

I have a confession – I've never been a big fan of Antony Gormley's work. 'Angel of the North' has always seemed a rather bombastic affair to me, more authoritarian logo than resonant artwork – populist, perhaps, but rather vulgar. It was not until 'Another Place', the group of figures looking out to sea set on Crosby beach like a cluster of wistful emigrants, that I began to feel some sense of insightful vulnerability about his work. So it was with uncertain expectations that I went along to the unveiling of 'Blind Light', described as "one of the most exciting and ambitious exhibitions of recent years" and the first major London show of Gormley's work for 25.

And when I got there, what did I find? Well it's certainly ambitious. For the art extends from the confines of the gallery out into the streets, walkways and rooftops of the city. One of the figures, a cast taken from his own body, stands naked and unashamed not far from the bus stop on Waterloo Bridge as if waiting for the number 4 – as I walked past, a group of teenagers was standing in the rain making jokes about its willy – while 31 others are poised like lookouts on both sides of the river on buildings as far flung as the Thistle Hotel, Charing Cross Station and the Union Jack Club.

Gormley is ubiquitous, and the effect is disquieting, like being watched by silent snipers or surveillance snoopers. These foreign bodies insinuate themselves within the cityscape, sitting on the skyline so the city appears reduced to the scale of a model. They certainly make us look at London with a totally fresh eye. Yet there is something inert about them, for they never quite achieve the edgy, existential vulnerability of those other figures created by the late Juan Muñoz in his Tate Turbine Hall installation 'Double Blind', which must surely have been an influence on Gormley.

Even before you enter the gallery, these sentinel forms signal his themes. Taking the body as his point of departure, Gormley explores how we orientate ourselves within the built environment and architectural space. He also seems to be asking questions about who the audience is, and who it is who's doing the watching, thereby suggesting that art is not something autonomous, simply to be observed by passive onlookers, but dependent on the interrelationship with the viewers, who become an integral part as they walk through it, and navigate and negotiate the spaces around it. Gormley has said he prefers the word "body" to "figure", wanting, no doubt, to distance himself from the figure within traditional figurative art. For these featureless incarnations appear to stand for something more universal. They are not individuals, and though their origins are unique, they can be endlessly reproduced.

Inside the Hayward, Gormley has mixed old works with new. Tilted precariously on its side is 'Space Station', a 27-tonne structure that looks like a gargantuan *Meccano* model, the sort boys made when Gormley was growing up. Full of peepholes into the interior void, it is a dark labyrinth, a prison-like space evocative of the vertiginous planes of Piranesi, though you can't help but think of a giant colander. It's only when you look down from a higher level that it becomes obvious that its genesis was a curled foetal figure. Dependent on the conceit of a small thing – a body – being made into a large thing, which itself is a metaphor for an even larger thing – a city – its apparent cleverness set me thinking about the fashion for gargantuan sculpture such as Anish Kapoor's 'Marsyas' or Louise Bourgeois' 'Spider', and I wondered too, why big increasingly seems to equate with beautiful, or at least innovative, recalling that some of the most powerful sculptures I've ever experienced are Giacometti's tiny evocative post-war figures.

'Space Station' is lit only by the glow from 'Blind Light', which, like 'Space Station', was newly commissioned for this show. Constantin Brancusi said that "architecture is inhabited sculpture", and 'Blind Light', a luminous glass room filled with dense cloud, seems to embody that. For from the outside, those who enter the vaporous space completely disappear, to become visible only as traces on the glass walls like the shadows in Plato's cave. While on the inside, the discombobulated viewer is entirely enveloped within the bright light and cloud. Architecture is supposed to give a sense of security, to be a refuge from the elements, but 'Blind Light' undermines all such notions by bringing the outside inside, so that being within is like being lost in a thick mist on the top of a mountain. Thus immersed, the viewer becomes an integral part of the work.

In another gallery stand the 300 sarcophagus-like life-sized concrete blocks of 'Allotment II', all derived from the actual

dimensions of citizens from the age of one and a half to 80 years, from Malmö in Sweden. Massed together, with apertures for the mouth, ears, anus and genitals, yet completely blind, they form intimate and moving relational groups. The grid structure also suggests a city with its high-rise buildings and, as I was standing looking down their serried ranks, the graves of the dead from the Great War.

Upstairs there are examples of Gormley's early works such as a rather droll piece made from slices of bread with a central figure cut into the middle, and the 'Matrices and Expansions' from 2006-07 – bodies made of steel rods and tubes that seem like fluid drawings in space. Actually, these are very beautiful, but still rather uninvolved, for there is something too calculated about them (literally, for they must have been generated on a computer) that is rather distancing. Then there is 'Hatch', a small built room, where a maze of aluminium rods of different lengths creates the illusion of solid divisions, but from which the body feels in constant peril of being spiked. To peer down the tubes also gives a kaleidoscopic view of other surrounding bodies.

And do I like Gormley any better than before? Well, a bit. It's hard not to be impressed by his grand aspirations, and sympathetic to his earnest intentions, for no one could accuse him of Postmodern indifference or ennui. But to make and install this work, with its ambitions of scale, must have cost a pretty penny or two, and at the end of the day I still remained curiously unmoved. For I kept thinking of the modesty and power of those tiny Giacometti figures, and how less, so very often, really is more.

Anthony Gormley
Blind Light
Hayward Gallery

The New Statesman
28th May, 2007

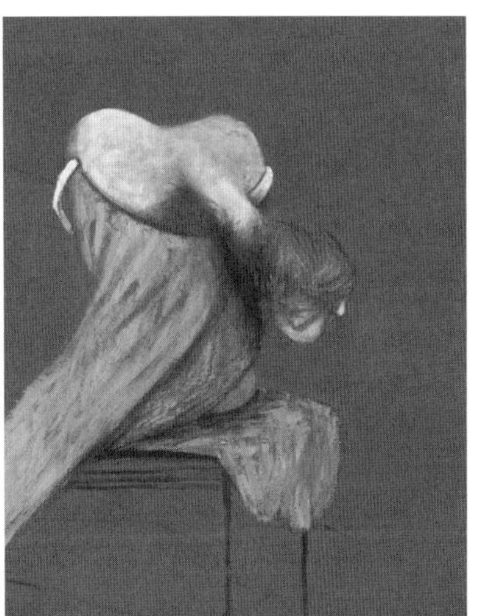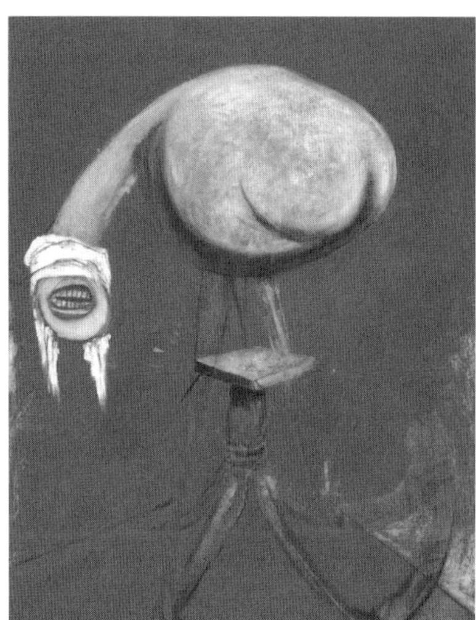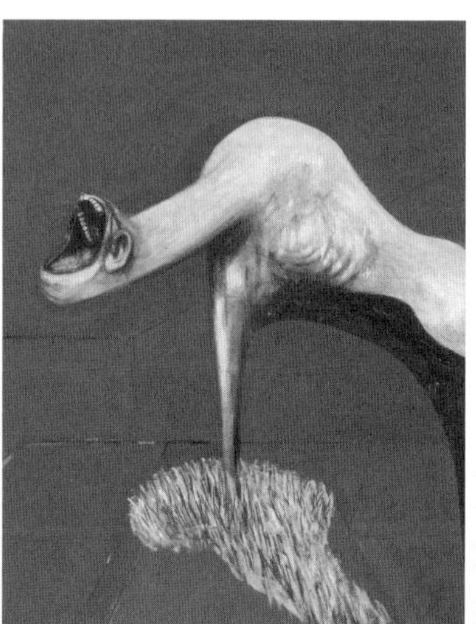

Francis Bacon, 'Study for Figure at the Base of a Crucifixion', *1944*

Francis Bacon
Three Studies for Figures at the Base of a Crucifixion, 1944

Francis Bacon's 'Three Studies for Figures at the Base of a Crucifixion' were painted over the course of two weeks in 1944 in his ground floor flat at 7 Cromwell Place, South Kensington, which had once been the studio of the artist John Everett Millais. During the day, the converted billiard room served as Bacon's studio, at night as an illicit casino. He recalled that, at the time, he was drinking heavily, painting in an alcoholic haze. Later he was to admit that he hardly knew what he was doing, though he believed that alcohol had loosened his style. Yet, despite this unpromising genesis, the triptych of three writhing, anthropomorphic figures, with featureless, scarcely human faces contorted into what might be either pain or exquisite ecstasy, set against a background of visceral oranges, reds and blacks, marks a watershed in British painting.

While Bacon had been painting the crucifixion since 1933, commissioned by his then patron Eric Hall, he considered these works unsuccessful and destroyed them, for a while abandoning painting. When he did return to the subject 11 years later, he was influenced by his reading of Aeschylus's savage drama 'The Oresteia' (itself a trilogy), which tells the tale of the curse of the House of Atreus and the pursuit, by the avenging Furies or Eumenides, of those responsible for murder. The 'Three Studies' is generally considered to be Bacon's first masterwork, and he was at some pains to suppress the showing of any paintings that pre-date it.

Executed in oil and pastel and, for economy, on light *Sundeala* boards rather than canvas, Bacon's Eumenides are barely recognisable as human figures, for they have no eyes, but only gaping, silently screaming mouths. The creature on the left, seated on a table of sorts, is the most recognisably human. Partially draped in a length of cloth, this bent form with its hunched white shoulders, its stumpy thalidomide arms and bowed head topped with a mop of dark hair, might be a mourner at some unnamed wake. While the figure in the central panel, with its grimacing mouth set directly into its elongated neck, is blindfolded by a white cloth – a motif taken, perhaps, from Matthias Grünewald's 'The Mocking of Christ' – and resembles some large flightless bird. The figure on the right appears to have most of its upper face missing. Its head is thrown back, its mouth stretched open to reveal its teeth as if in the grips of some bestial orgasmic spasm. The heads of all three figures point downwards, following a series of converging lines that radiate out from the central plinth, and imply a room or an enclosed space. The mood is one of bleak isolation and violent angst. This work is to painting what Sartre's 'Huis Clos' is to literature: a peon to existential despair. And this is also a crucifixion with a difference, for there is no evidence, not even a shadow, of the actual event. No trace of Christ or his cross, though Bacon did say in a letter in 1959 that 'Three Studies' was "intended to [be] use[d] at the base of a large crucifixion which I may still do". Yet how genuine this remark was is hard to gauge from this bleakly nihilistic non-believer who once said, "I think of life as meaningless; but we give it meaning during our own existence…" and "we are born and we die, but in between we give this purposeless existence a meaning by our drives".

Distortion and fragmentation are the tools that Bacon uses to explore these elemental states, for he is at enormous pains to eradicate what he sees as any figurative illustration. What he wants to convey is something visceral, a presence beyond mere likeness, beings controlled by chthonic urges and base instincts, the Dionysian Calibans of human existence rather than the Apollonian Ariels; his territory is what Freud would have called the Id.

The sense of futility that Bacon was trying to capture is not surprising given that it was 1944, and rumours of the death camps had already begun to leak out. Such nihilism is also present in much of the work of T. S. Eliot. Bacon had come to know Aeschylus through Eliot's 1939 play, 'The Family Reunion', in which the central character, Harry, is haunted by "the sleepless hunters/ that will not let me sleep". Here, the Furies embody the guilt and remorse felt by Harry, who harbours a dark family secret. Like many other artists and writers of the early 20th century, Bacon had read Nietzsche and shared something of his hypothesis of "a strong pessimism". He had been particularly attracted to 'The Birth of Tragedy', Nietzsche's passionate rejection of Christianity, and his affirmation for life resonated with Bacon who claimed: "… you can be optimistic and totally without hope. One's basic nature is totally without hope, and yet one's nervous system is made out of optimistic stuff". The American critic, historian and philosopher Donald Kuspit considers Bacon's figures to be "sick with death – not necessarily literal death, but rather the feeling of being nothing". Their

loneliness, he suggests, depicts a "general sense of oblivion".

Bacon had always been fascinated with images of the mouth, particularly the diseased mouth, after he found a second-hand book in which a number of these were illustrated in a series of coloured plates. He spoke of "the glitter and colour that comes from the mouth", and said that he "always hoped in a sense to be able to paint the mouth like Monet painted a sunset". He was also taken with a photograph by the Surrealist Jacques-André Boiffard in the radical magazine 'Documents' in which the editor, the French writer and philosopher of the abject Georges Bataille, had written a short text on 'La Bouche'. Bataille rejected traditional literature, arguing that the ultimate aim of all intellectual, artistic or religious activity should be the annihilation of the rational individual in a violent, transcendental act of communion. For Bacon, as for Bataille, the open, gaping, screaming wound of the mouth expressed something of our most intense emotional experiences, bringing us closer to our bestial selves. The linking of the noble and the base, of man and beast, so as to blur the distinction between them, was part of Bataille's attack on the "idealist deception" that man practices upon himself. The open mouth of Bacon's right-hand figure ends in a savage snarling snout of teeth. For the promiscuously gay and sado-masochistically inclined Bacon, the mouth had obvious sexual connotations. He was also, almost certainly, thinking of the scene in 'Battleship Potemkin' where the wounded nursemaid stands screaming on the Odessa steps, as well as making reference to the despairing mother in Nicolas Poussin's 'Massacre of the Innocents'.

First shown at the Lefevre Gallery in 1945, the triptych caused a sensation. The critic John Russell was shocked by "images so unrelievedly awful that the mind shut with a snap at the sight of them. Their anatomy was half-human, half-animal..." Yet by 1971, he was able to write, "there was painting in England before the 'Three Studies', and painting after them, and no one… can confuse the two". More than 60 years later, they have not lost any of their power.

Francis Bacon
Three Studies for Figures at
the Base of a Crucifixion, 1944
Tate Gallery

The Independent
31st August, 2007

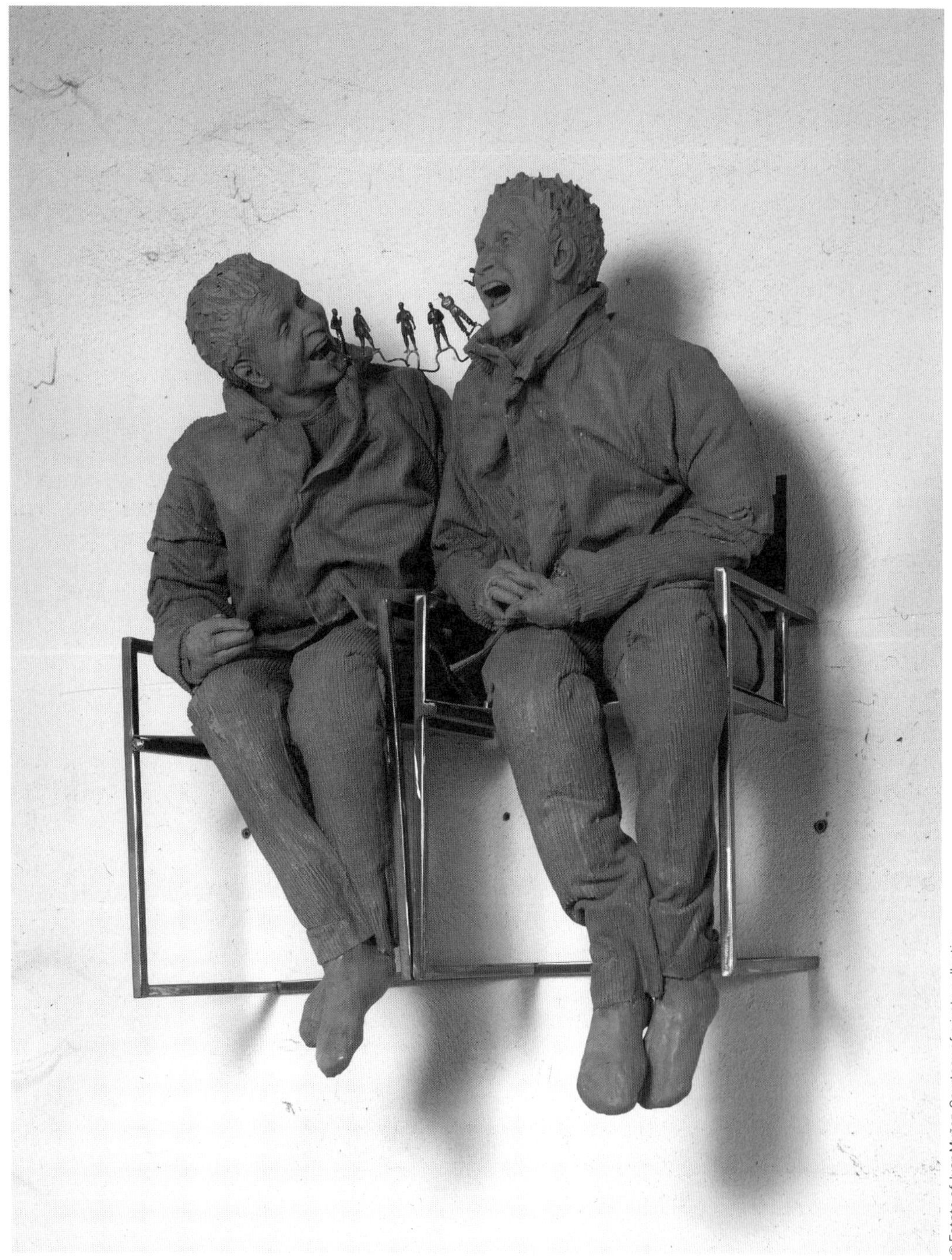

Juan Muñoz, 'Two Seated on the Wall', *2000*

Juan Muñoz
A Retrospective

A small, stooped, grey figure stands absorbed by his own reflection in a mirror at the gallery's edge. It is as if he's trying to assure himself that he exists. Reflection reflects reflection in an infinite series of regressions that blur the boundaries between illusion and reality. Preoccupied by this alienating act we, as observers, can only watch fascinated and excluded. For the sculptor Juan Muñoz, philosophical questions about the nature of the self, about time and the slippages between fact and fiction, run like a connecting stitch through all his diverse works.

Muñoz was the most significant Spanish sculptor to emerge after Franco's death in 1975, though much of his artistic education was acquired in New York and London where, for a time, he worked as a dishwasher. Best known for his powerful dystopian cityscape 'Double Blind', created in the Tate's Turbine Hall in 2001, Muñoz was just setting out on his sculptural career when it was brought to an untimely end by his sudden death at the age of 48 later the same year. 'Double Blind', with its false floors, its ambiguous levels and shadowy, half-glimpsed grey men going about their arcane business that seemed at once both boringly bureaucratic yet redolent with malice and threat, was the apotheosis of his short but substantial career.

It was an appropriate swan song for Muñoz, whose work was always concerned with architecture and the illusions of space. Architectural details such as lifts and handrails litter the gallery. Lilliputian metal staircases lead nowhere, while typical Spanish balconies are set high on the gallery wall beside a metal sign identifing a *Hotel* that manifestly has no rooms and no guests. Muñoz was significant among his generation of sculptors, who tended to be concerned predominantly with the language of art and materials. For, whilst never interested in "representational" art, he happily reintroduced the figure to act as both cipher and philosophical sign, and was as much influenced by the literature of Joseph Conrad, Günter Grass and T. S. Eliot, as he was by the work of Velásquez, Picasso, Bacon, Robert Smithson and Thomas Schütte.

Theatre was also an abiding influence, particularly the work of Samuel Beckett and Luigi Pirandello. In his 'Raincoat Drawings' he created large white chalk drawings on black gabardine of spare, often formally furnished, rooms that look like storyboards for old Hollywood films. All are devoid of human presence. A squashed sofa cushion, a half-open door into a long lit hall, evoke the absence of those who only moments before inhabited these spaces. They are places of silence and enigma, scenes pregnant with what is not there. Like Pirandello's famous characters in search of an author, these are locations in search of characters. Rooms become stage sets in which the Beckett-like failures of human life are played out. The silence becomes an existential hell, not quite of other people, as for Sartre in 'Huit Clos', but of silence and the impossibility of speech and meaning. His series of disembodied mouth drawings not only evoke Beckett's 'Not I' – where a disembodied mouth placed in a pitch-black space illuminated only by a single beam of light speaks, but says nothing – but also the silent screams of Bacon's popes.

Acrobats, mannequins, ballerinas without legs whose wobbly lower hemispheres reflect the floor of the room in which they are trapped, and dwarfs and ventriloquists' dummies, all provided Muños with his cast of characters: outsiders rendered mute or impotent in this Borgesian game of life. The dwarf, influenced by the Infanta Margarita's young maid of honour in Velásquez's 'Las Meninas', is a constant figure, and not only recalls the protagonist from Günter Grass's 'The Tin Drum' but the jester, the fool and the savant of Shakespeare. In 'The Wasteland' (the title is taken from Eliot's poem), a tiny ventriloquist's dummy sits on a metal shelf above a floor covered in a sea of complex marquetry. Unable to speak, he seems to be waiting for his master to come and give him a voice – a master who we, with our modern sensibilities, know is never, any more than Godot did for the waiting Estragon and Vladimir, likely to come. In 'The Prompter', a small dwarf stands in a prompter's box in front of an empty stage of black-and-white geometric tiles that create an optical illusion reminiscent of the floors of great Baroque houses. At the far end is a drum. If we peer into the prompter's box, we see that not only does the dwarf have no eyes, but he possesses no text. Both drum and prompter are mute – the drum waiting for a drummer, the prompter waiting for actors or a script. Both reflect Beckett's sentiments that human beings have the urge and imperative to express thoughts and emotions, but are forever unable to find the means. This sense of the impossibility of

communication is also played out in the large group of not-quite-life-size Chinese figures, all of whom gesture and smile the same enigmatic smile while frozen, like the characters on Keats's famous Grecian urn, in a timeless act of silence.

Muñoz died suddenly and shockingly on August 28th 2001, just months after the installation in the Tate of 'Double Blind'. And his loss? Well, without his existential and humanistic vision, the contemporary art world seems just that bit more glib and self-satisfied. Who knows what he would have gone on to make if he'd reached his full maturity, for here is an artist unafraid of the big questions, of what it means to strive to remain an individual in today's complex and uncertain world.

Juan Muñoz
A Retrospective
Tate Modern

New Statesman
14th February, 2008

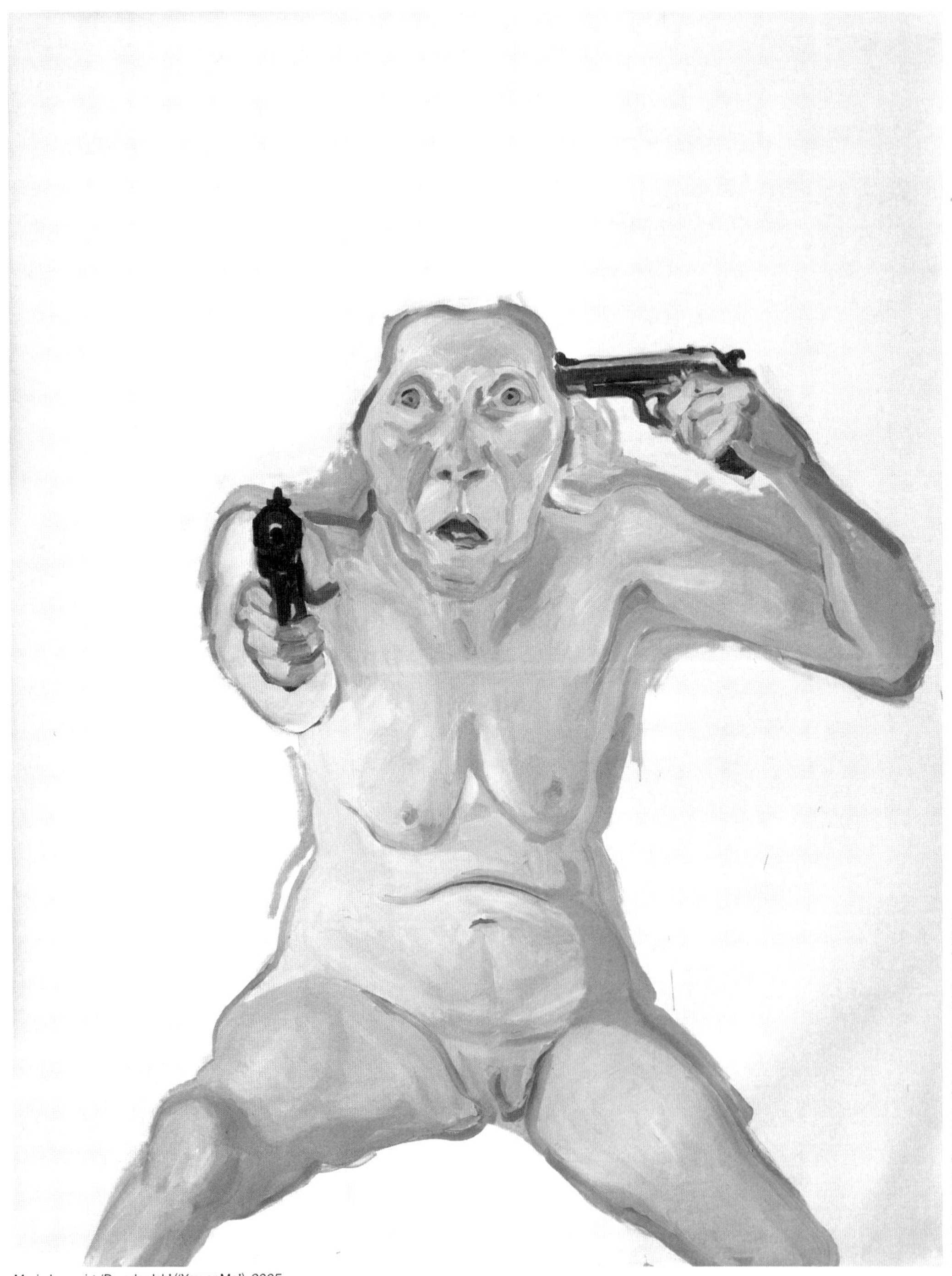

Maria Lassnig, 'Du oder Ich' ('You or Me'), *2005*

Maria Lassnig

Surviving into old age is a good career move for the creative woman. You may have been ignored during your middle years, but if you just hang on in there, you might be "discovered" and make it big. Never mind that you have been there all along just doing what you do. "Isn't she wonderful?" "Isn't it amazing?" the subtext will go, "Not only is she not dribbling in the corner, but she is even making new and challenging work". Think of Louise Bourgeois or the writer Mary Wesley, who both entered the public consciousness well beyond the age when they had collected their first bus pass. Now the Austrian artist Maria Lassnig, who is in her 90s, is having her first solo show in this country at the Serpentine.

As you enter the gallery, you are met by her naked self-portrait. Her green eyes pierce like bullets and her ageing body displays a bald, child-like pudendum. In one hand she holds a gun at her head, whilst pointing another point-blank at us, the viewers. It is quite a greeting, as if she is saying that we must accept these paintings on her terms, or one of us will cop it.

Arriving to meet her, I get a feisty message that she is in the middle of something and I will have to wait. I hang around, keeping an eye out for a little old lady, and fail to identify her in her polo shirt and trainers – she looks a good 20 years younger. It's hard to believe that she was born in Carinthia, Austria, in 1919, and has been producing these edgy, confrontational paintings for 60 years. Bleak, full of cruelty and implicit self-loathing, she appears in them over and over again. There are stumpy women without arms, like the torsos of thalidomide victims, and strangely morphed bodies with snubbed noses and pig-like tails, reminiscent of Paula Rego's early paintings of angry cabbages and murderous monkeys, set against an acid-yellow ground. In one, she is all Bacon-like open mouth and crooked teeth, blinded by a cooking pot that she wears on her head like a soldier's tin helmet, as if implying that she has seen more than her fair share of psychological battles. There is so much apparent pain here that if it were not for their flashes of humour and tenderness, these paintings would seem pathological.

She has coined the phrase "body-awareness paintings" to describe the visual language created to illustrate the sensations experienced from within, though it is hard to discern where physical sensation and psychological effect begin and end. "There are too few words," she has said, "and that is why I draw". When I ask if she ever suffered from an eating disorder – there is a large painting entitled 'Madonna of the Pastries', where she sits, a saggy nude, in front of an array of creamy gateaux – she dismisses the question, yet these uncomfortable paintings seem to embody the raw anxiety and trauma that so many women project onto their bodies.

She has had an interesting life. Trained in Vienna, she went to Paris on a scholarship in 1951 and met Paul Celan and André Breton, who brought her into contact with Surrealism. From 1968 to 1980, she lived in New York, where she made inventive, wacky animations on the complexities of relationships and her experience of being a woman artist, a number of which are on show here. On her return to Austria in 1980, she became the first female professor of painting in a German-speaking country.

And now, since this is being written just after the case was revealed of 73-year-old Josef Fritzl, who kept his daughter captive in a cellar for 24 years in an Austrian suburb, where she bore him seven children, the painting of a fat man crouched naked over a rag-doll of a child takes on a particularly disturbing resonance. 'The Illegitimate Bride', with her blank, backlit face and pendulous breasts, half hidden beneath a veil of stiff plastic, also suggests something potentially awful, while 'Spell' and 'The Power of Fate', where Lassnig painted models messing around in the cellar of her house wrapping themselves in clear plastic, imply something tainted and subterranean. Stark and often set in the middle of an empty canvas, her figures seem to float in their own space without reference to any wider world. "Background", she has said, "creates mood and atmosphere, and I don't need that".

Her models are from her region of rural Carinthia. 'Adam and Eve in Underwear' – where the pair might be embracing, or about to strangle each other – are her local priest and his girlfriend. Often, when painting herself, she lies on the floor beside the canvas as if looking into a mirror – daughter and mother of herself. Brides are a constant theme – most look sad – veiled and cut off from the world, separated from the connection sought in the act of marriage.

In many ways, Lassnig's work is totally idiosyncratic – a personal mix of dark humour and vulnerability – but there are links to Wols' paintings with their child-like influences and curious metamorphoses, as well as to the transmutations of Dorothea Tanning and Leonora Carrington. Alice Neel's Expressionist palette and Marlene Dumas's vulnerable exhibitionism also come to mind. Expressive, raw, and crude, Lassnig uses her bravura colour with consummate skill to construct her virtuoso figures.

Like Louise Bourgeois and Frida Kahlo, or the poets Sylvia Plath and Anne Sexton, she has mined the depths of her vulnerability to make art. There is nothing false, nothing done here for effect. Raw and real, you can almost hear her paintings scream.

Maria Lassnig
Serpentine Gallery

New Statesman
15th May, 2008

Shirazeh Houshiary, 'Breath', *2004*

Shirazeh Houshiary
Through Breath

"In the beginning was the Word, and the Word was with God and the Word was God", declares the first line of the Gospel According to St. John. The *Logos* was considered the highest manifestation of God, who, invisible, communicated with Man through divine language rather than visual form. But for the Iranian artist Shirazeh Houshiary, the Word, rather than being an incarnation of God as deity, is mantra – the starting point of a journey that leads through meditation to a visual realisation that is an evocation of the essence of all life. Houshiary makes religious art for an irreligious age, avoiding the symbols of specific creed and dogma. Her process is ruminative; there is a sense of a reaching towards something fragile, something tentative, rather than of the arrival at somewhere absolute. Using Sufi incantations or *zikr,* she creates monochromatic webs of light and dark, shadows and stillness based on the inhalation and exhalation of breath. "I set out to capture my breath, to find the essence of my experience", she has said, by "transcending name, nationality, cultures".

Placing the canvas on the floor, she "choreographs" her paintings by obsessively repeating a sacred word. In a devotional process of restrained calligraphic gestures, the visual coherence and linguistic meaning of the word dissolve to form a ghostly web of intricate white marks against a black ground. These interlaced loops, emphasised by the weave of the canvas, evoke many things: the veil worn by Muslim women, the Turin shroud, or the veil of St. Veronica, a fugitive trace of breath on garment or glass. Their resonance is poetic, suggestive. The shadow or imprint they leave appears like the afterglow of some emanation. Physical experience coalesces; seeing, hearing and feeling fuse into what the poet T. S. Eliot called, in 'The Dry Salvages', "the point of intersection of the timeless".

Houshiary's work is shaped by the experience of having been an exile for more than 20 years from her homeland, Iran. Hers is an Asian sensibility melded with a liberal western education. But her subject matter is broader than that of mere cultural or geographic displacement, for what she suggests is the sense of yearning within all human kind, the longing to find a place where "the past and future/are conquered, and reconciled," to quote Eliot again. As with all exiles, she is searching for a home. But that home is not simply material, but spiritual. In these minimal abstractions that pay homage to western painters such as Kasimir Malevich and Mark Rothko, she also appropriates a sensibility borrowed from an oriental culture where there is no figurative imagery, and where what is sacred is carried through the mysticism of the calligraphic mark. For a number of western artists, the model of calligraphy as gesture and somatic trace became an expressive end in itself, as in the mark-making of the French artist Henri Michaux in the 1920s. Resonant within these performative gestures was drawing and painting's relationship to the body. Through its physical manifestation, the mark was liberated from both code and symbol. This development can be seen in many of the Abstract Expressionists such as Jackson Pollock and Willem de Kooning for whom language – or more precisely writing – allowed for the *possibility* of saying what could not bc said overtly, what was beyond the confines of language. It is to these legacies – both oriental and occidental – that Houshiary aligns herself.

In the darkened room of the upper gallery is a four-part work, 'Breath'. As the viewer approaches the screens, pools of white light dissolve and reform in the blackness like the condensation of warm breath on glass, or a thin veil of material. Incantations emanate from each screen – the *Azan*, the Islamic call to prayer; a choir of Buddhist monks from Japan; a Jewish song to the invisible God; and a composition by the 12th-century Christian mystic Hildegard von Bingen – so faint that they are experienced by the listener/viewer more as a pulse than as specific sound. Yet in the darkened gallery it is well-nigh impossible to distinguish one chant from another – the Moslem from the Christian, the Buddhist from the Jew – reminding a world riven by religious bigotry and hate that the deep rhythms of human spirituality are essentially universal. In the empty space, the almost subliminal sound, along with the cycle of emergence and erasure of light and dark, seems to allude not only to a quest to seek out our divine nature, but also to the expansion and contraction of matter that makes up the very cosmos itself.

Shirazeh Houshiary
Through Breath
Lisson Gallery

The Independent
25th June, 2008

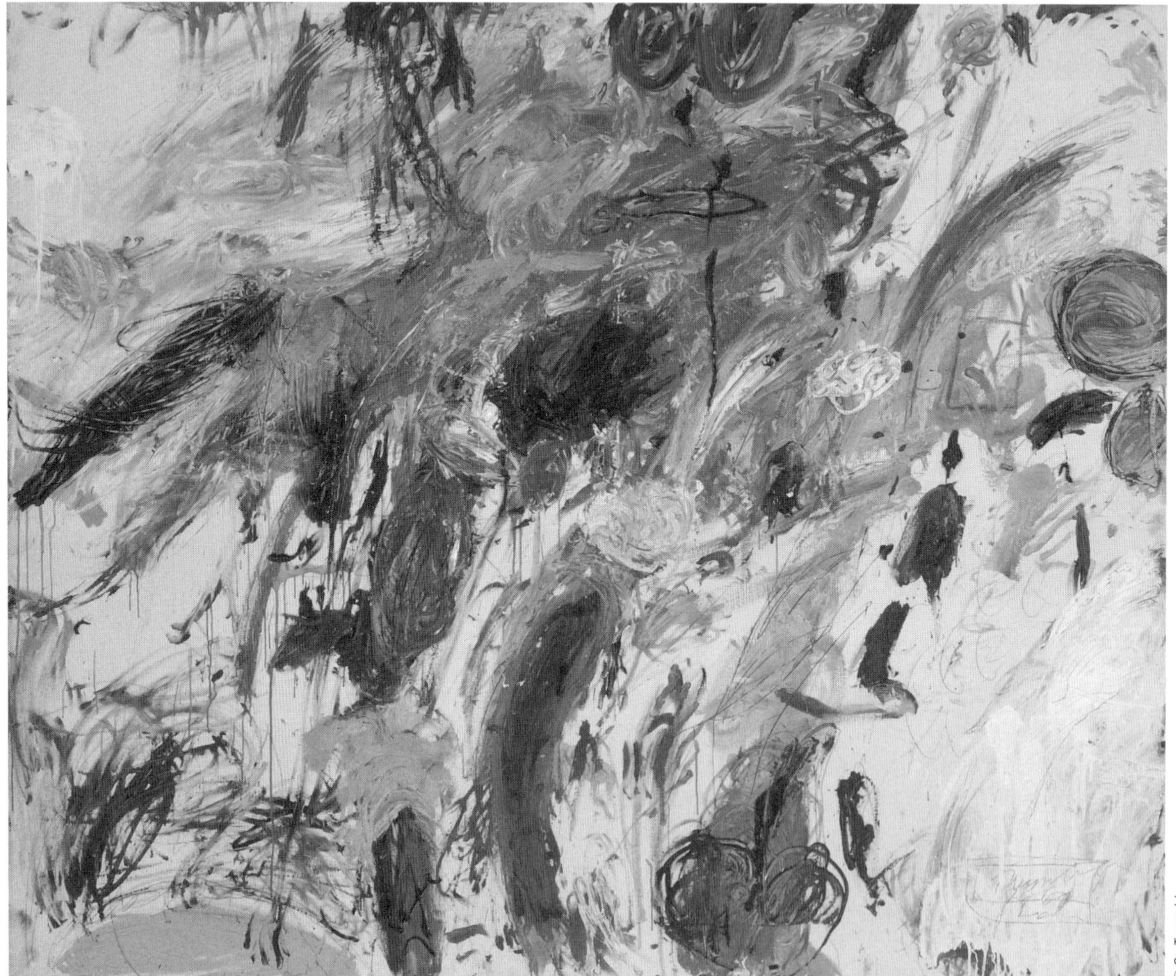

Cy Twombly, 'Ferragosto V', *1961*

Cy Twombly
Cycles and Seasons

In a recent article in 'The Times' Literary Supplement, Terry Eagleton wrote about the similarity between Samuel Beckett's and Theodor Adorno's language. "What is most drastically impoverished in Beckett is language itself," he wrote. "Adorno's style reveals a similar austerity as each phrase is forced to work overtime to earn its keep… Like Beckett's, Adorno's is a language rammed up against silence, a set of guerrilla raids on the inarticulable". For both these writers, the deficiencies and untruths of language had been revealed in the "crazed assurances of Fascism and Stalinism". Language itself had become discredited. Only what was indeterminate could in any way approach the truth, leading to Beckett's much-quoted remark about trying to fail again better. His favourite word, apparently, was "perhaps".

"Perhaps" might also be the favourite word of the American painter Cy Twombly, whose marks and expletives, hand-written quotes and dissolving textural pencil lines, stutter across the surface of his paintings like signs in search of meaning. A form of visual poetry, reminiscent in its arcane mark-making to that of the French artist Henri Micheaux, his appropriation of calligraphy – a point where art and writing become indivisible – creates something new in the interstices between both. Twombly never asserts; rather his paintings are an intuitive exploration. He is frequently described as a "graffiti" artist, but that is too narrow, and speaks simply of a style rather than of philosophical content. Language, and its inherent inability to articulate, is what concerns him, as much as experiments in the application of paint. For Twombly, just as for Beckett, there is a great compulsion to find a means of expression, but an awareness of the near impossibility of doing so. He once said of his work: "It's not described, it's happening… The line is the feeling". And for the French writer and philosopher Julia Kristeva, meaning can only ever be visible in the gaps and margins of the main narratives and prevailing discourses. Twombly's paintings are, essentially, about process, investigation and discovery – hesitant diagrams that attempt to chart intellectual and emotional experience.

"And what is it you do?" Jackson Pollock asked the younger painter on each of the four occasions they met in 1956, when Pollock was considered by many to be the high priest of modern American painting. Twombly's enormous body of work, with its scratches, scribbles and frenetic lines, can now be seen as a subversion of the dominance of Abstract Expressionism and of Pollock's *machismo* loops, drips, and swirls of paint. Here was the artist, not so much as hero, but as errant schoolboy, passing scribbling notes in lessons and writing "fuck" on the school-yard wall. For what Twombly understood was that in the modern world, there could be no dogmatic certainty.

Born in Lexington, Virginia, in 1928, Twombly studied in Boston, and then New York. It was there that he met Robert Rauschenberg at the Art Students' League in 1950. Later, he attended the influential Black Mountain College in North Carolina, where he studied under Franz Kline and Robert Motherwell. A number of things led to his interest in calligraphy, including the influence of Motherwell and that of the Surrealists, with their investigations into automatic writing and the nature of chance, along with his conscription as a cryptographer into the US Army, where he studied and deciphered code.

Influenced by his travels in North Africa, the early paintings in this major exhibition at Tate Modern, such as 'MIN-OE', emphasise a fascination with architectonic forms, as well as classical, archaeological and ethnic artefacts, and show the influence of artists such as Jean Dubuffet and Alberto Giacometti. His untitled sculptures – makeshift bits of wood lashed together with strips of dirty cloth and string – not only look like African fetishes, but show the influence of that guru of detritus, Robert Rauschenberg, with whom Twombly travelled during 1952-53.

In the spring of 1957, Twombly left America and set sail for Italy, leaving the citadel of Modernist painting for a world steeped in ancient mythology, and struggling with the aftermath of war. White and bleached, his paintings from this period are full of the effects of the harsh Mediterranean light. Crammed with classical and poetic references, his series 'Poems to the Sea' – executed in a single day – shows the influence of the poet Stéphane Mallarmé. "Whiteness", Twombly said of these spare, lyrical works that elide calligraphy, poetry and painting, "can be the classic state of the intellect, or a Neo-Romantic area of remembrance". There is an austere purity to all this classical whiteness as his snaking pencil lines, erased by the smears of

white paint, unravel into a syntax of approximate meaning.

Later, when he was working from a studio in the hot summer streets of Rome, in a part of the city frequented by prostitutes and petty thieves, his paintings became more scatological and transgressive with their scribbled genitals and orgasmic ejaculations of paint. His 'Ferragosto' series, named after a Roman fertility festival, seems to leak with putrefaction and overripeness, the canvases smeared with the blood and faeces of some ancient Dionysian rite. As Roland Barthes observed when writing on Twombly, he injected an aspect of the aberrant by "deranging the morality of the body". In contrast, the 'Bolsena' paintings look, with their manic scribble of apparently symbolic signs, their scattered vectors and meaningless measurements, like the crazed workings of some mad scientist who is determined to find order in chaos. Embedded in these works is the feeling that the struggle between opposing forces – reason and chthonic experience, Eros and Thanatos – is never far away.

This frantic sense of working out becomes ever more pared down in his 'Treatise on the Veil'. The initial influence for these huge paintings came from an Eadweard Muybridge photograph that Rauschenberg gave Twombly, which apparently showed a bride passing in front of a train. Finding in the mid-60s that he was being dismissed as outmoded by the *cognoscenti* of the New York Art world, Twombly violently changed trajectory to embrace that archetypal emblem of Modernist painting, the grid, along with more stringent Minimalist forms. Looking like enormous blackboards covered with sparse rectangles that imply some sort of geometric calculation, or even the storyboards for a film, these works stretch across whole walls of the gallery.

A graffito mark, according to the critic Rosland Krauss, is "a registration of absence".

It is the trace that remains as imprint and aftermath, as Jacques Derrida explains in his 'Of Grammatology'. What is left by the presence of the person who has done the tracing is a residue or, as Beckett might have implied, a pregnant silence. In the beautiful and melancholy 'Nini's Painting's', an elegy to the wife of Twombly's Roman gallerist, his tumbling seascapes of swirling marks stutter towards articulation only to dissolve into the incoherence of grief. In contrast, the rich reds and dark blues and greens, the thick impasto and rolling brush marks of his 1980s paintings of the sea, based on the legend of Hero and Leandro, seem to return to Turneresque experimentation of the expressive possibilities of paint. This watery theme is taken up in the astonishing suite of nine green paintings produced for the 1988 Italian Pavilion at the Venice Biennale, which seem to fuse Monet, Abstract Expressionism and the Baroque in an almost mimetic evocation of the watery canals of Venice, with their deep dark shadows cast by the crumbling Renaissance palaces.

Towards the end of the exhibition is the cycle 'The Four Seasons', painted in Twombly's mid 60s, which, in its intensity, explodes like a great choral work, assaulting the senses with its sensual colour and scribbled fragments from the poets Rainer Maria Rilke and Giorgios Seferis. The two series, each comprising four great paintings from the 1990s, one from the Tate collection and one from MoMA, New York, have been reunited here for the first time. But nothing quite prepares for the shock of the last room with its orgiastic swirls of red paint that loop and ooze across the canvas like the blood from some debauched Bacchanalian sacrifice. From the near silences of Cy Twombly's early monochromatic works, where marks stutter towards meaning and articulation, the exhibition ends with a great crescendo of euphoric, orgiastic and frenzied release.

Cy Twombly
Cycles and Seasons
Tate Modern

New Statesman
26th June, 2008

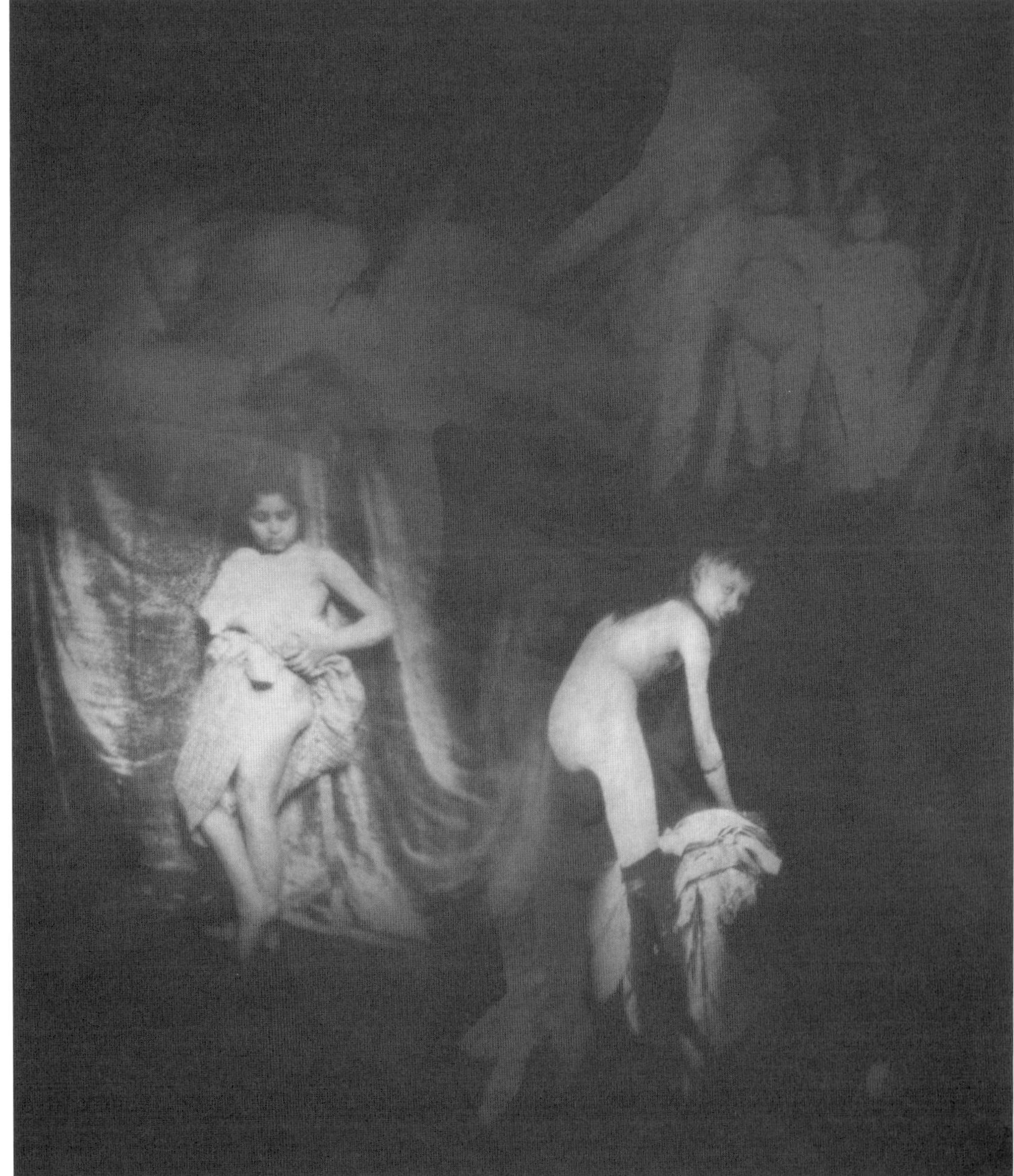

Mat Collishaw, 'Shooting Stars', *2008*

Mat Collishaw
Shooting Stars

After Freud, the world could never look the same, for we are all too aware of the worm in the apple. Myths and fairytales cannot be read without the filter of psychology and psychoanalysis. Innocence, along with religion and belief, is dead; we are all-knowing now. It is this territory that Mat Collishaw has colonised, blurring the distinctions between reality and fantasy, innocence and profanity. Walking into his new exhibition is like trawling the dark basements of the subconscious.

An animated video of the Swiss Symbolist painter Arnold Böcklin's 'The Island of the Dead' sets the tone. Böcklin's allegorical paintings, many based on mythical creatures, anticipated 20th-century Surrealism. His early style consisted of idealised classical landscapes. In the 1870s he turned to German legends, inhabiting similar territory to Richard Wagner. His later works, such as 'The Island of the Dead', became increasingly dreamlike and nightmarish. Collishaw's version is projected onto a two-way mirror in which the unsettling movement of shadows passes like an eclipse during a 24-hour period. Caught like some alienated figure in a Caspar David Friedrich painting, looking out into an existential void, is the reflected image of the viewer. The lone figure from Böcklin's original painting, which is absent here, has turned up in a recreated daguerreotype on an adjacent wall. Here the negative image of a girl appears positive only when passed over by the viewer's

shadow. The ectoplasmic nature of the work and the use of mirrors remind us of the tricks used in the 19th century by spiritualists and lovers of the séance.

Collinshaw's installation, 'Shooting Stars', has a disturbing, dreamlike quality. Photographs found on the Internet of Victorian child prostitutes in vulnerable, yet alluring, poses are projected onto the gallery walls and mingled with similar images restaged by the artist with an older model. Fired onto phosphorescent paint, they flare briefly before slowly fading from view. The ghostly after-images suggest the children's short, fragile lives, blighted by violence and sexually transmitted diseases. For many of these girls, comments Collishaw, "their lives were not much longer than the fleeting exposure of the camera shutter".

The top floor is dominated by a zoetrope, a cylindrical device that produces the illusion of action from a rapid succession of static images. The earliest projected moving images were displayed using a magic-lantern zoetrope as early as the 1860s. As it begins to spin in the eerie twilight, the small figurines of 'Throbbing Gristle' – a Minotaur ravaging a maiden, the Three Graces, a she-wolf and a wine-swigging cherub – begin magically to move. The effect of the flickering shadows is to conjure the dark underbelly of Victorian life with its deep and dominant concerns about death and sex.

In 1917, two cousins, ten-year-old Frances
Griffiths and sixteen-year-old Elsie Wright,
presented two photographs they'd taken
showing them in the company of fairies
and gnomes in a nearby glen. Their mother
gave the photos to Edward L. Gardner of
the then-popular Theosophical Society.
Through Gardner, the story reached Sir
Arthur Conan Doyle, who had become
obsessed with spiritualism after the death of
his son. Conan Doyle encouraged Gardner
to give cameras to the girls, in the hope they
would come up with new fairy portraits.
The cousins produced three new photos that
were accepted as genuine by Conan Doyle,
who wrote about them in the 'Strand'
magazine. As claims and counterclaims
about the pictures' authenticity flew, they
became the centre of one of the greatest
science-vs-superstition controversies of the
early 20th century. The effect of Collishaw's
series of backlit, ultraviolet light boxes is
to make these appropriated fugitive images
seem even more uncanny. Playing on
notions of the forbidden, Collinshaw throws
up questions about what defines personal
and social morality. The Victorians veiled
their transgressions behind a moral veneer,
while Collishaw reveals that we are all,
largely, a mixture of the dark and the light.

Mat Collishaw
Shooting Stars
Haunch of Venison

The Independent
17th July, 2008

Mark Rothko, Untitled, *1969*

Mark Rothko

"The sea-reach of the Thames stretched before us like the beginning of an interminable waterway. In the offing the sea and the sky were welded together without a joint... A haze rested on the low shores that ran out to sea in vanishing flatness. The air was dark above Gravesend, and farther back still seemed condensed into a mournful gloom, brooding motionless... The day was ending in a serenity of still and exquisite brilliance. The water shone pacifically; the sky, without a speck, was a benign immensity of unstained light; the very mist on the Essex marsh was like a gauzy and radiant fabric, hung from the wooded rises inland, and draping the low shores in diaphanous folds."

This famous description at the beginning of Joseph Conrad's 'Heart of Darkness', of the yawl Nellie waiting to set sail on the Thames, is as close an analogy of Mark Rothko's 'Brown' and 'Gray' paintings as literature provides. Conrad gives us a literary equivalent, expressing what it feels like to stand in the presence of such paintings, despite the fact that for Rothko they were remorselessly abstract. The sky welded to the sea, the vanishing flatness and gauzy mist, might all describe these sombre late works. Divided into two halves, the upper section is painted in a blackish-brown acrylic, while the lower half – though the ratios differ in different paintings – is made up of scrubbed, mud-flat greys. What has been removed, of course, is the ingredient that made up Rothko's classic paintings of the 50s: the deep veils of colour. Everything has been reduced to subtle and barely visible variations of tone and brushstroke. So what is going on?

There has been a tendency to see these late paintings as intimations of Rothko's suicide. But this powerful show at Tate Modern reveals a more universal concern. For as Rothko states: "The tragic experience is for me the only source of art". Elsewhere, he wrote, "I'm not interested in the relationship of color or form or anything else. I'm interested only in expressing basic human emotions such a tragedy, ecstasy, doom". As in Conrad's novel, these late paintings suggest a psychological journey, a voyage into that unknown heart of darkness at the centre of the self. Life and art here are stripped to the bone, as we the viewers are left staring into the inky void. Both a reassessment and a taking stock, these works are among the most profoundly existential paintings I have ever seen. Seeing is what all great art demands, but none more so than these late Rothkos – not a cursory "look", but a fully engaged relationship from the viewer. For, Rothko appears to be saying, this is all there is. As a Russian Jewish immigrant he might well have felt that, after the death camps, God was indeed dead, yet with this admission comes the anxiety of knowing that there is a spiritual void left at the centre of human experience. Rothko, it seems, wanted to do the impossible – to paint religious paintings for an irreligious world. For him, "The fact that people break down and cry when confronted with my pictures shows that I can communicate those basic human emotions... the people who weep before my pictures are having the same religious experience I had when painting them. And if you say you are moved only by their colour relationships, then you miss the point".

With these monochromatic paintings, Rothko seems to be suggesting that at the centre of the human psyche is a dualistic relationship between light and dark, between materiality and immateriality. Based on the strategy of repetition and variation not unlike that employed in Monet's 1890s haystacks, he illustrates his belief that, "If a thing is worth doing once, it is worth doing over and over again – exploring it, probing it, demanding by its repetition that the public look at it". For if we stand long enough, and really look until we see, we might, as T. S. Eliot suggests in 'Little Gidding', ultimately come to know this place for the first time.

Born in Latvia to Jewish parents, Rothko came from a largely secular and intellectual family. After he emigrated to America, where he won a scholarship to Yale before abandoning his studies for art, he was taught by Max Weber, a painter who helped introduce Cubism to the States, and was a contemporary of Barnett Newman, another exemplar of Abstract Expressionism. Both these men were also Russian Jewish émigrés. Rothko has been called a spiritual and a religious painter, but he is a religious painter for a secular age, providing what the French writer Gaston Bachelard, calls "a space to daydream". It is a space in which we can contemplate not only the natural grandeur of the world, but also the immensity within ourselves – the silence and stillness at the core of who we are. The Romantics called this the Sublime, while Freud referred to it as an oceanic feeling, this sense that connects

us to something within and beyond our very deepest selves.

The convoluted history of Rothko's Seagram murals has become one of the abiding myths of 20th-century art. In 1961, the Museum of Modern Art in New York honoured the 58-year-old Rothko with a major retrospective. At the centre were the sombre ox-blood paintings that form the core of this exhibition, originally commissioned to decorate the luxurious Four Seasons dining room of udwig Mies van der Rohe's iconic Seagram building on Park avenue. Rothko, at first, seized upon the project with enthusiasm, renting a former gymnasium that allowed him to simulate the dining room's proportions, and completing the work by early summer 1959, when he set sail with his family to Europe. Speculation has always been rife as to why he then withdrew the paintings. Some put it down to his socialist tendencies and his apparently vituperative remark that he hoped "to paint something that will ruin the appetite of every son of a bitch who ever eats in that room". The truth, more likely, is that he felt a mismatch between the putative function of the paintings and his desire to achieve very much more than his client wanted. There is also some evidence that he was exasperated with the general misinterpretation of his earlier, more lyrical and colourful, works, and felt the need to turn away from being (wrongly) seen as decorative. Tragic grandeur was what mattered. His paintings had "to be miraculous" and create a psychological and spiritual empathy between artist and viewer. Here, for the first time, the Tate's eight Seagram murals – Rothko bequeathed them to the gallery – are shown with a selection of those from the Kawamura Memorial Museum of Art, Sakura, and the National Gallery of Art, Washington. Though a final scheme for the Four Seasons was never devised, and the building could only accommodate seven paintings, Rothko executed 30.

With their floating frames and portals, these architectonic works have something ancient and atavistic about them. Rothko likened the effect to the claustrophobic atmosphere of Michelangelo's Laurentian Library in Florence, but walking around the Tate, I kept thinking of Stonehenge or the megalithic portal at the ancient citadel of Mycenae. Even the colours, the deep maroons and blacks, conjure something very ancient, suggesting the burnt pigments of cave paintings. There is here, too, something muscular, visceral and almost violent. This is the Rothko of Stravinsky's 'Rite of Spring' rather than the Rothko of floating veils of luminous colour. Architecture was to play an important role in his next commission. Following the Seagram murals, Rothko was invited by the patron Dominique de Menil to create a set of paintings for a non-denominational, purpose-designed, octagonal chapel in Houston. These hard-edged, stripped-down compositions, which are not in this exhibition, share something of the qualities found in his series of so-called 'Black-Form' paintings that, with their lack of hovering fields and feathered edges, mark a complete break with his colour-field paintings of the 1950s. At first glance totally black, it reveals, again only through the process of engaged looking, gradations of tone and texture. Perceptions are challenged by the complex layers that, rather than annihilating light, seem to radiate with an intense luminosity. Like some dark baptism they surround the viewer, so the experience becomes a form of sensual immersion. It is not so much that he has "abandoned" colour, but that there is an "absence" of colour. It is as if, through this lack of something expected, we are asked to consider what it is that is actually not present. Colour had become a man-made thing, something squeezed from tubes and slurped from tins, ready made rather than hand made from pigments. Rothko's blacks and greys are the opposite, arrived at by layering and mixing, and are both dense and radiant.

That Rothko suffered from depression and melancholia is well documented, but as the French philosopher Julia Kristeva has argued, and David Anfam pointed out in his catalogue essay, "the mind may be unable to countenance death, and the difference between clinical depression and an art born of melancholia is that the latter sublimates the former into eloquent speech". Black also has a history in Kasimir Malevich's canonical and "spiritual" 'Black Square' of 1915, in Robert Motherwell's 'Elegies to the Spanish Republic' and Ad Reinhardt's and Frank Stella's paintings of the 50s. As with Rothko's brown and grey works on paper, they seem like an heroic re-evaluation of everything that had gone before.

In his discussion of "late works", the writer Edward Said talked of them not as "harmony and resolution but as intransigence, difficulty and contradiction". As in the case of Henrik Ibsen's final play 'When We Dead Awaken', Said suggests that late work can "tear apart" and "reopen questions" that are supposed to have been long resolved. They stir up anxiety and tamper irrevocably "with the course of closure". Beethoven's last works, Said posits, "constitute an event in the history of modern culture: a moment when the artist who is fully in command of his medium nevertheless abandons communication with the established social order of which he is a part and achieves a contradictory, alienated relationship with it. His late works are a form of exile from his milieu". This abandonment and "exile from his milieu", is, I would suggest, exactly the territory of these late Rothko works.

Rothko was a bridge between the old and the new worlds, between the historic tragedies of Europe and the optimism of 20th-century America. He is one of the last great philosophical painters. After him, and his generation, art was fundamentally to change forever. No longer seen as existential investigators, the next generation of American artists were to deconstruct

notions of the uniqueness of the art object,
as suggested in Walter Benjamin's famous
essay, 'The Work of Art in the Age of
Mechanical Reproduction'. If a work of art
could be endlessly reproduced, as in the case
of Andy Warhol's silk screens, then it no
longer had value as a "sacred" object. Its
potential was changed from existential icon
into an object of commodification and
commercial exchange. Rothko is one of the
last to put aesthetics before money, and to
believe in the redemptive power of art:
an art that makes us ask who we are and
why we are here.

Rothko
Tate Modern

New Statesman
2nd October, 2008

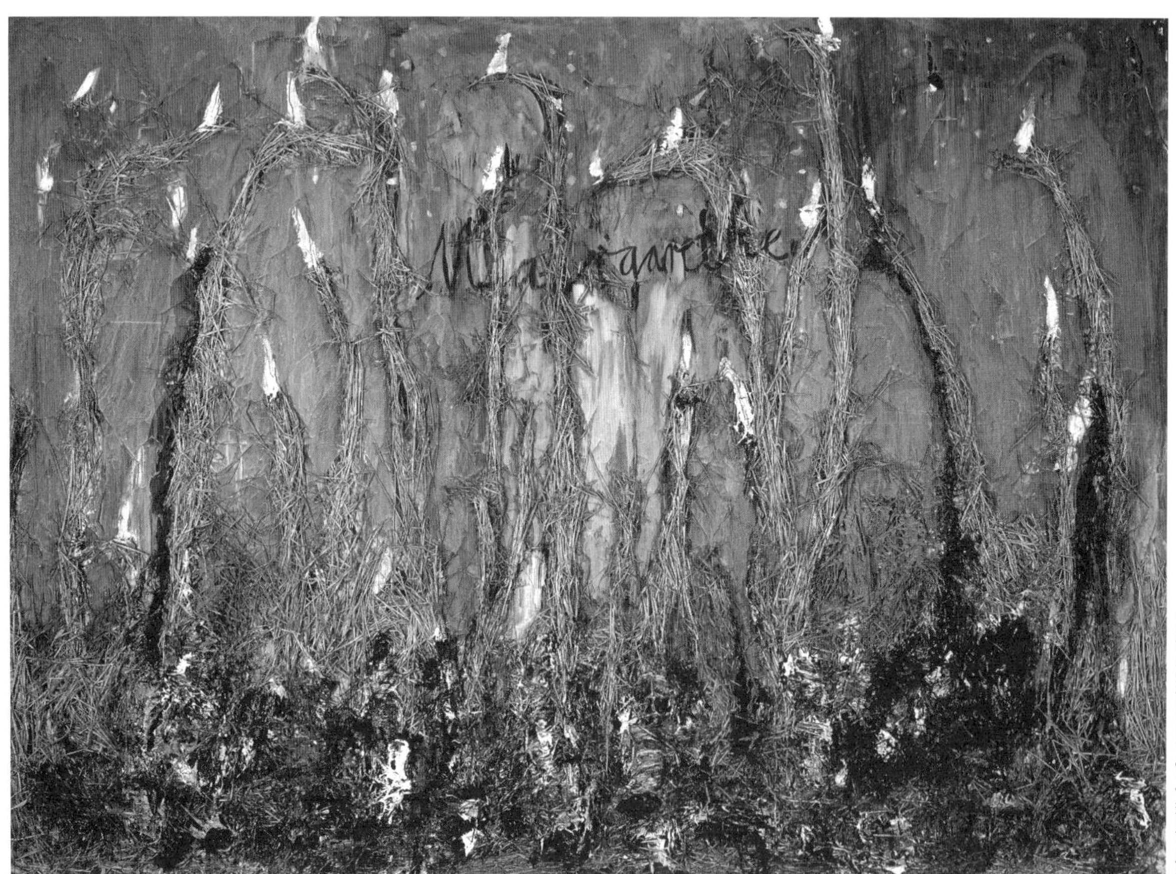

Anselm Kiefer, 'Margarethe', *1981*

Anselm Kiefer
Margarete, 1981

The poet Paul Celan was the only member of his family to survive incarceration in a concentration camp during the Holocaust, but then committed suicide in 1970 at the age of 49, after producing a body of work that included the searingly painful poem 'Death Fugue'. In this, he talks of the inhabitants of the death camp drinking black milk and digging graves in the sky. Two figures are contrasted in the poem and act as the central metaphor: Margarete, with her cascade of blonde Aryan hair, and Shulamite, a Jewish woman, whose black hair denotes her Semitic origins, but is also ashen from burning. The theme of Celan's poem has been an important preoccupation of the German painter Anslem Kiefer, for whom Margarete and Shulamite have become the metaphoric protagonists in a series of paintings, of which 'Margarete', *1981* is the concluding work.

Art and history often have a complex and uncomfortable relationship within Kiefer's work. In the 1970s he became increasingly concerned with depicting the land where historic events might have occurred. An archetypal landscape began to dominate where the earth was burnt or blackened and the high horizon line seemed to prevent escape. As Kiefer's 80s series on Margarete and Shulamite evolved, he, like Celan, developed a series of visual tropes that characterised the two women. Shulamite's black hair is usually painted, while Margarete's is depicted in straw embedded in the paint. By making them mirror images of each other, Kiefer implies that the destinies and cultures of these women were inextricably linked. Straw added to a painting of Shulamite suggests Margarete's golden tresses, while black lines or tangled areas of dense black paint in 'Margarete' imply the silent, erased presence of Shulamite. For Kiefer, Germany had maimed itself by the destruction of the Jews. By pairing these two women in paint, he attempts a restoration of wholeness.

Having already exploited the metaphoric resonances of lead and sand, Kiefer first used straw in the early 80s. With its potential to be burnt and turned to ash, it not only implied a landscape scarred and formed by human history, war and fire, but also the possibility of alchemical transformation. The glorified Margarete, indicated by straw, symbolises the old German love of land, and the nobility of the German soul, allowing Kiefer to play with complex notions of racial purity. The image of Margarete owes much to the vision of German womanhood created by Goethe. In 'Faust', Margarete, (also known as Gretchen) exhibits a pure and innocent love for Faust. But love leads to a series of deceits and the killing of her own baby. While lying in prison on a bed of straw, Faust, in a complex series of events, murders her brother. Thus Margarete's innocence is tainted. Goethe depicts women as sacred preservers of moral values, undone by male power, yet able to be both saved and redeemed. This is a model to which Kiefer often refers, though for him, there is an ambivalence about the implied purity of such women.

In 'Margarete', *1981* – the last of the series – Margarete's name is scrawled in black paint across the surface of the canvas like graffiti: part prayer and part memorial. Long tendrils of straw curl upwards like smoke from the death-camp chimneys, ending in small candle-like flames. Meaning is ambiguous. For this flourishing crop might imply resurrection, yet the soil from which it grows is charred, while the knots and tangles of black paint evoke the shorn piles of hair found at Auschwitz. Of his limited palette, Kiefer has claimed that only the French traditionally use a range of colours, and that as a German he is less familiar with the practice. The gloopy, textured surfaces bring to mind the "frottage" of another German artist, Max Ernst.

Born in 1945, Kiefer abandoned law in 1966 to turn to art. His intellectual and artistic evolution mirrored the concerns of a number of German artists. Along with contemporaries Georg Baselitz and Eugen Schönebeck, he rejected the overwhelmingly American influence of Abstract Expressionism, Pop and Minimalism to search for a uniquely German viewpoint that would reflect the upheavals of the country's war-torn past. Moving away from art for art's sake, he began to explore both the recent and distant past in order to learn lessons for the future. Influenced by Joseph Beuys, he saw art as a healing, spiritual process, and adopted myth and metaphor to investigate the "recent terror of history". This impetus for examining the Nazi era may have derived partly from the 1960s spirit of revolt against the legacy of previous generations. Sensing the unaddressed presence of World War II everywhere within contemporary Germany, he felt compelled to confront the silent taboos of post-war German society.

At times his depiction of land can seem shocking in the context of German idealism and sentimentality about *das Land*. Unlike the German Romantic attitude of *Sehnsucht* – a chthonic longing for nature – Kiefer takes an objective look at what happened to his country. Yet his often-ambiguous approach has lead to accusations that if, like the Nazis, he wants to turn away from international questions of art to explore German roots, doesn't that somehow make him a Nazi sympathiser at heart? Yet others see him as undermining the almost-sacred German attitude towards land to render it bankrupt. For the scorched landscape he depicts, he suggests, has been sullied by those who inherited Margarete's so-called "idealism". The painted words *dein goldenes Haar, Margarethte* (your golden hair Margarete) and *dein aschenes Haar, Sulamit* (your ashen hair, Shulamite) written across two earlier paintings evoke the question as to what horrific fate has befallen Shulamite.

Magical, poignant, and emotionally complex, these straw paintings are among the most powerful of Kiefer's works, and echo the German poet Rainer Maria Rilke's words: "For *beauty* is nothing but the beginning of *terror*, which we are still just able to endure…" In 'Margarete', straw acts a symbol for a range of emotions stirred by the idea of land within German history. There is, Kiefer seems to imply, a dark blemish on the soul of the German nation that it will still take generations to erase.

Anselm Kiefer
Margarete, 1981
Saatchi Collection

The Independent
24th October, 2008

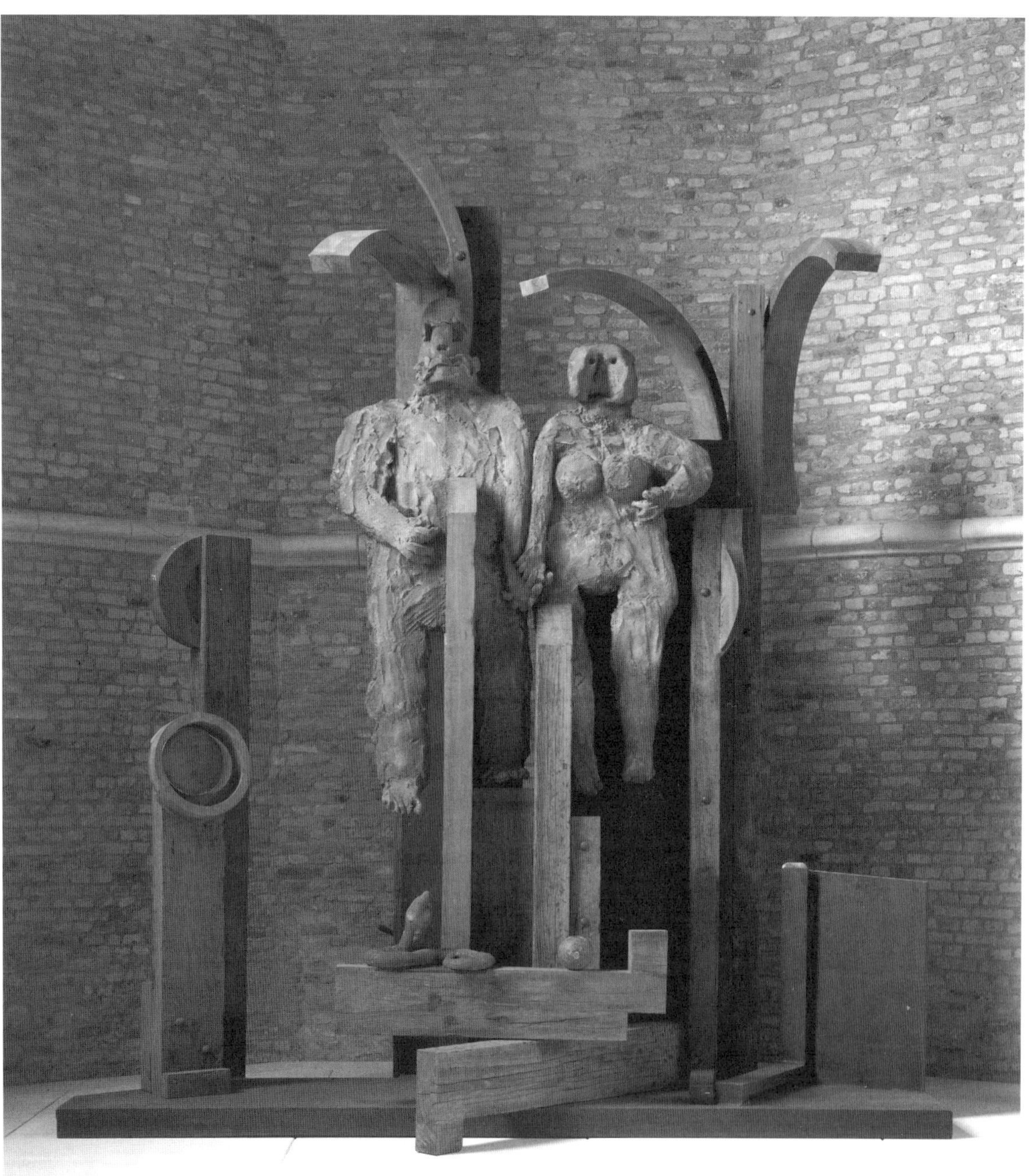

Anthony Caro, Chapel of Light – 'Paradise Garden', *2007*

Anthony Caro
Chapel of Light

In May 1940, an RAF plane crash-landed onto the roof of the church in the small northern French town of Bourbourg in order to avoid the people in the nearby market place. The roof caught fire and was destroyed. The following year, the chapel archway collapsed and the ornamental tiling was dismantled for use by the occupying German forces. In 1955, restoration work started on the central nave and transept, but the eastern nave remained hidden by a brick wall, cut off from the body of the church and closed for worship for 50 years. The church built by the monks of Saint Bertin was first mentioned in the 11th century.

The decoration of a chapel by a contemporary artist might be considered, as in the case of Matisse's in Ville de Vence, or the Rothko chapel in Houston, to be the zenith of a career. After all, it could still be standing in 1000 years. It was at the end of 1999 that Anthony Caro was approached by the Ministry of Culture and Communication to visit the ruined chapel at the church of Saint-Jean Baptiste. The most innovative British sculptor of his generation, Caro is the leading exponent of abstract and Constructivist sculpture. Using a wide variety of materials including steel and aluminium, ceramic and paper, he has continuously played with a sense of equilibrium, freeing sculpture from the constraints of the base. Yet, despite the influence of American thinkers such as Clement Greenberg, and sculptors like the late David Smith, he has always been primarily interested in an expressive lyricism. He is equally at home creating austere works of painted steel as expressive ceramic figures. When he first saw the church hunkered in a corner of this little provincial town, it made an immediate impression. Its spatial quality, its proportions and play of light, the sense of history, and the stories of conflict and war, seemed to be embedded in the mineral mass of the building.

The project has absorbed ten years of Caro's life. Now over 80, he has embraced it with the vigour of a man half his age. Working from a scale model in his Camden studio, he wanted the choir, which faces east and catches the morning sun, to be "both a baptistry and a chapel of hope". Despite his Jewish roots, his attitudes are entirely ecumenical. He claims no fixed belief, but is "against Dawkins' view that everything can be explained". He wanted to create a non-denominational space where anyone could go in order to seek spiritual nurture. With this in mind, he built an external circular steel porch that guides the visitor to the church's new wooden door on the south side. This creates a transitional space, both actual and metaphysical, between the outside world and the place of contemplation that allows those of different persuasions, or no persuasion at all, to enter without going through the main body of the church, and experience a sense of pilgrimage.

Caro has responded to the unique architecture of the choir, which seemed to offer itself up like an empty receptacle. With the original floor gone – a floor that, like a palimpsest, articulated the history of the building – he replaced it with flags of pristine white concrete. At the back of the nave, raised on three steps and surrounded by stained-glass windows that were a gift to the church earlier this century, he has installed a new baptismal font created from the same material. This double spiral, with its steps that allow for full baptismal immersion, rises from the floor like an open shell. Surrounding this in the apse wall are nine niches. Each contains a relief made from sheet steel and terracotta. Based in myth, each sculpture makes reference to the Creation, and to water as the source of life subject include 'The Deep' and 'Waterfall'. The waves and ripples of steel suggest continual movement, while hidden within its folds is an array of terracotta creatures – a squid, a crocodile, a frog – that will enchant children and adults alike. Since it's flooded by the blue and yellow light from one of the stained-glass windows, Caro decided to allow chance to play its role in the reading of the relief entitled 'Undergrowth'.

Bordering the main area are two wooden towers – 'Tower of Evening' and 'Tower of Morning' – that are part architectural and part sculptural. Made of French oak, they rise like giant pulpits almost five metres high and echo a previous work, 'Child's Tower Room', *1983-84,* which is on show in Dunkirk in one of the three retrospective exhibitions (the other two are in Calais and Gravelines) that accompany the opening of the chapel. To enter the womb-like space beneath the 'Tower of Morning', which is wrapped around an ancient pillar, is like sitting in the quiet of a confessional. On either side of the towers, in each aisle, are two works made of steel and terracotta. 'Paradise Garden' contains archetypal primitive figures that suggest Adam and Eve, while in 'Alleluia' a flurry of terracotta

hands reaches heavenwards in prayer or supplication.

A symbolic threshold between the liturgical space and the newly refurbished choir is created by a translucent glass screen that frames the priest's podium dividing the main body of the church from the choir. Here, Caro has created a cross, candelabra, lectern and tabernacle, as well as an altar formed from a huge rough stone found in the south of France. After 50 years of being abandoned, the choir of Saint-Jean Baptiste has been revivified by Anthony Caro. With its sensual generosity that melds myth and religious ritual, his contribution is expressive, humane and contemporary, as well as timeless.

Anthony Caro
Chapel of Light
Church of Saint-Jean
Baptiste of Bourbourg

Building Design
24th October, 2008

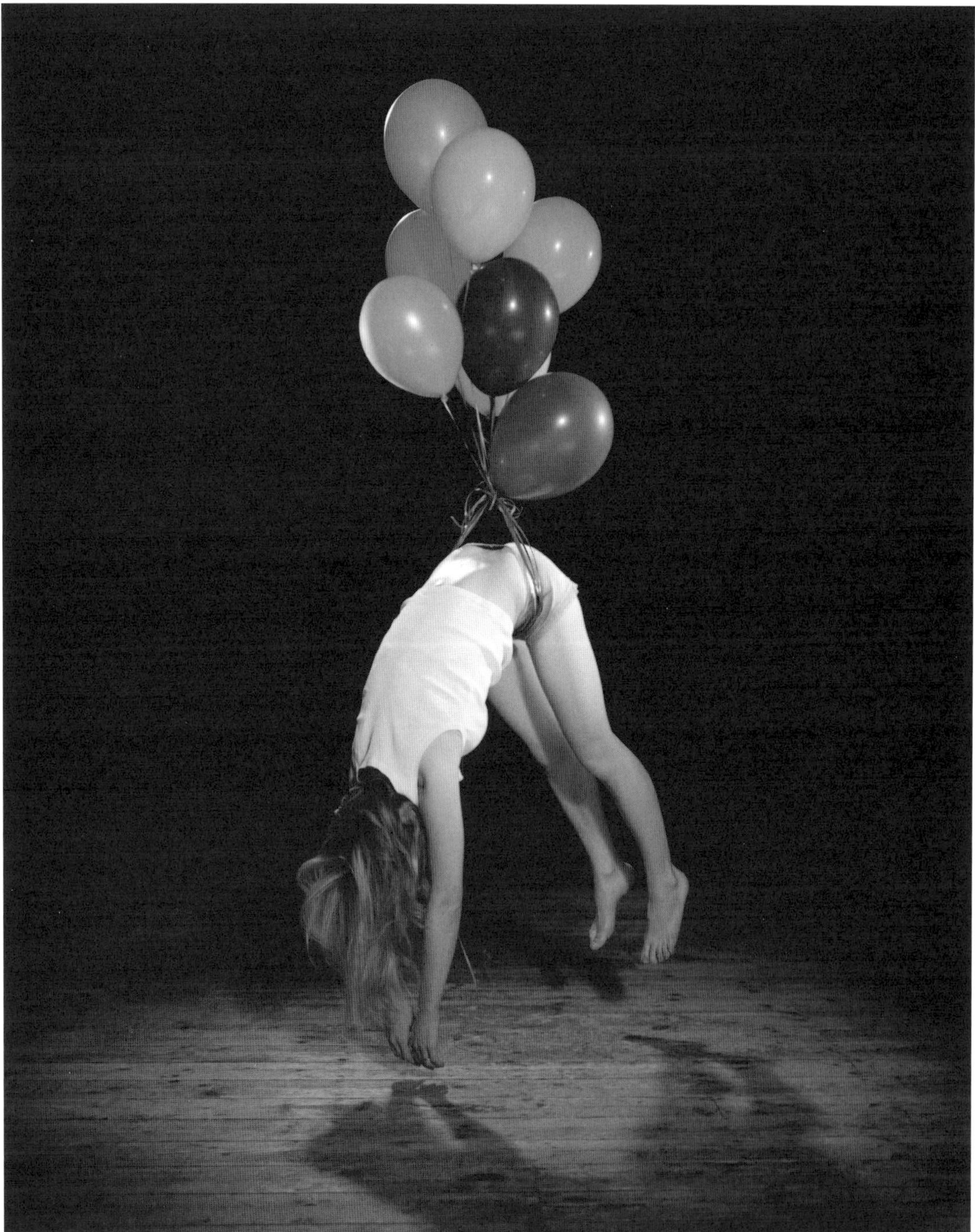

Sam Taylor-Wood, 'Escape Artist (Multicoloured)', *2008*

Sam Taylor-Wood
Yes I No

For a girl who grew up on a Peabody estate and then a hippie commune in Crowborough, East Sussex, where the inhabitants wore orange robes and the cats ate out of the chip pan, Sam Taylor-Wood has come a long way. It is not possible to write about her art without also writing about her life, for the two are inextricably linked. Abandoned by her biker father, her mother simply upped sticks one day after they had moved from London to the commune. Sam had no idea where she had gone, only by chance seeing her in a house just down the road where she had moved with another man. A sense of loss, and of the world not quite being in balance, was engendered early.

It was art school that saved her. At 16, she signed on at Hastings Art College, sharing a house with 12 men, many of whom were ex mental patients. But if Hastings saved her, it was Goldsmiths that made her. For it was there that she fell in love with Jake Chapman (half of the duo who produced the famed penile-nosed dolls), her boyfriend for the next nine years, and became sucked into that glittering whirlwind that defined an artistic generation, the Young British Artists (YBAs). The rest, as they say in Mills and Boons novels, is history.

Straddled across two sites, her new exhibition 'Yes I No' seems to illustrate – as does the title – something of the dichotomy at the centre of Taylor-Wood's work – the pull between celebrity and serious art making. Perhaps too, unintentionally, the two-part exhibition asks questions about the point and purpose of much contemporary art. In the elegant, shabby chic of 1 The Piazza, Covent Garden are two series of photographs, the 'Escape Artist' and 'After Dark'. The first shows the artist, her yoga-toned body in stylish *Agent Provocateur* vest and knickers, and her toenails immaculately manicured, hanging in mid-air like a rag doll, held up by coloured helium balloons. It is a trick, of course, like Yves Klein's faked 'Leap into the Void'. She employed the expertise of an S&M specialist known as Mr Rope Knot, whose ties leave no marks, and whose ropes were digitally removed from the final prints. In 'After Dark' a traditional clown, all greasepaint, big nose and baggy trousers, looks rather melancholy in a variety of abandoned industrial buildings and under dripping railway arches. Yet standing in front of these works, knowing that they are in many ways autobiographical – the artist as escapologist refusing to be pinned down, part drowning body, part Houdini circus act, and the clown as sad Shakespearian fool – it is difficult to feel other than rather manipulated. For these series of chic photographs might have been shot for a *Benetton* ad. There is an implied gravitas that, in reality, amounts to a good deal of style and rather less substance.

More than any other artist of her generation, even Tracey Emin, Taylor-Wood exemplifies the art of the X-Factor generation. She is probably best known for her series 'Crying Men', *2004,* of film stars weeping, and her video of David Beckham sleeping, the tattoos on his perfectly honed body gently lifting with each breath, which drew crowds of adoring women at the National Portrait Gallery in 2004. The human body has been central to her from her early 'Fuck, Suck, Spank, Wank', *1993,* and her 1995 video, 'Brontosaurus', of a skinny naked man with flailing genitals, manically dancing to techno music. Her most famous self-portrait shows her wearing an expensive black trouser suit, holding a stiff dead hare, for she has had a tendency to place herself in many of her works, appearing as the scantily clad Madonna clasping a hunky Christ in 'Pietà', *2001.*

Given this tendency for chic and self promotion, it was not surprising that the night after the opening of 'Yes I No' at White Cube, owned by the ubiquitous old Etonian Jay Jopling, Sam Taylor-Wood's husband of 11 years from who she has just split, saw her splashed across the free London papers with her pals Daniel Craig and the newly single Mr Madonna, Guy Ritchie. She is mates with Sadie and Kate, Elton and David. Hers is one of the most coveted address books in London. Her growing celebrity status allowed her to collaborate with the late Anthony Minghella on the film 'Love You More', which is to be shown in this month's London Film Festival, while she has just made a single with her downstairs neighbours, the Pet Shop Boys, and is soon to feature on 'The South Bank Show'. Yet undermining this gilded trajectory is the fact that she has twice suffered and recovered from bouts of colon and breast cancer which, she has said, makes her want to "do everything, try everything, be everywhere". It is difficult not to feel that this understandable "do it all, have it all" attitude colours both her life and her art.

Yet travel to Piccadilly, to Mason's Yard, and things are rather different – altogether quieter and more considered. In the upstairs gallery is 'Ghosts', a series of photographs taken around Haworth on the Yorkshire moors, and inspired by Taylor-Wood's first reading of 'Wuthering Heights'. What she has caught is not only the spirit of the novel, in this wild unpeopled landscape where a solitary sheep shelters from the buffeting wind in a hollow by a stone wall, and louring clouds race across the sky, but the essence of brutality, beauty and awe that is the essence of Romanticism. In her leafless tree, bent by the wind on the top of a lonely hill, she has found an image that not only speaks eloquently of the destructive passions of Cathy and Heathcliff, and stirs the voices of Ted Hughes and Sylvia Plath who also haunt this bleak landscape, but captures her own intimations of mortality.

But the *pièce de résistance* is undoubtedly 'Sigh', which had people clapping after each performance. In a darkened room, a circle of eight video screens shows a conductor conducting an orchestra with no instruments. Surrounded by the music, as if part of the orchestra, the viewer is drawn to the bowing hands of the violinists and their accurate, sensitive fingering, as well as to the pursed lips of the silent flautist whose every breath and swallow can be observed. And the effect? Well, it is very powerful. For these musicians are not miming, but silently playing the music, which emanates from their every pore. It is not their instruments that make the music, but them, for even with their loss, they are still music makers to the core. Poignant and evocative, this is an expansive metaphor that reminds us we are not simply defined by our outward trappings. If we were to speak of souls, this might give some hint as to where they reside. Should Sam Taylor-Wood choose to lose her celebrity address book for a bit, stop trying to do "everything" and be "everywhere", and take note of her own message, she might become a significant, as well as a fashionable, artist.

Sam Taylor-Wood
Yes I No
1 The Piazza, Covent Garden
and White Cube

New Statesman
10th November, 2008

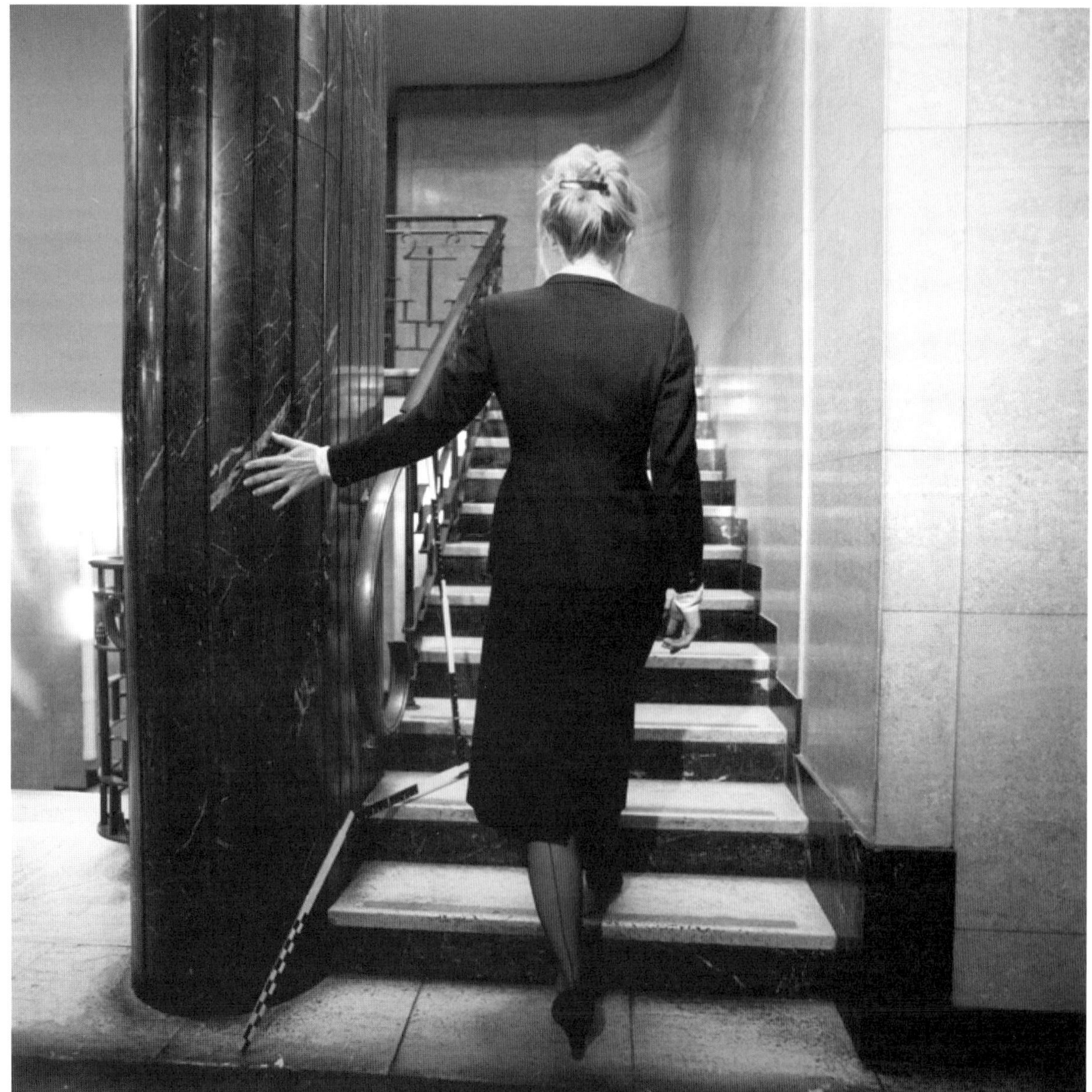

Jane and Louise Wilson, 'Unfolding the Aryan Papers', (still), *2008*

Jane and Louise Wilson
Unfolding the Aryan Papers

In 1976, the late filmmaker Stanley Kubrick travelled to New York to try and interest the Jewish novelist Isaac Bashevis Singer in writing an original screenplay for a project he was working on about the Holocaust. Kubrick was, in his words, looking for a writer who could create a "dramatic structure that compressed the complex and vast information into the story of an individual who represented the essence of this manmade hell". Not himself a Holocaust survivor, Singer declined, saying he didn't "know the first thing about the Holocaust".

The project was shelved until Kubrick read Louis Begley's short novel 'Wartime Lies', about a young Jewish boy and his aunt who managed to escape from Poland by pretending to be Catholics. In 1993, Kubrick made a deal with Warner Bros to make a film entitled 'Aryan Papers' (a reference to the documentation required to prevent deportation to the camps). The film was developed into pre-production. Sets were located, costumes designed, and Julia Roberts and Uma Thurman were considered for the main role of the boy's aunt, Tanya. Eventually Kubrick settled on the Dutch actress Johanna ter Steege. But the film was never made, though the reasons for this are not completely clear.

Being of Jewish Austro-Romanian and Polish origin, Kubrick had a lifelong fascination with the Holocaust, but was extremely sceptical as to whether any film could do it justice. When Frederic Raphael, who worked with him on the script of 'Eyes Wide Shut', suggested the subject of 'Schindler's List', Kubrick's acerbic response was, "Think that's about the Holocaust? That was about success, wasn't it? The Holocaust is about 6 million people who get killed. 'Schindler's List' is about 600 who don't. Anything else?"

Kubrick, like many Jewish thinkers and artists of his generation, had a very real anxiety about "the problem of how to do ethical and artistic justice to the depiction of the horror of mass extermination", echoing, no doubt, the German critic Theodor Adorno's belief that to write poetry after the Holocaust was barbaric. Kubrick was, according to his widow, very depressed whilst working on 'Aryan Papers'. He also learnt that Spielberg had started working on 'Schindler's List', and therefore shelved the project to concentrate on 'Eyes Wide Shut'.

Now the British duo Jane and Louise Wilson, who were nominated for the Turner Prize in 1999, have made a new work, 'Unfolding the Aryan Papers', based on the research they conducted, during a residency at University of the Arts London, into Stanley Kubrick's archive. The Wilson Twins have worked together for over 20 years on research-based projects that have dealt with, among other subjects, the dilapidated former Stasi headquarters in Berlin, Greenham Common and, in 'New Brutalists', the murky waters of colonialism. Using film, photography and sculpture, they have created theatrical and atmospheric installations that investigate the darker side of human experience.

This gallery installation concentrates on newly shot footage of Johanna ter Steege, along with stills from the wardrobe research, with period images of the Warsaw ghetto and other Holocaust subjects drawn from the pre-production period of 'Aryan Papers'. The film opens with a shot of the back of ter Steege's blonde head. The voice-over relates her experience of working with Kubrick, of how he made a point of observing the way she stood and her gestures, especially those of her hands. She recounts how he seemed to have something definite in mind, and was looking for a person and "a human being", not just an actress. He also apparently asked her not to change her accent, which could, he felt, have come from anywhere, and conveyed something universal.

Shot in the faded 30s grandeur of Hornsey Town Hall with its marble staircase, brass banister, heavy wooden panelling and Art Deco glass lamps, the Wilson twins' film concentrates on shots of ter Steege standing in the empty corridors and offices of this rather austere bureaucratic building, either in her petticoat, or dressed in period costume. During the shooting she speaks of her disappointment that the original film was never made and how, on its cancellation, she lay in bed for two years in a state of depression with a blanket over her head. Her beautiful face is just showing the first signs of ageing, but has become less bland with the passing of the years.

But what does the piece really amount to beyond the pleasure of the elegant cinematography and watching an attractive older women standing around in nice clothes in an interesting building? The Wilson twins say that it is not really about the Holocaust "as they are not qualified to make a film about something so dark", but

is rather the story of a woman and an actress, and the narrative of a film that was never made, which has now been rescued from invisibility.

And yet there is something uncomfortable about this work, as if the Holocaust can be reduced to a period backdrop against which to make a piece of contemporary art. Although Kubrick's motivation for dropping the original film is not completely clear, it is obvious that he took the ethical problems concerning this dark subject very seriously. Johanna ter Steege may have been resurrected from relative obscurity by this project, but the ghosts of millions of women lost to the gas chambers hover in the wings of this film, unacknowledged and unseen.

Adorno worried that attempting to condense the incomprehensible suffering of the Holocaust into a few lines of poetry would "violate the inner incoherence of the event, casting it into a mould too pleasing or too formal" and considered that silence was the only appropriate response to the tragedy, insisting that "Speechlessness alone could reflect integrity... to seek to portray reality with inadequate words would betray that reality and the voiceless dead at its core". The Holocaust is one of the darkest failings of the human imagination. In 'Unfolding the Aryan Papers', a fairly thin idea is, with Postmodern insouciance, given gravitas by association, diminishing this livid stain on our history to a stage set for a fashion show, and betraying those voiceless dead.

Jane and Louise Wilson
Unfolding the Aryan Papers
BFI Southbank Gallery

New Statesman
26th February, 2009

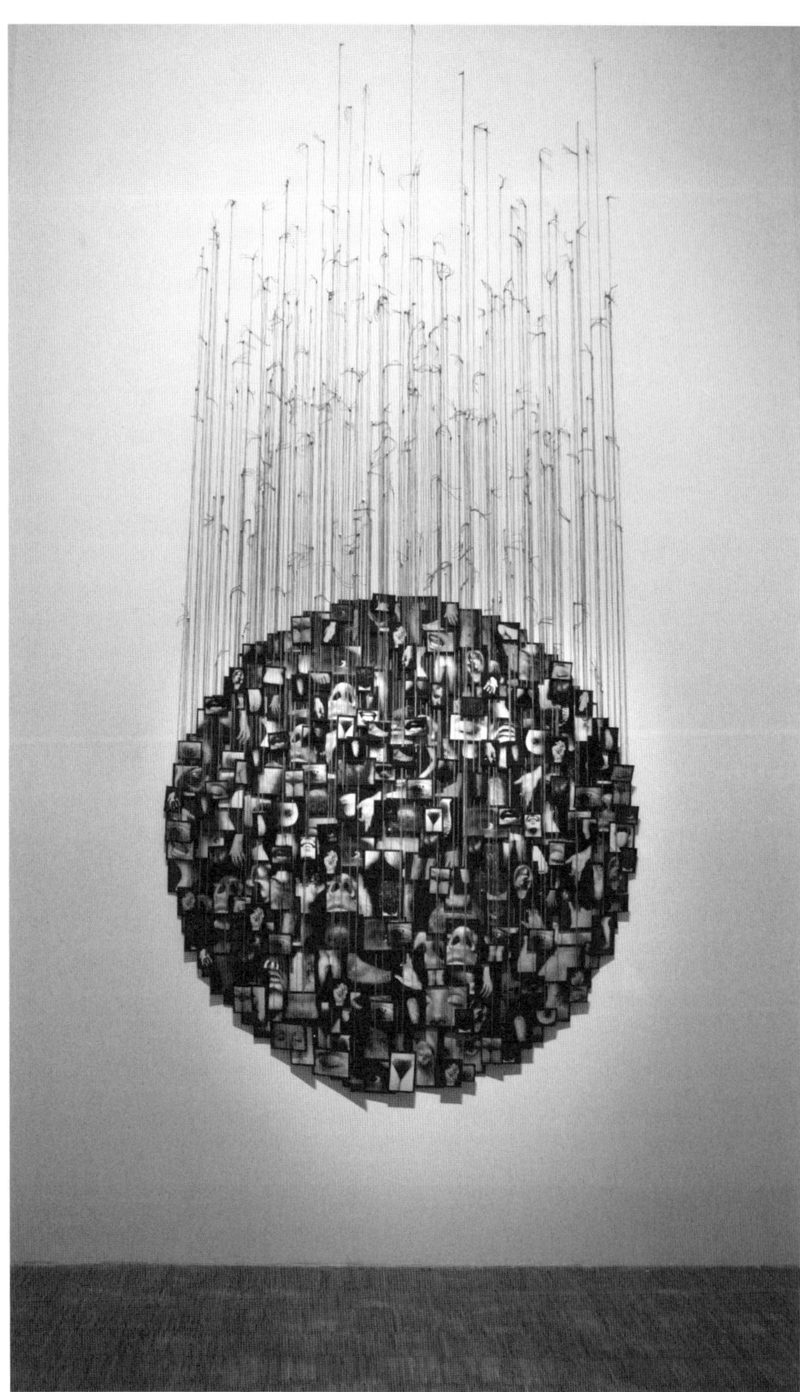

Annette Messager, 'Mes Voeux', *1989*

Annette Messager
The Messengers

In the late 1960s, the American critic Harold Rosenberg coined the term "Anxious Object" to describe works that seem deliberately to undermine their own status as "art" – for example Warhol's *Brillo* box. Ambiguity by its nature unsettles, which explains its appeal both to the Romantics and the avant-garde. Its mission is to disrupt the status quo and our ways of seeing. Freed from any functional use, objects become unstable – instead of anchoring us in the world, they upset our accepted readings to create feelings of unease, or what Sartre might have called nausea.

The French artist Annette Messager is not much known in England. Born in France in 1943, she attended the 'École des Arts Décoratifs', which she was eventually asked to leave because she spent more time poking around museums and sitting in cinemas than in college. The first woman artist to be invited to represent France at the Venice Biennale in 2005, she creates installations that use photography, drawing, knitting, embroidery and text, along with objects she has collected, to challenge fixed definitions of art, and the culturally assigned roles of women. Her work deals with sexual and physical abuse, the fragmented body, sin, obsession, fairytales, childhood, and the rites and symbols of religion, through the use of "female" materials, and techniques such as sewing. Her influences are varied, from French carnivals, Jean Dubuffet and that guru of squidgy objects Claes Oldenburg,

to religious votives and Hans Bellmer's disturbingly erotic dolls. This, her first major UK retrospective, includes work from the 1970s to recent large installations.

Fragments, particularly of the body, are used to explore small, obsessive everyday rituals. Her investigations revolve around the nature of identity, desire and cruelty, often lifting the lid onto the hidden, the transgressive and the taboo. In her disquieting installation 'Borders', rows of dead sparrows are dressed in doll-sized hand-knitted pink-and-lemon jackets and rowed in a glass case like stuffed objects of Victorian taxidermy. Others have been tied onto little iron bars in a way that recalls the often-sadistic behaviour of children's play. Looking at the tiny feathery corpses, I kept thinking of those last terrible minutes of James Bulger's young life. That some of the birds have batteries and clockwork motors attached, presumably to make them jump, is even more disquieting, and a reminder of the dark rituals and masturbatory fantasies of childhood. 'Children with Their Eyes Scratched Out', *1971-74*, includes photographs of babies with their eyes scribbled over in ballpoint in an act of apparent Oedipal violence.

Stuffed toys are another constant, but there's nothing very cuddly about them, lying discarded in funereal piles on the gallery floor or skewered on the ends of pikes like guillotined heads from the French Revolution. A disembowelled toy elephant, a flayed lion, a fluffy lime-green paw and a pink ear are just some of the disembodied parts nailed to the wall, which take on magical properties similar to those objects used in black magic or voodoo. And, without wanting to get too deeply psychoanalytical about it all, these fragmented "part objects" speak, as Melanie Klein might have done, of the lost mother and childhood rage.

Early on in her career, Messager played with issues of identity, creating two personalities to mirror the division in her activities carried out in her small Parisian apartment – "Annette Messager the Collector" and "Annette Messager the Artist". 'The Secret Room', a small sealed section of the gallery which, frustratingly, we can't enter, is full of diary notes, images cut from magazines, misogynistic terms for women embroidered onto fabric, and a series of black-and-white photos, 'Voluntary Tortures', from the early 70s, showing barbaric forms of beauty treatment. Elsewhere there is a display of her "best" signatures. Written over and over again in the manner of an adolescent schoolgirl practicing her name in the back of a textbook, these seem to be part of a search for her true identity.

Further on in the exhibition, 'My Vows' includes a large number of small photographic close-ups of body parts – a pair of breasts, a penis, a mouth – all framed in black and hung from bits of string in a unisex circle like those votive offerings found in Catholic churches. It is in this work, more than any of the others, that we can see the echoes of her partner, the great French artist Christian Boltanski.

This tendency to fragment, catalogue and name is everywhere. Many of the works, such as 'Lines of the Hand', incorporate text. Photographs of decorated female hands have been placed above a column of writing done directly on the wall, where a word has been repeated over and over like a prayer or mantra. This is very much a visual mirror

to the writings of the French feminist thinkers Hélène Cixous and Luce Irigaray, who deal with female identity and language, and of Julia Kristeva, who has written on the abject. Their presence lurks behind much of Messager's work.

Many of her recent pieces are more ambitious and, at times, absurdly humorous. 'Inflated-Deflated' is a kinetic display of intestines and other internal body organs that sigh and deflate in an erotic writhing mass, and in 'Dependence-Independence', lengths of fishing net and odd bodily shapes made from stuffed tights, some ripped to look like ghoulish faces, hang among black-and-white photos of children pulling odd expressions. In 'Articulated-Disarticulated', numerous heaving mannequins lie in a variety of abject positions, whilst the carcass of a stuffed cow is pulled by a small motor around the edge of the installation – a reference to the slaughter during the mad-cow epidemic. In the carnivalesque 'Casino', a menstrual flow of red silk is fanned by a wind machine to flow over hidden lights, and somehow involves the adventures of Pinocchio as Everyman. Yet these larger, more theatrical works are less successful. For it is the domestic scale and sense of personal transgression in installations such as 'Children with Their Eyes Scratched Out', or 'Borders', with its implied taboos and secret cruelties, that continue to resonate when the exhibition has been left behind.

Annette Messager
The Messengers
Hayward Gallery

New Statesman
26th March, 2009

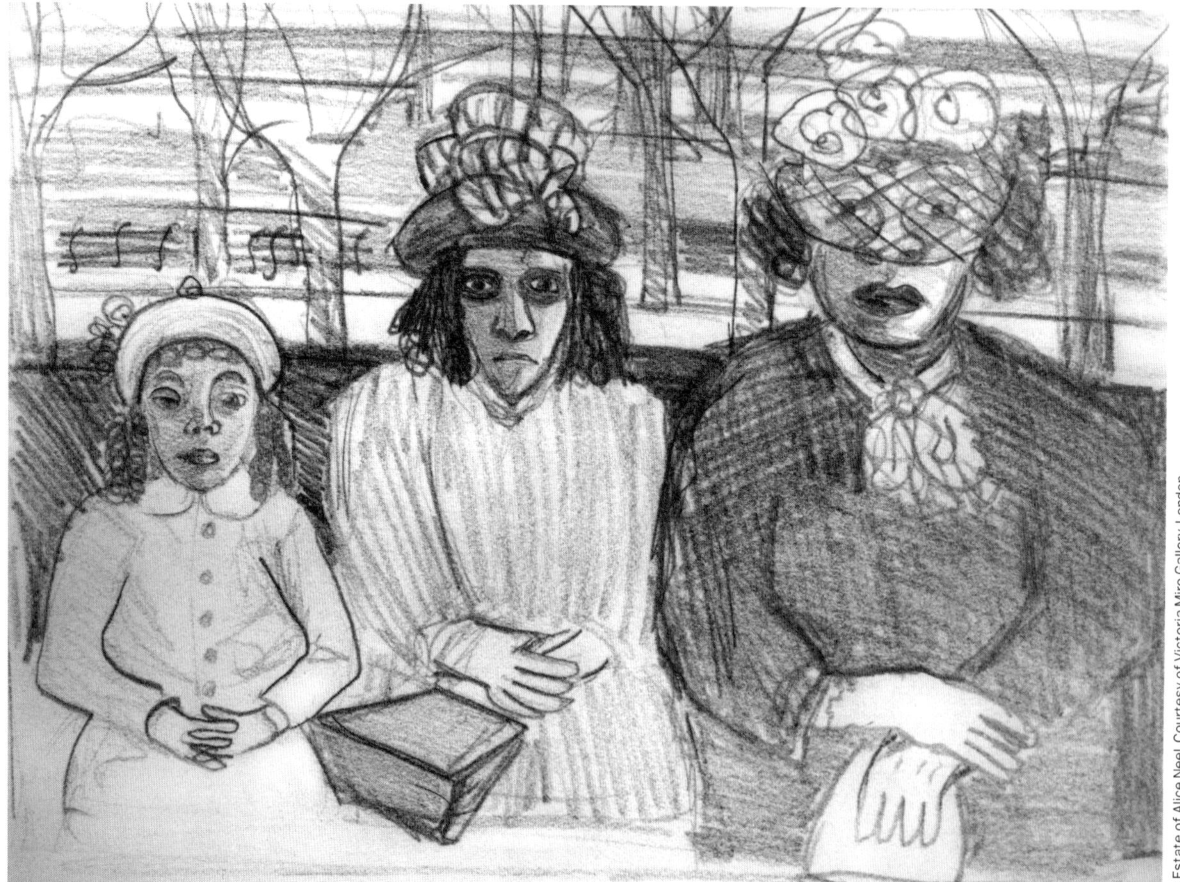

Alice Neel, 'Three Women on a Bus', *1940*

Alice Neel
Works on Paper

"Drawing", wrote the American painter Alice Neel, "is the discipline of Art". One of the great painters of the 20th century, she was a pioneer among women artists: a representational painter of people, landscape and still life in an era dominated by the essentially masculine language of Abstract Expressionism. Clement Greenberg, the high priest of formalism, had insisted that the canvas be freed of all personal narrative, autobiography and literary content. Influenced by Expressionism and realism, Neel overtly disobeyed this mantra of Modernism. Against this background of heroic male art she made sense of the world through an essentially female gaze that encompassed the body and personal emotion. She was not, she said, against abstraction, but could not stand that the abstractionists had "pushed all the other pushcarts off the streets".

What she produced were images of friends and lovers, poets, celebrities and the poor – Hispanics, blacks and the elderly – from Spanish Harlem where she lived in line with her strong social conscience and left-wing beliefs. Her cast of characters was portrayed with an incisiveness never clouded by sentimentality or illusion. Through the body's idiosyncrasies and vulnerabilities, she revealed, with searing honesty, the psyche and soul of her sitters, their suffering, endurance, courage and insecurities hidden behind carefully constructed facades. What she captured, in a form of "internal portraiture", was the inner texture of their lives. "Every person", she said, "is a new universe, unique, with its own laws emphasising some belief, a phase of life immersed in time and rapidly passing by".

Now there is a chance to see the first exhibition in this country of her works on paper. Her pencil, ink and gouache compositions from the 1930s to the 1960s include both individual portraits and closely observed scenes of daily urban life. "I love you Harlem", she wrote in her diary, "your life, your pregnant women, your relief lines outside the bank full of women who no dress in *Saks Fifth Avenue* would fit". Her stark graphic drawings include a row of old women with dishevelled hair and beaky profiles waiting patiently in line, no doubt for handouts, and one of three black women on a bus. With its penetrating observation, it is a prize example both of her compassion and her honesty. Executed in soft pencil on paper, it shows them in their veiled church hats and their gloves, staring out at the viewer, isolated, proud, dignified and afraid. Fundamental to her expression is her use of line, which at first glance appears casual but is, in fact, the product of great awareness, skill and economy. In these drawings we are allowed to see a record of her creative process in its most immediate and intimate form.

There is also an intense life-sized drawing of the American feminist poet Adrienne

Rich, with her awkward face. The two
ink-on-paper portrayals of Walter Gutman,
the New York stock-market analyst and
patron of underground art films and
projects, are almost caricatures. They show
him as a squat impresario dressed in a tight
raincoat holding his Homburg, a lid of lank
hair flipped over his balding patch.

Neel also has great sensitivity to children.
Her pencil drawing of a young girl done in
1930 not only evokes the finesse of Picasso's
early drawings, but reveals the vulnerability
of this short moment just before puberty.
With her hair in plaits, dressed in a polka-
dot swimsuit that reveals her still-flat
nipples, the girl in this little drawing is
a study in poignancy, while the children in
the park, executed in pen and ink, have the
blank stares and empty eyes that evoke the
existential alienation of Edvard Munch, and
emphasise Neel's belief that "Death, the great
void of life, hangs over everyone".

Alice Neel
Works on Paper
Victoria Miro

The Independent
7 May, 2009

Diane Arbus

"I really believe there are things which nobody would see unless I photographed them", wrote Diane Arbus. Her distinctive photographs of people, often on the margins of life, are rooted in an essential understanding of the relationship between photographer and subject. Attuned to the small tragedies and metaphors of contemporary life, she is to the photographic world what Raymond Carver was to literature. As John Szarkowski, organiser of the 1967 Museum of Modern Art exhibition 'New Documents' emphasised, "The portraits of Diane Arbus show that all of us – the most ordinary and most exotic of us – are, on closer scrutiny, remarkable".

Arbus was born to a wealthy Jewish family in 1923; her father was the son of a Russian immigrant, and her mother the daughter of the owners of Russek's Fur Store in NYC. The large apartment, the cooks, chauffeurs and maids led her to have a "sense of unreality" about her life, no doubt further complicated by her father's frequent absence at work and her mother's depression. At the age of 18, she married Allan Arbus, an employee in the advertising department of her parents' store, whom she had met when she was 13. It was he who gave her her first camera. They worked together in fashion photography until she went her own way professionally, after which their marriage broke down. In July of 1971, at the age of 48, she ended her own life with pills and a razor. Like Anne Sexton, Sylvia Plath and Janis Joplin, she was beautiful, tragic, romantic and complicated.

By the 60s, her commercial portraits for magazines such as 'Esquire' and 'Harper's Bazaar' had begun to assume a distinctive look. She would frame her subjects in ordinary settings, posed looking straight at the camera. Unblinking and quizzical, they assumed an air of disquiet, as if some secret were about to be exposed. No sentimentalist, she began to search out, rather than stumble upon, the sort of people she wanted to photograph: young children and socialites, nudists and dwarfs, transvestites and circus performers.

She has been accused of being interested only in aberration: a poor little rich girl getting her kicks from life's seamy side, from off-beat sexual practices, tortured sexual identities and the shock value of mental feebleness and physical deformity. And even now, many of her images seem, in the true sense of the word, shocking, in that they bring the viewer up short to experience the raw and damaged humanity behind the glitter, the showgirl outfits and the socialite dresses. Why did people agree to let her into the privacy of their bedrooms, and reveal themselves at their most vulnerable?

In this exhibition there are plenty of such examples: the stripper with bare breasts in her dressing room in Atlantic City, New

Jersey in 1962, the walls running with damp as she sits in spangled arm bands at her makeshift dressing table, not bothering to disguise her spare tyre; or the "naked man being a woman in his room in NYC" in 1968, posing provocatively with his hand on his hip and his genitals tucked away between his legs; or the nudist lady in a flower-petal hat and absurd diamanté swan sunglasses. There is something complicit in these images, as if the subjects needed Arbus as much as she needed them. Being photographed defined them, gave a moment of colour to their otherwise anonymous lives. For most of her photographs depended on her subject's active participation. People must have been flattered to be asked. Inside they simply felt themselves and didn't know or didn't see that in front of her lens, whether they were Mrs T. Charlton Henry, a raddled dowager in a negligee from Philadelphia, or a Puerto Rican woman in a nylon headscarf with heavily painted eyes and a beauty mark, they would both end up looking like axe murders.

But it is her untitled photographs taken between 1969 and 1971 of people in residences for what is euphemistically called "developmental difficulties", that are the hardest to look at. Those with Down's syndrome or other mental or physical oddities are dressed in masks, their faces painted as if for some mediaeval pageant. Arbus admitted that she loved "freaks". "There's a quality of legend about freaks. Like a person in a fairytale who stops you and demands that you answer a riddle. Most people go through life dreading they'll have a traumatic experience: freaks were born with trauma. They've already passed their test in life. They're aristocrats."

Perhaps, in the end, this is the true power of her images – that not only do they throw light on those who seem odd and dispossessed, but they illuminate our own responses when faced with the different, the damaged and the abject. In that sense, Diane Arbus is a revealer of souls.

Diane Arbus
Timothy Taylor Gallery

New Statesman
4th June, 2009

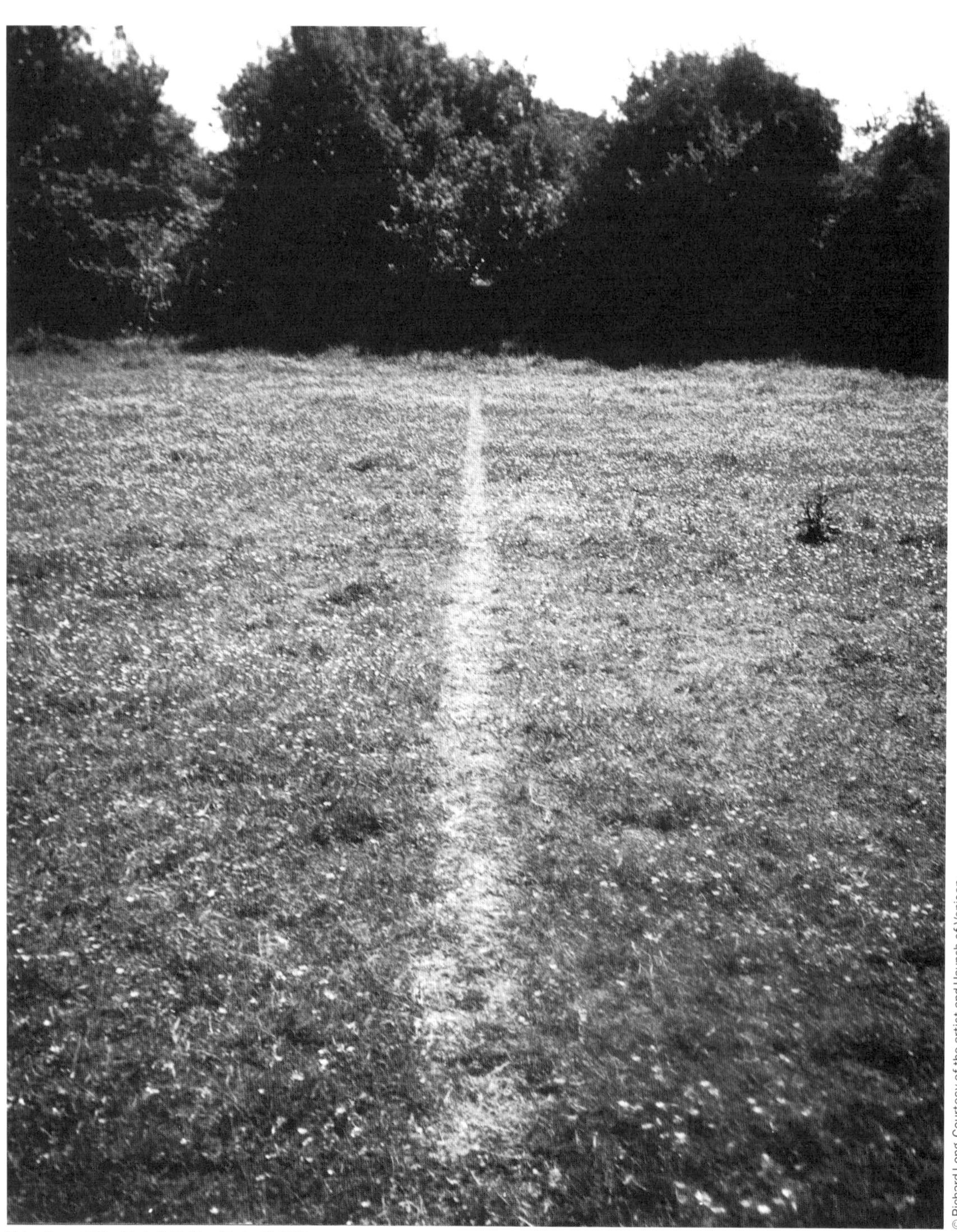

Richard Long, 'A Line Made By Walking (England)', *1968*

Richard Long
Heaven and Earth

The history of mankind has been about movement. People migrated on foot out of Africa and pilgrims have, through the ages, made journeys of prayer and penitence. In his remarkable book, 'The Songlines', about the ancient invisible pathways that criss-cross Australia carrying the songs that described the land's creation, the late Bruce Chatwin wrote, "by singing the word into existence... the Ancestors had been poets in the original sense of *poesis*, meaning "creation". No Aboriginal could conceive that the created world was in any way imperfect. His religious life had a single aim: to keep the land the way it was and should be. The man who went 'walkabout' was making a ritual journey".

Walking was also an inspirational habit for William Wordsworth. Thomas de Quincey estimated that Wordsworth's lifetime pedestrian rambles amounted to around 180,000 miles. John Clare walked as an imaginative catalyst. For walking is, as a way of being in, and part of, the natural world, an act of recollection and reflection. As a contemporary artist, Richard Long has found new ways to make and use walks, which not only connect him to these ancient wanderings, but have their own unique purpose. He likes common materials: stones, sticks, mud and water, with which he creates symmetrical patterns that link time and place, the wilderness and the gallery. He describes himself as a Modernist rather than a Romantic, and says that his talent

as an artist "is to walk across a moor, or place a stone on the ground".

It all started in 1967 when, at the age of 22, he made 'A Line Made by Walking' and in a significant way changed our understanding of sculpture. A student at St Martins, he took a train from Waterloo, got off at the nearest station, and found a suitable field, where he walked back and forth until the flattened grass became visible as a line in the sunlight. He then took a photograph, got back on the train and went home. There were no materials involved, no welding, and no "making". The piece simply involved an idea, a minimal physical act and a photograph. 'A Line Made by Walking' has been likened to Kasimir Malevich's 1915 'Black Square' in its impact, changing the face of sculpture as Malevich's work cancelled previous concepts of what constituted a painting. With this piece, Long moved away from formalism and the heroics of sculpture implicit in the work of artists such as Phillip King and Anthony Caro, placing it somewhere between the shamanistic performances of Joseph Beuys and Carl Andre's view of "sculpture as form – sculpture as structure – sculpture as place".

In 1966, Long went to the Saville Theatre in Shaftesbury Avenue, to a performance by the experimental composer John Cage. Cage's theories about the interchangeablity of art and life, and his interest in Zen Buddhism and Taoism, were to have a profound effect. This abiding interest is apparent in the opening room of Long's first major survey exhibition in London for 18 years, where the visitor is greeted by two hexagrams from the 'I Ching', which run from floor to ceiling. Here the lines of each hexagram, created by rhythmic hand strokes with Avon river mud, are set against black squares. Heaven has six solid lines, Earth six broken lines – yin and yang, dark and light. The hexagrams represent the dualities and balance to be found both in nature and in Long's work. Avon mud is a recurring material, whilst rivers and water are abiding themes. The Avon has the second highest tides in the world and it is from there, near where Long grew up, that he collects the mud. The four large mud works in the exhibition all display his interest in water, gravity and chance. Splashes and drips are integral to each work's character.

But it is his solitary walks, whether through the Dorset landscape or further afield on the plains of Canada, Mongolia and Bolivia, that are the backbone of his practice. His interventions are always minimal – a ring of stones arranged in the middle of the Gobi desert, a line of small standing stones on Cul Mor, Scotland, or a zigzag of camp-fire ash left by Lake Titicaca. Long understands the pull and longing in the human heart for wilderness and, through his modest interventions, forces us to evaluate the marks and traces we leave behind in the landscape. For a contemporary artist, there is no cynicism and even less ego. He simply disappears off into the wild where he creates his resonant archetypal forms, which he photographs so that, for a moment, the spare beauty of the world is revealed to us through his eyes. Other work is made specifically with the gallery in mind, and at Tate Britain the large central room is devoted to six major stone sculptures including the 'Norfolk Flint Circle', *1990,* an eight-metre stone circle of flints placed on the floor, and the beautiful 'Red Slate Circle', *1988.* Here, too, the configurations are the same – circles, lines and ellipses.

Long's explorations of the relationship between time, distance, geography, measurement and movement are also "mapped" in his text works directly applied to the gallery walls. Here the smallest incidents – the ritual moving of a stone, dragonflies on his tent, the chirrup of a skylark – are noted. The effect is rather like that of a haiku, but in fact these texts are verbal traces of his walks. There are no metaphors, no literary flourishes – he simply chronicles what he sees. As he says, "my work is neither urban, nor romantic. It is the laying down of modern ideas in the only practical places to take them. The natural world sustains the industrial world. I use the world as I find it... a road is the site of many journeys. The place of a walk is there before the walk and after it". In the contemporary brouhaha, there is something deeply refreshing about these still points in this endlessly turning world.

Richard Long
Heaven and Earth
Tate Britain

New Statesman
8th June, 2009

I received an email telling me it was over. I didn't
know how to respond. It was almost as if it hadn't
been meant for me. It ended with the words,
"Take care of yourself". I followed this advice to
the letter: I asked 104 women (as well as two
handpuppets and a parrot), chosen for their
profession or skills, to interpret the letter. To
analyse it, comment on it, dance it, sing it. Dissect
it. Exhaust it. Understand it for me. Answer for me.
It was a way of taking the time to break up: a way
to take care of myself.

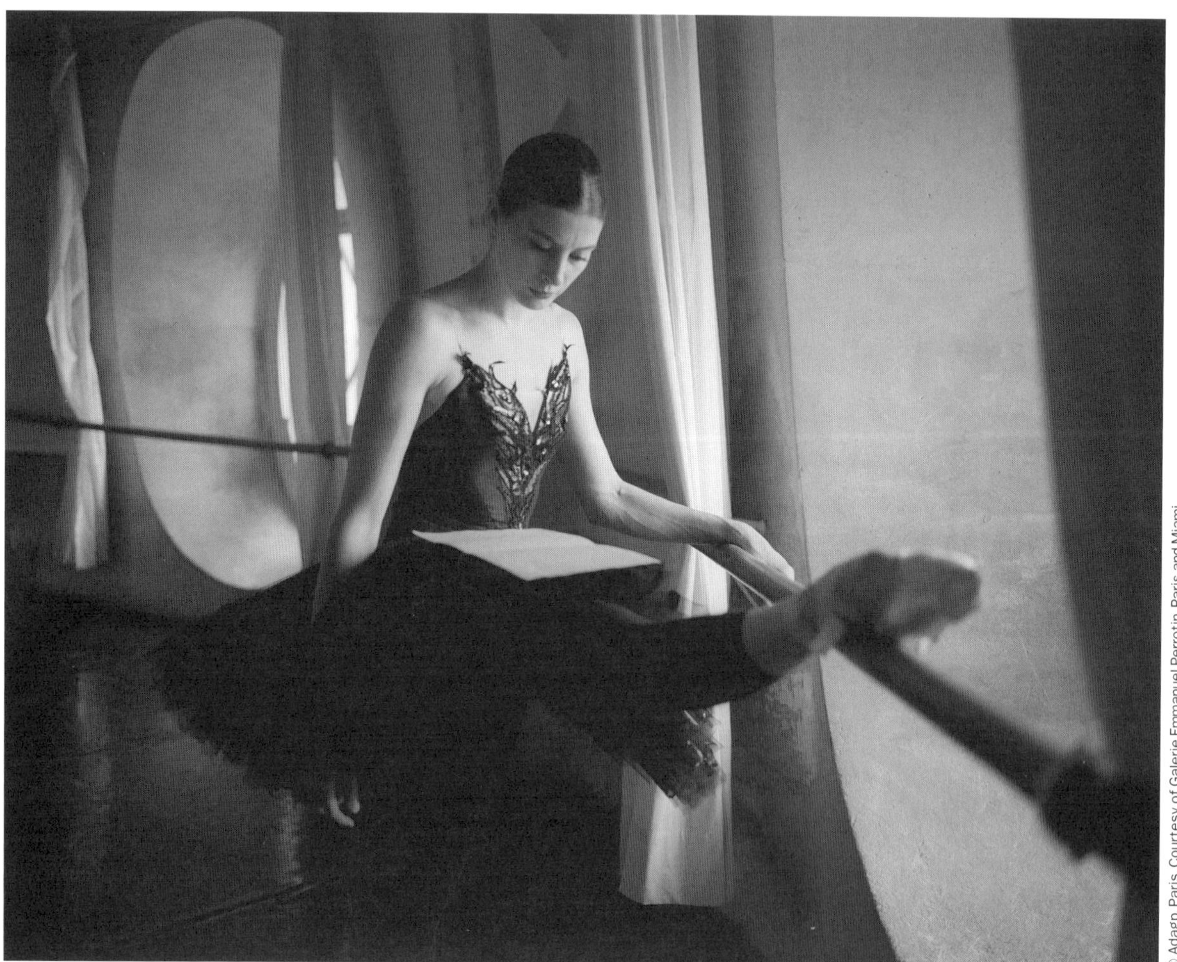

Sophie Calle, 'Take Care of Yourself' (detail), *2007*

Sophie Calle/
John Baldessari
Words, Images and
Playing Games

Sophie Calle

What do you do when your lover jilts you by email? Take to your bed and forget to wash, wander around in your pyjamas, cut up his suits or send him a poison-pen letter? If you are an artist there is another option: you can shame him by turning his self-justifying text into a large-scale conceptual art work using over 100 different women as allies. That is just what the French artist Sophie Calle does in her work 'Prenez soin de vous' ('Take Care of Yourself'), where she has invited lawyers, actors, accountants, singers and psychologists to comment on her lover's text though the lens of their professional vocabulary. A composer turns the letter into a musical score; a translator asks why her ex-partner uses the formal *vous* rather than *tu*, and what this says about their relationship; whilst a rifle shooter peppers the email with bullet holes.

From this single text, Calle weaves a web of female support. Spinning out the threads of the painful missive in which her lover admits that he is again seeing the "others", thereby breaking their contract in which he agreed not to make her the "fourth", she creates a complex polyphony of female voices rather like that of a Greek chorus. Using photographs, text and video, she creates a complex multi-layered narrative that arouses both distaste at her lover's self-indulgent musings, and a sneaking sympathy for his obvious inability to make any meaningful emotional commitment. As a clinical psychologist says: "He is an intelligent cultivated man from a good socio-cultural background, elegant, charming and seductive with a fine, fairly subtle, rather abstract intelligence. He is proud, narcissistic and egotistical".

Part photo-novella, part psychoanalytic text, this is a work in which fact and fiction, reality and artifice, are continually blurred. Like Cindy Sherman, Sophie Calle is a mistress of disguise. Never actually present within her work, she leads us to question the validity of the narrative "I". Who knows whether there really was a lover and an email, or if this is simply an intriguing artistic construct? The work turns at the same time into voyeurs, conspirators and dupes, never letting us settle into a single role. As with the novelist Paul Auster, who wrote one of the essays in the Whitechapel catalogue, she is concerned with how a subject sits within a constructed social and artistic framework, whilst always remaining very much the omniscient narrator. One of the underlying themes of her work is that of surveillance, whereby she uses photographs and texts to create a body of reportage and apparent documentation.

The first work she made, in 1979, was shown only in book form. Having come back to France after seven years travelling, she felt lost in her own town and took to following people in the street because she didn't know what else to do with herself. Choosing people at random, she let them dictate the course of her actions and neither wrote anything nor took photos. Following a man to Venice, she shadowed him for two weeks. Since he was a photographer himself, she tried to duplicate the kinds of images she imagined he might make, and created a book, 'Suite Vénitienne', about the experience. In her next work 'The Sleepers', she asked people she didn't know to come and sleep in her bed for eight hours, and then be woken by someone who would take their place. For the day shift, she invited those such as bakers who would normally sleep in the day. Staying by the bedside, she photographed these strangers every hour and wrote down what they said. This continued for eight days. The results are like the field notes and photographs of an ethnographer or anthropologist: objective rather than intimate.

This objective control is a central element of her work, making her into both *auteur* and conductor. In 'L'homme au carnet' ('The Address Book'), *1983*, she reportedly finds a fancy red notebook in a Parisian street and constructs the personality of the owner Pierre D. through a series of meetings and interviews with those whose addresses she finds inside its pages. Detailed descriptions were then published in the 'Libération' during the August of 1983. When Monsieur D. returned from Norway and recognised himself in the articles, the result was outrage and distress. He claimed it was a callous invasion of his privacy and demanded the right of reply. This was printed in the paper beside a photo of Calle, naked in a domestic environment, her features masked like those of a criminal. Who then was the victim – Calle or Monsieur D.? And is any of it true or do these Borgesian threads simply function as so many open-ended possibilities in a postmodern narrative? Chance, so beloved by the Surrealists, also plays its part in Calle's piece 'When and Where? Berck', a creative

game based on a journey of uncanny synchronicities dictated by her clairvoyant.

Her work is also about lack. About the lack of her central characters – her lover and herself in 'Take Care of Yourself', of Monsieur D. in the address-book piece – who are always off stage, hovering in the wings. It is this void that Calle fills with her complex, allusive narrative threads, standing in the middle like the spider weaving her complex designs. The persona she gives us is the one she wants us to see rather than the "true" Sophie Calle. But not all her work is so detached. The poignant tribute to her dead mother in 'Souci' captures, in text and works of black pigment, sand-blasted paper, lead and hair, her mother's last hours. It records her final pedicure, the final book she read, the last music she heard and her last smile. But, try as she might, Sophie Calle could not record her last elusive breath, which occurred somewhere between 3:02 and 3:12 in the afternoon, and proved impossible to capture: perhaps like truth itself.

John Baldessari

Language and text are also essential elements in the work of the Californian artist John Baldessari, who has been described as "a cross between Walt Whitman and a redwood tree". Born in 1931, he is an imposing figure of six feet seven inches tall, with a white beard and halo of prophet-like hair, widely regarded as the granddaddy of conceptual art. The current exhibition 'Pure Beauty' at Tate Modern brings together more than 130 art works in this most extensive retrospective of his oeuvre in this country. With iconoclastic wit and irony, Baldessari deconstructs the shibboleths that underlie much contemporary artistic practice, and questions the accepted rules of how art should be made. In the 1960s, he began to use words as most artists use images, saying "a word can't substitute for an image but is equal to it". Beguiling his viewers with humour, he aims to be as "disarming as possible". Instructions from art manuals and quotes from celebrated art critics painted onto the surface of his canvases drew attention to the prevailing aesthetic attitudes of the period. By painting words on canvas, he signalled that a "text" painting was just as much a "work of art" as a nude or a still life.

It's hard not to chortle at his 1960s 'Tips for Artists Who Want to Sell' and the deliciously tongue-in-cheek canvas that simply says: "*Everything is purged from this painting but art, no ideas have entered this work*". Baldessari has said that semiotics and, in particular, Claude Lévi-Strauss's structuralism, were major influences on his treating language as sign, and on his deliberate play between word and image, though it's easy to imagine that he might have had a career as a stand-up comedian. From the 1970s, he married his humorous pursuit of a new visual language to film. 'I Will Not Make Any More Boring Art', *1971* sees him record himself on videotape, writing the lines over and over again in a notebook. In 1970, he stopped painting to focus on photography and film, but not before he had burned all his paintings in 'Cremation Project', which was accompanied by an affidavit, published in the 'San Diego Union-Tribune'. His approach to teaching was equally playful and unorthodox, promoting what he called "post-studio art" based on the idea that "there is a certain kind of work one could do that didn't require a studio. It's work that is done in one's head". In his 1972-73 set of photographs called 'The Artist Hitting Various Objects With a Golf Club', he takes repeated swipes, in a form of intellectual crazy golf, at objects found in the city dump. There is also a set of photographs of him blowing cigar smoke to imitate a picture of a cloud, and another series 'Choosing (A Game for Two Players): Carrots', a sort of absurdist chess made up of arcane carrot-moving rules. It is both mad and rather funny.

Baldessari's work is full of paradox. It liberates, irritates, inspires and disarms, and has been an enormous influence on a whole generation of younger artists. Like looking through a kaleidoscope, we are presented with what is familiar with an unfamiliar twist, so that we are forced to think about things in a slightly different way. We are continually confronted by images that ask "Is this art?" and, if so, does such a definition matter as long as the work prods us and makes us look at the world afresh? Baldessari's own disarming answer, given in an early painting that escaped the 'Cremation Project', is 'God Nose'.

Sophie Calle
Whitechapel Gallery
John Baldessari
Tate Modern
Words, Images and Playing Games

www.3quarksdaily.com
16th November, 2009

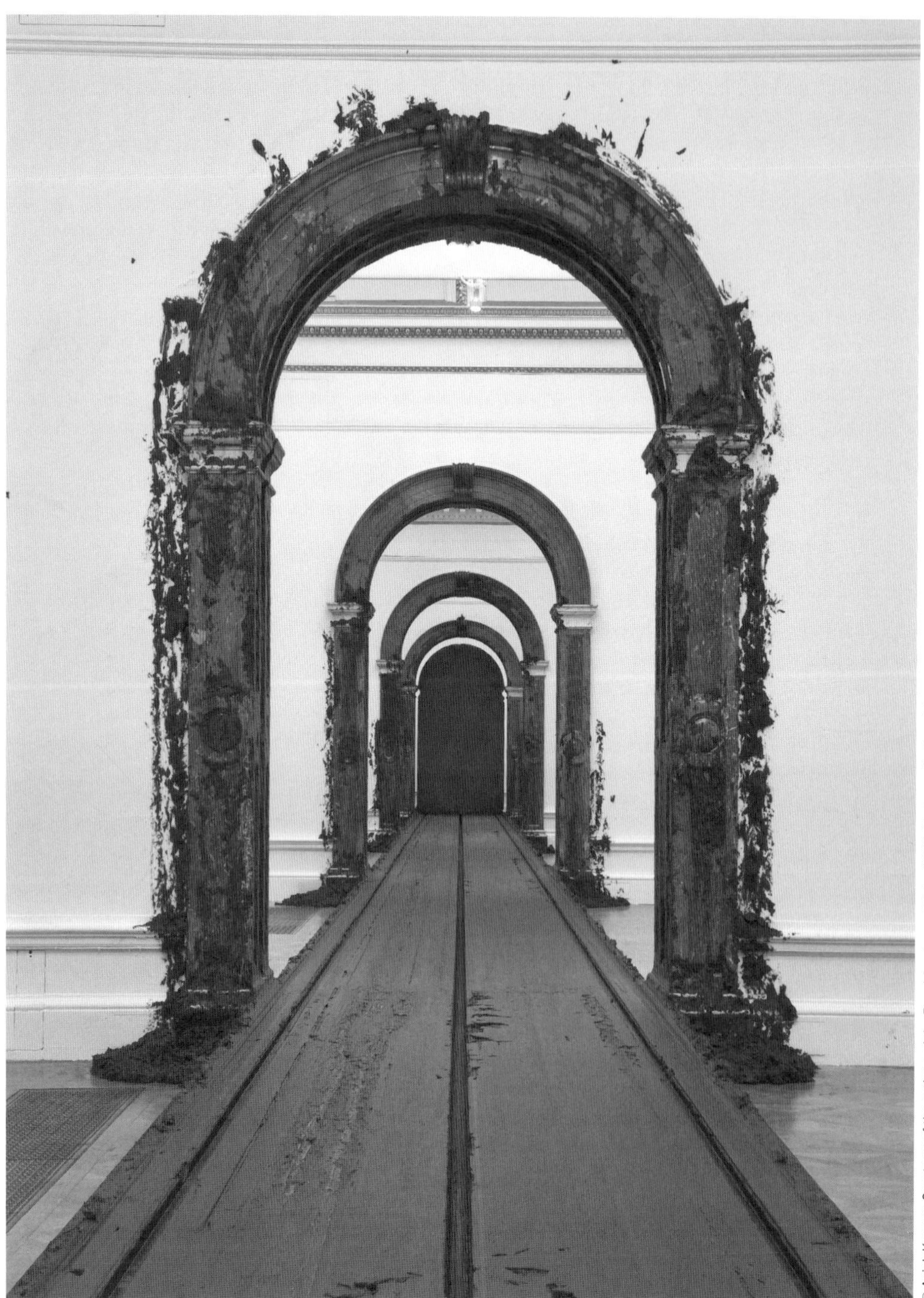

Anish Kapoor, 'Svayambh', *2007*

Turner Prize/ Anish Kapoor Seriousness Is the New Black

Many factors have lead to London's pre-eminence in the contemporary art world: the importance of Goldsmiths College to the Damien Hirst generation of Young British Artists, Charles Saatchi's ubiquitous influence as a collector, Jay Jopling's White Cube gallery, the founding of the annual Frieze Art Fair, and of course, the Turner Prize, that annual award set up in 1984 to celebrate new developments in contemporary art, and presented each year to a British artist under 50 for an outstanding exhibition in the preceding 12 months. It has always been a controversial affair. There was, of course, *that bed* (it didn't win) and Martin Creed's minimal light bulbs that simply went on and off. Last year, the shortlist was universally derided as opaque and pretentious. But looking back over its history, love it or hate it, the Turner Prize has become a barometer of the British art scene. Those nominated, often previously unknown outside the art world, usually end up as household names.

This year the short list feels subtly different; not only is there an absence of videos (accident, not design, it is claimed) but the work is thoughtful, complex, crafted and, in several cases, rather beautiful. There is little irony. Seriousness, it seems, is this season's new black.

Glaswegian artist Lucy Skaer (the only woman) has named her installation 'Thames and Hudson', a reference to both those mighty rivers as well as to the celebrated art publisher. Yet, somehow, the whole feels made up of rather too many disparate parts. A dismantled chair has been used to make some rather obtuse prints, while her 'Black Alphabet' is a version of Brancusi's 1923 sculpture 'Bird in Space', cast 26 times in compressed coal dust – though her purpose and message remain rather a mystery. Her *pièce de résistance*, however, is the skull of an adult male sperm whale (comparison with Hirst's formaldehyde shark is unavoidable) on loan from a Scottish museum. Suspended so that it is only partially visible through a series of screens, its sad bony hulk is reminiscent of Victorian curiosities peered at through fairground peep-holes.

Enter the second gallery and, at first, it seems to be mostly white. Yet, at the far end, a Baroque-style design made of gold leaf has been applied straight onto the wall. Standing in front of it, the viewer sees patterns begin to emerge: a pelvis, a spine and even female genitals. Elsewhere the gold bursts into a sunray, which made me think of Louis XIV, the Sun King, which then started me musing about the transient nature of power and provoked the thought that this rather beautiful piece would last only as long as the exhibition before being painted over and returned to being just another gallery wall. It could, therefore, be seen as a sort of contemporary *vanitas* painting. All this beauty, we are subtly reminded, will be erased to become so much whitewash, just as we too will eventually be erased. This is decorative art with a serious twist.

The next gallery comes as a complete contrast. Enrico David's installation, titled 'Absuction Cardigan' is fun, annoying and serious in about equal measure. I did not go much for his Humpty Dumpty black figures set on skis, but his *mise en scène,* raised on a sort of stage, is deeply unnerving. A huge black, stuffed-doll of a creature, with a neck and tail the length of the room, lies draped over a variety of disquieting props. Its face, a flat wooden mask, is comprised of nothing but bore holes. Part floppy toy, part dead animal and sexual playmate, it draws on Louise Bourgeois and Annette Messager's transgressive figures, and on Hans Bellmer's erotic dolls.

Roger Hiorn's work inhabits the final space. Here, lumpy sculptures of cast plastic have been injected with bovine brain matter, so that what was once sentient has been rendered inert and mummified. Metaphors of death are also strong in his beautiful, evocative landscape, in subtle shades of grey and black, made from an atomised passenger jet engine and scattered on the floor to resemble the Himalayas or the surface of the moon. Ashes to ashes, dust to dust – like all good art, it evokes a number of readings that range from the disaster of 9/11 to a globally warmed and violated earth.

Proof that the Turner Prize does sometimes get it right can be seen at the Royal Academy, where the 1991 winner, Anish Kapoor, has one of London's most outstanding exhibitions. There have been those who complain that it is sensationalist, too male and too reliant on gadgets and props. I admit that I never much liked his 'Masaryas', which filled Tate Modern's turbine hall – too much bravura engineering and not enough poetry. But this is one of the most evocative exhibitions I've come across in a long time. Not only technically brilliant and thought provoking, it displays

a scale that is heroic. It starts in the courtyard with a major new sculpture 'Tall Tree and the Eye', inspired, according to Kapoor, by the words of the German poet Rainer Maria Rilke. Made, apparently, of precariously balanced steel balls that reflect back the surrounding Palladian architecture, this work signals that Kapoor is not afraid of beauty. An unfashionable component in contemporary art, much is to be found inside Burlington House.

In the first room is a group of early pigment sculptures from the 70s and 80s that are strongly influenced by his Indian origins, and reinforce his reputation as a colourist. The unmixed heaps, built into pyramids and ziggurats of bright blue, cinnamon yellow and cayenne red, resemble rather sophisticated sandcastles, and evoke piles of Indian spices in a way that, although not particularly demanding, stirs a remembrance of things past.

Move through the galleries and you will find a barely visible pregnant lump protruding from the white wall, and another huge yellow wall where the indentation is concave. The effect is like standing in front of some Aztec shrine where one is seductively sucked into the sun-like void, and invited to think of beginnings and endings, origins and destruction.

Then there is 'Shooting into the Corner', a new work where gobbets of red wax are fired from a cannon through one of the Royal Academy's elegant 18th-century doorways. This happens three times an hour. Many visitors seem simply to have been taken up by the drama, in a man-fired-from-cannon sort of way, but I found it very disturbing. A gallery assistant dressed in black stands with military bearing, stuffing cartridges into the cannon. The explosion, when it comes, is deafening. In this palatial setting, as the red wax splatters the white walls and the surrounding Adam-style doorway, like the visceral effluvia of executed bodies, I kept thinking of the final moments of the last Tsar and his family, or Manet's 'Execution of Maximilian'.

A multiplicity of readings can also be applied to the monumental work 'Svayambh', *2007*. Although it has already been shown in previous locations, this is probably its most dramatic setting. 'Svayambh' means "self-generated" in Sanskrit, and the piece reinforces Kapoor's interest in sculpture that actively explores this process. Again, many viewers were taken with the theatre of the moving mechanism, running between galleries to watch as the vast block of red wax was slowly squeezed, like a great juggernaut, through the doorways of Burlington House. And certainly one is reminded of those huge Indian carts from which the name juggernaut comes, and of the annual procession at Puri in east-central India where worshippers throw themselves under the wheels of the huge wagon on which the idol of Krishna is carried. But for anyone with a poetic imagination, this red gash of an object, moving relentlessly along the rail tracks like a piece of raw meat, covering the doorways along the way with coagulated red carnage, must have historical resonances, evoking the trains that took thousands to their death in the Nazi transports, or those who gave their life's blood in acts of enforced labour to build railways in the Far East during the last world war. Huge and monumental, its movement almost imperceptible, it marks, as it slowly lumbers its way through the gallery like a slow birthing of the building itself, the passing of time. And yet despite all the layers of meaning that it invites, it is, ultimately, an abstract work of art, an act of the imagination and an exploration of the possibility of materials.

The exhibition is huge. There are beguiling sculptural mirrors that reflect the gold-leafed ceiling, and the self back to the self, blurring the lines between perceived and actual experience; and piles of coiled cement,

which suggest the history of pot-making and the touch of the human hand, but which, in fact, have been arrived at by a rough sketch being fed into a computer and attached to a cement-mixer, which, in turn, has been attached to a machine adapted from the food industry to excrete the cement like icing; and a vast, rusted-steel Richard Serra-like sculpture, 'Hive', an enormous pod splayed open at one end to reveal a deep central void, which is at once both erotic and chthonic.

Kapoor is not a philosopher, nor does he claim to have, as a visual artist, anything particular to say. The power of this work lies in its ability to provoke questions about origins, perception, belief and self-definition. Comparison can be made with the spiritual leanings of Yves Klein (homage is surely paid in Kapoor's early blue-pigment works), but where Klein's spirituality was derived from the arcane complexities of alchemy and Rosicrucianism, Kapoor's work is never didactic. There is an openness about his quest that is not wedded to a single belief system, but reminds us, as Keats once did, that there is, indeed, truth in beauty. This year's Turner short-listed artists still have some way to go.

Turner Prize
Tate Britain
Anish Kapoor
Royal Academy
Seriousness Is the New Black

www.3quarksdaily.com
19th October 2009

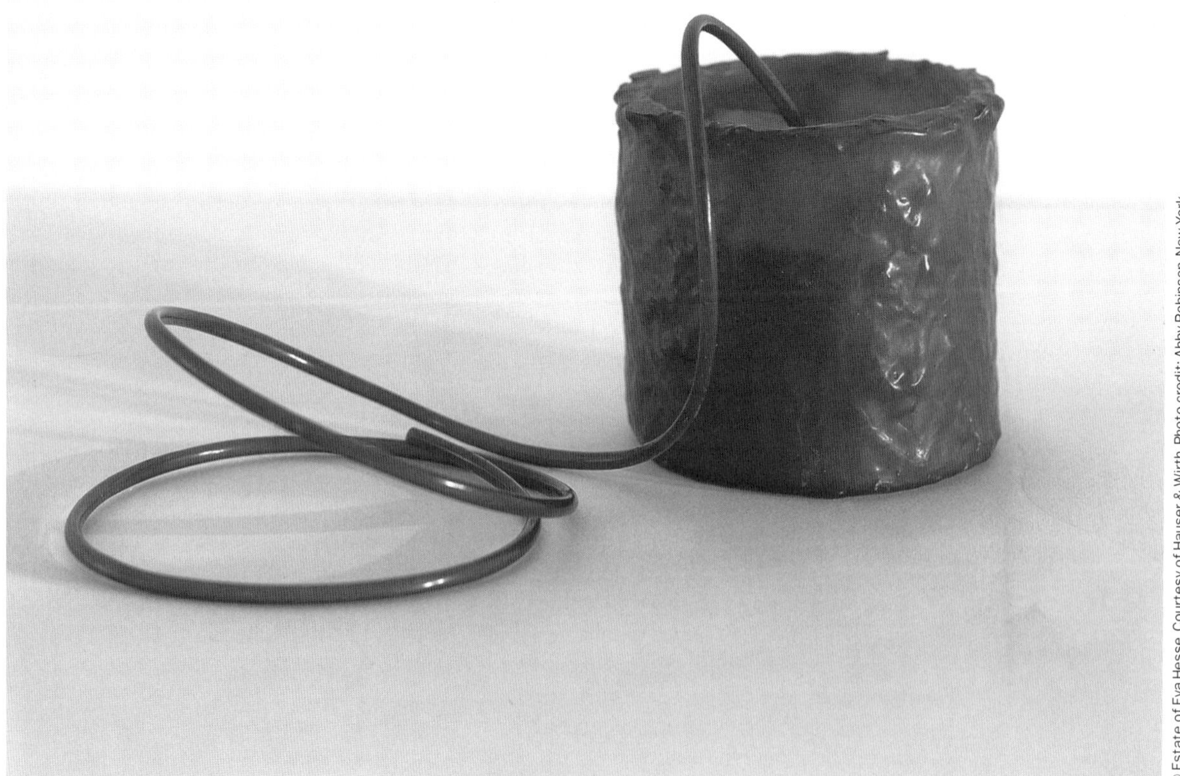

Eva Hesse, No title, *1967*

Eva Hesse Studiowork
Shards and Fragments

What is the purpose and function of art? The work of Eva Hesse challenges us to ask this question. Her history has been well documented. Born in Hamburg in 1936 to a family of observant Jews, she was, at the age of two, put on a Kindertransport arriving first in Holland, then England and, finally, America in 1939. A sense of tenuousness and the impermanence of things colours her work. The balls of screwed paper, the bits of flimsy gauze, mesh and cloth are like whispers rather than assertions, thought processes made physical, rather than finished objects. Her life was short. At the age of 34, when living in New York, she was diagnosed with a fatal brain tumour that cut short her career as a sculptor just as it was getting underway. The body of work she left was remarkable. Poetic, anxious and intense, it made manifest her inner, often turbulent, emotional life. A writer of diaries, she produced work for which autobiography was the base note.

Like the poets Sylvia Plath and Anne Sexton, Hesse suffered trauma in early childhood that strongly affected her emotional development, as did her parents' separation and divorce, and her mother's subsequent suicide in 1945. These events left her insecure and anxious, so that in 1954 she made a decision to enter therapy. Her subsequent analysis had a profound effect on her work as she began to examine herself more closely. "I think art is a total thing: a total person giving a contribution. It is an essence, a soul... In my inner soul, art

and life are inseparable." It is, also, not implausible to consider that on some level she must also have been haunted by the "what might have beens" that would surely have befallen her if she had failed to leave Hamburg in 1936, and faced the fate of many other Jews of her generation. The ghost of the Holocaust, as well as her own family traumas, shadows her work.

Hesse's creative talent had been evident since childhood. At the age of 16, she graduated from the New York School of Industrial Arts, later attending the Pratt Institute of Design. But by December 1953, she had dropped out to study figure drawing at the Art Students' League, whilst also working as a layout artist for 'Seventeen' magazine. Then, in 1957, she graduated from Cooper Union in New York, going on to study at Yale with the assistance of a Norfolk Fellowship.

There she worked as a painter, studying colour theory under Joseph Albers. Influenced by Abstract Expressionism, her work, during the five years from 1960 to 1965, was mostly small, and intensely personal. Her powerful drawings, with their circular and container-like shapes, anticipated her later sculptural configurations: her interest in the metaphors of inside and outside, of what is contained and what is left open-ended.

In 1962 she married the sculptor Tom Doyle, from whom she was later to separate, and moved to Ketturg-Am-Ruhr, Germany, where for a year they were guests of the textile manufacturer and collector F. Amhard Scherdt. When they arrived for their 15-month residency in the summer of 1964, Hesse was a painter who identified with Abstract Expressionism and the work of Arshile Gorky and Willem de Kooning, while Doyle described himself an "Abstract-Expressionist sculptor". This visit proved crucial to Hesse's development. Becoming frustrated with painting, she experimented with combining paint, collage and drawing. Her imagery became infused with the shapes of the machine parts she found in an abandoned factory. These machine drawings were the breakthrough for which she had been searching. According to Doyle, "she really had something, she'd found herself". Often humorous and reminiscent of the "erotic machines" of Francis Picabia and Marcel Duchamp, these drawings explored Dadaist notions of the absurd, which later Hesse was to incorporate into her sculpture. "If I can name the content, then… it's the total absurdity of life…. Absurdity is the key word. It is to do with contradictions and oppositions… I was always aware that I should take order versus chaos, stringy versus mass, huge versus small, and I would try to find the most absurd opposites or extreme opposites."

'Ring Around Arosie', *1965*, a pink breast-like protuberance of cloth and wire on a Masonite panel, was unashamedly sexual in nature, illustrating her growing interest in exploring definitions of the self in terms of the body and female experience. At the same time, she was beginning to break artistic convention and push against the prevailing dominance of the heroic and masculine influences of Abstract Expressionism, exploring the use of non-traditional materials such as plastic and industrial wire, in a quest for a more personal, immediate and feminised visual language. "My idea now is to counteract everything I've ever learnt or been taught about those things – to find

something inevitable that is my life, my thought, my feelings."

Her work defies categorisation, but Joseph Beuys, Claes Oldenburg, and Jean Dubuffet might all be considered to have had an input as Hesse became increasingly interested in ideas outside the conventions of sculpture, rejecting its "male" rigidity and the emptied forms of Minimalism, to follow her growing interest in the "female" and the internal. The critic Robert Hughes has described her as "the artist who did the most to humanise Minimalism without sentimentalising it". Too interested in debates about the essence and materiality of art to want simply to be categorised as a woman artist, she retorted to a list of questions sent to her by a journalist that "the best way to beat discrimination in art is by art", adding that "excellence has no sex".

Now the Camden Arts Centre in north London has put on an exhibition that explores Hesse's little known "test pieces". Throughout her career, she produced many small, experimental works alongside her large-scale sculptures. Constructed from a wide range of materials including latex, wire-mesh, wax and cheesecloth, these simple objects are not just technical explorations, but the physical embodiment of Hesse's creative thought processes. Previously considered peripheral to her main output, they have been renamed, by Professor Briony Fey, the curator of the show and a Hesse expert, as "studioworks".

After her death they posed something of a problem. What was all this "stuff" left in her studio? Her friend Sol LeWitt tried to make sense of it, calling what he discovered a series of "little experiments" or "studio leavings". Sometimes he insisted that what he found was "definitely not a piece" whilst on other occasions he would pronounce: "Yes, this is a piece". Yet, despite his close friendship with Hesse, maybe he was asking the wrong questions. Hesse was attracted to the modest, the discarded and the forgotten. Not only do these slight objects explore the limits of sculptural practice, but they resonate with compressed emotion and lost memories. They are less statements than expressions of feeling. Like Giacometti's tiny post-war figures, they leak existential anxiety and doubt, which is hardly surprising given Hesse's childhood and background. As in Samuel Beckett's novel 'The Unnameable', *1953*, where the last line insists that against the odds and the empty absurdity of life "things must go on", we intuitively feel Hesse's fragile grasp, overlaid by her determination to find a path through the bleak landscape of modernity and the raw, essential stuff of the human condition. These flimsy pieces are a philosophically visual encounter with nothingness.

Yet there is also something carnal, even scatological, about the fragments on show in their glass cases. Over time, the latex has darkened to the colour of tanned hide, and other pieces look like trusses or prosthetic supports for repetitive strain injury. A latex, cheesecloth, plastic and metal strip hangs from a hook on the gallery wall like a ribbon of flayed flesh. The possible interpretations are endless: a reference to Titian's 'The Flaying of Marsyas', the scourged body of Christ, or even Nazi lampshades made from Jewish skin. Meaning is never overt; each item entangles us in a web of questions and possible meanings about being and absence, art and non-art. Looking is an intense and uncomfortable experience. The pieces make demands on the viewer. They provoke, they needle, yet they resist interpretation. We can either see them as bits of junk or detritus, or if we look, really look, and give our imaginations free reign, we can read them as potent metaphors for loss, memory and the tragedy of human existence. Like Melanie Klein's part objects, they seem to stand in for something else, though exactly what that "else" is, is never made explicit. The fact that all the works have 'no title' – as opposed to that ubiquitous label of contemporary art 'untitled' – only adds to the feeling of uncertainty.

In one of the galleries, husks of papier mâché lie like empty pods on a large central plinth. Made of brown paper, they are dry and brittle: the apparent detritus of something left behind by a previous unnamed event, like shards of memory. Elsewhere two small pieces of stuffed canvas, covered with hair-like tendrils of string, lie hunkered in their glass case like some primitive copulating animal. Inside and outside, hard and soft, the pieces fold and collapse in on themselves. There are echoes of Louise Bourgeois' small latex works from the early 1960s; it is uncertain whether or not Hesse saw Bourgeois' work exhibited at the Stable Gallery in New York in 1964, but they both share the same sensual erotics of the abject, the same psychoanalytic undertow. The body is always implied. There are pieces that might be a string of coiled guts or turds, others made from latex, cotton and rubber look as though they could be used to administer an enema, or for some other taboo bodily function. Bits are wrapped up in string, squashed and crumpled. Many look like objects from a 19th-century ethnographic museum, though it's impossible not to think, also, of all those discarded leather suitcases and piles of shoes left at Auschwitz.

So what do these ephemeral objects, this body of "nearly, but not quite, art", amount to? To try and make sense of them as individual objects is to misunderstand their purpose. They are like the working manuscript or notebooks of a poet. In them, we can see Hesse's concerns: her obsessions with the self, with the body, with material and the fragile metaphoric possibilities of art. Engaging with them is an intimate experience, like watching the process of an artist's mind at work.

Eva Hesse Studiowork
Shards and Fragments
Camden Arts Centre

www.3quarksdaily.com
14th December, 2009

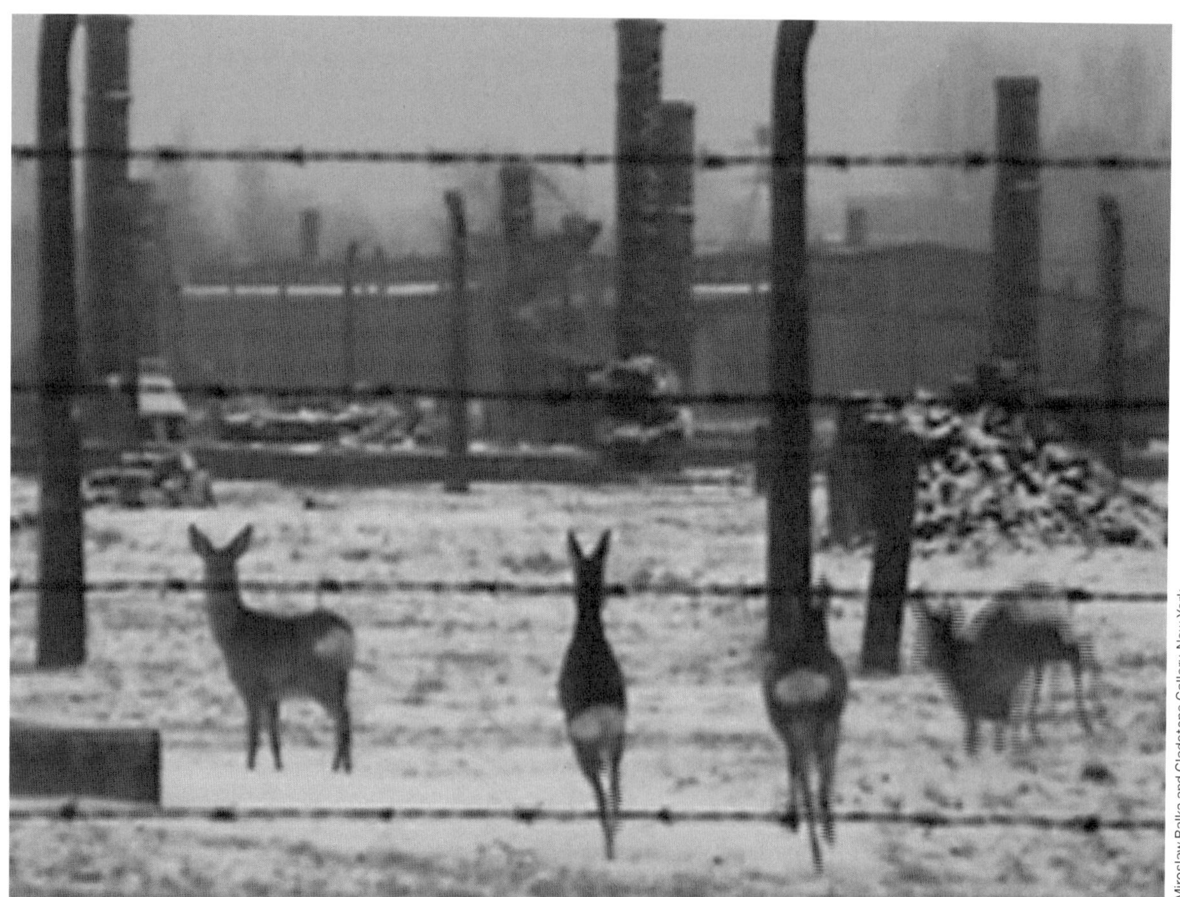

Miroslaw Balka, 'Bambi (Winterreise)', *2003*

Miroslaw Balka
Topography

It is, in case you didn't know it, "Polska! Year", an official campaign aiming to introduce Polish culture to the British public. One of the highlights is 'Topography' by the artist Miroslaw Balka, who is also the creator of Tate Modern's current Turbine Hall exhibit: a black box that is luring crowds into its dark centre. How we remember and how we choose to forget are his subjects. "Every day", he says, "I walk in the paths of the past". The grandson of a gravestone carver, Balka claims: "Contemporary time does not exist. We cannot catch the continuous".

In the flickering, black-and-white shadows of his videos, projected onto the gallery walls at Modern Art Oxford, images return, again and again, like troubling dreams. Born in 1958, Balka produces work cut by the shadow of the Holocaust. On the far wall of the gallery, there is a projection of a frozen pond surrounded by trees in a snowy landscape. The uncanny stillness and apparent silence tap into the Romanticism of Caspar David Friedrich and those half-remembered illustrations from childhood fairytales. It is a genuine shock, then, to learn that this idyll is the site of the concentration camp Auschwitz-Birkenau. Suddenly, we are forced to ask what this place has witnessed, what it remembers or keeps veiled behind this neutralising blanket of snow. In 'Bambi', *2003*, young deer forage in the snow looking for food. They leap over the ribbons of rusting barbed wire that encircle the ghostly vestiges of the camp's prison compound. The title implies the danger of Disneyfying history, of turning away from the truth by making such places into "Holocaust theme parks".

In recent works, such as 'Flagellare A, B and C', *2009*, Balka offers a more physical, less literal expression of both ritual and violence, drawing parallels between the two. Videos inserted in the floor show the shadow of a leather belt whipping the gallery floor, which seems to have transformed into a canvas of skin. The repeated swish suggests not only brutal torture but also Christian flagellation, with its motifs of guilt, redemption and reparation. There is something painterly about the way the soft blue-and-yellow light flits across the surface.

It is no coincidence that, within classical religious art, light implies the spiritual and the divine. These are complex, multilayered works. Sound accompanies a number of the videos: the burr of a truck-driver's foot on an accelerator accompanied by a Polish lullaby, or a clockwork wind-up toy shuffling around the studio. These both desensitise and disorientate.

Talking with Balka, I suggest that in Polish contemporary art, such soul-searching is much less common than among postwar German artists such as Anselm Kiefer, Joseph Beuys or Georg Baselitz. He tells me that, being younger, he has had to educate himself about the Holocaust, and that, having done so, he now has a responsibility to communicate his knowledge through his art. It is an idealistic and refreshingly uncynical view. "We are", he says, "so close to the erasure of the subject that, by making such work, maybe there can continue to be an honest dialogue".

Miroslaw Balka
Topography
Modern Art Oxford

New Statesman
14th January, 2010

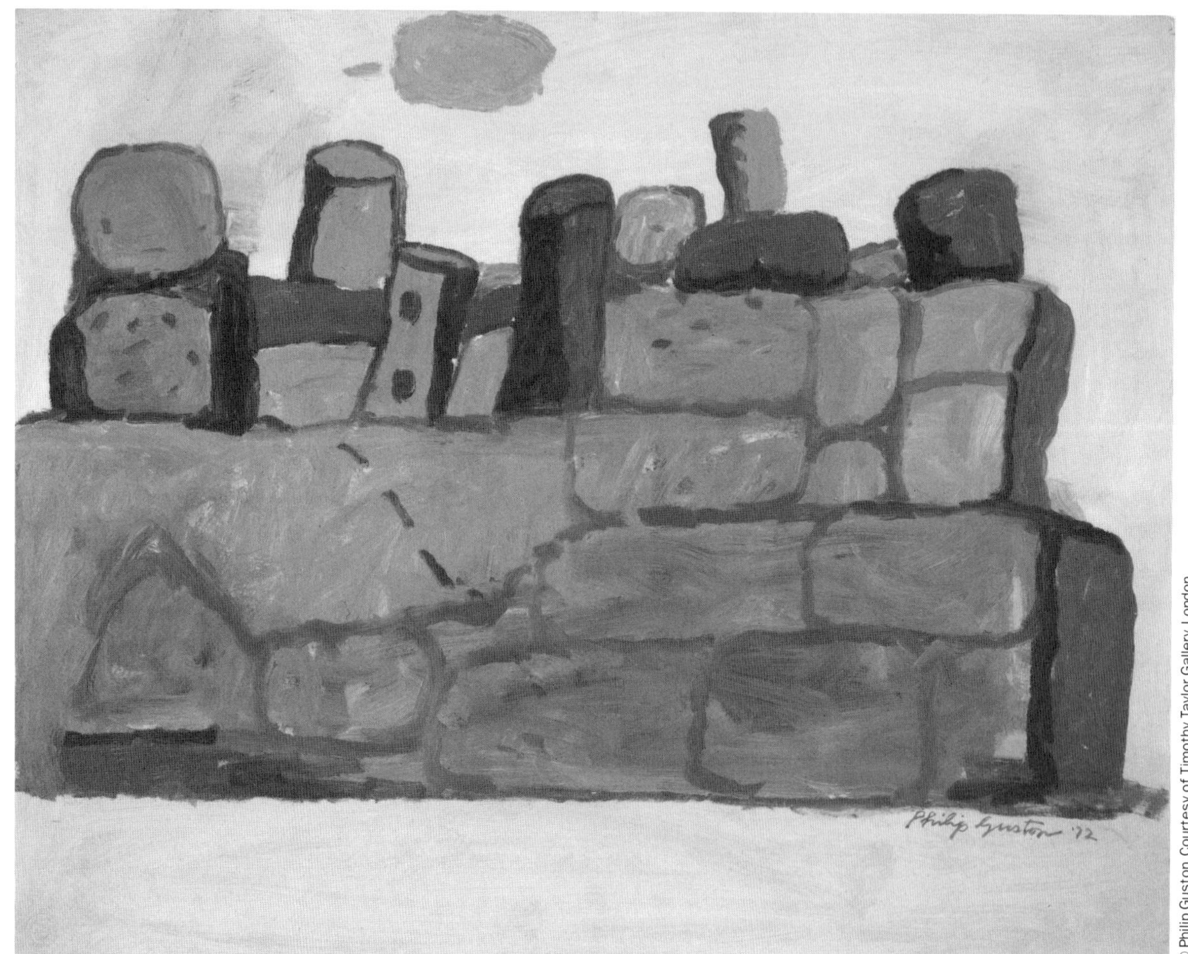

Philip Guston, 'Shoes', *1976*

Phillip Guston
Works on Paper

The return of the American painter Philip Guston to figuration, in 1967, was seen as a betrayal by many of his contemporaries. At the time, they were championing abstraction, particularly Abstract Expressionism, with an almost religious, not to say nationalistic, fervour. With its emphasis on the flat surface, which differentiated it from the perspectival concerns of the Old Masters, abstraction was modern.

Above all, it was American: a break with the traditions of Europe, and a heroic art fit for a New World. The critic Clement Greenberg was its guru and Jackson Pollock his star. Guston accounted for his abandonment, saying: "My quarrel with modern painting… was that it was too easy to elicit a response. Painters could put down swatches of colour and still get a response". As he argued: "Anything in life or art, any mark you make, has meaning – and the only question is: what kind of meaning?"

As an adolescent, Guston was obsessed with comic-book cartoons, and had shown a talent for drawing. His early career was spent as a politically motivated muralist, using his study of Italian Renaissance painters and the Mexican muralist Diego Rivera to underpin his work. In the 1940s, influenced by his high-school friend Pollock and the composers Morton Feldman and John Cage, Guston became fascinated with Zen Buddhism, and started to move his art

towards a more abstract language. But by 1967 he had begun to feel that the vocabulary of abstraction was "too thin".

The Timothy Taylor Gallery's exhibition of his works on paper shows how the immediacy of drawing pulled him back into figuration. The shift was gradual, as can be seen from the economic marks of 'The Hill', *1965*, with its ambiguous forms – two rectangles and a circle placed on a curve – that might be read as standing stones or henges. Guston began to create an idiosyncratic, pictorial alphabet of tragicomic forms. There are piles of shoes and legs and sinister, hooded figures, whose occasional resemblance to raspberry blancmange is even more disquieting at the realisation that they allude to the Ku Klux Klan. Although this personal grammar addresses the political upheavals and civil unrest of 1960s America, these images are, more than anything, metaphors and ideograms that give clues to Guston's internal world.

The meaning of the objects is always ambivalent. On the simplest level, 'Shoes', *1976* might have grown from seeing a pile of shoes chucked in the corner of his studio, but there are other allusions – to the mounds of footwear left by exterminated Jews before they perished in the Nazi death camps, or the writhing figures falling from the boat in the right-hand corner of Michelangelo's 'Last Judgement', their

immortal "souls" in peril. (Who knows
whether or not the pun was intended?)

Late in life, Guston repeatedly insisted that
what he did was not art. He called himself
a "laboratory scientist", a "fire-and-
brimstone preacher – a tortured Talmudist".
In his 1981 lithograph 'Painter', a figure
appears smoking a cigarette in front of a
canvas. His eyes and mouth are bound with
Band-Aids. Deprived of both language and
sight, the only things worth painting, Guston
seems to be saying, come from within.

Phillip Guston
Works on Paper
Timothy Taylor Gallery

New Statesman
1st February, 2010

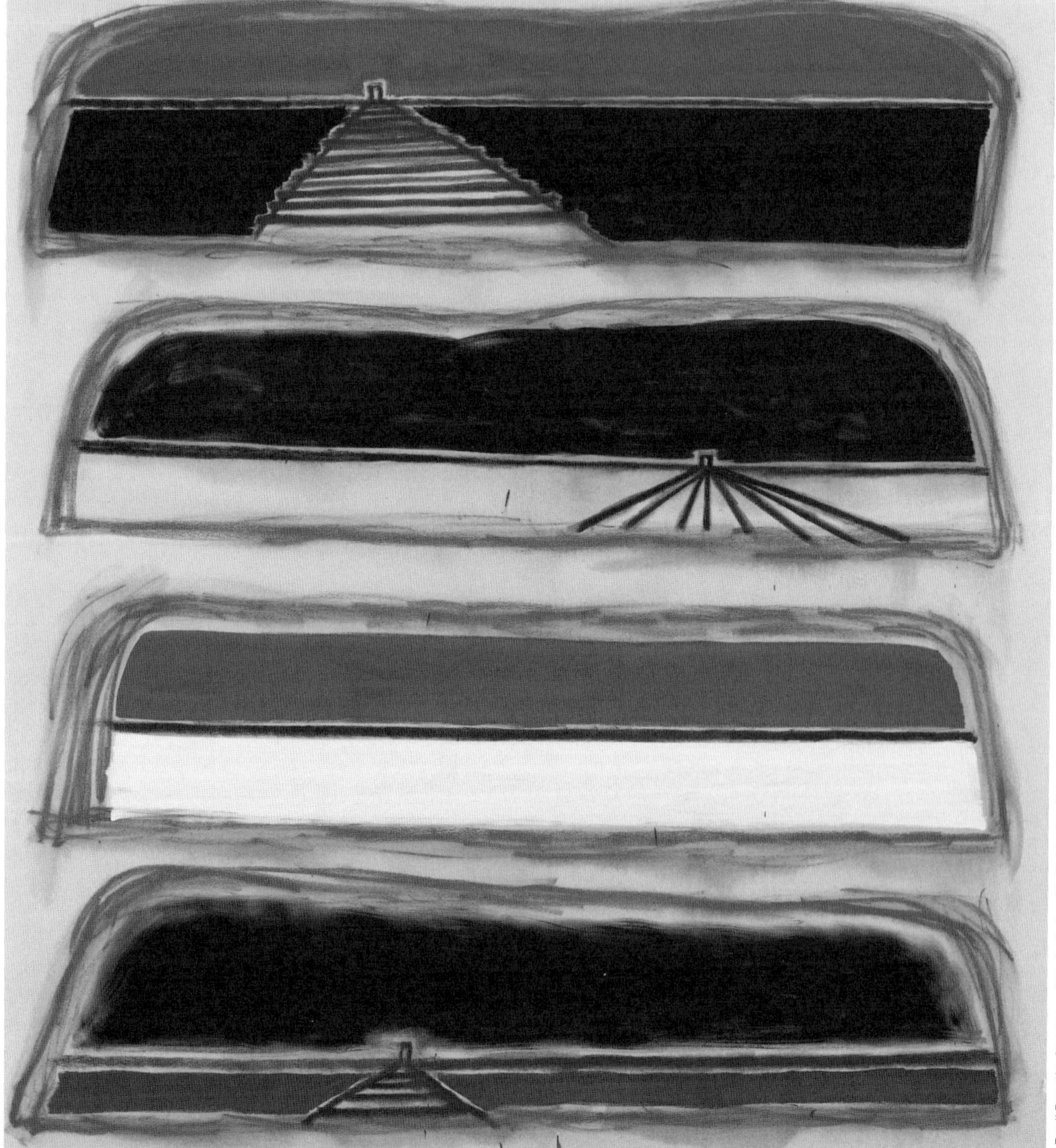

Basil Beattie, 'When Night Sidles In' (Janus series), *2007*

Basil Beattie Paintings from the Janus series II, 2010

"To find a form that accommodates the mess, that is the task of the artist now."
Samuel Beckett

He was the Roman god of beginnings, the guardian of gates and doors who presided over the first hour of each day, and the first day of each month and, as his name, suggests, January. Depicted on Roman coins with a double-faced head, one side bearded, the other clean-shaven, Janus represented both sun and moon. A sort of Roman yin and yang, he symbolised the light and the dark within human experience. Facing both east and west, the doors of his temple at the Forum marked the beginning and end of each day, whilst many Romans began their morning with prayers to him. Worshipped during the time of planting, he was also evoked during rites of passage such as birth and marriage. Throughout Rome, a number of freestanding structures – ceremonial gateways known as *jani* – were used as thresholds to make symbolically auspicious entrances or exits. Emblematic not only of new beginnings, Janus represented the transition between primitive life and civilisation, between the rural and the urban, youth and old age, whilst having the ability to look simultaneously back at the past and into the future. So what relevance does this obscure Roman god have for a contemporary British painter?

Born in 1935, in West Hartlepool in the north of England, Basil Beattie is often referred to as an "artist's artist". Such a phrase denotes a high degree of respect among peers, whilst tactfully acknowledging that his is not a name that tumbles freely from the lips of the general public. Beattie's work has never received the recognition that it deserves, despite his being described as "one of the most significant of bridges in the generations of contemporary British painters". Also, as a teacher at Goldsmiths College, he taught some of this country's most successful young artists such as Gary Hume and Fiona Rae. In 1994, the Tate Gallery, whose director, Nicholas Serota, is a long-term admirer of Beattie's, bought two of his paintings, while Charles Saatchi, who planned to mount an exhibition of neglected, older British artists, bought three. But for some reason, the exhibition never materialised. Though in 2007, Beattie did show work at Tate Britain as part of the BP New Displays.

Basil Beattie's career spans the emergence in Britain, in the late 1950s, of Abstract Expressionism, through to his more recent emphasis on figurative signs that meld gritty northern muscularity with a voluptuous sensuality towards the painted surface. Yet his uncompromising, expressive canvases, with their ambiguities and ironies, their depth and intelligence, are, perhaps, too demanding to be "popular" in these times that insist on easy access and constant novelty. In many ways, his sensibility is that of a 50s existentialist. His work feels more akin to Giacometti or Philip Guston than to the now not-so-Young British Artists. Best known for his evocative abstract paintings featuring architectural motifs, Beattie typically employs a muted palate of earthy colours and expressive, gestural brushstrokes to create an array of archetypal images and pictographic signs such as stairs, steps, ziggurats, ladders, gateways and tunnels. These are not intended to be read literally, but to act as psychological "thresholds" into the subconscious, much like those Roman *jani*. "Landscape", as Fernando Pessoa's heteronym, Bernardo Soares, writes in 'The Book of Disquiet' "is a state of emotion".

An only child, Beattie missed a lot of school. Because he was often ill with bronchitis, his mother worried about "lung disease". Yet he knew that he could draw, and remembers listening on the wireless to the BBC Home Service's broadcast of Dylan Thomas's 'Under Milk Wood', whilst copying pictures from adventure stories. He can still recall the embarrassment of being in the same room as his parents when Myfanwy Price dreamt that Mog Edwards, "a draper mad with love", would "warm her sheets like an electric toaster".

As a student at the Royal Academy, he painted like Willem de Kooning, though, he says, he was looking at Mark Rothko. The problem he had with English painting of the period was that it always felt "too well done". He admired the way Guston stuck his neck out, embracing an idiosyncratic figuration when abstraction was considered to be the only possible language for a serious painter.

It was in the late 1980s that Beattie began to relinquish the influences of American Abstract Expressionism, with its formal grammar of colour, gesture and relationship to the flat surface. The titles in the Janus series: 'No Known Way', 'Been and Gone', 'Dancing in the Night', 'Beginnings and Endings', 'Touching Distance', 'The

Approaching Night', 'Night Embrace', read like lines from a Samuel Beckett text, and function as poetic and philosophical underpinnings to his imagery, whilst all the while refusing literal translation. There is an inert silence about these canvases, where the only evidence of human presence is the linear traces incised across the empty landscape. One senses that Beattie might well be tempted to substitute the word "painting" for "writing" in Beckett's 1969 statement that: "Writing becomes not easier, but more difficult for me. Every word is like an unnecessary stain on silence and nothingness".

Comprising a purposefully limited repertoire of stacked domes tiered in threes and, occasionally, fours, like a series of "portals" that open out onto an illusionary space, the images in the Janus series act as a framing devise and suggest a car mirror in which viewers cannot be certain whether they are looking at a reflection or an actual view. As in Plato's cave, there is confusion as to what is real, or simply a reflection or shadow of reality. It is as if, speeding through these barren terrains, we are forced to witness our lives unfurl in front of us as in a silent film, so that, like Janus, we find ourselves looking both back at the past and forwards into the future.

"Birth was the death of him", Beckett once wrote with ironic black humour. Drawn into Beattie's series of vistas, where horizon lines, ploughed fields and railway tracks disappear into a series of classical vanishing points, we are made aware, in the underlying existential emptiness of this Godless landscape, of the continuum from birth to death. Eschewing easy autobiographical interpretations, Beattie nevertheless talks of being a young boy visiting his father's signalman's hut and watching for oncoming trains down the distant track, as his father pulled the lever. There are, too, other dim memories of listening to the disembodied voices of war correspondents on the radio as they recounted the chilling evidence of the death camps. For it is impossible not to see the incised lines, cutting aggressively across these scrubbed fields towards a distant tower on a far horizon, as the railway lines that ended beneath that infamous iron gate, topped with the words: *Arbeit macht frei*. Then, too, there were journeys Beattie undertook across Germany on the way to training exercises as an impressionable young soldier, whilst doing National Service in the mid-1950s.

Yet despite the allegory and allusion inherent in these works, their meaning ultimately resides in the physical reality of the paint. Clotted, thick and deceptively casual in its application, it emphasises both mass and absence. Whilst offering a basic illusion, Beattie's work is infused with tension that comes from the constant attempt to deny that illusion, whilst simultaneously accepting that the viewer is already reading his lines, as they disappear into the horizon, as journeys.

"I wonder if my apparently negligible voice might not embody the essence of thousands of voices, the longing for self-expression of thousands of lives, the patience of millions of souls resigned like my own to their daily lot, their useless dreams and their hopeless hopes", wrote Fernando Pessoa. These lyrical, yet visceral, paintings, in which the whole of life appears to unfurl as we head towards inevitable extinction, seem to echo Pessoa's bleak words.

Basil Beattie
Paintings from the
Janus series II, 2010
Abbot Hall Art Gallery, Kendal, Cumbria

www.3quarksdaily
8th February, 2010

Sue Hubbard
Adventures in Art
Selected Writings
1990–2010

Published in 2010
by Other Criteria
14 Welbeck Street
London W1G 9XU
www.othercriteria.com

ISBN 978-1-906967-21-5

Especial thanks are due to
David Halpin for his careful
reading and copy editing of
these essays; to the artist and
writer Simon Morley and the
gallerist Emma Hill for their
invaluable and insightful advice
and comments; and to the Cill
Rialaig Project, Co. Kerry for
providing the space to write
the introduction and rework
some of the essays.

"... not for glory and least of all for profit, but to create out of the materials of the human spirit something which did not exist before."
William Faulkner

"At the end of the day, people are more important than paintings."
Damien Hirst

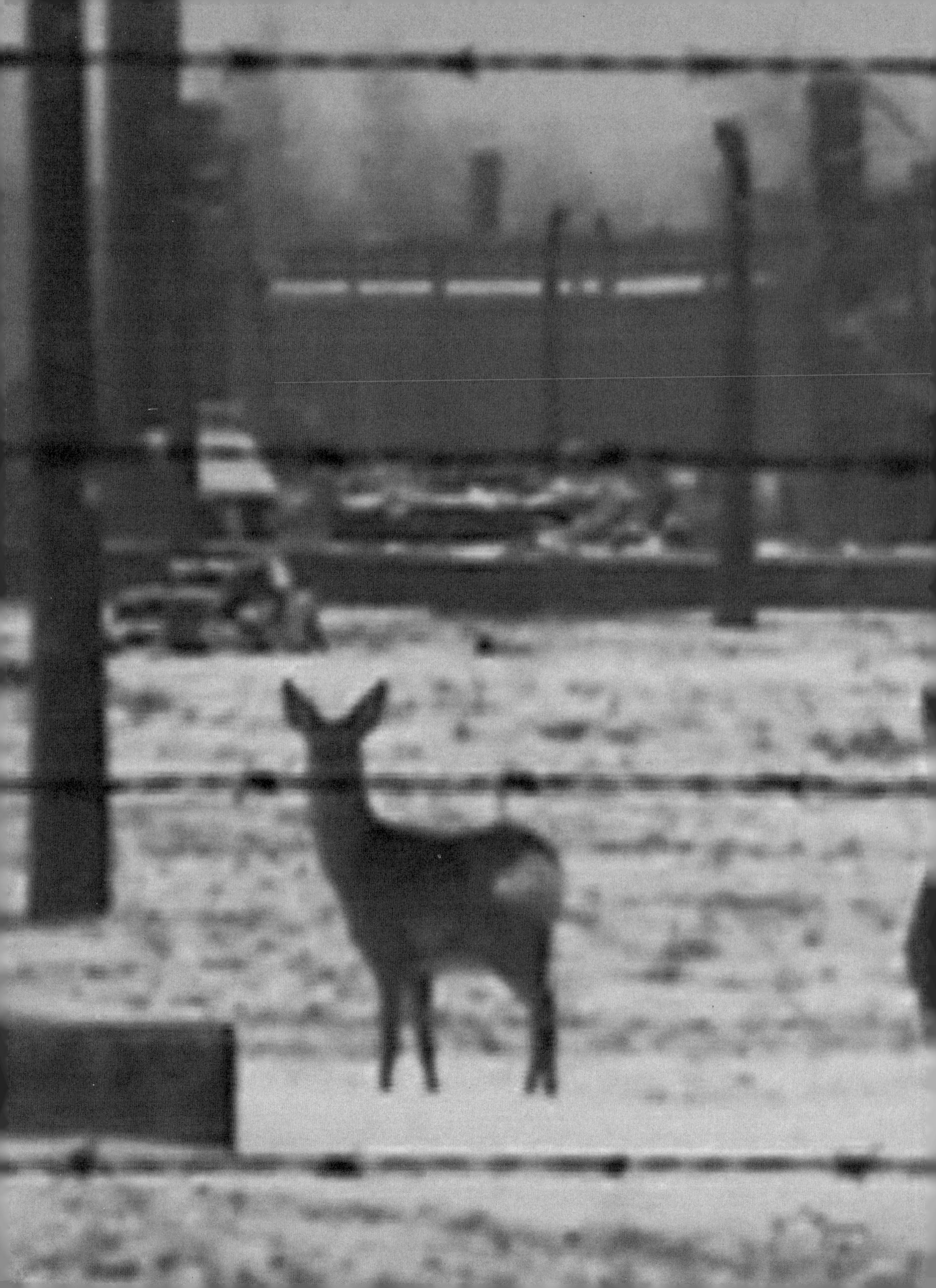